FROM CHILD TO ADULT

Studies in the Anthropology of Education

John Middleton

received his D.Phil. from Oxford in 1953. He has taught anthropology at Capetown, Northwestern, and New York universities, and at present he is professor of African anthropology at the School of Anthropology and African Studies, University of London.

He has done field research in Uganda, Zanzibar, and Nigeria. He is the author of *Black Africa* and *Lugbara of Uganda*, and, with David Tait, he edited *Tribes without Rulers*. Dr. Middleton also edited four other volumes of the Texas Press Sourcebooks in Anthropology series: *Comparative Political Systems*, with Ronald Cohen; *Myth and Cosmos*; *Gods and Rituals*; and *Magic, Witchcraft, and Curing*.

Texas Press Sourcebooks in Anthropology
were originally published by the Natural History Press, a division of Doubleday and Company, Inc. Responsibility for the series now resides with the University of Texas Press, Box 7819, Austin, Texas 78712. Whereas the series has been a joint effort between the American Museum of Natural History and the Natural History Press, future volumes in the series will be selected through the auspices of the editorial offices of the University of Texas Press.

The purpose of the series will remain unchanged in its effort to make available inexpensive, up-to-date, and authoritative volumes for the student and the general reader in the field of anthropology.

From Child
to
Adult

Studies in the Anthropology of Education

Edited by John Middleton , 1921–

University of Texas Press

Austin and London

Library of Congress Cataloging in Publication Data

Middleton, John, 1921–   comp.
    From child to adult.

    (Texas Press sourcebooks in anthropology; 9)
    Reprint of the ed. published for the American Museum of
Natural History by the Natural History Press, Garden City, N.Y.,
in series: American Museum sourcebooks in anthropology.
Bibliography: p.
Includes index.
1. Educational anthropology—Addresses, essays, lectures. I. Title.
II. Series. III. Series: American Museum sourcebooks in anthro-
pology.
[LB45.M53 1976]   301.2'1   75-44039
ISBN 0-292-75416-0

Published by arrangement with Doubleday & Company, Inc.
Previously published by the Natural History Press in cooperation
with Doubleday & Company, Inc.

CONTENTS

THE PURPOSE of this collection of essays is to place our educational system into a wider, comparative perspective, so that we can see it critically but from a less rigid and culture-bound viewpoint than we usually do. To ourselves, involved in it, our own system of education may appear unique and "natural" to our way of thinking. We may be aware of flaws in it and the problems that we face in trying to make it effective and socially just; some appear inevitable, others not, but we almost always consider them to be unique to ourselves. However, although we know that our educational system has been largely determined by our country's history and particular social conditions, we often find it difficult to look at these critically and objectively, and we ignore the knowledge available to us about other societies and their systems of education that might help us see our own more clearly. All societies are different, in varying degree; yet all are essentially similar, despite variations in their cultures and forms of organization. It is therefore useful for us to stand back from our own problems and to learn something of the range of possible educational systems as they are found in the many societies of the world outside our own.

First, it is useful to consider both the nature of human society and also that of education. A human society cannot be understood merely as consisting of an aggregate of people, like a herd of animals or a nest of insects. Rather, it consists of people who regard themselves as belonging to it because they possess a common culture or way of life, a common language, the recognition of certain common interrelationships, and the acceptance of common values and sanctions that order and maintain these interrelationships. These are but rarely invented by the members of a society: They exist apart from its members, before they were born and after they have died. The essential fact is that one of the basic features of man's social condition is that culture is learned and not genetically inherited. The human being who learns none of his society's culture—by being autistic, for example—is a human being in the sense of being an animal, but he is little more. All animals learn, but they learn little more than physical movements and the recognition of a few vocal and other signs: of danger, the presence of food, and the like. Man, being an animal, also learns these things from the moment of birth. But he is a social animal and must learn the culture of his society, a more complex task than learning movements and signs. He must also learn to transmit his culture to his descendants; consequently, throughout most of his life man is both learner and teacher.

In this regard our basic questions are how culture is transmitted from one generation to the next, how individuals share in this transmission, and how learning and transmitting culture are related to society's social organization. One way of answering these questions is to look critically at the process of education, as it is found in different societies. Education may be viewed as a "program" that is part of a person's social development from a child to an adult. During his lifetime a man must learn enough of his culture to act competently as a member of society. The culture of any society is too rich and too broad for any one person to know all of it, but there is always a minimum that anyone must know to be regarded as a social being at all. This comprises certain techniques and items of knowledge that vary from one people to another: to speak one's language, to move one's body in certain ways, to recognize common signs of action and emotion in others. Beyond this minimum there is an immense range of cultural behavior that is part of his society's heritage of which a person can choose a portion—although his freedom of choice may largely be determined by his parents, teachers, and others. This cultural behavior does not consist of signs but rather of symbols that are meaningful only to the members of a particular society or community. A man who does not understand them and the ways in which they are linked together into a cultural pattern does not participate fully in his culture and cannot conceive of himself as being a full member of his society. We see this in our society in the cases both of children and of adults who are mentally or psychologically unable to learn our particular "pattern of culture" (as Ruth Benedict called it), and of socially deprived sections of the total population who may not be given the chance to learn all of this pattern and may thus be left on the margins of society.

Education is the learning of culture. The various activities that we in Western industrialized societies refer to under this rubric are only part of the whole educational process. Education, although mostly the concern of the child, is a continuing process throughout the lifetime of any person. And, of course, it includes far more than the rather narrow program of formal training that we usually think of when we talk about school activities. In general, teachers in Western countries think of education as concerned with the acquisition of technical competence, in terms of physical skills and vocational and professional knowledge. Teaching these skills is the task of the educational specialist. These matters form part of any educational program, in any society; but the proportion of a program devoted to them varies from one society to another, as do the importance and meaning given them. But the major parts of any educational program concern the inculcation and understanding of cultural symbols, moral values, sanctions, and cosmological beliefs. In our own society we separate out these parts from "formal" education and leave them mainly to families, friends, priests, psychoanalysts, and guides and advisers of many kinds. But most societies, as the essays in this volume show, do not separate these various aspects of the total educational process. We are unusual in this respect— or more accurately we may say that literate societies tend to differ in this way from pre-literate ones. Societies, both literate and pre-literate, have different demands and ideas of the educational process, and there is great variation in the content and transmission of the educational program from one society to another.

Different beliefs, values, and symbols are associated with variations in the cultures and organizations of different societies. When we speak about variations from one culture to another we are really referring to the different ways in which people see themselves as forming communities, families, and other groups: We are referring to forms of organization. The organization of every society is unique, a consequence of historical, climatic, economic, and other factors that have affected different societies in slightly different ways. By the organization of a society is meant, essentially, the arrangement of social positions (or statuses) that are held by its many members. Any one person typically occupies many positions, some of which are formally defined (such as son, or father, or teacher), others of which are not (such as friend, acquaintance, or casual passer-by in the street). Any society has its own arrangements and constellations of social positions that form the basis for its way of life.

Social positions or statuses are acquired by a person during the course of his lifetime, as he progresses from that of a baby to the many statuses implied by the term "adult." Some statuses are ascribed (by birth, by sex, by age) and others are achieved, by a man's own efforts, by obtaining good education, wealth, prestige, and so on. The portion of his total culture that a man learns reflects his social position, his aspirations and those of his parents for him. In our own society, as with other Western industrialized nations, most statuses are achieved: Social mobility is both necessary and valued, and a man's progress through life is ideally measured by the acquisition of new and ever higher positions. We should expect the main thrust in our education to be in technical, vocational, and professional training; and in general this is so. Education in non-vocational matters (with learning one's social organization, values, beliefs, and assumptions that are also part of our culture) is regarded as of less educational importance (at least in practice—our theory is often a little different). This is due partly, of course, to the fact that in a rapidly changing society no one is ever very sure about what are the best values, assumptions, and beliefs; but we also generally accept these as being less important than vocational skills and as being something best left to others to trouble their heads about.

However, the essays in this book are concerned rather with peoples who do trouble with these matters and who regard them as being central to their various programs of education. In these "traditional" societies, those with a minimum of observed social change, with most recognition given to ascribed and formal statuses, and with little importance given to social mobility and the achievement of higher social positions, the education given to children and adolescents is devoted mainly to such matters as kinship, mythology, and cosmological values and moral sanctions that are at the heart of their various cultures. Training in physical and vocational techniques is largely incidental and regarded merely as a sign of normal growing up. Learning social roles and values is done by participating in adult activities, not so much as a child, cut off from adults (as among ourselves), but rather as an incomplete but developing adult.

To become an adult member of one's society means more than merely learning its skills, however difficult these may be. A man must also be given recognition by the remainder of society: Adulthood is defined socially, not in terms of physical or psychological maturity alone. We all know people who have many skills but who may be denied full adult status. A man who acquires skills at school or college is not formally regarded as having done so until he is given a certificate to that effect; a man who is physically adult may not be permitted to marry, or to vote, or even to be regarded as an independent and mature citizen. Social maturity may also be given to people (such as the son of a king or of a very wealthy person) who may not in fact have acquired the skills normally expected of adults.

In studying education we are studying processes of maturation, which is both physical and social. Physical maturation is in fact usually not very important in itself—and it takes place in any case. What is of more significance is how it and social maturation are defined and recognized in cultural terms. In most societies, puberty is selected as an important stage, for obvious reasons, as are other fairly easily definable stages, such as giving birth to a child. But even such apparently obvious phases as puberty are rarely defined in physiological terms but rather in cultural terms, so that "puberty" may be reckoned at anywhere from eight to twenty or more years of age, and the educational program adapted to that. So long as society defines it clearly, its members can adapt to it. What is difficult is when it is not clearly defined, as among ourselves; from this uncertainty spring so many of the difficulties of adolescence and the associated educational problems in Western society today.

II

The essays in this book have been chosen to illustrate, in varying ways and in varying degrees of detail, the main points made above. Most are concerned with small-scale "traditional" societies that have either experienced little rapid social change or that have experienced it only very recently. They enable us to understand something of the relationship between education and society as it is found among peoples very different from our-selves (and, of course, equally different from one another). This objective, non-evaluative view of other societies throws our own educational system and its relationship to the remainder of our social life into a less rigid perspective than that we usually hold when we are caught up in everyday problems of education and social maturation.

Despite its obvious importance for our understanding both of traditional societies and those undergoing rapid change and de-velopment, there is remarkably little information published on systems of education within their social contexts. There is a great deal of work published on the psychological processes of infant and child training and conditioning. The actual processes of learning, as a psychological activity, would seem fairly similar in all societies throughout the world, and these accounts almost all ignore the social contexts. I have therefore not included them in this book. What varies from one society to another, and what therefore I have considered it most valuable to include for pur-poses of comparison, is the content and context of learning and conditioning. The accounts that consider these matters deal mainly with traditional forms of educational programs, set in their social contexts. They illustrate certain common points: The many societies known to us vary from small to large, and from simple to complex in organization; the aims of their educational programs can be understood only by examining the social posi-tions for which they equip the children being educated; education is a gradual and usually non-specialized process that involves all members of a social group, without formal pedagogical methods of instruction. Other accounts deal with education in traditional societies undergoing rapid social change, in most of which some form of "Western" education is given to the children of de-veloping non-Western countries.

I have selected the papers from these latter kinds of material, in which the content and context of education are the basic fields of interest and analysis. They are by anthropologists, although there are surprisingly few good accounts in the anthropological literature; but the writings of non-anthropologists almost all neglect the cultural and social settings except in terms that are too general for adequate understanding of the data. The choice available has therefore been small, both in terms of geographical coverage of the world and in types of social systems represented. The available material deals mainly with education in small-scale pre-literate societies; there is little on the larger non-Western societies with literate traditions, such as China, India, or Japan.

III

It may be useful to list some of the more important and interesting anthropological sources on educational systems, especially on these systems in the more "traditional" societies. This list cannot hope to be complete, and it has to omit references to the vast literature on government and mission-controlled educational programs in developing countries, as well as those to Western societies.

There are first a few general and comparative accounts of traditional forms of education. Among those devoted to the anthropological analysis of education, as distinct from psychological studies of learning, are the volumes and papers by Spindler (1955), Helser (1934), Gruber (1961), Kneller (1965), Mead (1940, 1942, 1943), Paulsen (1961). There are summaries of the problems involved in research by Henry (1960, 1961) and Hilger (1960).

There are a good many monographs and shorter accounts that deal with education in particular societies. Although they are uneven in quality, the following sources all contain information of anthropological significance. It is convenient to list them by ethnographic area.

North America There is a good deal of anthropological material on education among North American Indians; here I have included only accounts of the content of more or less traditional societies, ignoring the many writings on the educational problems of the Indian reservations and government agencies. Some general works include those by Pettitt (1946), Erikson (1948), Havinghurst (1957), and Havinghurst and Neugarten (1955). For the Eskimo and Indians of Canada there are the bibliography by Carney and Ferguson (1965) and descriptive works by Lantis (1960) and King (1967). For the Northwest Coast there are accounts by DeLaguna (1965) on Tlingit and Wolcott (1967) on Kwakiutl. There are many writings on the Southwest groups: Leighton and Kluckhohn (1947) on Navajo; Thompson and Joseph (1944), Goldfrank (1945), Eggan (1956), Dennis (1940, 1941) on the Hopi; Williams (1958) and Joseph, Spicer, and Chesky (1949) on Papago; Opler (1941) on Apache; Smithson (1959) on Havasupai. Other accounts that may be mentioned for other areas include those by Erikson (1943) on Yurok; Searcy (1965) on Potawatomi; Wax, Wax, and Dumont (1964) on Sioux; and Polgar (1960) on Mesquakie.

South and Central America There are far fewer sources to be quoted on these areas. For the Indians of South America may be mentioned the works of Hilger (1957) on the Araucanians and Reichel-Dolmatoff and Reichel-Dolmatoff (1961) on the Indians of Colombia. For Middle America there are accounts by Redfield (1943) on Guatemala and Hunt and Hunt (1967) on Mexico. On the Caribbean there are writings by Landy (1959) and Brameld (1959) on Puerto Rico, and Keur and Keur (1961) on the Dutch Windward islands.

Africa There are a good many books and articles, many by modern anthropologists, on indigenous systems of education in Africa; most of them include reference to the problems involved in rapidly changing countries today. For the peoples of southern Africa there are writings by Krige (1937), Hoernlé (1931), Kidd (1906), Smith (1934), Blacking (1964), Pauw (1963), and DeRidder (1961), all on the Nguni- or Sotho-speaking groups; and there is the work of Childs (1949) on the Ovimbundu of Angola. For those of central Africa there are writings by Read (1968, also 1955a, 1955b, 1956) on the Ngoni of Malawi and other peoples; Richards (1956) on the Bemba of Zambia; Wilson (1951) on the Nyakyusa; Vincent (1954) on Ruanda-Urundi; Turnbull (1960) on the Congo Pygmies. For eastern Africa accounts include those by Raum (1938, 1940, also 1956, 1967) on the Chaga of Tanzania; LeVine and LeVine (1966) on the Gusii of Kenya; Gatheru (1964) and McGlashan (1964) on the Kikuyu of Kenya; Spencer (1965) on the Samburu of Kenya; Musgrove

(1953) on Uganda; and Lewis (1965) on the Amhara of Ethiopia. Finally, for western Africa there are writings by Fortes (1938) on the Tallensi of northern Ghana; Foster (1966), Kaye (1962), and Rattray (1932) on other peoples of Ghana; Nadel (1942) on the Nupe of Nigeria; Herskovits (1938, 1943) on Dahomey; Leis (1964) on the Ijaw of Nigeria; Little (1952) and Watkins (1943) on the peoples of Sierra Leone; Gay (1967) on the Kpelle of Liberia; Griaule (1952) on the Dogon; and Knapen (1962) on the Kongo of Congo.

Near East For this region there are the works of Ammar (1954) and Granqvist (1947, 1950) on Arabic societies, and of Spiro (1958), Neubauer (1965), and Rabin (1965) on Israel.

Asia There is surprisingly little material available on the educational systems of the great literate societies of Asia. For China there are works by Chiang (1952) and Yee (1963); for Japan those by Dore (1965), Passin (1965), and Singleton (1967); for Burma the article by Nash (1961); for Thailand the book by Phillips (1965); and for India the writings of Kapadia (1957), Narain (1964), Mencher (1963), Gorer (1938), and Minturn and Hitchcock (1966).

Oceania For Melanesia there are works by Mead (1930, 1935, 1949, 1956) on various peoples of New Guinea and the Admiralty Islands; Whiting (1941) on the Kwoma; and Hogbin on Wogeo (1943, 1946). For Polynesia there are writings by Mead (1928, 1935) on Samoa; Firth (1936) on Tikopia; Hogbin on Ontong Java (1931); and Ausubel (1961), Earle (1958), and Richie (1963) on the Maori of New Zealand. For Micronesia there is the book on Okinawa by Maretzki and Maretzki (1966). There is a good deal on the peoples of Indonesia: Mead and MacGregor (1951) and Bateson and Mead (1942) on Bali; DuBois (1944) on the Alorese; Williams (1969) on the Dusun; Geertz (1961) on Java; and on the Philippines the works of Guthrie (1961), Guthrie and Jacobs (1966), and Nydegger and Nydegger (1966).

There are many other works that are more particularly concerned with problems of social psychology, although the boundary is difficult to draw, such as those by Kluckhohn and Murray (1949), Whiting and Child (1953), Mead and Wolfenstein (1954), Hsu (1961), and Hunt (1967). Others are listed in the Bibliography at the end of this volume.

FROM CHILD TO ADULT

Studies in the Anthropology of Education

1 OUR EDUCATIONAL EMPHASES IN PRIMITIVE PERSPECTIVE

Margaret Mead

The following chapter is by an anthropologist who has written many accounts of non-Western systems of education in the light of her comparative field experiences (Mead 1949, 1964). The author discusses the contrasts between pre-literate and Western educational programs, and thus presents some of the basic points with which this volume is concerned.

The pre-literate programs occur in societies that are relatively static. Their members are tolerant of outsiders and interested in education for the maintenance of continuity of culture and helping children to develop within that traditional culture. Western programs, by contrast, exist in societies which are in a state of continual change; their members have stronger notions of their own cultural superiority; they are interested in education as a means of changing individuals, of improving their social status, and of ensuring discontinuity and development. They believe in the power of education to create something new, rather than to perpetuate something old. The paper contains references to Dutch and British colonial systems that are now out of date, but it is a clear presentation of basic principles of educational processes and policies.

IN ITS BROADEST sense, education is the cultural process, the way in which each newborn human infant, born with a potentiality for learning greater than that of any other mammal, is transformed into a full member of a specific human society, sharing

Reprinted from *American Journal of Sociology* 48, 1942–43: 633–39, with permission of the author and of the editor, *American Journal of Sociology*.

with the other members a specific human culture.[1] From this point
of view we can place side by side the newborn child in a modern
city and the savage infant born into some primitive South Sea tribe.
Both have everything to learn. Both depend for that learning upon
the help and example, the care and tutelage, of the elders of their
societies. Neither child has any guaranty of growing up to be a
full human being should some accident, such as theft by a wolf,
interfere with its human education. Despite the tremendous difference in what the New York infant and the New Guinea infant
will learn, there is a striking similarity in the whole complicated
process by which the child takes on and into itself the culture of
those around it. And much profit can be gained by concentrating on these similarities and by setting the procedure of the
South Sea mother side by side with the procedure of the New York
mother, attempting to understand the common elements in cultural transmission. In such comparisons we can identify the tremendous potentialities of human beings, who are able to learn not
only to speak any one of a thousand languages but to adjust to as
many different rhythms of maturation, ways of learning, methods
of organizing their emotions and of managing their relationships to
other human beings.

In this paper, however, I propose to turn away from this order
of comparison—which notes the differences between human cultures, primitive and civilized, only as means of exploring the processes which occur in both types of culture—and to stress instead
the ways in which our present behavior, which we bracket under
the abstraction "education," differs from the procedures characteristic of primitive homogeneous communities. I propose to ask,
not what there is in common between America in 1941 and South
Sea culture which displays in 1941 a Stone Age level of culture,
but to ask instead: What are some of the conspicuous differences,
and what light do these differences throw upon our understanding of our own conception of education? And, because this is too
large and wide a subject, I want to limit myself still further and
to ask a question which is appropriate to this symposium: What
effects has the mingling of peoples—of different races, different
religions, and different levels of cultural complexity—had upon
our concept of education? When we place our present-day concept

---

[1] This paper is an expression of the approach of the Council on Intercultural Relations.

against a backdrop of primitive educational procedures and see
it as influenced by intermingling of peoples, what do we find?

I once lectured to a group of women—all of them college
graduates—alert enough to be taking a fairly advanced adult-
education course on "Primitive Education" delivered from the first
point of view. I described in detail the lagoon village of the Manus
tribe, the ways in which the parents taught the children to master
their environment, to swim, to climb, to handle fire, to paddle a
canoe, to judge distances and calculate the strength of materials.
I described the tiny canoes which were given to the three-year-
olds, the miniature fish spears with which they learned to spear
minnows, the way in which small boys learned to calk their canoes
with gum, and how small girls learned to thread shell money into
aprons. Interwoven with a discussion of the more fundamental
issues, such as the relationship between children and parents and
the relationships between younger children and older children,
I gave a fairly complete account of the type of adaptive craft
behavior which was characteristic of the Manus and the way in
which this was learned by each generation of children. At the end
of the lecture one woman stood up and asked the first question:
"Didn't they have any vocational training?" Many of the others
laughed at the question, and I have often told it myself as a way
of getting my audience into a mood which was less rigidly limited
by our own phrasing of "education." But that woman's question,
naïve and crude as it was, epitomized a long series of changes
which stand between our idea of education and the processes by
which members of a homogeneous and relatively static primitive
society transmit their standardized habit patterns to their children.

There are several striking differences between our concept of
education today and that of any contemporary primitive society[2];
but perhaps the most important one is the shift from the need for
an individual to learn something which everyone agrees he would
wish to know, to the will of some individual to teach something
which it is not agreed that anyone has any desire to know. Such a
shift in emphasis could come only with the breakdown of self-
contained and self-respecting cultural homogeneity. The Manus
or the Arapesh or the Iatmul adults taught their children all that
they knew themselves. Sometimes, it is true, there were rifts in the

[2] This discussion, unless otherwise indicated, is based upon South Sea
people only.

process. A man might die without having communicated some particular piece of ritual knowledge; a good hunter might find no suitable apprentice among his available near kin, so that his skill perished with him. A girl might be so clumsy and stupid that she never learned to weave a mosquito basket that was fit to sell. Miscarriages in the smooth working of the transmission of available skills and knowledge did occur, but they were not sufficient to focus the attention of the group upon the desirability of *teaching* as over against the desirability of *learning*. Even with considerable division of labor and with a custom by which young men learned a special skill not from a father or other specified relative but merely from a master of the art, the master did not go seeking pupils; the pupils and their parents went to seek the master and with proper gifts of fish or octopus or dogs' teeth persuaded him to teach the neophyte. And at this level of human culture even close contact with members of other cultures did not alter the emphasis. Women who spoke another language married into the tribe; it was, of course, very important that they should learn to speak the language of their husbands' people, and so they learned that language as best they could—or failed to learn it. People might compliment them on their facility or laugh at them for their lack of it, but the idea of *assimilating* them was absent.

Similarly, the spread of special cults or sects among South Sea people, the desire to *join* the sect rather than the need to make converts, was emphasized. New ceremonies did develop. It was necessary that those who had formerly been ignorant of them should learn new songs or new dance steps, but the onus was again upon the learner. The greater self-centeredness of primitive homogeneous groups (often so self-centered that they divided mankind into two groups—the human beings, i.e., themselves, and the nonhuman beings, other people) preserved them also from the emphasis upon the greater value of one truth over another which is the condition of proselytizing. "*We* (human beings) do it this way and *they* (other people) do it that way." A lack of a desire to teach *them* our ways guaranteed also that the *we* group had no fear of any proselytizing from the *they* groups. A custom might be imported, bought, obtained by killing the owner, or taken as part of a marriage payment. A custom might be exported for a price or a consideration. But the em-

phasis lay upon the desire of the importing group to obtain the
new skill or song and upon the desire of the exporting group for
profit in material terms by the transaction. The idea of conversion, or purposely attempting to alter the ideas and attitudes of
other persons, did not occur. One might try to persuade one's
brother-in-law to abandon his own group and come and hunt
permanently with the tribe into which his sister had married; physical proselytizing there was, just as there was actual import and ex-
port of items of culture. But, once the brother-in-law had been
persuaded to join a different cultural group, it was his job to learn
how to live there; and you might, if you were still afraid he would
go back or if you wanted his co-operation in working a two-man
fish net, take considerable pains to teach him this or that skill as a
bribe. But to bribe another by teaching him one's own skill is a
long way from any practice of conversion, although it may be
made subsidiary to it.

We have no way of knowing how often in the course of human
history the idea of Truth, as a revelation to or possession of
some one group (which thereby gained the right to consider itself
superior to all those who lacked this revelation), may have appeared. But certain it is that, wherever this notion of hierarchical
arrangements of cultural views of experience appears, it has profound effects upon education; and it has enormously influenced
our own attitudes toward education. As soon as there is any
attitude that one set of cultural beliefs is definitely superior to
another, the framework is present for active proselytizing, unless
the idea of cultural superiority is joined with some idea of hereditary membership, as it is among the Hindus. (It would indeed
be interesting to investigate whether any group which considered
itself in possession of the most superior brand of religious or
economic truth, and which did not regard its possession as limited
by heredity, could preserve the belief in that superiority without
proselytizing. It might be found that active proselytizing was the
necessary condition for the preservation of the essential belief
in one's own revelation.) Thus, with the appearance of religions
which held this belief in their own infallible superiority, education becomes a concern of those who teach rather than of those
who learn. Attention is directed toward finding neophytes rather
than toward finding masters, and adults and children become
bracketed together as recipients of conscious missionary effort.

This bracketing-together is of great importance; it increases the self-consciousness of the whole educational procedure, and it is quite possible that the whole question of methods and techniques of education is brought most sharply to the fore when it is a completely socialized adult who must be influenced instead of a plastic and receptive child.

With social stratification the possibility of using education as a way of changing status is introduced, and another new component of the educational idea develops. Here the emphasis is still upon the need to learn—on the one hand, in order to alter status and, on the other, to prevent the loss of status by failure to learn. But wherever this possibility enters in there is also a possibility of a new concept of education developing from the relationship between fixed caste and class lines and education. In a static society members of different caste or class groups may have been teaching their children different standards of behavior for many generations without any essential difference between their attitudes toward education and those of less complex societies. To effect a change it is necessary to focus the attention of the members of the society upon the problem, as conditions of cultural contact do focus it. Thus, in present-day Bali, the high castes are sending their daughters to the Dutch schools to be trained as schoolteachers because it is pre-eminently important that learning should be kept in the hands of the high castes and profoundly inappropriate that low-caste teachers should teach high-caste children. They feel this strongly enough to overcome their prejudices against the extent to which such a course takes high-caste women out into the market place.

As soon as the possibility of shift of class position by virtue of a different educational experience becomes articulately recognized, so that individuals seek not only to better their children or to guard them against educational defect but also to see the extension of restriction of educational opportunity as relevant to the whole class structure, another element enters in—the relationship of education to social change. Education becomes a mechanism of change. Public attention, once focused upon this possibility, is easily turned to the converse position of emphasizing education as a means toward preserving the status quo. I argue here for no historical priority in the two positions. But I am inclined to believe that we do not have catechumens taught to say "to do my duty in that state of life into which it has pleased God to call me" until we have the beginning of movements of individuals away from their birth positions in society. In fact, the whole use of education to defend vested interests and intrenched privilege goes with the recognition that education can be a way of encroaching upon them. Just as the presence of proselytizing religions focuses attention upon means of spreading the truth, upon pedagogy, so the educational implications of social stratification focus attention upon the content of education and lay the groundwork for an articulate interest in the curriculum.

Movements of peoples, colonization, and trade also bring education into a different focus. In New Guinea it is not uncommon to "hear" (i.e., understand without speaking) several languages besides one's own, and many people not only "hear" but also speak neighboring languages. A head-hunting people like the Mundugumor, who had the custom of giving child hostages to temporary allies among the neighboring peoples, articulately recognized that it was an advantage to have members of the group be well acquainted with the roads, the customs, and the language of their neighbors, who would assuredly at some time in any given generation be enemies and objects of attack. Those who took the hostages regarded this increased facility of the Mundugumor as a disadvantage which had to be put up with. But the emphasis remained with the desirability of learning. Today, with the growth of pidgin English as a lingua franca, bush natives and young boys are most anxious to learn pidgin. Their neighbors, with whom they could trade and communicate more readily if they knew pidgin, are not interested in teaching them. But the European colonist is interested. He sees his position as an expanding, initiating, changing one; he wants to trade with the natives, to recruit and indenture them to work on plantations. He needs to have them speak a language that he can understand. Accordingly, we have the shift from the native who needs to learn another language in order to understand to the colonist who needs someone else to learn a language so that he, the colonist, may be understood. In the course of teaching natives to speak some lingua franca, to handle money, to work copra, etc., the whole focus is on teaching; not, however, on techniques of teaching, in the sense of pedagogy, but upon sanctions for making the native learn. Such usages develop rapidly into compulsory schooling in the language of the colonist or the conqueror, and they result in the school's being seen as an adjunct of the group in power rather than as a privilege for those who learn.

Just as conquest or colonization of already inhabited countries brings up the problems of assimilation, so also mass migrations may accentuate the same problem. This has been true particularly in the United States, where education has been enormously influenced by the articulate need to assimilate the masses of European immigrants, with the resulting phrasing of the public schools as a means for educating other peoples' children. The school ceased to be chiefly a device by which children were taught accumulated knowledge or skills and became a political device for arousing and maintaining national loyalty through inculcating a language and a system of ideas which the pupils did not share with their parents.

It is noteworthy that, in the whole series of educational emphases which I have discussed here as significant components of our present-day concept of "education," one common element which differentiates the ideas of conversion, assimilation, successful colonization, and the relationship between class-caste lines and education from the attitude found in primitive homogeneous societies is the acceptance of discontinuity between parents and children. Primitive education was a process by which continuity was maintained between parents and children, even if the actual teacher was not a parent but a maternal uncle or a shaman. Modern education includes a heavy emphasis upon the function of education to create discontinuities—to turn the child of the peasant into a clerk, of the farmer into a lawyer, of the Italian immigrant into an American, of the illiterate into the literate. And parallel to this emphasis goes the attempt to use education as an extra, special prop for tottering continuities. Parents who are separated from their children by all the gaps in understanding which are a function of our rapidly changing world cling to the expedient of sending their children to the same schools and colleges they attended, counting upon the heavy traditionalism of slow-moving institutions to stem the tide of change. (Thus, while the father builds himself a new house and the mother furnishes it with modern furniture, they both rejoice that back at school, through the happy accident that the school is not well enough endowed, son will sit at the same desk at which his father sat.) The same attitude is reflected by the stock figure of the member of a rural school board who says, "What was good enough for me in school is good enough for my children. The three *R*'s, that's enough."

Another common factor in these modern trends of education is the increasing emphasis upon change rather than upon growth, upon what is done to people rather than upon what people do. This emphasis comes, I believe, from the inclusion of adults as objects of the educational effort—whether the effort comes from missionaries, colonizers, conquerors, Old Americans, or employers of labor. When a child is learning to talk, the miracle of learning is so pressing and conspicuous that the achievement of the teachers is put in the shade. But the displacement, in an adult's speech habits, of his native tongue by the phonetics of some language which he is being bullied or cajoled into learning is often more a matter of triumph for the teacher than of pride for the learner. Changing people's habits, people's ideas, people's language, people's beliefs, people's emotional allegiances, involves a sort of deliberate violence to other people's developed personalities—a violence not to be found in the whole teacher-child relationship, which finds its prototype in the cherishing parent helping the young child to learn those things which are essential to his humanity.

We have been shocked in recent years by the outspoken brutality of the totalitarian states, which set out to inculcate into children's minds a series of new ideas which it was considered politically useful for them to learn. Under the conflicting currents of modern ideologies the idea of *indoctrination* has developed as a way of characterizing the conscious educational aims of any group with whom the speaker is out of sympathy. Attempts to teach children any set of ideas in which one believes have become tainted with suspicion of power and self-interest, until almost all education can be branded and dismissed as one sort of indoctrination or another. The attempt to assimilate, convert, or keep in their places other human beings conceived of as inferior to those who are making the plans has been a boomerang which has distorted our whole educational philosophy; it has shifted the emphasis from one of growth and seeking for knowledge to one of dictation and forced acceptance of clichés and points of view. Thus we see that the presence of one element within our culture—a spurious sense of superiority of one group of human beings over another, which gave the group in power the impetus to force their language, their beliefs, and their culture down the throats of the group which was numerically, or economically, or geographically handicapped—has corrupted and distorted the emphases of our free schools.

But there has been another emphasis developing side by side with those which I have been discussing, and that is a belief in the power of education to work miracles—a belief which springs from looking at the other side of the shield. As long as the transmission of culture is an orderly and continuous process, in a slowly changing society, the child speaks the language of his parents; and, although one may marvel that this small human being learns at all, one does not marvel that he learns French or English or Samoan, provided that this be the language of the parents. It took the discontinuity of educational systems, purposive shifts of language and beliefs between parents and children, to catch our imagination and to fashion the great American faith in education as creation rather than transmission, conversion, suppression, assimilation, or indoctrination. Perhaps one of the most basic human ways of saying "new" is "something that my parents have never experienced" or, when we speak of our children, "something I have never experienced." The drama of discontinuity which has been such a startling feature of modern life, and for which formal education has been regarded in great measure as responsible, suggested to men that perhaps education might be a device for creating a new kind of world by developing a new kind of human being.

Here it is necessary to distinguish sharply between the sort of idea which George Counts expressed in his speech, "Dare the Schools Build a New Social Order?" and the idea of education as creation of something new. Dr. Counts did not mean a new social order in the sense of an order that no man had dreamed of, so much as he meant a very concrete and definite type of society for which he and many others believed they had a blueprint. He was asking whether the teachers would use the schools to produce a different type of socioeconomic system. His question was still a power question and partook of all the power ideas which have developed in the long period during which men in power, men with dominating ideas, men with missions, have sought to put their ideas over upon other men. His question would have been phrased more accurately as "Dare the schools build a different social order?" The schools of America have these hundred years been training children to give allegiance to a way of life that was new to them, not because they were children to whom all ways were new, not because the way of life was itself one that no man had yet dreamed of, but because they were the children of their parents. Whenever one group succeeds in getting power over the schools and teaches within those schools a doctrine foreign to many of those who enter those doors, they are building up, from the standpoint of those students, a different social order. From the standpoint of those in power, they are defending or extending the old; and, from the moment that the teachers had seriously started to put Dr. Counts's suggestion into practice, they would have been attempting by every method available to them to extend, in the minds of other people's children, their own picture, already an "old" idea, of the sort of world they wanted to live in.

It is not this sort of newness of which I speak. But from those who watched learning, those who humbly observed miracles instead of claiming them as the fruits of their strategy or of their superior teaching (propaganda) techniques, there grew up in America a touching belief that it was possible by education to build a new world—a world that no man had yet dreamed and that no man, bred as we had been bred, could dream. They argued that if we can bring up our children to be freer than we have been—freer from anxiety, freer from guilt and fear, freer from economic constraint and the dictates of expediency—to be equipped as we never were equipped, trained to think and enjoy thinking, trained to feel and enjoy feeling, then we shall produce a new kind of human being, one not known upon the earth before. Instead of the single visionary, the depth of whose vision has kept men's souls alive for centuries, we shall develop a whole people bred to the task of seeing with clear imaginative eyes into a future which is hidden from us behind the smoke screen of our defective and irremediable educational handicaps. This belief has often been branded as naïve and simple-minded. The American faith in education, which Clark Wissler lists as one of the dominant American culture traits, has been held up to ridicule many times. In many of its forms it is not only unjustified optimism but arrant nonsense. When small children are sent out by overzealous schoolteachers to engage in active social reforms —believed necessary by their teachers—the whole point of view becomes not only ridiculous but dangerous to the children themselves.

Phrased, however, without any of our blueprints, with an insistence that it is the children themselves who will some day, when they are grown, make blueprints on the basis of their better upbringing, the idea is a bold and beautiful one, an essentially democratic and American idea. Instead of attempting to bind and limit the future and to compromise the inhabitants of the next century by a long process of indoctrination which will make them unable to follow any path but that which we have laid down, it suggests that we devise and practice a system of education which sets the future free. We must concentrate upon teaching our children to walk so steadily that we need not hew too straight and narrow paths for them but can trust them to make new paths through difficulties we never encountered to a future of which we have no inkling today.

When we look for the contributions which contacts of peoples, of peoples of different races and different religions, different levels of culture and different degrees of technological development, have made to education, we find two. On the one hand, the emphasis has shifted from learning to teaching, from the doing to the one who causes it to be done, from spontaneity to coercion, from freedom to power. With this shift has come the development of techniques of power, dry pedagogy, regimentation, indoctrination, manipulation, and propaganda. These are but sorry additions to man's armory, and they come from the insult to human life which is perpetuated whenever one human being is regarded as differentially less or more human than another. But, on the other hand, out of the discontinuities and rapid changes which have accompanied these minglings of people has come another invention, one which perhaps would not have been born in any other setting than this one—the belief in education as an instrument for the creation of new human values.

We stand today in a crowded place, where millions of men mill about seeking to go in different directions. It is most uncertain whether the educational invention made by those who emphasized teaching or the educational invention made by those who emphasized learning will survive. But the more rapidly we can erase from our society those discrepancies in position and privilege which tend to perpetuate and strengthen the power and manipulative aspects of education, the more hope we may have that that other invention—the use of education for unknown ends which shall exalt man above his present stature—may survive.

2 SOCIAL AND PSYCHOLOGICAL ASPECTS OF EDUCATION IN TALELAND

Meyer Fortes

Despite many general studies, we know remarkably little about educational programs as they are actually carried out by the members of "traditional" societies. This chapter is one of the few detailed accounts of a traditional system of education in the available literature. The Tallensi are a people of northern Ghana, in west Africa, described in many papers and in two books by Meyer Fortes (1945, 1949). The author places education within the social context of this small-scale farming society in which the basic principle of organization is in the system of patrilineal clans and lineages. Technical abilities, moral and cosmological values, and the sanctions that uphold them, are shown both to form a coherent pattern and also to be an integral part of the general system of household, family, lineage, and neighborhood. Neither the educational system nor the social organization would persist over time without the other, and we see clearly the part played by education in ensuring continuity of culture among these people who yet are still little affected by the outside world. The paper includes a description of the psychological aspects of this educational program, and presents a classic account of childhood in a traditional African society.

INTRODUCTION

THERE is no lack of disquisitions on the role of education in the simpler societies. Africa, in particular, has received enormous attention in this connexion. Commissions and congresses have

Reprinted from *Africa*, Supplement to Volume 11 (4), 1938, with permission of the author and of the Director, International African Institute. The paper is reprinted in *Time and Social Structure, and Other Essays*, by Meyer Fortes (London School of Economics monograph series).

delivered judgment on education in one or another African society. Missionaries, anthropologists, itinerant journalists, travellers, Government officials, and innumerable others have vouchsafed opinions on the subject until it has become smothered in platitudes and generalizations. But empirical studies of a sociological or psychological kind in field or school are far from numerous. In this paper I shall attempt, in outline, such a study.[1]

THE SOCIOLOGICAL APPROACH

We can commence from two axioms which must be regarded as firmly established both in sociological and in educational theory. It is agreed that education in the widest sense is the process by which the cultural heritage is transmitted from generation to generation, and that schooling is therefore only a part of it. It is agreed, correlatively, that the 'moulding of individuals to the social norm is the function of education such as we find it among these simpler peoples' (Hoernlé 1931; see also Dewey 1961: ch. 1) and, it may be added, among ourselves.

Starting from these axioms, anthropologists have explored the conditions and the social framework of education in pre-literate societies. It has been shown that the training of the young is seldom regularized or systematized, but occurs as a 'by-product' (Hoernlé 1931; Malinowski 1936) of the cultural routine; that the kinsfolk, and particularly the family, are mainly responsible for it; that it is conducted in a practical way in relation to the 'actual situations of daily life'.[2] It has been observed that manners and ethical and moral attitudes are first inculcated within the family circle in association with food and eating and with the control of bodily functions. A good deal of discussion has been devoted, also, to what appear to be overtly educational institutions, such as initiation schools and ceremonies, age grades, or

---

[1] An outline of this paper was first presented in a lecture on 'Play Activities of Primitive African Children' which I gave in March 1936 at the invitation of Paul and Marjorie Abbatt. Dr. Lucy Mair and Dr. E. E. Evans-Pritchard have assisted me greatly with their comments and criticism.

[2] R. Firth, 1936: 147 ff. This is the most valuable empirical and theoretical contribution to the subject of recent years. There have been various attempts to utilize this principle in planning curricula of schooling in Africa. Cf. W. B. Mumford 1930 and A. D. Helser 1934.

secret societies.[3] It has been proved that direct instruction in tribal history, sexual knowledge, and ritual esoterica is promoted by these institutions.

In this way a good deal of information has been accumulated about *what* is transmitted from one generation to the next in preliterate societies, about the circumstances of this transmission, and the institutional and structural framework within which it occurs. Of the process of education—*how* one generation is 'moulded' by the superior generation, *how* it assimilates and perpetuates its cultural heritage—much less is known. The problem has, indeed, never been precisely formulated,[4] with the result that alleged discussions of primitive education not infrequently prove to be merely descriptions of social structure slightly disguised.

The problem formulated. Education is a social process, a temporal concatenation of events in which the significant factor is time and the significant phenomenon is change. Between birth and social maturity the individual is transformed from a relatively peripheral into a relatively central link in the social structure; from an economically passive burden into a producer; from a biological unit into a social personality irretrievably cast in the habits, dispositions and notions characteristic of his culture. The problem presented by this function of society is of an entirely different order from that presented by the religious or economic or political system of a people. The former is primarily a problem of genetic psychology, the latter of cultural and sociological analysis. In studying education in a particular society we ought, ideally, to be able to take its cultural idiom for granted, whereas the first task of sociological analysis is to discover the cultural idiom. Thus, in Taleland one often finds a pair of small boys disputing with childish earnestness as to who is senior. Unless one has observed the scope of the principle of seniority in the social structure one is liable to dismiss this as mere childish play of no importance.

Education, from this point of view,[5] is an active process of

---

[3] Cf., *inter alia,* E. W. Smith 1934 for a useful commentary on this and other general points referred to in this paper; and J. H. Driberg 1932:232 ff.

[4] I refer to Africa here. Margaret Mead 1928:193 and Firth 1936, have done much to clarify it for Oceania. Attention is drawn to the problem in Rev. E. W. Smith's essay, cited above.

[5] An excursus into genetic psychology would be out of place in this paper, but the reader will observe how much it owes, *inter alia,* to F. C. Bartlett,

learning and teaching by which individuals gradually acquire the full outfit of culturally defined and adapted behaviour. In this paper I shall try to delineate briefly how it occurs in one African society, that of the Tallensi of the Northern Territories of the Gold Coast. As it will be impossible to compass the whole process of social maturation within the limits of this paper, some of the more conspicuous changes and activities only will be examined.

The sampling problem. My observations were made in the course of a field study of the Tallensi the object of which, in accordance with the usual ethnographical method, was the entire society and its culture. It is impossible in such a case—as other anthropologists have found—to follow up a special psychological problem in a manner commensurate with the criteria of experimental research in England. That will only be achieved when specialists can be induced to take over these investigations.

Such material as I am able to present consequently suffers most from sampling deficiencies. Social behaviour among primitive people appears to be more standardized than among ourselves. Yet variations occur, distributed perhaps in accordance with the normal curve of error as among ourselves but perhaps not. The problem has still to be investigated. Ethnographers are principally interested in 'patterns of behaviour', hence they neglect or slur over variations, and sometimes indeed build whole theories on a single occurrence. For most problems of social anthropology variations are of minor importance as compared with the 'typical', and an all-round knowledge of a culture is a sufficient check of typicality. For problems of developmental psychology variations may be of the utmost importance. For example, the first case of thumb-sucking I observed was that of a girl infant 3–4 years old whose mother had recently died. Could it be assumed that this was a clear-cut instance of the thumb being substituted for the nipple? Some time later I came across another little girl, about the same age, thumb-sucking, but her mother was alive and she was

Remembering; K. Koffka, *Growth of the Mind;* S. Isaacs, *Intellectual Growth of Young Children; Social Development of Young Children;* C. E. Spearman, *Nature of Intelligence;* and to the writings of Jean Piaget (*Language and Thought of the Young Child,* &c.). I have borrowed also from the anthropological writings already cited and from those of Malinowski and Radcliffe-Brown, particularly from their writings on kinship.

not yet fully weaned. Further observation brought a few more cases of this habit to light, but it is so infrequent among Tale children that a single year's observation does not yield sufficient instances to suggest any correlation.

Generally speaking, therefore, small samples form the basis of the observations recorded in this paper. Where norms of development are implied it will be understood that an appreciable, though indeterminable, variability exists.

SOCIAL SPHERE OF THE TALE CHILD

The process of education among the Tallensi, as among a great many other African peoples of analogous culture, is intelligible when it is recognized that the social sphere of adult and child[6] is unitary and undivided. In our own society the child's feeling and thinking and acting takes place largely in relation to a reality —to aims, responsibilities, compulsions, material objects and persons, and so forth—which differs completely from that of the adult, though sometimes overlapping it. This dichotomy is not only expressed in our customs, it comes out also in the psychological reactions which mark the individual's transition from the child's world to the adult's—e.g. the so-called negative phase or adolescent instability which has been alleged to be universal in our society.[7] It is unknown in Tale society (cf. also Mead 1928). As between adults and children, in Tale society, the social sphere is differentiated only in terms of relative capacity. All participate in the same culture, the same round of life, but in varying degrees, corresponding to the stage of physical and mental development. Nothing in the universe of adult behaviour is hidden from children or barred to them. They are actively and responsibly part

----

[6] I am aware that the unqualified manner in which this proposition is formulated here invites the immediate objection that it cannot possibly hold for the new-born infant, or even for the child who is inarticulate and does not yet walk or crawl. I would suggest in answer that it is impossible empirically to observe the point at which the child's affective orientation to its cultural environment first receives its bias; and also, that recent psychology and anthropology would support me in attaching basic importance to the earliest infantile responses of a child as determinants of later interests.

[7] See G. Murphy 1937:429–32 for a critical discussion of this question.

of the social structure, of the economic system, the ritual and ideological system. Psychological effects of fundamental importance for Tale education follow from this. For it means that the child is from the beginning oriented towards the same reality as its parents and has the same physical and social material upon which to direct its cognitive and instinctual endowment. The interests, motives, and purposes of children are identical with those of adults, but at a simpler level of organization. Hence the children need not be coerced to take a share in economic and social activities. They are eager to do so. This does not mean that Tale children are altogether passive in the hands of their parents. Temperamental idiosyncrasies in children strike the observer at a glance. Tantrums, disobedience, destructiveness, and other aggressive outbursts occur sometimes. Among youths and adults misfits and incompetents can be found. But even they live for the same ends and have the same objective values and interests as the majority.

The unity of the social sphere is the more marked in Tale society since they have almost no social stratification within a genealogical or local community. There are no class or rank cleavages, nor highly organized and exclusive economic, political, or ritual associations cutting across the local, genealogical segmentation; and the social division of labour is rudimentary. The pattern of existence is the same for all members of a given community, varying only in texture or tone from individual to individual. The social sphere is differentiated only as between communities which are generally localized clans or lineages. Thus, the blacksmith lineage of Sakpee is unique, as compared with its neighbours, in respect to those components of its culture connected with its craft. Only sons of that lineage may be taught the craft of the smith; and even those who through lack of inclination or ability do not learn it share the ideology associated with it and submit to ritual and moral constraints in virtue of this. Because of their traditional craft the men of Sakpee do not eat the hedgehog until they have successfully made a piece of ironwork; and when they were driven from the Tong Hills, abandoned their homes and property but carried with them the sacred anvils. Similarly, the social sphere of the Hill Tallis contrasts in many respects with that of their Namoo neighbours on account of their different ritual systems.

Yet it is necessary to note that these differences do not detract
from the essential homogeneity of the social sphere for all the
Tallensi. They are differences in the substance of some cultural
definitions, not in the forms and functions of institutions. The
totemic taboos of the Hill Tallis are exactly paralleled by the
prohibitions of first-born children eating the domestic fowl among
the Namoos. What their sacred groves and initiation rites mean
to the former, their first ancestor, sacred drums, and the chiefship
mean to the latter. The psychological substratum of social behaviour is the same in both groups and in their associated clans, with a
sole exception. The initiation cult of the Hill Tallis does give a bias
to their ideology and so to their social sphere which the Namoos
lack (Fortes 1936a). In our present inquiry these differences may
be neglected since the dynamic relationships of the individual to
his community are the same everywhere in Taleland. Whether a
child is trained as a blacksmith or as a farmer, and whether
he is inducted into the ritual and ideology of the ancestor cult
alone, or into that of the sacred groves as well, the principles are
the same.

This background will be continuously discerned in our study of
Tale education. But a few clinching observations may be cited
here to show that the child is not merely a supernumerary
element of his society but thinks and feels himself to be a part of
it.

1. I was walking with Samane and his two small sons (8–9
years)[8] across a recently sown field of early millet already a
few inches high. I chanced to tread on a shoot. Immediately one
of the small boys stooped and carefully raised and replanted the
blade of millet. 'Why did you do that?' I asked. 'Don't you know
that is our food?' he replied reproachfully.

2. Every small boy of 6–7 years and upwards has a passionate
desire to own a hen, and many of them are able to realize this
ambition. If you ask a small boy why he wants a hen he will
reply in almost the same words as an adult uses to explain the
importance of 'things' (*bon*). 'If you have a hen it lays eggs, and
you take the eggs and breed chicks, then you can sell the chickens
and buy a goat, and when the goat breeds you can sell its offspring

---

[8] All ages are estimated, but the probable error of such an estimate is
at least 12 months.

and buy a sheep, and when the sheep breeds you can sell its offspring and buy a cow, and then you can take the cow and get a wife.'

3. Maanyeya, a little girl of about 9–10 years, said that she had eaten none of the meat of last night's sacrifice. 'Why?' I asked. 'When they sacrifice to Zukɔk', she explained gravely, 'women don't eat of the meat. If they do, they will never bear any children, they become sterile.' 'What's that to you?' I said. 'Am I not a woman? Who wants to be sterile?' she responded almost indignantly.

4. I was playing with Tarəmba and Yindubil (8–9 years), sons of the same joint family, and their friends. We were discussing parents. Tarəmba and Yindubil, speaking together, told me the story of the latter's mother. Three or four years ago she had run away from their father to marry another man. They said, in the very words that an adult member of the family would use, speaking seriously: 'She ran away and took our belly [that is, she was pregnant by their father] and went and bore over there, so our child is there. Then she bore another child there. When our child is big enough we will separate it [*pɔhg*—the technical legal term] and bring it home.' These two were thus identifying themselves completely with the family, mother–child attachments notwithstanding.

Such examples could be multiplied tenfold, but they will suffice at this stage.

The adult attitude about education. Education is not an entirely unwitting process among the Tallensi. They set a high, and indeed over-determined, value on their culture, and are fully aware of the fact that its continuity depends upon adequate transmission to their descendants. Their social structure, which is built up on the lineage system, and their economic organization put a premium on this, and a significant motive for stressing the continuity of their culture arises from their ancestor cult. Every Taləŋa desires sons so that there may be some one left to pour libations and make sacrifices to him after his death. The ancestor cult and family morality combine to imbue every man and woman with an intense sense of their continuity, both physical and psychological, with their parents on the one hand and their children on the other. A man feels a moral compulsion to pass on his private possessions, his craft, tools, and knowledge to his son, a woman to her daughter. He has the same feeling about carrying on a craft or cult which had been practised by a parent. Ironwork is not merely a profitable craft to the blacksmiths of Sakpee; it is a religious duty to their ancestors.

The most conspicuous affective moment in the religious system of the Tallensi is this sense of moral obligation to parents and children. It is the counterpart of the notion that the sins of the fathers will be visited on the offspring even unto the third and fourth generation. Last year, for instance, Kuwaas had to promise heavy sacrifices to expiate the sin of his grandfather, who was responsible, three generations ago, for the ravaging of his clan settlement by the Hill Talis.

The idea of education is, therefore, not only understood but also frequently formulated in discussions and conversations. A chief once observed to me that children learn who their fathers and ancestors (*banam ni yaanam*) were by listening at sacrifices. 'Our ancestor shrines are our books', he said. Nyaaŋzum, a man of 45–50, put these conceptions neatly and precisely one day when we were discussing some particularly secret ritual matters. His 'grandson',[9] a youth of about 25, was with us. 'Shall we send him away?' I asked. 'No,' he replied, 'if he listens it doesn't matter. He will not gossip to any one. And when some day I am no longer here, is it not he who will take it on? If he listens will he not know, will he not acquire wisdom?' When children are very small, he explained, they know nothing about religious things. 'They learn little by little. When we go to the shrine they accompany us and listen to what we say. Will they not [thus] get to know it?' His own small son Badiwona (6–7 years) is extremely devoted to him. One day, affectionately patting the child, he said: 'When we come out in the morning, and if he doesn't see me, he seeks about for me. If he doesn't find me he won't rest. That is why I had him initiated last year. Whatever I do he also sits and listens. Will he not get to know it thus? And when I am gone will he not say that when he was a child he used to go about with his father and used to see how his father did this and that? This is my child and I am teaching him uprightness. If he is

---

[9] Kinship terms placed between inverted commas are translations of native terms indicating classificatory kin.

about to do anything that is not seemly I tell him, so that when he grows up he will know upright ways.'[10]

Education, it is clear, is regarded as a joint enterprise in which parents are as eager to lead as children to follow. In consequence of this attitude adults are very tolerant of children's ways and especially about their learning. A child is never forced beyond its capacity. This is seen most clearly in relation to the pivotal economic activity, agriculture. However skilful a boy may be with his hoe, he will not be forced to do as much work as an adult. Men often restrain their sons of 12–14 from joining the adults in hoeing on the grounds that over-exertion is harmful. Again, women do not take daughters of 9–10 on firewood expeditions to the bush.

That skill comes with practise is realized by all. When adults are asked about children's mimetic play they reply: 'That is how they learn.' Thus when a boy is 7 or 8 his father buys him a small bow so that he can go and learn marksmanship in play with his comrades. Yet the existence of individual differences in ability, both amongst children and amongst adults, is recognized and cited with reference to the acquisition of skill. Rapid learning or the acquisition of a new skill is explained by *u mar nini pam,* 'he has eyes remarkably', that is, he is very sharp. A friend of mine who was a cap-maker told me how he had learnt his craft, as a youth, from a Dagban by carefully watching him at work. When he was young, he explained, he had 'very good eyes'. This conception of cleverness is intelligible in a society where learning by looking and copying is the commonest manner of achieving dexterity both in crafts and in the everyday manual activities.

At the same time, no one hestitates to punish when it seems to be merited. A child who neglects a task entrusted to him or her may expect to be rebuked or even chastised. Incidents such as the following occur frequently. Strolling through Puhug one morning in June when the early millet was ripening, I stopped to chat with Tampɔyar, a young man of 25 or so. Suddenly there came the sound of furious railing from his father's house-top. 'Your ears don't listen. Can't you look after your cattle

---

[10] He learns—*u bamhɔra,* cognate with *baŋ,* to know; I teach him—*mpaanumi.*

properly, you good-for-nothings, you things-with-sunken-eyes.
. . .' A voice from a neighbouring house-top joined in to the
same effect, adding: 'I'll come down and thrash you.' The
objects of these fulminations were two small boys, about 9–10
years, who were driving some cattle out to pasture. They were
dawdling and their beasts stopped to munch at the millet. The
rebuke had the desired effect. Tampɔyar's comment was to point
to a scar on his body where for the same crime he had been
so severely whipped, as a small boy, that a suppurating wound
resulted.

Disciplinary punishment is also administered at times. A small
boy is told to go and scare the birds from the fields. He refuses.
A hard smack on the haunches sends him scampering.

Nevertheless, I have never observed vindictive punishment or
malicious bullying, either of children by adults or of young children by older ones. Indeed, punishment appeared to me to be
extremely rare among the Tallensi, as compared with ourselves.
It is thought to be necessary sometimes to use rough measures
in teaching morals and manners, but not in teaching skills. A
very intelligent elder once declared, 'If you don't harass your
child, he will not gain sense.' This view is held by many. But, as
the context of conversation showed, what he meant was not so
much corporal punishment as that constant supervision is necessary in the training of children for life.

The concept of 'yam'. Tallensi often use the concept *yam*
when discussing social behaviour. It corresponds to our notion of
'sense' when we refer to a 'sensible man', or 'sound common
sense'. As the Tallensi use the term it suggests the quality of
'insight'. Its range of usage is wide. If it is said of some one
u mar yam pam, 'he has a great deal of sense', the implication
is that he is a man of wisdom, or is intelligent, or experienced in
affairs, or resourceful. If some one commits a *faux pas,* or shows
lack of understanding, or misbehaves morally the comment is
u ka yam, 'he has no sense'. The concept is used to refer
both to qualities of personality and to attributes of behaviour.
It is applied also in a genetic sense to describe the social development of the child. A normal child between the ages of about
6 and 9 years is said to 'have sense at length'. It knows how
to behave in the social situations which confront it, whereas an
infant of 3 or 4 years old does not. Yet a 4-year-old having

learned bladder and bowel control is said to 'have sense' as compared with a 2-year-old. Similarly Nindɔyat, (17–18 years) telling me of his sweethearting, waxed scornful about his own boyish friendship with girls two years before. 'I still had no sense then', he explained. The concept, it will be seen, is generally used relatively to a particular situation.

Children's attitude to education. In Tale society every pupil becomes in some situations a teacher. At the one extreme there are specialized ritual performances which some men do not learn till they are grey, and at the other, the toddler leaning over to play with his nursling brother is teaching the latter something about his environment. This holds right through the age-scale. Considering also the unity of the social sphere, one is not surprised to find that children have the same attitudes about education as their elders. Hence children are rarely unwilling to learn. As a rule, too, they are not ashamed of confessing failure, ignorance, or inability to do or make something. Conversely, children laugh good-humouredly at one another's deficiencies in skill or knowledge, they never jeer. Ridicule is reserved for the correction of uncouth manners, disgraceful morals, or aberrant interests.

Fundamental educational relationships. It will be evident from the preceding analysis that Tale children receive their education not only from the adults but also from older children and adolescents who are always transmitting what they know of the cultural heritage to their younger brothers and sisters and cousins. From the age of 5 or 6 years until they become fully absorbed into the economic system children often go about in small groups. These groups[11] usually consist of siblings, half-siblings, and ortho-cousins of close agnatic kinship, from the same joint family or sublineage group. The composition of a children's group depends upon various factors. The most important of these are the following:

Age and mobility. Infants still requiring care are often carried about by boys and girls attached to a group of older children. Generally speaking, children of the same degree of mobility tend to go about together. Thus one often finds a group comprising children of about 6 to 10 years. But the stage of social develop-

---

[11] See M. Fortes 1936a for ancillary information about these groups. Also M. and S. L. Fortes 1936 for an outline of their structural context.

ment reached by a child is important in this connexion. Hence young children under 10–11, children between 10–11 and the beginning of pubescence, and adolescents all tend to form separate groups.

Sex. Before the age of about 6 years small boys very frequently go about with girls' groups, and small girls, though more rarely, accompany older brothers. After that age as mobility increases and interests diverge the sexes tend to separate. A well-defined sexual dichotomy runs through Tale social life and thought, and the children begin to adopt the cultural definitions of the roles of the sexes in relation to each other about the time that single-sex groups become common. This is associated with a differentiation of their activities on the periphery of the economic system. Thus cowherds are always boys, whereas it is the girls who help with the housekeeping.

The social situation. Yet none of these children's groups resemble gangs. They have no permanent structure. They generally crystallize out in particular situations and the composition of a group depends largely upon the situation. In ritual situations one often finds a somewhat amorphous group of children and young people of a wide age-range. In games and imaginative play, however, it is more usual to meet with small groups of restricted age-range. Pairs and trios of either sex and of nearly the same age, who are almost always siblings or ortho-cousins, often have a more lasting companionship in work and play and provide a nucleus for larger temporary groups, especially in the dry season.

The most fundamental educational relationship of the Tallensi is, however, not that of children to children but of children to parents. It is a complex relationship, as defined in Tale culture, but its principal moments can be readily discerned. On the plane of rational, everyday economic and social activities there is co-operation, friendliness and tolerance, almost equality. This is more marked between father and child than between mother and child. A father is always addressed by his personal name, a mother is always called *mma,* my mother. Affectively, however, a powerful tension exists between parent and child. A parent's authority may not be flouted, though he or she is expected to be affectionate and indulgent. Sin, in Tale ideology, is primarily an offence against the person, status, or rights of the living parents, or the parent-images—the ancestor spirits.

The structure of this relationship makes it possible for children to acquiesce immediately in the commands and teachings of their parents or parent-substitutes. Children are, as a rule, very obedient. If they refuse to carry out an order there is usually some very valid reason—acknowledged as such by both parents and children—such as that it is some one else's turn. But the parent-child relationship is educationally fundamental in another sense—it is the paradigm of all moral relationships.

It is worth noting, by contrast, that the relationship between grandparent and grandchild is the reverse of that between parent and child. In this case equality, compatibility and partisanship, as if in league against the generation between them, are emphasized, more particularly by the joking relationship—mutual ragging among the Tallensi—permitted between grandparent and grandchild.

The social space. How these relationships function in the educational development of a Tale child is determined by its social space.[12] An individual's social space is a product of that segment of the social structure and that segment of the habitat with which he or she is in effective contact. To put it in another way, the social space is the society in its ecological setting seen from the individual's point of view. The individual creates his social space but is himself in turn formed by it. On the one hand, his range of experiences and behaviour are controlled by his social space, and on the other, everything he learns causes it to expand and become more differentiated. In the lifetime of the individual it changes *pari passu* with his psycho-physical and social development.

In Taleland an infant remains confined to the house for the first three to six months or even longer. During this period its social space is extremely restricted. It has effective social relationships with its mother, sometimes its grandmother or a co-wife of its mother, of an older sibling or half-sibling, and its father—in this order of frequency and intensity. At the age of 3 to 4, when it is beginning to talk fluently and can run about, its effective range of contacts includes all the members of the joint family and probably those of closely neighbouring related joint families.

---

[12] This term is employed here for want of an apter one. It has been used in a different sense by Simmel and others.

It is beginning to associate with groups of other related children belonging to its immediate milieu and to know the topography of its parental homestead and its immediate surroundings. By the age of 6 or 7 it is being taken on visits to its mother's brother's house and begins to incorporate into the texture of its life its relationships with its mother's people and their settlement. A little later it commences to take a share in very simple economic duties. In this way the child's social space is continuously expanding as it grows older. The educational agencies to which it is subjected become more numerous and more diverse and its experiences more variegated as it participates in an ever-increasing range of social situations. With adolescence a great increase in mobility ensues and a new interest emerges—the opposite sex as potential spouses. This coincides with the beginning of real economic responsibility. When he reaches adulthood, the individual's social space is a function of the entire social structure in its complete ecological setting.[13] He should be capable of appropriate behaviour in any social situation which may confront the normal Taləŋa. He is a full citizen—which means that he is actually or potentially subject to the whole gamut of constraints inherent in Tale society.

In the evolution of an individual's social space we have a measure of his educational development. In Taleland this is brought about not only by accretion to, but also by differentiation of, his or her field of social activity. Sex, for example, is a differentiating factor of great significance. From childhood on a person's relation to the economic system is chiefly determined by sex. In the kinship system sex operates as a differentiating factor from an equally early age, from the time, in fact, when a child learns to designate like-sex siblings by different terms from opposite-sex siblings. Local, lineage, or family institutions also act as differentiating factors, though not in the same way. This is a consequence in part of the peculiarities of Tale political

---

[13] A person's social space is not equivalent to the entire social structure since it is included in the latter, which is never fully known to or acted on by the individual. Take, for instance, the Tale joint family. As a structural unit it can be easily distinguished and described by the anthropologist; but each member's view of the whole is unique—that of the head of the joint family is different from that of his wife or son—yet all derived from the same single unit of structure.

structure. Local groupings, clans and lineages are asymmetrically linked *inter se* and with communities outside the Tale area proper by political, genealogical, territorial, or ritual ties. The most striking case of this sort is presented by the Hill Talis who have immemorial ritual links with villages and genealogical groups among Dagomba, Mamprussi, Bulisi (Builsa), Woolisi (Kassena), Mossi, and other neighbouring peoples. Each of the Hill communities has its exclusive associates in these foreign areas. The people of Sii were traditionally associated with the Bulisi, the people of Gorogo with the Woolisi, the Kpata'ar clan with certain villages of Black Dagomba, and so forth. There was in former times, and is even more so now, a constant traffic between the Tong Hills and the outside areas linked with the clans dwelling there—pilgrims coming to the Fertility Shrines in the Hills and Talis paying ceremonial visits to their associates. But the economic and political by-products of this traffic were most important. In this way a range of geographical and social contacts was, and is, available to a member of the Hill clans which no Namoos had, and among the Hill clans themselves the actual contacts varied from clan to clan. The Namoos again have their traditional political associates among the Mamprussi. It is especially interesting to note that the Mamprussi associates of the Hill Talis and the Mamprussi associates of the Namoos belonged to a single political structure; yet the latter would not, a generation ago, have hesitated to overpower and enslave any Hill Talis they encountered defenceless.

Factors of this sort become significant only after adolescence and more so in the life of men than of women; but they are operative even in childhood. The Black Dagomba guests at a Kpata'ar elder's homestead are familiar figures to his children; and one sign of the interest taken in them by the children is the fact that most Kpata'ar youths understand and easily speak the dialect of the Black Dagomba, whereas other Tallensi do not.

The specific genealogical links of a family act in a similar way. In the extreme case, they may alter a person's whole life. The story of Puvɔləmra is typical, though such occurrences are not usual. He was a Kpatia man whose parents had died in his boyhood. For special reasons he had come to live with his mother's brother at Gbizug. There he grew up, and when I met him, a man of 35–40, he was to all intents a Gbizug man, a complete partisan of that lineage, professing its ideology, subject to its ritual restrictions, and practising the craft of leatherwork as he had learnt it from his mother's brother. He will probably return to Kpatia when he succeeds to his patrimony, there to be assimilated to a rather different ritual system, but transmitting to his sons and grandsons the art of leatherwork and the habits of industry learnt from his mother's brother. Many Tale lineages trace peculiar features of their residence or kinship, or the possession of special ritual, medical, or technological knowledge, to an ancestor with a history like that of Puvɔləmra.

Finally, the phase of family history coinciding with an early period of a person's education—the status of one or more senior members of his family, or the holding of ritual or political office by any of them—may have a significant differentiating influence on his or her social space. The homestead of a lineage or clan head is the focus of intercommunication both of the constituent parts of that grouping, the sublineages and joint families, and of the lineage or clan with its neighbours, not only in secular affairs but also in ritual matters. This is even more evident with people who hold offices. There is a constant coming and going of people at the house of a chief or clan-head: a complainant has brought a case to lay before the chief; the elders of the clan have come to consult him about the rain; somebody's daughter recently married has deserted her husband and the indignant son-in-law is brought to the clan-head to discuss the affair; a distant cognatic kinsman has brought a goat to sacrifice to the spirit of the supreme ancestor of the lineage; orders have been received that the young men must turn out for rest-house repairs in two or three days; and so forth. Transactions of this sort generally take place in public and the children of the house are always avid listeners. If any one has to be summoned or a message delivered a youth or a small boy is sent.

The members of such a house, especially those who have reached or passed adolescence, have a wider range of direct contacts with the social structure and their culture than their less privileged contemporaries. In Taleland, it is true, these differences tend to get smoothed out in the course of a person's lifetime owing to the uniformity of the culture and the homogeneity and cohesion of the social structure. Every lineage or clan member is at home in the house of the head, and important affairs are never discussed unless every branch of the grouping is represented. Again, eldership and office circulate from sublineage to sublineage, and the classificatory kinship system spreads the range of identification between the units of the structure widely. Nevertheless, the differential influence of this factor is significant from the educational point of view since our emphasis is on the stage of an individual's life-history at which it operates. The effects are strikingly observable both at the time it is operating and especially in the character of the mature man or woman. An amusing instance of the former is the following: Deǝmzeet of Puhug was elected elder under somewhat dramatic circumstances. Next morning, near his homestead I met his small grandsons of about 6–7 years old. Quite spontaneously they started telling me the story of the exciting events of the past two or three days, obviously repeating the talk that they had heard and only half understood in the family circle. They told me what the other elders had said and what the chief had said and how Deǝmzeet had summoned a diviner to consult. 'Deǝmzeet is the father of all of us,' said one of them, 'and he has a big farm.' They ran off to show me the boundaries of the farm he had recently inherited as head of the sublineage. As we passed the family graves they pointed out, solemnly, the tomb of Deǝmzeet's predecessor, who had no doubt been frequently referred to in the last few days. These were all matters which would normally not have occurred within the purview of children of their age.

Instances of the effect on his adult character of such an expansion of an individual's social space during his youth were so numerous as to suggest a general rule. I always found that, allowing for variation in ability and personality, men whose fathers had been elders or office-holders at a time when they themselves were old enough to take an interest in public affairs as spectators or participants were better informed than the average person, and tended to assume the lead in social and ritual activities. The natives themselves recognize this. It often happens that a man who has not had the advantage of such a training succeeds to eldership or office and has to depend upon the advice and assistance of younger men who have been more fortunate in this respect.

THE DYNAMIC CHARACTERS OF TALE EDUCATION

Learning and teaching proceeds within the structural framework and subject to the cultural conceptions outlined in the preceding pages. We must now investigate its dynamic characters. The educational development of a Tale child may be regarded as the gradual acquisition of an ensemble of *interests, observances* and *skills*. What these are and how they are acquired constitutes our next inquiry. It is basically a psychological problem, tantamount, up to a point, to analysing the observations already recorded at a different level of behaviour.

An exhaustive investigation will not be attempted in this paper. The detailed exposition of Tale child psychology which should be the foundation of such an investigation cannot be undertaken here, nor would it be practicable to try to follow out the complex pattern of Tale education in all its ramifications in a limited space. I propose, therefore, to discuss only a few of the major trends and significant processes. Learning and teaching is a composite process, a network of interacting factors. For the purpose of analysis it will be necessary to isolate some of the variables, but it will have to be borne in mind that in the actual life-history of a Tale man or woman they occur only in interaction with one another and with numerous others.

The determinants of social behaviour. From the genetic point of view social behaviour is determined by four groups of factors —physiological, psychological, social, and cultural. If we observe a child learning to walk, we can easily distinguish these factors. It cannot start walking until it has reached a certain degree of physiological maturity. As it practises it learns to plan its efforts so as to avoid falls or trying to accomplish too much at a time—a psychological achievement, depending partly on its level of intelligence. Again, a child learns to walk in response, partly, to stimulation, encouragement and even training given by some or all of the people who come into its social space. The most important of these is, universally, its mother or some one who acts as mother. Finally, there will be culturally defined ways of encouraging and stimulating or restraining a child in these efforts.

In Taleland these factors of social behaviour are notably intercorrelated. In general there is a marked parallelism between the trend of physiological and psychological development and that of social and cultural development—unlike our own society in certain strata of which social development lags behind psychophysical development. A girl of 16 or so in Taleland is not only physiologically mature but has accepted the role of a mature woman in the psychological and social sense. She is married, she has economic duties to perform, she is socially responsible. A boy of the same age is pulling his full weight in the economic system, and it is regarded as entirely reasonable that he should be thinking of marriage and sex life, though it may be four or five years before he finds a wife. It should be added that physiological development among the Tallensi is probably somewhat slower than among ourselves. Accurate age norms could not, as will readily be appreciated, be established, but I have estimated that the average age of walking is about 2 years, of talking about 3 years (though single words like *mma,* my mother, and names of members of the family are used with infantile approximation at about 2 years). As far as one can judge by somatic indications, pubescence in boys commences at about 14 years. Girls, according to my wife's observations, do not as a rule menstruate before the age of about 15–16 years, by which time they have frequently been married for a year or two.

This close correlation between psycho-physical and social development is reflected in the notion held by the natives that physiological growth is a natural process, like the growth of plants and animals. The Tallensi have no elaborate transition rites to mark the passage from one stage of growth to another. Unlike many other West African peoples, they accept the onset of puberty in boys and girls, which they recognize by special terms, with the same casual rationality as they accept the cycle of time itself. Health and well-being of the body must be safeguarded with all the resources of their empirical and magical knowledge, but growth in itself is not a matter of cultural emphasis. It is of the very nature of human life. It emanates from *Naawun,* Heaven, the *ultima ratio* of Tale philosophy, corresponding in this context to our notion of Nature.

In keeping with this conception of physical growth, children are *expected* to acquire, in due course, the elementary bodily skills—sitting, crawling, walking, running, hand-eye-mouth co-ordination in eating, and so forth. There is no deliberate training

in these skills. Parents and older siblings take an affectionate
and attentive, though sporadic, interest in an infant's psycho-
physical development, but do not resort to special methods of
fostering it. An infant beginning to crawl is allowed to practise
more or less at will, watched by mother or sister, brother or
father, lest it injure itself. An infant beginning to walk is supported for a bit, now and then, by an older child, or a parent,
or any one to whose care it happens to be entrusted. There is no
such thing as regular training in these skills. The attention given
to an infant in these respects is a function not only of its stage
of physiological development, but even more so of the practical
exigencies of the situation with which the parent or older child
has to cope at the moment. It is quite usual to see incidents
such as this: a woman is gathering guinea corn-stalks for her
fire some 20–30 yards from the homestead. Her infant son of
about 2½ years totters along the path to her calling out *mma,
mma* (my mother). She appears to take no notice until he reaches
her. He stands beside her, clutching her thigh tightly, while she
finishes tying the bundle of guinea corn-stalks. She puts the bundle
on her head and, as she wants to get back into the house as
quickly as possible, swings the infant—by one arm—up to her
hip and marches off. If she were not in a hurry she might walk
back slowly, allowing the infant to follow her and throwing back
encouraging remarks to him.

Since nobody thinks infants need special training by particular
persons, the natives have a habit of bandying them about from
one member of a family to another, though grandparents, co-
wives, and other children of the same mother are the most usual
nursemaids. A Tale child must, from earliest infancy, learn to
co-operate to its fullest capacity with the demands of practical
necessity: it must learn to adapt itself to such facts of reality
as the economic preoccupations of its mother. I have often seen
children of about 12–18 months left sitting in the shade for half
an hour or longer, quite alone, while their mothers are busy with
some household task. A healthy infant will remain sitting thus,
almost motionless, playing with a fragment of calabash, a stick,
or the sand—for the idea of giving an infant a toy or some attractive trinket to occupy it when it is left alone does not occur
to the Tallensi. On the other hand, when an infant clamours for

attention there is always some one of its kinsfolk near at hand to render it.

The native point of view about physical growth was well illustrated in the case of two infants belonging to a single extended family which I knew well. The younger infant was a lively, healthy, inquisitive girl of about 2½–3 years old already toddling about and exploring the world. The other infant, a boy about 3 months older, had been puny and ailing from birth and, though obviously intelligent, was chronically fretful and dependent and had not yet begun to walk. In Taleland the number three is symbolical of maleness, four of femaleness. Hence it is said in their folk-lore that boys begin to walk and talk in their third year, girls in their fourth. Yet the glaring discrepancy in development between these two infants caused no anxiety to the parents of the boy, except about his health. They realized clearly the connexion between his retardation and his health, but were entirely complacent about the former. That he would walk and talk in due course was taken for granted.

The expectation of normal behaviour. It will be evident from these examples that in the cultural idiom of the Tallensi age is not conceived as a significant factor in psycho-physical or social development. Yet relative seniority determines status and rights even in children's groups and their notion of time is explicit and clear. They think of genetic development primarily in terms of maturity, which is a synthetic concept embracing both physiological and behavioural signs. Growing up, in other words, is the evolution of one's social personality as it approximates closer and closer to the fully grown, mature adult. Just as this point of view precludes deliberate and standardized methods of training children in the rudimentary bodily skills such as walking, talking, and eye-hand co-ordination in eating, so it would be incompatible with a didactic attitude about bowel and bladder control or about sexual habits and knowledge.

This point of view gives rise to a factor of great importance in Tale education, the *expectation of normal behaviour*. In any given social situation everybody takes it for granted that any person participating either already knows, or wants to know, how to behave in a manner appropriate to the situation and in accordance with his level of maturity. An effort to learn is thus evoked as an adaptation to the demands of a real situation. It is not that people expect one another to act with automatic and machine-like precision; for in point of fact Tale culture tolerates considerable elasticity in the patterns of behaviour. We have an analogy in our own culture in the expectation entertained by most adults that little girls want to play with dolls and little boys with toy engines. We act on this expectation whenever we buy presents for children. How exactly this influences the play of Western children has not been investigated, but there can be little doubt that it does. We expect children to know how to play without being taught.

In contrast to this, many Western mothers nowadays do not expect their children to acquire clean habits simply in the normal course of development, and therefore set out to train them deliberately from earliest infancy in these habits. Tale mothers never train their children deliberately to be clean. When they reach the stage of walking and talking easily, children are expected not to defecate indoors in the daytime but to be asked to be taken outside or to run out themselves. A lapse meets with an expression of disapproval and a reprimand: 'You are big enough already. Can't you go outside to defecate?' The child learns in response to the expectation that it is capable of normal behaviour in that respect.[14] Similarly, infants are expected to understand or to be eager to understand the language of adults, and no one would think of using 'baby talk' to them.

As normal behaviour is always expected, no one hesitates to

---

[14] The example is intended to illustrate how the expectation of normal behaviour acts but, of course, other factors are also involved in the Tale child's acquisition of clean habits. These habits are learnt gradually, not all at once. Before it can walk or talk, its mother or an older child sometimes takes it outside when it shows signs of wishing to defecate. By the time it is expected to be clean it is being drawn into the play-activities of slightly older children, most of which take place out of doors. The need to adapt itself to the habits and standards of its older playmates is a strong stimulus to the child to learn not only bowel and bladder control but also the rules of etiquette. As the Tallensi have no special sanitary arrangements, but excrete in the open anywhere near the homestead, taking care only to keep a little way from the paths and from any people who may be about, it is easy for a child to learn the adult convention from the example of older children and adults. Clean habits, like other skills, are learnt as organic responses (see below). I shall refer to this matter again, in another context, in a later section.

correct a child or adult who behaves inappropriately through ignorance, and the correction is generally accepted with alacrity and ease. If children are allowed to be present at the activities of adults, they are assumed to be interested in and to understand what is being said and done. No one would inhibit his conversation or actions because children are present, or withhold information upon which adequate social adjustment depends from a child because it is thought to be too young. Tallensi, therefore, are not surprised at the comprehensive and accurate sexual knowledge of a 6-year-old, though direct instruction in these matters is never given. As with the ordinary skills and interests of daily life, they expect children to want to know such things. *Naawun mpaan ba*, 'Heaven teaches them', they say, or, as we should put it, it is perfectly natural.

It is known that some people learn more quickly and accurately than others, that variations in skill and ability exist. But the idea of precocity or retardation as a quality of a child's character has no place in Tale thought. A child may intrude on a situation where some one of his or her degree of maturity has no business to be and will be categorically dismissed then; but it would never be rated for being 'old-fashioned'. Every child is expected to be eager to know and to do as much as its social space and its stage of psycho-physical development permits. Hence, though it is clearly recognized that knowledge, skill, and capacity for social adjustment grow cumulatively, the Tallensi have no technique of isolating a skill or observance from the total reality and training a child in it according to a syllabus, as, for instance, we train children in dancing, the multiplication table, or the catechism. Tale educational method does not include drill as a fundamental technique. It works through the situation, which is a bit of the social reality shared by adult and child alike.

The conceptions and practices we have been considering constitute the significant factors in education by participation in practical tasks which is often described as the distinctive method of primitive societies and is as conspicuous in Taleland as in every other pre-literate country. It may be observed that even in Western society the principal method of education is by participation. A child repeating the multiplication table is participating in the practical activity appropriate to and defined by the school; but measured by the total social reality it is a factitious activity, a

training situation constructed for that purpose. The Tallensi do
not make systematic use of training situations. They teach through
real situations which children are drawn to participate in because
it is expected that they are capable and desirous of mastering
the necessary skills.

Corresponding to this contrast in method we can observe a contrast in psychological emphasis. The training situation demands
atomic modes of response; the real situation requires organic
modes of response. In constructing a training situation we envisage a skill or observance as an end-product at the perfection
of which we aim and therefore arrange it so as to evoke only
motor or perceptual practice. Affective or motivational factors
are eliminated or ignored. In the real situation behaviour is com-
pounded of affect, interest and motive, as well as perceptual
and motor functions. Learning becomes purposive. Every advance
in knowledge or skill is pragmatic, directed to achieve a result
there and then, as well as adding to a previous level of adequacy.

The expectation of normal behaviour and organic response
operate also in the education of a Western child, e.g. when it is
learning speech or manners. In Taleland it is the most effective
factor in the inculcation of a wide range of social behaviour from
bowel and bladder control to ritual notions, and from economic
skills to sexual habits.

Interests, skills, and observances. We have seen, now, that a
Tale child acquires the interests, skills and observances which
comprise the repertoire of adult social behaviour not in discrete
categories but in a synthetic combination. But it is necessary, for
analytical purposes, to define such categories of behaviour. They
refer to forms of overt behaviour and not to the psychological
functions or mechanisms subsumed therein.

Interests. By *interest* I mean simply the observable fact that,
according to their level of maturity, Tale children and adults
spontaneously show preference for some activities rather than
others; that they have a selective orientation in their social space,
e.g. reacting to some people more readily than to others; that
they obviously seek to satisfy aims and desires in their activities
and show a sense of purpose and sustained effort. Food, for example, is one of the dominant interests of Tale children. In 1936
the ground-nut crop surpassed all anticipations in some districts.
An elder, referring to this in conversation a week or two before

the crop was harvested, said: 'We have a surfeit of ground-nuts this year. Look at the children. They don't care about their mothers, they don't care about their fathers.' When food is scarce, he explained, children are for ever running in to their mothers clamouring for something to eat. Now they are out all day, and if they feel hungry they simply pull up a handful of ground-nuts to chew and are satisfied. Food, indeed, remains one of the dominant interests of a Taləŋa from childhood to old age, and with the confluence of other interests and motives has a great effect on Tale economic life. Between the ages of 6 and 14 the interest of boys in food becomes linked up with other interests which have been developing during that period, e.g. in learning to use the bow and arrow, in the comradeship of boys of about the same size, in primary economic and technical processes such as herding and hoeing, in exploring the environs of the settlement, and so forth. Thus, a group of boys out herding cattle often have their bows and arrows with them, and when the cattle are grazing quietly they will search around for cane rats or birds to shoot as titbits.

From a very early age—before they can walk or talk—until adulthood children show a marked and explicit interest in the activities of their parents and older siblings and other adults with whom they come in contact. This is due, in part, to the unity of the social sphere. The children thus begin to adopt the cultural values of their society in infancy, as has been indicated above in our discussion of the social sphere. It may, however, be worth while repeating that children express a keen interest in farming, in livestock, in ceremonies, dances and recreations, and in the conspicuous current activities of their households, in their kinship relationships, and so forth, from the age of 3 upwards, long before they can actively participate in these affairs. But it is shown quite clearly in their attitudes when they are allowed to be present at adult activities, and in their fantasies as revealed in their talk and play, which revolve round the themes of adult social life.

Another group of interests significant for the educational development of Tale children is connected with their habitat. By the age of 9 or 10 the children are thoroughly familiar with the ecological environment of their clan settlements. They know the economically important trees, grasses, and herbs, e.g., a girl of

about 9 once named and showed me nine varieties of herbs used
for making soup. They have a fair idea of the gross anatomy of
the fowl, small field animals, and larger live stock. But apart from
these achievements which lead one to infer the existence of an
interest in the natural environment, I was able to obtain some
direct evidence thereof. The natives say that small children frequently ask questions about people and things they see around
them. However, listening to children's talk for 'why' questions
(Isaacs 1930), I was surprised to note how rarely they occurred; and the few instances I recorded refer to objects or persons foreign to the normal routine of Tale life. It would seem
that Tale children rarely have to ask 'why' in regard to the people and things of their normal environment because so much of
their learning occurs in real situations where explanation is generally coupled with instruction, and because they hear so much
adult discussion, in terms of cause and effect, as these are understood by the Tallensi, of the things they are interested in. Yet two
examples will prove that even quite small children react with
exploratory interest to what is new and unusual. I gave some
tiny tin figures of animals to a group of small children to play with.
A little boy of about 5 looked intently at the figure of a horse.
'Why does he stoop like that?' he asked, speaking to himself
rather than to his companions. But immediately he answered his
own question, 'He is eating grass.' On another occasion I observed the 3-year-old son of our cook, pointing to the garbage tin,
ask the horseboy: 'Why has that got a lid?'

Again, making clay figures is a favourite diversion of small
boys and adolescents. The standard figures are men and women,
cows and horses. But a youngster of about 9 or 10 once produced a motorcycle, explaining that he had recently seen the
Agricultural Officer arrive on one. Another boy, a little older, once
made a roan antelope, explaining that some two years previously
he had seen one of these animals which, fleeing from a hunting
party, had entered the settlement and been surrounded and killed
there.

I have not attempted to give an exhaustive account of the interests which Tale children develop in the course of their education. I have tried to indicate only some typical interests and their
relation to the educational process.

Skills. The acquisition of skills also commences in early infancy, with the child's first experiments in motor co-ordination and speech. Bodily dexterity provides merely the foundation upon which are subsequently built up the socially important skills of adult life. They include not only the predominantly manual skills, such as are connected with farming and care of live stock, with hunting, fishing, building, thatching, cooking, housekeeping and gardening, and the technology of specialists, but also non-manual skills, such as a knowledge of the kinship system, of ritual and ceremonial, of economically useful herbs and roots and of others used as drugs to cure illness, of buying and selling, of law and custom—in short, of the whole body of cultural definitions which guide the Taləŋa in his daily existence. Such skills are the end-results of education; and it will be obvious that they represent merely the cognitive and motor aspects of activities rooted in developing interests and fostered by the expectation of normal behaviour. Typical skills will be referred to as we proceed, but one general feature must be noted here. Children in Taleland are remarkably free from over-solicitous supervision. They have the maximum freedom and responsibility commensurate with their skill and maturity. On the one hand they can go where they like and do what they like, on the other they are held fully responsible for tasks entrusted to them. Thus, a 6-year-old is quite often charged with the care of an infant for several hours at a stretch. Girls of 9 or 10 can be seen in large numbers in every market, selling or buying things for their mothers or themselves. Boys of this age and even younger swarm in the markets. One market day I discovered a boy of about 10–11 selling a basketful of leaves used as a food for animals which he had himself collected in the bush near his settlement. He hoped to earn a penny or twopence to buy arrow-heads for himself. Another day a boy of about the same age offered his services to the butcher. He earned a tenth of a penny which he spent on a feed of locust-bean flour for himself and a friend. Similarly, when there is dancing at a homestead, the children of about 6 years and upwards from the whole neighbourhood congregate there and remain till dawn. They might tell their parents where they are going, but would not be sent for to come home.

Numerous instances could be added to illustrate further the freedom allowed to children. Of the responsibility allotted to them in applying their skills and their appreciation of it, one

good example may be quoted. I was chatting with a group of
boys, aged about 7–11 years, at sunset one day, when Duunbil,
the oldest of them, suddenly exclaimed, clasping his hands in a
gesture expressing both amusement and consternation: 'Ma! I've
forgotten to untie the goats; I'll get a whipping.' 'You'd better
run,' one of the others advised, as he dashed away. His companions explained that he had pegged his father's goats out in the
morning to graze and that it was his duty to bring them home
again. Goats cannot be left out all night lest hyenas catch them.
A few days later I met Duunbil again and he told me, with a grin,
that he had not managed to bring the goats in till after dark, but
that he had been let off with a mild beating.

Children and adolescents share economic tasks in accordance
with their skill and maturity, and they have a strong sense of the
rights to which they are entitled in consequence. An adolescent
has the right to be adequately fed and supported by his or
her parents in return for co-operation in agricultural or domestic
work. I have known of youths running away from home when
they considered themselves to be badly treated in these respects.
Children expect to have their services acknowledged in a similar
way. Yindɔl, aged about 11, an intelligent and enterprising lad,
was already giving his father valuable assistance, both in the care
of live stock and in farming. When the great dances came round,
Yindɔl wanted a new loin cloth. His father refused to buy him
one, whereupon Yindɔl went on strike, neglected the chickens,
the donkeys, the goats and refused to go to the bush farm even
after a beating. In the end his father had to yield. *Bii la mar
buurt*—'The boy has justice on his side'—he said, when he told
me the story.

A similar incident occurred with a man who supplied us with
milk for a short while. Money is scarce in Taleland and 2*s.*
6*d.* a month is an enviable addition to family resources. Yet one
day he came to tell me apologetically that he could no longer sell
me milk. Why? His small son, whose job it was to herd the cow,
had rebelled. He used always to milk the cow during the day, in
the pasture, when he became hungry; but if he was not going to
be allowed to do this because the white man must be supplied
with milk, he would no longer drive the cow out to graze.

Increasing skill and maturity, therefore, bring increasing responsibilities but also concomitant rewards—that is, ever closer

integration into the system of co-operation and reciprocity which is the basis of Tale domestic economy (see M. and S. L. Fortes 1936). The unity of the social sphere, the interest of children in the world of adult activities, and the rapidity with which each advance in educational achievement is socially utilized constitute a ring of incentives which help to explain the eagerness of Tale children to grow up and take their full place in adult life.

Observances. Finally, there are the observances which every Taləŋa has to learn in the course of his or her life. These comprise ritual, moral and ethical values, norms and obligations, as well as rules of etiquette and standards of correct conduct in general. Some of these types of observances can be readily identified in Tale culture. It is not so easy to determine what exactly are moral and ethical norms and obligations and their place in this culture. Certainly an exhaustive study of this, the most recondite and perhaps fundamental aspect of Tale education, could not be ventured without first precisely establishing the nature of these observances and how they are maintained. For the limited purpose of this paper it will be sufficient to select some representative examples of rules of conduct the violation or neglect of which is repugnant to the cultural idiom of the Tallensi or, otherwise expressed, would be considered blameworthy or disgraceful, sinful or wicked, uncouth or embarrassing to others. To ask how they are learnt is to ask how they are experienced by the growing child at different stages of its development.

To the native these norms have an arbitrary quality as if they require no validation, other than the fact that normal and equable social relations would be impossible without them, that they are indispensable for satisfactory social adjustment.[15] In Taleland, it is true, learning the correct observances has many points in common with learning skills, but there is a significant difference. When a child is learning a skill he has the test of objective achievement to evaluate his progress and to stimulate him to further effort; when he is learning how to behave properly the only test of attainment is the reaction of other people and his own sense of the adequacy or inadequacy of his conduct. One can observe, in consequence, that both children and adults are very sensitive to

---

[15] The argument of this section owes much to the stimulus of Durkheim's *L'Education morale* (1925).

ridicule of a lapse in manners or morals but are fairly indifferent
to ridicule of poor skill. The contrast between observances and
skills is evident when we compare the way in which a child learns
to model clay figures, gradually perfecting his technique, with the
'all or none' way, associated sometimes with corporal punishment, in which he is taught to respect other people's property, or
the way he is taught his totemic taboos.

Among the Tallensi, as in many other primitive societies, manners and morals are acquired almost as a by-product of the normal social relations between the growing child and the people who
constitute his or her social space. The unity of the social sphere
and the expectation of normal behaviour have a correspondingly
greater influence than in the acquisition of skills and interests. But
the critical factor is the tension inherent in the fundamental
educational relationships, the authority of parent over child and
of senior over junior.

In Tale ideology this is epitomized in the danger attributed to a
parent's resentment. If any one who has reached years of discre-
tion behaves in such a way as to incur the resentment and hostility
of a parent, some calamity will certainly befall him or her unless
he comes formally to beg forgiveness and the injured parent
ritually abjures his or her anger.[16] It very often happens that
two children of about the same age and members of a single
joint family are related as parent and child. They can be seen
playing together amicably, squabbling at times, and working together. But when the 'child' is questioned about his playmate, he
will say, 'I fear (respect) him, because he begot me.' This
is not merely a formula. Sinkawol (aged 23–25) used to order
his 'father,' Kyekambε (aged 12–13) about when the lad was
helping with the housebuilding and even scold him if he bungled
a task. This was legitimate technical instruction. But he declared
emphatically that he dare not strike the boy, *ɔn ndɔɣam la
zugu*. From the authority of parent over child is derived that of
elder sibling over younger. It is equally absolute. A youth or girl
has no hesitation in restraining or correcting a younger sibling
with a cuff which often sends the latter off howling at the top of

---

[16] The connexion between one particular aspect of Tale morality, their
notion of incest, and the background of kinship has been discussed in my
paper 1936b.

his voice. The authority of seniors in general over juniors is accepted by custom (e.g., among herdboys), though not so absolutely and unquestioningly. It is often maintained by force, or in virtue of superior skill. It is intelligible, therefore, why the Tallensi usually say 'our forefathers' matter is this' when they are asked to account for an observance, and why their children say, 'the grownups have told us so'.

Just as all Tallensi, children or adults, recognize the force of authority, even though they sometimes flout it, so they accept the principle of equal rights for equals. One can see this, not only in standardized patterns of behaviour, but, e.g., in the spontaneity with which children share things and activities. When a small boy snares a bird or kills a mouse or lizard he will always share his catch with friends or siblings, apportioning it according to sex and age. A favourite pastime of boys of all ages, from 5 upwards, is wrestling. Sometimes bigger youths stand by to supervise, but always scrupulous fairness is insisted upon, and thus instilled. It is as correct and even praiseworthy to demand what one is entitled to as it is reprehensible to take what one has no right to. A nice illustration, showing incidentally how such principles are sometimes taught, came to my notice during an evening ceremony which had been unduly dragged out. A dozen or more small boys aged from 5 upwards had gathered at the ceremony to wait for a share of the feast which would follow the religious rites. The food was sent out and distributed by an adult, one or two boys of equal size to a dish. Suddenly an elder called out, 'Where is Zuur?' (a small boy of about 5) and rose to look for him. Zuur lay fast asleep in a corner. The old man shook the child roughly to awaken him, and dragged him towards a dish of food upbraiding him, 'Where do you think you will find food after it has all been eaten? You can't control yourself at all.' Zuur, still somnolent, sat whimpering as he ate, while some one else commented that if you want your share of food you must be there to receive it.

The principle of reciprocity which is thus early learnt in association with siblings and age mates is one of the basic moral axioms of Tale social life. If a man refuses to come to the assistance of a neighbour who has invited a collective hoeing party, the latter will retaliate by refusing assistance to the former at a later date. Often at mortuary ceremonies some one, not obliged by custom to do so, will bring an animal to be slaughtered for

the dead, 'because when my father died, he brought a sheep to
be killed'. A girl of about 10, after her grandmother's funeral,
showed me how half her head had been shaved in the customary
way. But her spontaneous explanation was: 'Because, at the feast,
when they cook the beans they give me a whole dish to myself.'
This moral aspect of Tale social relations, as we can now see, explains the rights which increasing economic skill confer upon a
boy or a girl. Those who work for you *deserve* their keep.[17]

---

[17] I have not attempted to track the Tale attitudes towards authority and
justice to their roots in infant psychology, as would be necessary for an
exhaustive analysis. Some of the phenomena which should be observed in
this connexion are not accessible to study by the behaviouristic methods
of the field worker. But it may be worth mentioning that one can
readily observe the constraint and force which, at some times, the affection
and indulgence which, at others, are expressed in the way parents treat
their infant children. From the day of its birth an infant is subjected to
the agonizing ordeal of a daily bath in steaming medicated water which
is so hot that it becomes rigid with pain on the first douche. One sees
infants of a few days to about 12 months old arbitrarily held down on
their mother's laps while medicated drinking water is forcibly poured
down their throats as they struggle and splutter. A few minutes after an
infant has been treated thus roughly it will be lovingly suckled, fondled,
and caressed by mother or sister, or affectionately dandled by its father.
A 3-year-old suddenly frightened runs to its father, or more characteristi-
cally to its mother to bury its face between her knees, clutching her
thighs, or to snatch at the breast. The same 3-year-old, in a fit of temper,
will nag, whimper petulantly, strike its mother with its little fists. No
one beats an infant for this. The mother tries to soothe it, or patiently
calls some one—husband or co-wife—to come and take charge of the
unruly child. This indulgence extends to the excretory processes, and
to masturbation, which is overt until puberty in boys. Until it is weaned,
at about 3—when it can walk—it has very complete possession of its
mother. After weaning, which is generally mild, the child becomes more
detached from its mother, who now resumes regular intercourse with her
husband. At this age, or even younger, children are often playfully
threatened by their fathers. 'I will slaughter you if you do so and so',
but they always seem to react with complete equanimity to this. Yet a
boy of 4–5 years, suspiciously eyeing me from the security of his mother's
lap, was heard to say that he was afraid I might cut off his penis. The
Tale infant, in short, appears to be permitted to gratify all its wish
impulses without restraint; yet it must do so in a social world over which
it has no control, in which it is a weak dependent. Here, I think, still

Like ourselves, the Tallensi recognize that some observances are merely matters of convention, others are matters of conscience, and a great many have elements of both. Their emphasis, however, differs conspicuously from ours. For example, the notion of cruelty to animals as delinquent or reprehensible would never occur to them. Small boys often catch mice or birds and keep them, tied with a strip of strong grass, to play with for days and eventually kill and eat them. It is, indeed, a crude form of nature study, for they learn a great deal about the habits, the anatomy, and physiology of the animals and birds they ostensibly maltreat in this way. They are never checked, and the suggestion that this was bad (the Tallensi have no expression, as far as I am aware, for our notion of cruelty) was received with amused laughter. It is a natural interest of children and not a moral problem; and it does not produce a general attitude of cruelty to animals. Both children and adults often show great affection for domestic dogs, for example.

Many rules of conduct are observed 'because it is befitting' —or because non-conformity is 'unbecoming'—i.e. it rouses embarrassment or ridicule or public criticism. Thus when greeting a superior, a man must sit with legs flat, crossed at the calves, bare-headed, eyes lowered, whereas a woman must crouch on all fours or sit with thighs close together and legs tucked under the buttocks. This latter posture in women is a matter of modesty. Up to about 9 or 10 years of age a little girl can sit in any way, legs spread out if she wishes, although from babyhood she has learnt to sit with legs tucked under. As she approaches puberty she will often be admonished 'sit properly' if she does not sit decorously. It is unbecoming for women to eat the domestic fowl, and I have often heard little girls of 9 or 10 boast that they are already refraining from it. A woman goes naked until she is advanced in her first pregnancy. After that she must wear a perineal band even at night, in the privacy of her own room, for the sake of modesty. Not to do so

speaking in terms of superficial psychology, is the germ of the later domination of respect for authority in the child's moral development. It seems probable, from these observations, that the deeper psychology of the process is not unlike that which has been recorded by students of our own children, such as Dr. S. Isaacs.

'is embarrassing' for her and others. Similarly it is indecorous
for a young man, especially if he is married, to go about
without a loin cloth. His comrades would scoff at him, womenfolk jeer, and his wife be ashamed. Yet the Tallensi have
not the slightest sense of shame about the naked body or any
physiological functions, all of which they discuss publicly and
openly. Ask any one, child or adult, the sex of an infant and the
answer will be to open its legs and expose the genitals with the
word 'boy' or 'girl'. An infant's excretory processes arouse no
embarrassment and meet with no attempts at regulation. As we
have seen it is expected to learn cleanliness in due course. The
child is made to understand that excreting indoors is a nuisance
to those who have to keep the house clean. No one would dream
of chastising an infant for this misdemeanour. These are all matters of decency and decorum learnt without formal instructions as
direct adjustments to the social space, through the influence of the
expectation of normal behaviour.

It is otherwise with the morality of property. A thief incurs disgrace and universal opprobrium, and even small children of 6
and 7 express contempt for one. A child that steals, like one who
neglects a task, can expect a severe beating if his father is a conscientious citizen. 'Don't let Tii (a boy of about 6) come and see
your things,' said Batiignwol, a little girl of 7 or 8, to me one
day, 'he's a thief. He stole his mother's ground-nuts and meat and
his father beat him and tied him up.' Theft is immoral as well as
criminal. Lying, by contrast, is considered merely foolish and
contemptible. It causes annoyance and a liar's comrades distrust
him, but one would not punish a child for lying unless it led to
serious consequences. Such misdemeanours, nevertheless, go beyond what is merely 'unbecoming'. They are not nice, *a pu maha*.

Finally there is a type of observance which is a matter of conscience rather than of public approval or reprobation. Many of
these have a ritual character and most of them are associated with
mystical notions. There are food taboos which must be observed
from infancy; there are ritual obligations such as those connected
with mourning, which a person may escape till he reaches adulthood, but which children of 9 or 10 are fully familiar with and
the compulsion of which they experience to the same degree as the
adults; and there is the whole body of implicit moral norms which

regulate the day-to-day life of the family and emerge in the duties of children to one another and to their parents.

I have already mentioned the prohibition in some clans against the eating of fowl by first-born children. By contrast with the voluntary abstention from fowl meat practised by women, this is a taboo of supreme mystical value for these clans and is exactly parallel to the totemic avoidances of other clans. The Hill Tallis, for instance, may not eat tortoise, some may not eat crocodile or python, and others taboo dog. A 5-year-old knows his or her personal or clan taboo, and can state it emphatically. The remedy for a chance infringement of such a taboo is extremely simple —e.g., in the case of the fowl, crushing some fowl droppings in water and giving the child the fluid to drink. Again the supernatural penalty for a breach is of a vague and general kind. In some cases it is thought that it would lead merely to an eruption of scabies on the head; in others it is said that the offender would slowly lose health and strength. These sanctions, however, are not the effective agencies maintaining the observances. Breaches of these rules are exceptional, both among children and among adults. A Taləŋa submits to a food taboo in virtue of a configuration of positive habits and dispositions built up in childhood, not through fear of the sanctions. From the time that it is a babe in arms a child is prevented from tasting or even touching any food which it is prohibited from eating. Later it will be called away from where its companions are sitting over a fire roasting titbits of food forbidden to it—'Come here, you mustn't eat that; it is forbidden.' I once observed a child of about 5 standing aloof while a group of his brothers and sisters were consuming a dish of python meat—a prized delicacy. 'I don't eat python, it is my taboo,' he explained, with an expression of complete aversion.

A vivid example of how food taboos are inculcated was provided by a biographical reminiscence of the chief of Tongo who, as a first-born, may not eat fowl. There was talk in his courtroom of crops and famine in the old days, when an elder wondered if a man would eat a forbidden animal if he were starving. The chief, holding with some of his elders that it would be too repugnant even for a starving man to do so, told this story of how he had himself, on two occasions, violated his taboo. When he was a child of perhaps 5 or 6 he was the favourite of his

grandfather, as often happens. Some one brought the old man a
gift of eggs which he promptly had roasted. He had to go outside
to attend to some matter and he left his small grandson to see that
no one purloined the eggs. Now an egg is a potential fowl, and is
therefore equally taboo with the latter. The chief described how
there was a brief struggle between his conscience and his desire,
and how he succumbed and ate the eggs. His grandfather was
furious when he returned and the child in trepidation lied, accus-
ing a girl who was in the next room. The girl denied the accusation
and the small boy's father was called in to adjudicate. He at once
suspected his son, but the grandfather angrily defended the boy,
who was now too terrified even to speak. The matter was dropped;
but the small boy, afraid of his father, remained with his grandfather till nightfall. Then he slunk out, only to be caught at once
by his father, who had been waiting for him. His father said nothing, but grimly called for a feather and a large gourd of water.
'Drink,' he commanded, and compelled the child, now sobbing
with terror, to swallow the whole gourdful of water. 'Open your
mouth,' said the father, and began to tickle the child's throat
with the feather until he vomited. 'And now,' said the father,
grasping the child's arms tightly and striking him right and left, on
buttocks, back and head, 'I'll teach you to eat fowl and steal
and tell lies.' 'That was how I learnt not to eat fowl,' the chief
concluded amid general laughter. But, he continued, many years
later, at the time of the great famine, he with two companions
was on his way to a neighbouring district and stopped for the night
en route. They were extremely hungry, not having had a proper
meal for days, and when they were offered porridge and a
cooked fowl ate ravenously. Now two of them tabooed the fowl,
but they were too hungry to resist. The meal finished, they rose,
when suddenly the other man who was not allowed to eat fowl
was overcome with nausea and began to vomit. Immediately he
himself also began to vomit. They had not, after all, been able to
stomach the fowl.

How strongly quite young children feel the compulsion of a
ritual obligation was brought home to me when a boy of about
10–11 was telling me one day about his dead mother. 'I want
them to complete her funeral', he said at length, sadly, 'so that I
can have my head shaved' (a ritual obligation). 'Why?' I asked.

'Well, is it not my mother?' he said. 'If I don't have my head shaved it is dirt' (ritual uncleanness).

This is typical also of the moral attitudes to the living, to parents and siblings, engendered in the normal course of family life. That is how children learn to be obedient, considerate of others, ready to co-operate, careful of household property, and so forth.

It is evident from the above examples that adjustment to authority and adjustment to equals act together in the child's acquisition of moral observances. But my observations have led me to conclude that authority is effective from an earlier age than the pressure of opinion from equals. From earliest infancy commands, accompanied by acts or gestures, are constantly being addressed to children. 'Go to your father', 'Take this', 'Come here'—as the child is lifted up, or pulled away from some object it must not touch. Until the age of 3–4, when they are walking and talking well, children appear to be indifferent to the presence of other children or indeed of adults other than their parents and members of their own family. I have watched two infants of 2–2½ years old, both walking, remain for over an hour within a few feet of each other without showing the least interest in each other. By the age of 3½–4 the Tale infant has emerged from this stage of egocentricity (as Piaget has termed it [1959]). It will now run to join another child of this age or older, and likes to play with younger infants. It has now also become sensitive to public opinion to a degree not far short of an adult, and therefore capable of adjustment to others, as the following incident illustrates: I was chatting with Ɔmara and a few other adult members of his house when his little daughter Sampana, aged about 3½ years, who knew me as a familiar and friendly visitor, ran out to see me. 'Give me some money,' she asked; and her manner, intonation, and posture were so like those of the grown-up women who often half-playfully asked me for money, that the whole company burst spontaneously into loud laughter. Sampana, obviously taken aback, turned tail and fled indoors where we found her sobbing with chagrin. 'She is ashamed at our laughter,' said Ɔmara, still amused. When the child's mother tried to soothe her she first struggled and struck at her, venting her chagrin on her mother. It was fully ten minutes before her mother was able to quieten her by playing with her and distracting her by making her a toy of wet clay. 'They will laugh at him (or her)' or 'His comrades will laugh at him' is the commonest motive alleged for correct behaviour. If you ask a boy of 6 or 7 why he no longer plays with the little girls he says, 'If I do my comrades will laugh at me'; and little girls say the same. Adolescents, talking about their sweethearts, who are usually clan 'sisters', explain why they avoid the girls of their own section—'because our comrades will find out and laugh at us'; and the adult is equally sensitive to public opinion.

The total pattern and its genetic development. We have seen that these categories of social behaviour are not learnt in isolation one from the other but as patterns in which interests, elements of skill, and observances are combined. The Tale housewife, going several miles into the bush to collect firewood, is using knowledge of the bush tracks and of the best places for firewood acquired over a period of years; but she is impelled also by the sense of duty to her family and her own self-esteem. The Tale farmer's devotion to his agricultural pursuits is due to a passionate interest in land and crops and to a sense of moral responsibility towards his family and his ancestor spirits. His skill is but one of the factors that affect his general efficiency.

These total patterns which constitute the texture of Tale cultural behaviour are not built up bit by bit, by addition, during the course of a child's life. They are present as *schemas*[18] from the beginning. My observations suggest that the course of development is somewhat as follows: at first the child acquires a well-defined interest associated with a postural diagram of the total pattern. The postural diagram is, as it were, a contour map, extremely simplified and crude but comprehending the essential elements and relations of the full pattern. Further experience strengthens and amplifies the interest at the same time as it causes the details of the postural diagram to be filled out, making it more and more adaptable and controllable, producing more discriminatory responses to real situations, and linking it up with other patterns of behaviour and with norms of observance. The total pattern is not built up brick by brick, like a house, but evolves from the embryonic form.

---

[18] I have taken this concept from Prof. F. C. Bartlett's *Remembering*, pp. 199 ff., though its bald application here hardly does justice to the significance given to it by Prof. Bartlett, and to its value for an understanding of primitive education.

A simple demonstration of this principle is provided by a child's learning to dance. A favourite amusement of women with infants just beginning to walk is to let them dance. The tiny tot, barely able to maintain an upright posture for ten minutes or so, is set up on its legs. A couple of women—usually the women of a homestead play with an infant thus when they have no work on hand—calling out to it, with laughter and warmth, 'Come on, dance', begin to sing and clap a dance rhythm and execute a few steps. Tale infants respond with every sign of pleasure to such stimulus and by the age of about 3 have learnt, in a sketchy and diagrammatic but specifically recognizable way, the rhythms and the main steps of the festival dances. The 6-year-old has advanced so far that he or she can sometimes join the real dancing of the adolescents. His sense of rhythm is accurate, he learns the songs quickly, and he has the pattern of the dance clearly. But his dancing is extremely crude still. It tends to be mechanical and monotonous, completely lacking the improvizations and variations, the delicate tracery of step and gesture with which the skilled adult fills out the formal pattern. Every year improves the child's style, but even the adolescent has not yet perfected his or her technique. Yet from babyhood to maturity dancing ability grows continuously.

A child's knowledge of the kinship structure evolves in the same way. The schema, rudimentary and unstable as yet, can be detected in the 3–4-year-old. He or she discriminates kinsfolk from non-kinsfolk, equating the former mainly with people living in close proximity. He knows his own father and mother precisely, but already calls his mother's co-wives 'mother'. Similarly, he knows that 'father' is his own father, but that other men—in the first instance those of the same joint family—are also 'fathers', and he knows that the other kinsfolk frequently seen are brothers, sisters, grandfather, grandmother. But he is still incapable of discriminating genealogical differences; he groups people by generation and by spatial proximity. Thus an adult brother may be described as a 'father'. A child learns the fundamental kinship terms and has the idea of distinguishing its relatives according to generation and genealogical distance long before it can couple this knowledge accurately with differential behaviour towards kinsmen. The 6-year-old knows the correct terms and appropriate behaviour defining its relations with the members of its own paternal family and has grasped the principle of classification according to descent. But in practice he still confuses spatial proximity and relative age with kinship, beyond the limits of his own family. The 10–12-year-old has mastered the schema, except for some collateral and affinal kinsmen, the terms for whom are known though he cannot describe the relationships.

Biological drives and cultural motives combine to produce variations in the rates of evolution of different schemas. I have not the experimental data to give accurate or even sample norms, but a rough indication is possible. If the 6-year-old is compared with the 12-year-old in respect to e.g. knowledge of the kinship structure, of agricultural processes, of ritual, and of sex life, the 6-year-old is least advanced in knowledge of the kinship structure and ritual, and most advanced in his or her knowledge of sex life, while knowledge of agricultural processes could fall somewhere between these two levels.

FUNDAMENTAL LEARNING PROCESSES

In the course of the preceding discussion I have given several indications of how Tale children are taught and learn. But our investigation would be incomplete without a special consideration of the three fundamental processes utilized by the child in its learning—mimesis, identification, and co-operation. These are not the only learning techniques observable among the Tallensi, but they are the most important; and they usually appear not in isolation but in association with one another. They are most intimately interwoven in play, the paramount educational exercise of Tale children.

Mimesis. Writers on primitive education have often attributed an almost mystical significance to 'imitation' as the principal method by which a child learns. The Tallensi themselves declare that children learn by 'looking and doing'; but neither 'imitation' nor the formula used by the Tallensi help us to understand the actually observable process. Tale children do not automatically copy the actions or words of older children or adults with whom they happen to be without rhyme or reason and merely for the sake of 'imitation'. For hours at a stretch mimetic behaviour may be unnecessary, but in certain types of situation it is the child's readiest form of cognitive adaptation.

Mimesis occurs (*a*) as a response to direct stimulation; (*b*) as an adaptation to a situation the child does not know how to deal with on the basis of its attainments at the time; (*c*) in play, when it is rehearsing in fantasy its interests and the life of the world about it. The Tale boy who learns the leatherworkers' or blacksmiths' craft by closely studying his father at his work and listening to his explanations, tentatively repeating the procedure with scraps of leather or iron and gradually perfecting his skill, is no more learning by imitation than our own children do when they learn arithmetic by copying procedures demonstrated on the blackboard. If he does not understand the craftsman's procedure the lad will never learn it.

We have already had examples of mimesis in response to direct stimulation—e.g. when an infant begins to learn to dance. A child's first efforts at talking are constantly stimulated in this way. At the babbling stage its mother or grandmother, or whoever is looking after it, will frequently in playful mockery mimic its babblings, 'What are you muttering there?' says the woman, 'gba-gba-gba-ma-ma . . .', and the infant is thus stimulated to repeat these sounds again and again. I have often observed incidents such as the following: Duun was playing with his little daughter of about 2. He called her, 'Kologo-o-o ee!' and she replied 'm!'; and again he called, and she replied; and so on for about five minutes. Then he said, 'Call the dog, wo-ho, wo-ho!' The infant repeated, 'Wo-wo!' Again he called the dog and the infant repeated the call, and so on several times. Some one spoke to him, and turning his attention from the child, he answered. The infant, still influenced by the set of the game, repeated, as well as she could, a word or two, much to his amusement. As we have seen, the expectation of normal behaviour influences parents to talk to infants as if they understand everything.

When there is a pair or a group of children together, the oldest or most self-possessed generally gives the cues to behaviour which the others follow. This is logical, since collective action must be common or co-operative. Tale adults behave in exactly the same way. In an unfamiliar or difficult situation the best adaptation is to copy the actions and words of any one who understands the situation. Small children, whose schemas are still very rudimentary, are peculiarly apt to encounter unfamiliar elements in situations, and therefore readily resort to mimesis. Between the ages of 3 and 6 years, when the child is eagerly exploring its social space, this happens so often that it seems to develop a habit of mimicking older children in whose activities it is trying to participate. Thus, whenever I encountered little groups of children at play, pegging out goats, gleaning ground-nuts, or doing anything else, and asked the youngest, 'What are you doing?', one of the older children would reply, and the youngest repeat this reply in the same words. One evening I met four or five children from a neighbouring compound idling on a path. One was a girl of about 8 who had her brother of about 5 in tow. She noticed another child some way off and called out a message to him. The little brother, equally interested in the other child, called out and repeated the message in the same words and intonation. He was obviously not merely repeating automatically what he had heard, but endeavouring to draw the attention of the distant child and using the same method as his sister. A great deal of language learning goes on in this way.

Mimesis in play will be considered later.

Identification. A striking feature of social development among the Tallensi is the degree to which children overtly identify themselves with older siblings and parents. It is noticeable in children of 5 and 6 and becomes more marked as they grow older. The parent of the same sex is the model according to which the child regulates its conduct and from which it derives its aspirations and values. Though unwitting, the process is unmistakable. Character appears to run in families. An aggressive, loud-spoken man's children tend to become aggressive and pushing; an industrious man's sons apply themselves to work from early childhood; the dishonesty and unreliability of shifty parents tend to be reproduced in their children; and so forth. The social structure of the Tallensi with its emphasis on family and lineage solidarity, and the unity of the social sphere, encourage such identification. If one asks a child, 'Who are you?' the answer is invariably, 'I'm so-and-so's child', or 'of so-and-so's family', accompanied by a manner or posture which leaves no doubt in one's mind as to who is his father or her mother. Nindɔyat of Zubiung, for instance, was notorious for his selfishness, his arrogance, and his insincerity. His son Sapak, aged 6, was his father in miniature—self-assertive, greedy, combative and refractory. Lɔyani, clansman and near neighbour of Nindɔyat, was a complete contrast to him and the most popular man in the clan. His children were among the quietest, most respectful, and most good-tempered I knew. Once they were visiting me when Sapak thrust himself upon us. Within ten minutes he had managed to offend one of the other boys and but for my presence they would have come to blows. A similar contrast in character existed between Nɛnaab's small daughters and Saandi's. Indeed, it would be possible to cite a dozen examples of the way parental character reappeared in children, if space permitted.

A child says, 'This is *our* dog, *our* sheep, *our* land, *our* child, *our* wife', identifying himself completely with his family. Some of the examples given in our discussion of the unity of the social sphere show how identification operates to constitute that unity. It is, obviously, the mechanism mainly responsible for the child's acquisition of interests, and therefore generates powerful motives for following out these interests derived from the world of adult activity. Hence Tale children all want to grow up. I often asked boys of 10 to 12 why they were so keen on hoeing though it was far more arduous than herding or playing about with their friends. The question puzzled many, though they were always emphatic about preferring work on the farm to herding or play. But discussion generally resolved their motives into this: 'We want to hoe because we want to be among the men and help to bring in more food'; and girls have the same attitude about domestic work and childbearing. One day I found a small boy of about 5 struggling with a large goat. 'Where's your father?' I asked. 'Hoeing his bush farm,' he said. 'What about you,' I said, 'can you hoe?' 'Of course I can,' he replied proudly, 'didn't I hoe the whole compound farm?' I teased him a bit, asking him about the details of farming, and eventually he said, 'No, I can't hoe. I'm still too small.' Similarly, a little girl of about 8 told me that she had accompanied some older girls to the bush for firewood the previous day. Her mother burst out laughing and called to me: 'Don't believe her, she's much too small.' But these innocent fabrications illustrate the contents of children's identifications with adults.[19]

---

[19] This exposition of identification is over-simplified in order not to burden the general argument. In Taleland, as elsewhere, it is not the sole determinant of character formation. It has been stressed here in order to underline its educational importance.

Co-operation. Mention has previously been made of children's co-operation in the ordinary social and particularly economic activities in a manner and to an extent commensurate with their maturity at the time. But it must be referred to again in order to emphasize why it is specially important for children's learning. The little girl who goes with her mother to the water-hole and is given a tiny pot of water to carry is making only an infinitesimal contribution to the household's water supply. Yet it is a real contribution. She learns to carry her little pot of water in relation to a real need of the household. The boy at a sacrifice called to hold the leg of a carcass while it is skinned not only receives his first lessons in anatomy thus; he is performing a task necessary for the completion of the ceremony. The children summoned to carry balls of swish for the men building a house are contributing valuable labour. The child's training in duty and skill is always socially productive and therefore psychologically worth while to him; it can never become artificial or boring.

Yet as long as the child's co-operation is limited to subsidiary assistance—that is, until he reaches adolescence—it includes an element emanating from the child's own psychology, an element of play. Upon the adult Taləŋa the economic system bears down with a disciplinary and constraining effect. The house must be built, plastered, and thatched in time, before the rains come; the crops must be planted, hoed, harvested at the right moment, and the penalty for negligence is severe. The child cannot yet experience this. Its co-operation is still partly wish-fulfilment and has for it the attractions of an imaginative experiment. Thus, whenever there is building in progress, they play at building as well as help carrying swish; and the play part is for the child of equal importance with the work.

Play in relation to social development. The concept of play is well defined and clearly recognized by the Tallensi. The play of Tale children, it has been pointed out, emerges partly as a side-issue of their practical activities. It is also an end in itself, and has a noteworthy role in their social development. In his play the child rehearses his interests, skills, and obligations, and makes experiments in social living without having to pay the penalty for mistakes. Hence there is always a phase of play in the evolution of any schema preceding its full emergence into practical life. Play, therefore, is often mimetic in content, and expresses the child's identifications. But the Tale child's play mimesis is never simple and mechanical reproduction; it is always imaginative construction based on the themes of adult life and of the life of slightly older children. He or she adapts natural objects and other materials, often with great ingenuity, which never occur in the adult activities copied, and rearranges adult functions to fit the specific logical and affective configuration of play.[20]

A typical play situation. How vividly these motifs appear in the play of Tale children will be evident to the reader if I describe shortly an actual play situation as I observed and recorded it. I shall describe a typical play episode among children at the transition from infantile egocentricity and dependence to social play and participation in peripheral economic activities. It will be noted how recreational and imaginative play are interwoven with practical activities and how infantile habits still persist. The children's interests fluctuate from moment to moment, egocentric attitudes alternate with co-operative play, and the economic task receives only sporadic attention. Later on we shall consider these factors in relation to the phases of development of children's play.

On a morning in June I found Gɔmna, aged about 7, his half-sister Zɔŋ, aged about 6, and his friend Zoo of about the same age out scaring birds on the home farm. They sat astride the trailing branch of a baobab tree on the boundary of Gɔmna's father's farm and Zoo's father's farm. They slid down to talk to me, and a bigger lad, Tɔŋ, aged about 10, joined us. Gɔmna had wandered off a few yards and now came running up with three locusts. He called to his sister and Zoo. Eagerly they squatted round the locusts. 'These are our cows,' said Gɔmna, 'let's build a yard for them.' Zoo and the little girl foraged around and produced a few pieces of decayed bark. The children, Gɔmna

---

[20] In this respect Tale children resemble our own children; cf. S. Isaacs 1930: 99–102. She sums up: 'Imaginative play builds a bridge by which the child can pass from the symbolic values of things to active inquiry into their real construction and real way of working. . . . In his imaginative play the child recreates selectively those elements in past situations which can embody his emotional and intellectual need of the present, and he adapts the details moment by moment to the present situation. . . .' Cf. also the same author, 1933: 425, 'Play . . . is supremely the activity which brings him [the child] psychic equilibrium in the early years.'

dominant, giving orders and keeping up a running commentary, set about building a 'cattle-yard' of the pieces of bark. Tɔŋ, the older boy, also squatted down to help. He and Gɔmna constructed an irregular rectangle with one side open of the pieces of bark. Zoo fetched some more pieces of bark which Tɔŋ used to roof the yard. The little girl stood looking on. Gɔmna carefully pushed the locusts in, one by one, and declared, 'We must make a gate-way.' Rummaging about, the boys found two pebbles which they set up as gate-posts, with much argument as to how they ought to stand. Suddenly the whole structure collapsed and Tɔŋ started putting it up again. The little girl meanwhile had found a pair of stones and a potsherd and was on her knees, 'grinding grain'. Suddenly the two small boys dashed off into the growing grain, shouting to scare the birds. In a minute or two they returned to squat by the collapsed 'cattle-yard'. They appeared to have for-gotten all about the 'cows', for they were engrossed in a conversa-tion about 'wrestling'. Some one called Tɔŋ, who departed. Zɔŋ, finishing her 'grinding', came up to the boys with the 'flour' on a potsherd and said, 'Let's sacrifice to our shrine.' Gɔmna said in-differently, 'Let Zoo do it.' Zoo declared that Gɔmna was senior to him, and an argument ensued as to who was senior. Eventually Gɔmna asserted, 'I'm the senior.' Zɔŋ meanwhile had put down her 'flour' which was quite forgotten; for Zoo challenged Gɔmna's assertion. Gɔmna retorted that he was undoubtedly senior since he could throw Zoo in wrestling. Zoo denied this, and in a few minutes they were grappling each other. Gɔmna managed to throw Zoo and rolled over him; but they stood up in perfectly good temper, panting and proud. Suddenly with a shout Gɔmna began to scramble up the baobab branch, followed by Zoo, call-ing out, 'Let's swing.' For a minute or two they rocked back and forth on the branch and then descended. Now Gɔmna re-membered his cows. Vehemently he accused his sister of having taken them, and when she denied this challenged her to 'swear'. 'All right,' she said placidly. Gɔmna took a pinch of sand in his left hand and put his right thumb on it. Zɔŋ licked her thumb and pressed down with it on Gɔmna's thumb-nail. He stood still a moment, then suddenly withdrew his thumb. (This is a children's play ordeal.) Gɔmna examined his sister's thumb and found sand adhering. 'There you are,' he said, rapping her on the head with a crooked finger. The 'cows' were completely forgotten though, for now they turned their attention to me, asking me various questions. After a while Gɔmna, who had been observing my shoes, said, 'Let's make shoes,' and took a couple of pieces of the decayed bark previously used to build the cattle-yard to make shoes. He and Zɔŋ found some grass and old string lying about and tried to tie the pieces of bark to the soles of their feet. Gɔmna now noticed his 'cows' and picked them up, but he was still trying to make 'shoes'. The 'shoes' refused to hold together so he abandoned them and squatted over his 'cows' for a moment, moving them hither and thither. 'I'm going to let them copulate,' he burst out with a grin, and tried to put one locust on top of another. Looking up, he noticed a flutter of birds' wings. 'Zɔŋ,' he cried, jumping to his feet, 'scare the birds!' and he raced into the grain, followed by his companions, shouting and stooping to pick up handfuls of gravel to fling at the birds. For the next five minutes they were engrossed in bird-scaring. The entire episode lasted over half an hour.

The developmental phases of play. Infant play. Up to the age of 6 or 7 a good deal of play, especially that of boys, consists in sheer motor exuberance. Small boys run about, leap and prance for the pleasure of it, frequently in a totally unorganized way. But even 3-year-old boys often introduce mimetic themes, spontaneously or in response to suggestions from older children. They 'ride horses', using a long stick as a horse, with a wisp of grass attached as bridle. In the Festival season they love 'playing drums'. Cylindrical tins discarded by our cook and useless as receptacles were in great demand for this purpose. A remnant of goatskin tied over one end with a strip of bark or grass makes a satisfactory diaphragm, and a hooked twig serves as a drumstick. Often an older boy of 8 or 9 manufactures a toy drum for himself or an infant brother. A small discarded calabash is covered with a piece of skin—a remnant of goatskin or the skin of a rat caught by the boy himself and prepared by himself. The skin is cleverly attached to the calabash with strong thorns. Small boys delight in walking round, tapping out a rhythm on a toy drum, sometimes executing a few dance steps. Another instrument they like to copy is the *kolog,* a single-string fiddle. I once saw a boy of about 6 singing to a 'fiddle' which consisted of a large bow made of a green stick and a thread of grass—the 'fiddle'—and a smaller bow of the same materials—the 'bow'.

A bow of the very same sort with a short piece of thick
reed as arrow is the 4- to 6-year-old's introduction to the
handling of bow and arrow. They very soon develop an accurate
aim at a dozen yards or so. Play of this kind is generally very
egocentric. I have watched groups of children playing side by
side—a boy with a 'drum' absorbed in his banging, another
lying on his back absorbed in fantasy, a couple of little girls
playing at housekeeping—all indifferent to one another's activities.

The little girl of 3 to 6 plays in much the same way at times;
but she is already being drawn into the family play of slightly
older children, and, like the small boy with the toy bow, she
tends to mimic simpler features of older girls' play when she is
playing alone. Hence one often sees a little girl of this age sitting
and playing at 'grinding millet'—one stone as metate, a smaller
stone as muller, and a handful of sand or a potsherd as the grain.

Play in early childhood. Between the ages of about 6 and 10
the play of both sexes becomes more social and more complex.
This is the period when the child is beginning to co-operate in
real economic activities, subject to real responsibility, and is
acquiring a knowledge of his social space. His or her play reflects
these experiences and reflects also the interests and activities
characteristic of the stage of maturity just ahead of it. There is,
in all Tale children's play, this feature of looking ahead, as it
were, experimenting tentatively with what lies just beyond the
present psychological horizon.

During this period the younger children, both boys and girls,
have charge of the goats, scare the birds from the newly planted
fields and the crops, run errands, nurse the infants, and so forth.
The boys help in sacrifices to domestic shrines; the girls assist
in household tasks such as sweeping and carrying water.
Towards the end of this period boys whose fathers own cattle go
out with the cattle-herds and girls are beginning to help in the
preparation of food. A 10-year-old girl can prepare the majority
of usual dishes. At the age of 6 or 7 brothers and sisters often
play together; at 9 or 10 the sexual dichotomy has become firmly
established.[21]

---

[21] Nevertheless, this sexual dichotomy is not so absolute as to prohibit a
girl or a woman from stepping into a breach if there is no male available
for a man's task; and men often undertake women's work in an emergency.

At this stage the play of infancy develops in three directions. The sporadic motor exuberance is transformed into recreational play—organized group games and dances; the rudimentary mimetic play becomes elaborate and protracted imaginative and constructive play; and the rude toy-making of infancy grows into children's arts and crafts.

Tale children have a great many organized games, passed on from one generation of children to the next by drawing younger ones into the games played by those who already know them. The games are traditional, and often built round themes derived from the cultural idiom—farming, hunting, marriage, chiefs, etc. But their value is predominantly recreational. Children play them for the pleasure of collective singing, rhythmical physical activity, and sensory and bodily stimulation. The ordinary dances of moonlight nights in which both adults and children participate are regarded as 'play' of this kind.

Kuobon is a game of this sort. Both boys and girls from 7–8 to about 15 years play it on moonlight nights in single-sex groups. A group of about the same size forms a ring, clasping each other and standing on one leg. The other leg is extended towards the centre of the ring, and the children arrange themselves so that their extended legs cross one another. The group then commences to revolve, singing as they go round and round, 'fruits of farming, yee, how nice'. The game goes on until they are tired and the extended legs begin to drop. It breaks up with much laughter, only to start again after a rest. Similar games are played by boys only and others by girls only; but for both sexes dancing is the supreme recreation. In both the mixed dances and the single-sex dances one invariably sees a few small boys or girls at the tail end of the line. At the beginning of the festival season one often meets a group of children about 6–9 years old practising the dances in their play, crudely but recognizably.

At this stage, and till pubescence, boys spend a great deal of their leisure improving their dexterity with the bow and arrow. They now have bows like a man's but smaller, and real arrows with unbarbed heads. They go about in small groups practising marksmanship—shooting at a guinea corn-stalk or a chunk of wood. Sometimes they challenge one another and shoot according to certain rules. The loser forfeits an arrow to the winner. All this is recreational play; but it has a very practical aspect, recognized by adults and children. In Taleland the bow is the symbol of manhood; and every man must know how to wield it. The long years of practice necessary to become an accomplished shot begin with the small boy's first toy bow and extend through the play of childhood and pubescence. Part of this play-practice is the hunting of small field animals and birds. To the boy it is a real hunt, demanding knowledge and alertness and yielding a favourite titbit. Yet it is play as well, being neither obligatory nor dangerous, and being mimetically derived from an adult activity. This has great educational importance. The boy in his play identifies himself with the men, accepts their practical valuation of the bow and arrow, and tries out, as it were, what it feels like to be a man in this respect. Boys often hunt thus in groups, especially when they are out herding cattle, and share the spoil, thus training themselves in co-operation and fair dealing. By the age of 11–12 boys begin to accompany their fathers or elder brothers to real hunts, though they remain onlookers for the most part, whose principal task is to help carrying home anything killed. Not till adolescence will they be allowed to use barbed and poisoned arrows; but quasi-playful hunting thus shades over into the real activity for which it is a preparation.

Imaginative play is rich and frequent during this period, though its themes appear to be few. Family life, the principal economic activities, and domestic ritual supply the mimetic content. Sometimes children are entirely preoccupied with such play for hours at a time; often it is interwoven with practical activities or appears as a resonance of practical activities in which the children co-operate.

On any day in the dry season or the first half of the rainy season one can find a group of girls playing at housekeeping. Most commonly they consist of a group of sisters and ortho-cousins—two to four active participants with, perhaps, a couple of infants attached. Often one or two small boys of about 5 or 6 are in their company, sharing in their play or absorbed in their own separate play. In play, as in the simple economic duties, there is as yet no marked sex dichotomy at this age; and small boys are not ridiculed for 'grinding grain' and 'cooking porridge', or small girls for 'building houses' in play. The girls generally constitute a mixed age group, varying from 6 to 10–11 years, for even those who are already capable of real cooking enjoy playing at it. When they are of about equal maturity their play tends to be loosely organized. Each cooks for herself, but they help one another, lending one another 'utensils', 'grain', 'firewood', and exchanging 'dishes of porridge' like co-wives. When one girl is older than the others she tends to take the lead, and the smaller girls assist her on the pattern of daughter helping mother in real cooking. Infants are 'our children'; and reliable informants have told me that small boys are said to be the 'husbands'—but I have never observed boys being addressed thus, though I have watched housekeeping play very frequently. According to my observation, it is merely implied in the manner of distributing the 'cooked porridge', which follows the pattern of family feeding. Older girls sometimes introduce dolls as the 'children'—clay figures of people made by themselves or, more usually, for them by their brothers.

The essentials of the play consist in 'grinding flour', 'cooking sauce' and 'porridge', and 'sharing out' the 'food'. Every feature of the real processes is mimicked, but with the most ingenious imaginative adaptations. A pair of flattish stones or a boulder and a large pebble serve as 'grindstones'. For pots, dishes, calabashes, and ladles various things are used—old sherds chipped into roughly circular pieces the size of a half-crown or crown, fragments of old calabashes, the husks, whole or bisected, of *mɔlǝmɔk* or *kalǝmpoo,* spherical fruits of common trees varying in size from that of a large marble to that of a cricket ball, and even old tins or bits of tins, while some girls make little pots of clay. Pebbles make a fire-place, a thin piece of millet-stalk is the stirring-stick, some dried grass the firewood. Sometimes a real fire is lit, but usually it is merely imagined. Real grain is never used in such play—it is too valuable to waste thus, as the children themselves would be the first to insist. A piece of potsherd pounded up or a handful of sand serves as grain; but a much more realistic effect is sometimes achieved by using dry baobab stamens. These can be 'winnowed' and the 'grain' ground. Green weeds and leaves are vegetables.

The children play with great zest and earnestness, yet never forget that it is but play. As they grind they hum in a low voice a grinding song they have heard from mother or elder sister. They examine the 'flour' to see that it is fine enough, try to get the right proportion of water, stir the 'porridge' thoroughly, 'dish'

it out with scrupulous fairness. There is a constant interchange
of conversation and commands to the smaller children: 'Bring me
that dish', 'Lend me your broom', 'That's my firewood', 'Don't
stir so fast', 'Come and fetch your porridge', and so on. As a
rule they play together most amicably. I have observed argu-
ments in such groups about who should do some task or another,
but never quarrels. There is real co-operation, based on a distribution of tasks in play.

Such play is occasionally associated with a 'house' built of mud
by a brother who often does not share the play, or actually uses
the 'house' for his cattle play while his sisters are 'cooking' nearby.
It is said, also, that housekeeping play sometimes branches into
sexual play, little boys and girls pretending to be husband and
wife and trying to copulate. Detailed inquiry shows that this is
not common. The usual method of sexual experimentation at
this stage of development follows the pattern of adolescence.
Small boys 'woo sweethearts' with little gifts, and sexual experiments occur in connexion with dancing or by chance opportunities
(Fortes 1936b).

Girls' housekeeping play ceases with the beginning of pubescence. Not only are they by then already taking a full share in
real housekeeping but their interests are turning to youths and
marriage. Housekeeping play, in which the child rehearses the
interests which it has as yet neither the skill nor the degree of
social development to satisfy, and expresses the wishes which
pubescence brings near to realization, has served its purpose.

The corresponding play of boys at this stage is 'cattle-keeping'.
It occurs more sporadically than the girls' play, particularly with
older boys; but as much fantasy and invention go into it. Sometimes, indeed, it seems like an overt day-dream of leisure
hours. One boy alone, or two, usually play. When the group
is bigger more boisterous or recreational play ousts it—they wrestle, shoot arrows, gamble with ground-nuts, or at certain seasons
pitch bangles and hoops of plaited reed. Boys of all ages are far
less placid than girls.

The 'cattle' play involves constructing a 'house' in which the
'gateway' and the 'stable' are prominently indicated and finding
something to serve as 'cattle'—sheep and goats never seem to
enter. These activities, and moving the cattle about in and out of
the 'stable', with murmured remarks in monologue or addressed

to a companion, constitutes the play. I have never been able to record this accompanying speech as I have always had to watch cattle play from a distance. Boys say that it is 'about bulls and cows'.

'Cattle' play has more of pure fantasy and less reproduction of real activities than 'housekeeping' play. Sometimes the 'house' and 'stable' are built of mud—a circular 'wall', 9 or 10 inches in diameter and 2 inches high, with a space left for the 'gateway', and a smaller circle of mud adjoining it as the 'stable'—to last for a whole dry season. Often it is constructed *ad hoc*—two circles drawn in the sand or made of heaped-up sand may be enough. A great variety of objects serve as 'cattle'. Boys who like modelling may make clay figures of cows and bulls for their play; bits of sticks, leaves of a common shrub which can be opened so as to stand up on their edges, pebbles, and other things are used. Yet despite the meagre materials and the paucity of mimetic content the play fascinates boys from the age of 5 or 6, when they are still too young to go out with the herds, to about 12, when they may be full-blown herd-boys. Even if their families have no cattle and they have never followed a herd regularly, they play at it. The interest and identification are active nevertheless.

At this stage, too, domestic ritual begins to be reflected in the play of boys. A boy's or girl's schema of ritual and religious ideology at the age of 9 or 10 includes the main structural principles of the system. As his knowledge has been acquired by attending at sacrifices, he knows most about the ritual acts and conventional formulas connected with sacrifice and least about the beliefs and theories. He is familiar with all the concepts of Tale religion and magic but cannot assign them accurately to their relevant contexts. He knows that ancestor spirits and medicines are different, and can even describe some of the latter by their functions, but cannot elucidate these differences. He knows also and believes that health, prosperity and success depend on mystical agencies, that sickness, death, and misfortune are caused by them, and that sacrifices must be made to placate them or to expiate offences. He has heard talk of all this and seen consultations of diviners. As an infant, perhaps, he has been called by his mother to get off a partition wall 'lest the spirits push you off', or has seen food put out 'for the spirits' during the ritual festivals. He knows what different types of shrines look like and what are their appurtenances. But it is surface knowledge, confused in details and full of gaps.

Ritual is men's business, though women are well versed in it. Hence it emerges mostly in the play of boys and not of girls. Significantly, it is permitted till pubescence, that is, as long as a boy is not likely to take a responsible part in real ritual. After that he is liable to have to accept an ancestor spirit demanding real sacrifices and may no longer play at it. At 13 or 14 years of age, when a boy's ritual schemas approximate those of an adult, he fully understands and acquiesces in this prohibition. It suggests, however, that playing at ritual has a different value for children than actual ritual has for adults. Children share the adults' interest in ritual and accept its prescriptions, but not the adults' emotional relationship to ritual. In their play they express this interest and their identifications, rehearse their knowledge, and integrate it with the rest of their educational achievements.

Small boys build shrines a few inches high for themselves in a corner of the cattle-yard. They take great pains to achieve verisimilitude and neatness, and their inventiveness is remarkable. *Kaləmpoo* husks are turned into medicine-pots; fragments of calabash or potsherd represent the hoe-blade which is essential to many ancestor shrines; a pronged twig is a shrine's 'tree'; the tail of a stillborn kid or lamb, tied with string and feathers in the same way as adults do, is a shrine's 'tail', another object commonly dedicated to real shrines. There are 'roots'—of grass —as in adult medicine-pots, and other appurtenances. Whenever they build miniature houses, during the building season, 'shrines' are added and, as in real life, each has his own.

Play with these shrines is woven into other play activities, and it revolves around sacrifice. When a small boy goes out hunting for fieldmice or birds, if he happens to have a 'shrine' he will 'give it water', i.e. pour a libation to it. Ashes represent flour, which is stirred up in water as in a real sacrifice. He invokes the shrine, 'My father' (but never mentioning names as in real sacrifice since his own father is probably still alive), 'accept this water and grant that I have successful hunting. If I kill an animal, I will give you a dog.' Some time later he may catch a live mouse, and when he has played with it to satiety he 'sacrifices' it on his shrine—this is the promised 'dog'. A nestling bird found alive

is 'sacrificed' as a 'fowl' or 'guinea-fowl'. If he finds a live mouse
or bird by chance it will always be taken home and 'sacrificed'
thus before it is cut up and eaten. Taboos like those of adults
are invented for his shrines. Fetishes, like those of adults, accept only red and black 'fowls'; other shrines only white ones.
Siikaɔni, a small boy of about 7 or 8, built himself a *loo*
fetish, which can be dispatched to 'tie up' any one who might
interfere with one's enterprises. Siikaɔni pretended to use his *loo*
to keep the parents of his 'sweetheart' out of the way when he
went to see her—a frequent use of a real *loo* by young men.

Of the imaginative and constructive play produced as a response to current social activities in which children co-operate, I
shall instance only building. During the building season a favourite preoccupation of the children is to build miniature rooms or
houses. It is a co-operative group enterprise, boys and girls frequently working together, led by a boy of about 12–13. It is
carried on in the intervals between helping the men. Sometimes
they are content to build only walls, a few inches high, but when
the leader is keen they undertake a complete replica of a house
—walls a foot or more high, several rooms properly arranged,
a roof, a beaten inner court, and shrines. The work goes on for
days on end and needs planning and organization. The girls and
smaller boys make the swish and roll it into pellets, the older
boys do the actual building, often with extraordinary skill. When
the 'house' is built and roofed and the walls have dried, if the
enthusiasm for building still lasts, the girls plaster the walls and
beat the inner court in the way they have learnt by assisting
their mothers with these tasks in connexion with the real house.

Children's arts and crafts have a play value in that they are
practised purely for pleasure and have a seasonal incidence.
But they demand considerable skill of eye and hand, and individual differences in ability are noticeable. Towards the end of the
rainy season a strong and supple reed springs up in profusion
along the watercourses. Young people and children pluck these
reeds to plait bangles, necklets, small panels to hang over the
chest as decorations, and waistbands. These things are worn by
young and old at the festival dances. But whereas the young men
and women plait sporadically a few things for themselves, their
sweetheart, or a child, children do so continuously and ab-
sorbedly. From July to September one sees them sitting about or

strolling about in small groups, plaiting reed decorations. The boys have a game played by tossing or bowling the reed bangles and waistbands at a mark. A group plays, and the winner collects all. Girls of all ages love decking themselves from head to foot in this reedware. The technique of plaiting these articles, which is the same as that employed in the manufacture of a number of utilitarian objects, is fairly elaborate. It is gradually learnt between the ages of about 8 and 11.

Less widely practised is the art of modelling clay figures. Girls sometimes model, but it is chiefly a diversion of boys. Cattle and other animals, humans, horses accoutred and with riders astride are the usual subjects. A taste for modelling appears to depend on talent to a great extent. Many boys never acquire the art; others take such delight in it that they devote the whole dry season to producing dozens of clay figures for themselves, brothers and sisters, and friends. Gifted boys model extremely cleverly. I knew two boys of 12 or 13, sons of a chief, who made clay horses and manufactured saddlery and trappings of old rags and bells and ornaments of pieces of tin to adorn the figures. Older boys or youths teach small boys by correcting errors they make in modelling; but I have never found a boy of under 8 or 9 years able to model well.

Play from pubescence to adolescence. The last stage of childhood coincides with the rapid absorption of the child into the economic system and his or her gradual acquisition of a responsible status in the social structure. By the age of 14 or 15 most girls are already married or being courted in marriage. They take their household duties more lightly perhaps than older women with children, but their childhood education is complete. Their education in the duties and responsibilities of wifehood and motherhood lies outside the scope of this paper. 'To play' now means to join in the dance or to dress up and go to market, there to gossip and flirt. These are recreations merely, like conversation in the evening after a good meal, when the whole family sits or sprawls about in one of the inner courts or in front of the gateway. Such 'play' is educative in quite a different sense to that of childhood.

Boys, too, between the ages of 12 or 13 and 16 to 18 are at the stage of transition from childhood to young manhood. The imaginative play still prominent at the beginning of this period is given up by degrees and usually altogether abandoned when puberty is established. Like the adolescent girl, the boy of 16 or so finds his principal recreation in the dance at certain seasons. He, too, begins to frequent markets when time permits, for he is greatly preoccupied with the opposite sex, with courtship and flirtations and even transient love affairs, and there is no place like the market for pretty girls. An adolescent youth is already applying the deftness and skill acquired in juvenile play or in the arts and crafts of his boyhood to practical ends. A 16-year-old takes an active part in building and thatching and in the manufacture of bows and arrows, or in the practice of crafts like leather-work or the forging of tools and implements.

The transition from boyhood to manhood can readily be observed in the development of farming interests and skill during this period. The boy of 10 to 12 is extremely keen to plant, hoe and weed. Helping his father, he sows ground-nuts for himself amongst his father's early millet. Frequently he has a small plot of cereals, a few yards square, in a useless corner of one of his father's fields. He hoes and plants and weeds his plot with great energy and zest, though somewhat crudely, borrowing one of his father's discarded hoes for this purpose. He assists his mother to farm her ground-nuts and beans. But his efforts make no difference to the family commissariat or to the care and sustenance given him by his parents. He is still experimenting without responsibility, though with great earnestness. Two or three years later the play element has vanished. If he cultivates a personal plot he makes an effort to beg land which is agriculturally good, and works with the avowed purpose of obtaining a crop which, though minute compared with the needs of the family, suffices to buy himself a cap or a loin-cloth. The time he can now devote to his own plot or to his own ground-nuts must be adjusted in accordance with his responsibilities as a contributor to the family economy.

With boys, therefore, as with girls, the completion of their childhood education marks the end of childhood play. Mimetic and imaginative experimentation becomes redundant when the individual attains social responsibility and maturity. The play of Tale children changes, as we have seen, *pari passu* with their advancing maturity, contributing at each stage to the elaboration and integration of those interests, skills, and observances the mastery and acceptance of which is the final result of their education.

SYNOPTIC CHART OF EDUCATIONAL DEVELOPMENT

In conclusion, and in order to bring the preceding analysis of the education of Tale children to a focus, I append a synoptic chart setting out the main trends of the development of their interests and skills as these are reflected in their economic duties and activities, on the one hand, and in their play on the other. The reader will realize that these norms are necessarily crude and approximate. I have not ventured to include observances in the chart, since the trend of their acquisition cannot easily be analysed into approximate stages.

CHART OF DEVELOPMENT

BOYS

Economic Duties and Activities	*Play*
3–6 years	
None at first. Towards end of this period begin to assist in pegging out goats; scaring birds from newly sown fields and from crops; accompany family sowing and harvesting parties; using hoe in quasi-play to glean ground-nuts in company of older siblings.	Exuberant motor and exploratory play. Use mimetic toys (bow, drum, &c.) in egocentric play. Towards end of period social and imaginative play with 'cattle' and 'house-building' commences, often in company of older children of either sex, as well as recreational games and dancing.
6–9 years	
These duties now fully established. Help in house-building by carrying swish. Assist in sowing and harvesting. Towards end of period begin to go out with the herd-boys, and to care for poultry.	Imaginative 'cattle' and 'house-building' play common, the latter often reflecting current economic activity of adults. Practise with bow and arrow in marksmanship competitions, and 'hunting' with groups of comrades begun. Recreational games and dancing established. Modelling clay figures and plaiting begun. Ritual play begun.

9–12 years

Fully responsible cattle-herding. Care for poultry. Assisting parents in hoeing and care of crops, but without responsibility. Farming own small plots and groundnuts but in quasi-play. Sons of specialist craftsmen assist fathers in subsidiary capacity—'learning by looking'.

Further development of preceding forms of play, especially of ritual play. Clay-modelling and plaiting established. Recreational games and dancing more skilful. Quasi-play farming.

Sexual dichotomy in work and play established.

12–15 years

Duties as in preceding period but more responsible. Responsible care of poultry, sometimes own property. Leaders of herd-boys. Real farming of own plots and in co-operation with older members of family established by end of period. Sons of specialists experimentally making things.

Imaginative play abandoned. Dancing the principal recreation. Ritual play abandoned. Modelling gradually abandoned. Plaiting for personal decoration mainly. Regular sweethearting commences.

GIRLS

Economic Duties and Activities   *Play*

3–6 years

None at first. Towards end of period the same duties as small boys. Frequent nursing of infants. Accompany mothers to water-hole and begin to carry tiny water-pots. Help in simple domestic tasks such as sweeping.

Exuberant motor and exploratory play. Attached to older sisters and drawn into their 'housekeeping' play. Towards end of period begin to take active social part in the latter and begin recreational play and dancing. Often found in mixed sex groups.

6–9 years

Duties of previous period established. Responsible co-operation in water-carrying and simpler domestic duties. Help in cooking and food-preparation, such as searching for wild edible herbs. Accompany family parties at sowing and harvesting. Carry swish at building operations and assist women in plastering and floor-beating, but still with a play element.

'Housekeeping' play usual. Recreational play and dancing established. Begin to learn plaiting. Participate in 'building' play of boys, mimicking current women's activities, e.g. plastering.

9–12 years

All domestic duties can be entrusted to them by end of this period—water-carrying, cooking, care of infants, &c. Assisting in building and plastering, &c., more responsibly. Often sent to market to buy and sell. Help in women's part of the work at sowing and harvest times.

'Housekeeping' play continues, gradually fading out at end of this period. Dancing becomes principal recreation. Plaiting both for decoration and use established. Begin to have sweethearts but not yet with serious intent.

Sexual dichotomy in work and play established.

12–15 years

Responsible part in all domestic duties of everyday life, and of those associated with ceremonial occasions. Go for firewood and collect shea-fruits in the bush, and help to prepare shea butter. (Marriage a very near prospect.)

Note. Care of infants and children is a duty of girls at all ages. Boys also are frequently entrusted with this task.

Imaginative play abandoned. Dancing the main recreation. Courtship and hetero-sexual interests occupy a great deal of time and attention. Actively participate in the social side of funeral ceremonies, &c., in the role of marriageable girls.

3 EDUCATION IN TIKOPIA

Raymond Firth

Raymond Firth's We, the Tikopia *(1936) is one of the classic
monographs in anthropology. The* Tikopia, *who number only
about twelve hundred people, are Polynesians occupying a small
and remote island in the western Pacific. The book from which
this chapter is taken deals mainly with the family and descent
groups of the islanders. It is a rare account of traditional education, which shows clearly how education is inextricably a part
of everyday family and social life and not the world of specialists:
education is not something marginal to the child's development
as a member of his family, but an essential part of it. The general
principles of education are thus very like those of the Tallensi
from Africa described in the previous chapter, the differences
being related to differences in social organization and values between the two peoples.*

EDUCATION AND KINSHIP

THE CARDINAL points of education in a native society such as
Tikopia are its continuity in both a temporal and a social
sense, its position as an activity of kinsfolk, its practicality—
not in the sense of being directed to economic ends, but as arising from actual situations in daily life—and its non-disciplinary
character. A certain subordination to authority is required and is
sometimes impressed by forcible and dramatic methods, but these
are sporadic and the individual is a fairly free agent to come
and go as he likes, to refuse to heed what is being taught him.
All this is in direct contrast to a system of education for native
children wherever it is carried out under European tutelage.
Such consists usually of periodic instruction with segregation, in-
termitted by intervals of relaxation and rejoining of the normal

Reprinted from *We, the Tikopia*, London, Allen and Unwin, 1936, pp.
134–146, with permission of the author and the publisher.

village life, and imparted not by kinsfolk of the children but by strangers, often from another area, even when non-Europeans. This instruction is given not in connection with practical situations of life as they occur, but in accord with general principles, the utility of which is only vaguely perceived by the pupils. Moreover, it is disciplinary, the pupils are under some degree of direct restraint and may even suffer punishment for neglect of appointed tasks.

The divorce from the reality of the native social life, the staccato rhythm of instruction and the alien methods of restraint undoubtedly are potent factors in retarding the achievement of the aims of so much of what is rather falsely termed "native education."

In Tikopia we have an example of a people largely free from European influence, where education is not an imagined preparation for social life but is actually a vital part of it, hinging upon the participation of the child in all ordinary activities from early years, and arising out of the inevitable lacunæ in its knowledge when called upon to face practical situations. The observer is impressed almost immediately by the absence of any institutionalized education. The training of children is a private affair, and is very largely a function of the kinship situation, the parents of a child playing the most important part as instructors. The residential factor must by no means be left out of account however, as in the case of orphans, or of "adhering children", for much of whose teaching the elder members of the household where they live are responsible.

Since education may be considered to include all social processes which serve to fit the human individual more adequately for his social environment, it is clear that much of the descriptive part of this book may be comprised under this head. What is desired here, however, is merely to indicate some of the more obvious fields of education in Tikopia, and particularly by means of examples to show the mechanism of the social processes involved. Specific spheres in the education of a child are instruction in the manners and moral rules of the society, training in arts and crafts and imparting knowledge of traditional lore and ritual formulæ. Formal lessons are rarely given in these departments, but advice, explanation and commands tend to cluster around the performance of any activity, or the onset of any social situation.

The kinship factor in education is extremely important, and by the natives themselves it is continually stressed. Tuition in points of etiquette is frequently given by parents, and they are held responsible for breaches of manners on the part of their children. Discipline, especially in the field of obedience to the authority of father and of clan chief, is inculcated by them as a moral duty but is not apt to be insisted upon in ordinary affairs. In the economic sphere too they severally play leading parts. The training of a boy, however, is often due to the interest of one of his mother's brothers in him. If this man is an expert in any branch of knowledge he will probably see to it that his nephew receives some of the results of his experience. If he is a noted canoe-voyager and fisherman he will pass on his store of information in the finer points of his craft to the lad: especially will he show him the location of fishing-banks, a prized set of data not possessed by all fishermen. In dirges composed to the memory of mothers' brothers reference is not infrequently made to this sort of assistance. A grandfather may take a great interest in a child's upbringing and may provide him with traditional lore, names of family ancestors and their history, tales of ancient fights and immigrations, of the origins of the land and the doings of the gods. The transmission of details of family ritual and more esoteric information concerning the family religious life is essentially the role of the father, and not infrequently does the head of a house lament the fact of his own comparative ignorance due to his father's early death. Individual circumstances vary considerably in this respect, but as a rule in such cases the gap is filled more or less adequately by a father's brother or even a father's sister, who will be acquainted in some degree with the requisite information. A mother's brother is of little use here, since family ritual and religious formulæ are secret property, jealously conserved, and transmitted essentially through the male line. Education of the last type applies particularly to the heirs of family headships.

This brief outline of the educational system of the Tikopia will allow the detailed descriptive material which follows to be set in perspective.

Even before the child is of an age to comprehend properly

what is being said to it, it is addressed quite solemnly by its
elders, with a view to promoting its understanding and education. The Ariki Kafika, for example, shows quite an interest in
Arikifakasaupuke, his young grandson, a light-skinned plump
youngster with a round face and a seriously determined expression. The old chief gets the child to bring him little things
which he requires, and gives him directions carefully. In preparing his betel mixture he splits the areca nuts with the butt
end of his spatula, puts them down in front of him in a row and
gets Saupuke to pick them up one by one, take out each kernel
in turn and hand it to him. He speaks to him solemnly all the
while, then sits and looks at him steadily for a space. If the infant
does not do as he is told the chief sometimes says to him calmly
without the least spark of annoyance, "May your father eat filth,"
the conventional curse of Tikopia. Saupuke is treated with considerable indulgence in the house of the chief; perhaps because
he is the offspring of a younger son, he is by way of being the
old man's favourite. His gluttony and bursts of ill-temper are indulged, so long as they do not interfere too much with the peace
of the household, or imperil the dignity of his grandsire. And
even such a disgraceful exhibition as his beating the end of the
house with a stick while he shrieked with rage at being stopped
from entering called forth no more than a mild remonstrance
from his grandmother. His education, however, is not altogether
neglected. His father, his father's brothers and cousins reprove
him as they do each other's children, and he is taught, like all
other junior members of the household to respect the interior
of the dwelling and in particular the presence of his grandfather
the chief. His elder cousins, children of six to nine, take a considerable hand in his upbringing, and the little girls in particular
give him severe commands as to how to conduct himself. Here
is one instance. He sits and eats food that has been given him,
then goes and gets the coconut water-bottle, taking off an empty
bottle from the hook first, then the full one, and then carefully
replacing the empty one again. He raises the nut with both hands
to his lips and drinks. As he goes to put back the plug his cousin
intervenes, "Give the plug here," then "Run and hang it up"
she says, sticking in the plug firmly and giving him the bottle.
Then as he quietly complies, "Go to the back," an injunction to
retire to the rear of the house away from people of importance,

and finally as a parting shot the order comes, "Don't go walking about on the mats"—all of which he obeys without a murmur and sinks down in obscurity. This is a sample of the way in which children are continually ordered about by their elders, a process in which a few years gives an immense advantage, so that the Tikopia kingdom of youth tends to be one which is ruled on the basis of seniority. Girls rather than boys tend to act as mentors of the young.

Instruction in Tikopia in matters of etiquette and decorum in the house begins at a very early age, almost before the child can fully understand what is required of it, but as the essence of the system for the young is quietness and self-effacement, the general lesson is soon learnt—though apparently as soon forgotten, or disregarded, perhaps as the result of over-repetition. As always, instruction is given in relation to concrete situations, rather than to abstract principles. For instance, to *pe tua*, "throw the back" to people of superior status is bad manners. Firimori was sitting thus in Motuapi, facing away from his grandfather the chief. Nau Nukunefu, his father's brother's wife, spoke to him sharply, "Do not turn your back on your grandfather," whereupon he shifted round slightly. So children learn.

The child soon comes to take part in the work of the community, and so useful is it that a household without one is at a distinct loss. At first it goes out with a relative to the cultivations and intersperses its play with fetching and carrying things. Gradually most of the economic minutiæ are allotted to it by its elders, including others than the parents, and its performances, small in themselves, act as the emollient which allows the household machinery to run smoothly. Girls go and fill the water-bottles, carrying them in kits on their backs at morning and evening; it may be for a considerable distance. They bring back loads of firewood from the orchards, they go and pluck the yellow leaves of *ti* from which the family decorations are made for the dance. At some part of the day, according to the state of the tide, they are to be found accompanying their mother or their father's unmarried sister in her scoop-net fishing on the reef. Boys also go fishing on the reef, but with them this is apt to be more a matter of personal sport than actual work, since the obligation of combing the reef daily is primarily a woman's task. But they too have their place in the economic scheme. They are sent on errands, as to fetch a fire-stick, to borrow betel leaf, or some lime, to return a net to its owner, or to take a message about fishing. They accompany older brothers to the orchards to pluck breadfruit or green coconuts or to cut a bunch of bananas. Anything to be carried to another house is given to a child, and the injunction *"Feti o sau mai . . ."* "Run and fetch me . . ." is one of the commonest phrases heard addressed to young children in Tikopia.

The little one is speedily made aware of its subordination to authority and its function as an element in a larger group. These limitations on its freedom of action are not always kindly received, and sternness, threats or even physical coercion may be necessary to exact obedience. On one occasion a group of men sat yarning under the trees at the head of the beach and began as usual to chew betel. Lime was wanting, and Mosese, a chubby little three-year-old, was sent by his father to get it from their house some fifty yards inland. He got some yards off, then stood still, wriggled, whined and objected to going any farther. "He wants to listen to the talk of the men," said his father with a smile. But he insisted, speaking sharply to the child, who after some urging disappeared, to return as commanded.

Another scene in illustration may be given from the house of Pa Niukaso, a Christian teacher newly returned from Anuta with his wife and small son, Allen. This is a chubby child with a soft chocolate brown skin, darker than most, and an attractively solemn expression in repose—which is not, however, his constant state. His only vesture consists of a string round his neck, suspending a bone of a phalange type, said to be that of a turtle, and worn not as an amulet but for ornament. While his mother and father are inside the house Allen is ranging up and down outside with a stick, battering the walls and roof, to his evident pleasure. A small girl—a naked little urchin like himself—begins to crawl out of the doorway, and he turns to lunge at her a couple of times, for which he is reproved by his mother. She draws back, then attempts to emerge again a little later. This time Allen's aim is more accurate, to judge from her cries as she re-enters. Frightened by the success of his exploit he begins to yell too, but soon quietens down. A short time afterwards he comes in and is given some ends of taro, which he passes to his father, saying, *"Dudi, dudi,"* meaning *"tutia, tutia,"* "Cut, cut." This is done. Then he gets hold of the knife, and when it is taken from him he lies on his back on the floor and yells, then kicks and screams. Gradually he is pacified by his father and mother, frequent references being made, since I am there, to what the white man will think. When we leave he comes too, and howls on being ordered to go back. He is appeased only by being carried along on his father's back, and from this point of vantage prattles away cheerfully with many questions, all of which his father answers patiently and seriously.

The cleanliness of the child in its early years is the care of the mother; later it is supposed to have learned to look after itself.

Native peoples may be classified into two types—those who wash and those who do not. The Tikopia must be put most distinctly into the former category. Frequent washing by children is encouraged by the parents, and those who are reluctant may soon find themselves the object of derisive remarks from their companions or elders. Such is Kapolo of Matautu, a poor half-wit with a cleft palate who was continually being mocked by his fellows for his dirty state. In the south-east trade wind season the air in the early morning is sometimes decidedly chilly, and children may then have to be driven to wash. Scenes such as the following, which I noted, are common in the village soon after sunrise. A woman approaches the aqueduct mouth carrying a child on her arm and leading another by the hand. The latter —a three-year-old—is urged to get under the spouting water and wash. He grumbles and refuses to stir. "Jump into the water, friend!" says his mother. Still he hesitates, upon which she takes him firmly, stands him under the stream and rubs his face and body hastily with her hand. "There! you are wet!" she says rather unnecessarily. Then he is released, to stump off up the path, still querulously grunting. The younger child is treated with more care. Towels are unknown on the island, so that such of the moisture as is not stripped off by the fingers must evaporate from the body surface, leaving a chilly feeling for some time.

It is a canon of the society that parents are most fitted to coach their offspring in manners and customs and that the obligation of so doing lies on them. Of a child which is a nuisance at public gatherings, which wilfully misbehaves itself, or shows itself to be lacking in some of the elementary notions of decorum, people

say, "Why do not its parents instruct it? Why is it not told by its
parents not to act thus?" In a family which cares for the proper
upbringing of its children—and such families exist in Tikopia
society and can be distinguished from others of a more slovenly
habit—considerable attention is paid to the child's ways of
speech. It is taught by mother and father two main principles.

The first is to avoid rude and indecent expressions. They listen
to its talk, and hearing objectionable words say to it, "Your
speech that is made is bad speech, give it up! But use good
speech," or again they say, "When you go out, do not call out to
people; you hear, is the speech of the land made thus?" *"Ea?"*
replies the child in wonderment. "These words that you use are
evil speech; abandon them," the parents answer. The child is
thus early taught to distinguish two categories of expressions:
taraŋa laui and *taraŋa pariki*—good speech and bad speech. It
soon learns that the latter is not permissible in public, or in the
presence of certain relatives, or of members of the opposite sex,
though regarded as amusing, and even allowable among groups of
its own kind and status. It is well known that children of three
or four years of age pick up expressions relating, for instance,
to the sexual act, as *fekoni,* "copulate," which are not used in
polite conversation. When they repeat them in the home parents
take this opportunity for correction. Some children are said to
"grow up foolishly," *somo vare;* they do not listen to any instruction from their parents, but repeat every new phrase they
hear, calling it out to strangers, to the amusement of the vulgar
and the shame of their relatives. Young folk draw attention to
these lapses with a laugh, chiding the child, yet turning the matter
to a point of humour. I noted once a child babbling meaningless
syllables to itself, "La—la—la—la." It was overheard by a
group of unmarried people. "May its father eat filth! It utters
evil speech—the *lala!"* cried a girl (*lala* signifies female genita-
lia, in particular the clitoris). This was with an affectation of disapproval but a giggle at the end for the benefit of the boys near.

The second rule which is impressed on a child, with rather
less success, is that it must refrain from calling out to passers-
by, strangers, or people at large. The mere fact of shouting out
to them implies some degree of ill-breeding on the part of the
child, and moreover, there is always the likelihood of its using

some objectionable remarks. In this as in other cases the parents are concerned not so much with abstract rules of conduct as with the possibility of offending other people, and even bringing down the wrath of an insulted chief on their heads. Instruction in good manners has a distinctly practical side.

PUNISHMENT AND OBEDIENCE

The sanction for good manners in Tikopia is the fear of social disapproval rather than that of physical retaliation. The attitude of the community towards the punishment of children for offences may be summarized as one full of promises but rather empty of performance. In any case where direct action is taken corporal punishment of a mild type is adopted; more subtle methods of inflicting discomfort on an offender, such as restriction of liberty or deprivation of food, are never practised. Execution is always immediate, and there is nothing comparable to the refinement of mental torture practised in some European families of leaving a sentence hanging over the child's head till the return of the male parent to act as vehicle of chastisement. The punishment, it may be noted, is to be interpreted as a reaction of anger on the part of a parent or other elder, not as retribution for an offence. It is regarded as deterrent in that promises of its infliction are held out as warnings, threats to strike, but it appears to be actually inflicted as a result of the emotions aroused to an explosive point. Again, it is the act of beating rather than the severity of the punishment which is regarded as being so serious. Often the blows are delivered with a fan, the result being that the spirit rather than the body is bruised. When the daughter of Pa Paŋisi was suspected of an intrigue with a boy of whom she was obviously enamoured, her mother threw her down, made uncomplimentary remarks about her morals and beat her in this way. The girl escaped, crying, and went off to Raveŋa to other relations where she stayed for a few days. The whole village talked about the incident. It is the affront to self-esteem that is the greatest wound. The argument that such punishment is really immaterial because it is so light would not appeal to a Tikopia. Young children are not often struck, and are not thrashed by successive blows. Occasionally a child is hit with a stick, but, light or hard, a single blow normally suffices.

In later years, when there is a likelihood of its being punished, the child takes care to avoid the issue by discreet absence and stays with relatives elsewhere till the storm has blown over. This is rendered extremely simple by the ramifications of the kinship system, and by the ordinary habit of the natives of spending a night or so away from home for casual reasons of work or pleasure. The final resort of the adolescent or young adult who wishes to avoid punishment or wipe out its stigma is, of course, suicide at sea. It is with this in mind that the father—presuming that he is the responsible parent—sometimes goes in search of his child, from *arofa,* affection, as the natives say, and brings it back with harmony restored.

To strike a child or to threaten to strike it is frequently done, not in punishment for any specifically wrong action committed but merely to induce it to go away, the offence consisting in its obstruction or inquisitiveness. A couple of samples show the type of action. Seteraki, son of Pa Raŋifuri, was making a nuisance of himself in the house. *"Taia ke poi ki fafo!"* "Strike him so that he goes outside," said his father fiercely to one of the daughters. As his sister moved towards him, however, the little boy fled. Another child continued to play with a wooden bowl after being told not to. "You want to cry, eh? You don't listen," its parent said, announcing what was in store if it persisted. So it stopped.

There are various expressions in the native vocabulary to denote the different modes of action in getting rid of the encumbrance of unwelcome youth. The general term is *fue,* meaning to drive away, while *fakarei* and *fakakiro* have a similar meaning. These describe the uttering of injunctions to go, accompanied by a toss of the head or a wave of the arm, the usual way of shooing children off. *"Oro kese ŋa tamariki,"* "Go away, children," is an injunction uttered continually and almost automatically by people at public gatherings—and hardly heeded by the objects of it. *"Fakareia ke poi,"* "Let them be driven away," it is said. *Fakakiro* may represent rather more vigorous methods. Thus *"Fakakiro tau soa ke kiro,"* a command addressed to someone to chase away a persistent child, may be freely translated as "Quieten our friend; hit him with a stick." *Teteŋe* is used of striking with a stick, *"te rekau ke teŋe."* Any light piece of wood is used and the blow is often very mild. I once observed Nau Taitai, my neighbour's wife, getting angry with her little child for his obstinacy, catch up a stalk of the betel creeper, a pliant green twig not more than six inches long, and strike him on the hand. The blow was the merest tap, but the child broke into a roar and stamped the ground in his indignation.

"I talk, talk; you do not listen to me," she explained to him and to the world at large, in part anger, part extenuation, as she lifted him up and bore him off. Such incidents of petty punishment are frequent and instructive to the observer in the light they throw on family relations and the guardianship exercised by elders. Thus a lad who struck a younger child with what appeared to be insufficient provocation was promptly smacked by his grandmother, half-smiling as she did so. The commonest method of punishing a child or clearing it out of the way is a light smack on the head, the term for this action, *patu,* meaning to hit with the hand. A person who is driving a child away may give it one clout on the back of the head to send it off, or more leisurely and in playful mood may strike it on the temple, the forehead, the other temple and the back of the head, counting as he does so, "One, two, three, four!" Having thus "boxed the compass," as it were, he tells it to go. If an adult is in a callous frame of mind he tells another, *"Fakamimo ko a mata o tau soa,"* "Make the eyes of our friend swim"—a command to bang the unfortunate intruder on the head without ceremony. I have seen a child which tried to enter a house in which adults were busy, given a resounding smack on the arm with the flat of a paddle. It withdrew without a cry, but with an extremely hurt expression.

Another method of punishing a child or dissuading it from some act is to pinch its cheek just at the corner of the mouth with some force. This is termed *umoumo.* On one occasion the treatment of Saupuke by his mother's father, Pa Porima, provoked the whole household of Kafika to discussion. The child, it was said, insisted on following his elder down to the sea and would not go back when spoken to. Pa Porima was reputed to have struck him—actually it was only a pinch, which had however broken the skin, since examination established a slight scratch. This caused quite a hubbub for a few minutes and called forth a scornful remark from Nau Kafika, "What kind of a grandparent is he?" During the washing operations connected with the manufacture of turmeric a child was taken down to bathe by one of the workers. A wave came up and soused them, some water going up the child's nose. It yelled, and was pinched by its angry parent, at which it yelled the more. Finally it was pacified by being told to help in cleaning the turmeric roots, the spot that had been pinched was rubbed and peace was restored.

The subject here has departed somewhat from the immediate sphere of family relations, but the treatment of children when outside the household circle by parents and by outsiders in the matter of punishment is very much the same. The use of the word friend, *soa*, in the linguistic example given above implies that the child stands in no very close kinship relation to the speaker.

Since promises of punishment are much more frequent than the act itself children, knowing this, are apt to stand their ground despite all commands made to them. Though these be uttered in most peremptory tones the youngsters merely smile. Repetition is necessary to produce any effect, and so much is this a habit that most orders are given automatically three times over at the start! Much talk and little obedience is the impression gained of family discipline in questions of ordinary restraint. The most blood-curdling threats may be used to make children go away, the object being merely to frighten them. Thus to generalize an incident often witnessed—a band of children on mischief bent come to the side of a dwelling-house and stamp on the ground, peer in, or make objectionable noises, to the irritation of people within. A man inside calls to them to go away, but without effect. He says then, "I shall come out to you, take a stick and split open your heads!" but no notice is taken. Or he curses them, saying, "May your fathers eat filth! If I come out, you will die on the spot!" This horrific threat may silence them for a short space, but a recrudescence of their efforts by the bolder spirits begins almost at once and now it produces no effect whatever. Finally he has to crawl out of the door to disperse them. As soon as he is perceived a general stampede ensues, the sound of running feet is heard in all directions, and he stands there to pursue them with words alone.

In addition to the performance of small services and the observance of good manners, the child must also conform to the rules of *tapu*. These are manifold, consisting of a set of prohibitions that can only be learned after long experience. A few of the most obvious, however, speedily come within the infant's comprehension. It soon comes to mingle mainly in the affairs conducted by people of its own sex, to keep clear of the elders and people of rank in its neighbourhood, and be moderately quiet in their presence. It learns also to avoid touching large canoes, certain house-posts and spears or clubs hung up, and to refrain from walking on the *mata paito* side of the house. Here constant instruction from its parents when a breach of *tapu* has been made or seems impending speedily impresses on it its duties, and the verbal restraint in such case is usually translated into physical terms more rapidly than with the ordinary social rules discussed above. "It is prohibited, do not grasp it" is a frequent warning, which the child learns to accept, with wide eyes, sensing something strange beyond its ken, but recognizing from the solemn tone that here are matters to be heeded, things to be avoided. If it does not obey immediately, then it is grabbed and shaken. Such habits of avoidance inculcated in early years when no reason is understood, save the command of a parent, form the basis of the system of rules to which such attention is paid in later life.

Thus the child Mataŋore inquired of her father regarding articles belonging to her grandfather, the Ariki Kafika. "Things of your *puna;* do not go and interfere with them," he said. *"Toku puna, te Ariki Kafika?* My grandfather the chief of Kafika?" "Yes, don't speak of him, it is *tapu.*" "It is *tapu?*" "Yes." "My grandfather the chief of Kafika," she repeated. Here the prohibition does not represent a definite social regulation—children are permitted to speak of their grandparents, even by name—but the anxiety of a man as chief's son and as parent lest his small daughter wander further in speech and unwittingly infringe the bounds of propriety. In wide-eyed acquiescence Mataŋore subsided and soon began to prattle of other things.

Even in matters of *tapu* the obedience of the child is not always so easily procured. A father brought his small son to a kava rite of ordinary type in Kafika lasi, one of the sacred houses in Uta, and tucked it between his knees. Children are welcome at these functions—much as children in European God-fearing families are encouraged to go to church—so long as they remain decorous. This child, however, began to grizzle, and the father's efforts to pacify it were useless. The child's complaint swelled to a roar, when suddenly the father, abandoning his soothing words and gestures, shook it roughly and shouted, "May your father eat filth! The house is *tapu!*" At the moment this had no effect, but soon the cries subsided to a whimper. No one else present paid any attention.

A couple more examples of the disobedience of children may be given. Seteraki, walking with some older people, climbed up on a rock. "Come down," he was sternly ordered. But he stayed where he was and nothing was done to him. Some days before his initiation Munakina was wanted. His mother's brother ordered him to go. He adopted a policy of passive resistance and did not budge. Various people told him, "Go when your uncle tells you." He still sat tight, until laughingly holding back he was dragged to his feet and led off struggling. As he went he grasped the waistband of another boy, to the latter's discomfiture and the general amusement. On this occasion Munakina's sister took a leading part in the chiding.

Usually little action is taken to compel obedience. The individuality of the child is respected and its freedom allowed, even when this freedom involves discomfort or additional work on the part of its elders. Conformity to the will of a senior is regarded as a concession to be granted, not a right to be expected; an adult behaves to a child as one free spirit to another, and gives an order to another adult in just as peremptory a fashion. Indifference to commands, as indicated above, is common on the part of children and persists in adult years. Often children answer angrily to an order, or make no reply at all. The father in turn speaks angrily, but rarely takes direct steps to enforce his will. In spite of the recognition of the general obligation of filial obedience, moreover, practically no specific moral instruction is given to children on the point.

Children are apt to react petulantly if thwarted and to commit violent actions, till they get their way and allow themselves to be pacified. From my seat in Taramoa, during the ritual celebrations of the fishing season, I watched a small child attempt to enter. It tried to crawl in at the seaward door, but since this is the men's entrance, it was rebuffed by those sitting there. It began to cry, then petulantly threw away the taro tuber which it had just been given to eat. Pa Fenuatara, observing it, said angrily—the gift was from his house—"May its father eat filth!

It has cast away its food!" Soon afterwards the child was allowed to enter and then quietened down.

Children are kept in control by the near relatives of their parents as well as by these latter. Here is an incident of common type. Saupuke, the small grandson of the Ariki Kafika, stands up in the dwelling-house and begins to wander about. He is immediately grabbed by a cousin of his father's with the exclamation, "Whither? the house is sacred, sit down!" The immediate factor here is the presence of the chief, who is lying asleep, and who must be respected. In the ordinary domestic life a child is constantly being reproved for shouting, for rattling a stick, for standing up in front of its elders. *"A mata tou mana!" "A mata tou puna!"* literally "Face of your father!" "Face of your grandfather!" *i.e.* colloquially, "Mind your father!" etc., are commands frequently given and enforced. By this means the child gradually learns the rules of etiquette proper to a house, and how to behave in front of people.

Of specific instruction in technology I saw very little; the child is usually told how to carry out a process only when the article itself is required for practical purposes. I did see, however, a cross-piece of wood, lashed together with sinnet braid in a complex style, specially prepared. This was a model of the *sumu,* the lashing used to fasten the roof-tree of a house to the supporting posts. The prevalence of gales, rising at times to a hurricane, makes a secure lashing important, especially for the large ancestral temples. When I asked the maker, Pa Niukapu, what the model was he said that it was for his son—"that he may know how it is done." The process needs knowledge and considerable skill, and few men are adepts, hence the unusual care.

Craft instruction is normally given by parents. "Boys are taught by their fathers. When men plait sinnet, they are instructed by their fathers." The first piece of work, it is said, is often poor; the second is better. But some boys and girls do good work from the beginning; of such people the expression is used "they have grown up as experts" (*e somo tufuŋa*). So also in the dance. When a person masters the complicated movements of hands and feet known as the *auŋa* while still a child, then it is said *"e somo purotu."*

In a great deal of the economic co-operation between parents and children the latter can hardly fail to absorb knowledge of technical processes. For instance, a little group consisting of a man, his wife and children, is to be seen in the angle formed by two stone walls of a fish corral. The man, armed with a long-handled net, stands at the junction of the walls, and blocks the exit of the fish, while the other members of the family, with scoop-nets in their hands, half-walking, half-running, sweep inwards from the open water. Small fish are thus caught, and the children by shouted commands are taught how to perform their part.

4 SOME ASPECTS OF INDIGENOUS EDUCATION AMONG THE CHAGA

Otto Raum

Otto Raum's book Chaga Childhood *(1940) is a valuable account of indigenous African education, in which the author traces the intimate relationship between a tribal education and the culture of which it is a part. He also explores the role played by children's peer groups in the process of education—a child is taught by his parents and by other children, rather than by specialists who separate out a formal program of training from his everyday development. In this chapter Raum presents a general outline of the argument of his book, and it is thus an excellent introduction to it. Again, as with the Tallensi and Tikopia, we can see how the differences in the form and values of the society and local community are reflected in the variations in aims, content, and methods of education.*

PRELIMINARY METHODOLOGICAL REMARKS

OF ALL THE sociological sciences, Education is the least advanced. The reasons for this are partly to be found in the past connexions of Education with Philosophy and partly in the educational situation itself. It is obviously difficult for an outsider to *observe* the educational process in a family fairly. This difficulty is increased among native peoples, as parental sensitiveness and the shyness of children are often fixed by tradition at a much higher pitch than in our society. It may, for instance, be assumed that the scarcity of observed cases of corporal punishment is partly due to this modifying factor.

Reliance on informants clearly suffers from the presence of many sources of error, such as the suggestibility of children, in-

Reprinted from *Journal of the Royal Anthropological Institute* 68, 1938: 209–21, with permission of the author and of the Council of the Royal Anthropological Institute.

tentional bias in statements made by parents, and the unconscious colouring of reminiscences by natives who are neither parents nor children. Statistical methods, so useful in other sociological sciences, could therefore only be applied with great caution, and are in fact seldom or never used.

It is clear that the fundamental difficulty is the definition and classification of educational phenomena. From the educational point of view it is necessary to find an answer to the question of how a given people, such as the Chaga,[1] deal with a certain educational situation, *e.g.,* how they treat a disobedient child. We would falsify our observations if we did not consider under the heading of disobedience the type of behaviour to which the Chaga themselves apply that word, but used European standards. Viewing it from this angle, the field-worker, by a careful combination of methods and by avoiding generalisations at an early stage of his study, will be able to collect adequate material on indigenous education.

Sociologically education can be defined as the relation between consecutive generations. This relationship, like all other social relations, possesses the characteristics of mutuality and reciprocity. It is usually assumed that in the educational process the child is subjected to a multiplicity of formative forces, *e.g.,* family, play group and tribal organisation. If one tries to visualise the situation, one is easily led to imagine the child crushed by the action of many social forces. There are, however, three factors which restore the balance.

First, the sociological significance of the child is extraordinarily great and contrasts strongly with its biological dependence. The possession of a child raises the status of the parents among the Chaga. A young woman, who is called *mbora* from the time of her circumcision, receives the status of a *malyi* after the birth of her first child and that of *nka* after the arrival of her second. The status of her husband, too, is raised. His father gives a heifer to the young couple when the first child is born. On the other hand, barrenness in woman or man is considered a fault in character and leads to divorce. The death of a child is put down to the agency of sterile women or co-wives resorting to sorcery out

---

[1] The Chaga live on the slopes of Mount Kilimanjaro; aspects of their culture have been described by B. Gutmann (1926 and 1932–35) and by C. Dundas (1924).

of envy. Sociologically the Chaga child is therefore the founder of a stable marriage, just as marriage procures for the child the status of legitimacy.

Secondly, the psychological significance of the child for the parents must not be forgotten. Its trustfulness, simplicity, light-heartedness and fancifulness produce pleasurable emotional responses. Even the polygynous Chaga father cannot escape these influences. He fondles his baby, tickles it and addresses it respectfully by his father's name. The mother's lullabies have not only the purpose of quieting the child, but are an expression of her own experiences in adult society, as an examination of the texts reveals. Very significant in this respect are the names given to children. In many cases they embody a story, or hint at an event which is of importance to the parents.

Thirdly, the child is not a passive object of education. He is a very active agent in it. There is an irrepressible tendency in the child to become an adult, to rise to the status of being allowed to enjoy the privileges of a grown-up Chaga. The child attempts to force the pace of his "social promotion." Thus, at five or six years of age, a little boy will surprise his mother one day by telling her that he wants to be circumcised. The mother will hear nothing of it and threatens to beat him if he repeats the request. But the demand will be made with increasing insistence as the child grows up. In former times it was the clamour and restiveness of the adolescents which decided the older section of Chaga society to start the formal education of the initiation camp.

THE CHILD'S SOCIAL ENVIRONMENT

The child's position in the Chaga family is determined by the fact that Chaga marriage is as a rule patrilocal, and not infrequently polygynous. Since the households of the wives do not form a kraal but are scattered over the district, this means that the father is only an occasional visitor to the child's home. The early intimacies between father and child are superseded by a period when the father is held up as a bugbear to the toddler by the mother. Later he comes to be feared for his disciplinary interventions. The mother's mediation prevents this fear from becoming a permanent mental state. But when the father departs from the compound the children cannot but make merry, and the mother joins in laughingly, saying: "When the bull is gone, the lizards slip out to sun themselves!"

The child's attitude towards the mother is determined by the closeness and continuity of the contact. She knows the worries and troubles of her little flock. The sharing of trivial experiences in field and hut and her partial exclusion from affairs of court and community make a woman a member of the children's group. She stands out in it because of her wider knowledge, but the confidential relationship which she maintains with her children often makes it difficult for her to enforce discipline. She allies herself, therefore, to the father's authority and reports to him when the children have broken rules of conduct. As her mediation may, however, be favourable to a particular child the children are ready to do their mother a good turn; *e.g.,* the boys, by taking a piece of roasted meat from the slaughtering place, circumvent for their mothers the taboo which prohibits them from cooking meat before the husband's return from the butchering party.

The Chaga family can thus be looked upon as having three layers of disciplinary authority. The bottom layer is formed by the children, for even among them the boys and the older girls rule the others. The top layer is represented by the father and the central one by the mother. She holds a crucial position, much more so than she can possibly do in a monogamous marriage, where the attempt is usually made for the parents to take up an identical attitude. The three layers find their expression in the rules of etiquette observed.

These rules can be sub-divided into terms of address and polite manners. Within the first two or three years a child learns all the names, proper, descriptive, and classificatory, of the members of the family group. The parents, notably the father, occasionally test the knowledge of the child as regards these names. The parents are differentiated from the children's group by the descriptive terms *awu* and *mai,* or the classificatory terms *baba* and *mama,* respectively. The latter terms are used by smaller children, who also, when they want to confide something to one parent, use the proper name of the other parent.

The teaching of polite manners starts later than that of terms of address, as I was able to establish in my observation of Chaga family life during a number of years. It takes place between three and six years of age. The formalised kinds of behaviour comprise such acts as handing over things to older people with two hands and getting up from seats on the arrival of important persons. Polite manners to some extent imply the employment of a new and elaborate set of terms of address, involving the use of the clan name and other ceremonial phrases. Confusion with the ordinary set is unavoidable and is looked upon as normal. The method of training used is not one of attempting to ensure that "right for the first time is right for all time," but rather of gradually restricting the originally vague boundaries of application to the appropriate persons.

Etiquette undoubtedly enhances the authority of the parents. Yet it is not a mere bolstering up of prestige, but a necessary factor in all family life, as it helps to create "social distance" under the levelling conditions of close contact. That this is so is shown by the fact that parents observe some sort of etiquette towards the children, as they do, in turn, among themselves. The parents are particularly polite to the eldest son, and there is a formalised way of dealing with the youngest child. Again, the children, besides taking up a "parental" attitude towards their younger brothers and sisters, address the eldest brother as *wawa* and habitually submit to his authority and give him precedence. This is not only of educational significance, but is an important element in the social organisation of the Chaga. The classificatory application of the term *wawa* to eldest sibling, father, and paternal uncles implies potential identity of sociological function: if the father dies, the paternal uncle or the eldest brother assumes his position as regards ritual leadership and control of hereditaments.

The terms of address and manners which the child should adopt in its relations with grandparents, paternal and maternal uncles and aunts are first taught so early that the child cannot have the slightest idea of what it is all about. When the infant is a little more advanced, it is the members of the child's narrower family circle who comment on or check any misbehaviour in the presence of these relatives. The male members of the parental generation are all addressed as *baba,* the female ones as *mama.*

The attitude of the children towards the kindred has three components. First, according to native theory, the behaviour of the children towards their parents is also extended to uncles and aunts since they, on their part, exercise disciplinary authority

like that of the parents over the children. To this corresponds
the system of vocative terminology. Secondly, the general attitude towards the parental generation is modified in practice by
the behaviour of the parents towards the individual members of
the kindred group. The greater deference shown by the parents
towards the senior mother's brother and father's brother, as well
as the more confidential relationship between a man and his eldest sister, are reflected in the children's attitude and symbolised
by indices of individuation, *e.g.,* the father's brother is called
awu o kawi, "second father." Thirdly, special attitudes are ingrained towards those persons who are of ritual or social importance to the child, *e.g.,* the mother's brother who carried out
the ear-piercing ceremony. Behaviour towards these relatives is
less static than that examined so far. It looms large when the
control of a relative becomes decisive to the child, *e.g.,* at the
stage of initiation or marriage, and may weaken when the ties
are not reinforced by social intercourse, *e.g.,* if spatial separation
makes such intercourse difficult.

The relations of the children with their grandparents, especially
the paternal ones, are very close. Frequent visits are paid to
them. In fact, the parents' possessive rights in their children are
restricted in favour of the grandparents. The first child is claimed
by the paternal grandfather. The claim rests on the assistance
which he rendered the young couple in setting up a household.
The second child is claimed by the maternal grandfather. However, he must compensate its parents by the payment of a goat.
If the first child is a girl and the second one a boy, the father
usually insists on having his heir left with him. But the mother's
people's claim is only postponed, not cancelled thereby. It appears from this and other factors that the system of child trans-
ference to kindred is different from what has been called fosterage, where children are sent to friends of their father's for their
education. In fosterage a definite educational purpose is present,
while in the Chaga system, as in the similar one reported of the
Baganda, the emphasis lies on fulfilling a kinship obligation. Accordingly the claim of the maternal grandfather is inherited by
the maternal uncle.

Children are generally sent to their paternal grandparents at
the time of weaning. The grandmother attempts to console the
child for the separation by cooking food which it likes, and care

is taken not to beat it lest it be reminded of home. This laxity in grandparental education is said to result in rudeness of manners and stupidity. However, the statement may very well be only an expression of jealousy, as the boy who grows up with grandparents may inherit from them.

The relationship of cross- and parallel-cousins among the Chaga is not based on common play, but on more or less ceremonial meetings. Thus when an animal has been butchered, the mother allows the children to invite their half-siblings and the children of the father's brothers to eat with them those parts of the animal which are reserved for children. The children of the other kindred are only invited if they happen to be neighbours. Similar children's parties take place at harvest time, and when a cow is newly in milk, for the beestings are consumed by children only. In adolescence the motive for meeting shifts gradually from the ceremonial to the utilitarian. It is especially paternal parallel-cousins who are bound together by the reciprocity of cooperation.

Within the cousin-group marriage is prohibited, with the exception that in certain circumstances marriage with the daughter of a mother's brother is allowed, but this is not a preferential marriage. It is only allowed after Ego's mother is dead. Cousin relationship, however, does not involve avoidance in play groups. Erotic elements enter very early into play imitative of married life. It sometimes happens that boys play such games with their sisters or cousins. When this is discovered the children are not scolded. They are asked in a sarcastic tone, "Who would ever marry his sister?" As this happens at a time when the erotic impulse is vague, the boys' choice of playmates for wives becomes by degrees canalised, *i.e.,* limited to girls that stand outside the cousin relationship. Boys who ask their parents why one does not marry one's cousin are simply told, "It is bad!"

In the foregoing sketch two types of relationships can be distinguished. First, the relationship to a definite individual, such as a mother or a father's father. This is the only type experienced by the smaller child. The primary relationships to members of the family are gradually extended to members of the kindred, and form a set of derived individual relationships. Secondly, there is the relationship of the child to a social unit as such. The older the child grows the more intimately his interests are interwoven with the welfare of the family. Through evasions of kinship obligations, through the fear experienced by the family as a whole regarding neighbours suspected of practising witchcraft, through petty quarrels between the different households of a polygynous family, loyalties are formed which have unique emotional value. By analogous processes the child finds its place in the play group, the clan and later the tribe.

THE PARENTAL MEANS OF EDUCATION

The Chaga parent is fully aware of the process of education. There exists a great number of proverbs and tales concerning the effects of negligence, bias, harshness and other educational factors.

One of the most important means employed by parents is supervision of the smaller child. Infants are hidden in the "sleeping corner" of the hut when anybody suspected of possessing the evil eye comes to call on the parents. This area is separated from the central passage by a beam which serves both as seat for the mother when cooking and as boundary for the infant in the crawling stage. The storage place for food and milk is forbidden territory to children of both sexes. For boys, in addition, it is considered a disgrace to touch a calabash. The Chaga child is prevented from handling the many implements which might injure it; they are tucked away out of reach in the thatch of the hut. A small child is also watched lest it come too near the open fire on the hearth.

However, the essential problem of education is how direct means of behaviour control, such as supervision, punishment and reward, which have only a temporary effect, can be superseded by an indirect mechanism which will determine the actions of the child in the absence of the parents and for a longer period than an ordinary command. This can only be done by the creation of a set of inhibitive factors in the mental make-up of the child itself. Accordingly, the older children are warned by terrifying, but quite probable, stories concerning the fate of disobedient children who kindled a fire or stole honey from the storage place.

In this indirect control of the child's behaviour magic plays an important role. If the mother wants the child to stop crying she calls the *irumbu*-spectre. If the baby does not drink its soup, a brother is sent behind the Dracaena hedge to produce the growl of his ghost. A loitering child is warned that the low-sailing clouds will carry it off. The speedy return of a child messenger is secured by spitting on the palm of his hand saying, "If you are not back before the spittle is dried up, you will vanish like it!"

Taboos can be classed with this kind of magical behaviour control. The effect of these rules is to place the children into definite behaviour groups as they grow up, since the taboos differ according to age and sex. It is unnecessary to describe them in detail. It is of educational importance, however, to examine the way in which they are supposed to act. In general, the transgression is said either to have a detrimental effect on some person to whom the child is attached, usually the mother, or to react on the child itself by handicapping its future assumption of full adult status. Many food taboos are sanctioned by the threat that the mother will die, or that the transgressor will behave in a cowardly way during circumcision. Appeal is therefore made to the two most powerful sentiments, those centring round one's mother and one's own social aspirations. The educative function of these taboos consists thus in ensuring that the prescribed behaviour should appear to serve the interests of the children themselves.

A special class of sanctions, best called religious, threatens the child with death if it breaks certain rules. The mother tells the child in angry tones, "If you won't obey, I shall call the spirits to kill you!" When the excitement has subsided, the parents usually repudiate the curse in a solemn manner. Of special efficacy are grandparental curses. Hence children who live with their grandparents are warned not to enrage them. Their nearness to death magnifies, in the eyes of the Chaga, their potentiality for interference.

Among the Chaga several kinds of punishment can be distinguished according to their nature, such as deprival of food, incarceration, disgrace, corporal punishment, and torture. But it is also possible to define them with reference to the situation from which the conflict ending in punishment arises. There is first the class of punishments which is inhibitive, conditioning or habituating. They occur mainly during the first half of childhood and can be easily observed. The kind of punishment most suitable for this purpose is a quick unexpected slap, and the Chaga mother makes frequent use of it, *e.g.,* when the child comes too near the fire, eats earth or dung, or refuses food when it is being weaned. When punishing, mothers act under an affective strain. Then the physiological exhaustion of the emotion of anger being complete, the opposite reaction is released. The mother who slapped her baby a minute ago proceeds to fondle and even lick it.

The other type of punishment is much more difficult to observe. It arises out of a conflict between the paternal and filial generations, and increases in frequency the older the boys grow. During the first six years there is little disciplinary differentiation between sons and daughters. Between eight and ten the girls enter into effective co-operation with their mother and gradually come to share all her burdens and rights, except marital ones. The occasions on which mother and daughters may fall out with each other are therefore limited to cases where the degree of diligence or thoroughness considered necessary for a particular job is in dispute. When the boys start looking after the cattle, however, the growing cleavage between mother and sons shows its effect in an increased disciplinary tension. It is at this time that boys become attached to a play group, and its influence makes the separation irrevocable. Moreover, the father deems it fit to inculcate in his sons a feeling of contempt for all womenfolk. But boys do not quarrel only with their mothers. Soon they will be passing out of their father's tutelage also, and at puberty a struggle ensues as to the time at which full adult status is to be granted to the striplings.

In this struggle deprival of liberty is a recognised form of punishment. Disobedient children may be shut up in an empty hut and left there without food for some time. Loiterers may be tied to the middle post of the hut and sometimes have to spend the whole night in this uncomfortable position. Deprival of food is common, probably because it lends itself to being administered in varying degrees. A lazy child does not get its share when an animal is slaughtered. The nurse who eats the baby's food may not get anything to eat for one or two days.

Degradation, the public deprival of one's honour, is not unknown as an educational method. A negligent herd-boy gets the excrements of a slaughtered animal smeared on his face in the presence of all the male members of the kinship group, who forgather on such an occasion. A persistent loiterer is given a goat's horn to drink out of during a carousal, a sign of utter disgrace. Quite distinct from degradation is humiliation, which is employed when the child has not given cause for complaint. For instance, a child that is being brought up in the home of his grandparents is made to remove their faeces from inside the hut without showing any signs of disgust. It is in this way that one earns the grandparents' blessing. Again when an elderly person emits wind, it is the child who is blamed for it. Children must not deny any such charge, because they are told that by their acquiescence they prevent the disgrace of their fathers.

Corporal punishment is also used as a means for settling disputes between father and son. A boy who loses a cow on the pasture gets fifteen strokes with a stick, this being the traditional measure. In the exercise of their disciplinary rights, parents are subject to the control of the community in which they live. Cruelty is condemned and indulgence ridiculed. Individual cases are dealt with on their own merits. In spite of this check, the existence of stories of torture and the use made of them for intimidating a child into obedience suggest that they might in certain circumstances serve as justification for the summary punishment of young offenders.

When an interval is placed between the punishable act and the corrective reaction, opportunity is given for the elaboration of the punitive process. The necessity is felt, especially with adolescent children, for a confession to justify the punishment. When the child is young the reconciliation ritual may be a quite informal act, such as seizing the father's beard. But if the boy already possesses a semi-independent household of his own, the procedure is quite formal and takes place in the presence of the kindred, some of whom may act as mediators. Usually the ceremony consists in expressions of repentance, the handing over of a fine by the son to his father, and a symbolisation of restored confidence on the father's part. It is important to notice that both the affective reconciliation noted above, and the ceremonial one, are initiated by the parent concerned. The explanation of this is the fact that not only the punishable act but also the punishment itself violates the principle of mutual assistance upon which family life is based. It is restored only if the parents resume the relations of affectionate attachment which amplify the biological bond existing between parents and children. These attempts at reconciliation clearly distinguish educational from legal punishment.

Rewards are, of course, extensively used by parents in their attempt to make the children conform to their standards. The technique of rewards implies the lavish use of promises, controlling child behaviour by anticipation. Thus when the mother goes to market, the children are promised a small present, such as a locust, a banana or a few beads, if they do not cry. The father who interests himself in his sons at a later stage deviates sometimes from the customary law of inheritance by assigning special gifts to a son who is obedient and exhibits good manners, thrift and diligence, and he ensures the carrying out of his will by a curse on anyone who should deprive his favourite of his claims.

A most important educational factor is training in work. It is impossible to distinguish play and work genetically. A great amount of childish energy is directed to the acquisition of techniques, and this is done spontaneously and in a style which differs little, if at all, from play activities. A condition of this state of affairs is the simplicity of the tools employed and the scarcity of toys. It is sometimes difficult to decide whether at a particular moment a child is using an implement as a tool or as a toy.

Actual training in work takes place at a much later date and consists chiefly in an impressive lesson in the necessity of diligence and thoroughness in work. From the above generalisation professional training in one of the non-hereditary crafts must be excluded. This takes place after initiation and is surrounded by elaborate ceremonies to ensure the secrecy of the methods taught and to protect the teacher from future competition by the pupil.

As regards the content of training in work, the education of the girls is concluded much earlier than that of the boys. Both sexes learn first together all the domestic tasks of a Chaga household. At about eight years of age the division of labour is gradually imposed on this common base. For the girl this means continuation lessons in domestic tasks, with greater refinement and independence. For the boy this is the opening of a new chapter in life. As an informal process of social education he is taken to public meetings, where he gleans information about the political authorities, the distribution of wealth and influence, and legal procedure. He is also introduced to tasks reserved for men only, such as hunting and forest work.

We must next consider some of the methods employed in training for work. Extensive use is made of models. Oral explanation is rarely given, except to a very inquisitive child. The degree of skill attained in the basic tasks is ascertained, and proficiency made a pre-condition of advance in status. The training terminates in the handing over of some of the parental stock and land to the care and for the use of the adolescent child. The first-fruits of his labours are expected to be given to the parents, and later on annual gifts are the rule. Thus the adolescents grow into the adult system of kinship obligations.

Ceremonies hold a special position in the educational process. The Chaga *rites de passage* divide childhood into different stages. The infant has to undergo the rite of the "First Tooth" and of receiving a name. From the time of the latter rite to the appearance of the second set of teeth the child is called a *mwana,* but thenceforward a *ndentewura.* About three years later the ear-piercing ceremony takes place and simultaneously the two lower incisors are knocked out, the child acquiring the status of a *ndaka.* At adolescence the boys form groups that loiter about and make a nuisance of themselves. In some districts a special *kisusa* rite is held to discipline the most forward of these stripling individuals. If the *"kisusa* spirit," as the rebelliousness of youth is called, cannot be curbed, the demand for tribal initiation and the formation of a new age-class is raised before the chief.

The educational function of these rites has often been described. The special diet, the quaintness of the ceremonies and the tiring repetition of the ethical teaching all help to make the impression indelible. Yet if one has seen native children during the longer rites, haggard, drowsy, often insensible to what is going on around them, one doubts whether the educational importance of ritual lies entirely in its immediate effects. Much more important are, indeed, two other factors neglected hitherto. First, the anticipation of the rite influences childish behaviour long beforehand. Negatively this means that the parents make admission to the rite conditional on conformity to their demands, and positively that the child definitely strives to make himself worthy of acceptance. Secondly, the rites introduce the child into wider social circles. This rise in status, implying ever-increasing responsibilities, is the topic most discussed among the children. Their wish for social advancement is so strong that the children of third-generation Christian families are sometimes "infected" by it and run away from their parents to take part in the rites, showing how effectively social pressure is still diffused in the society of the children.

THE SELF-EDUCATION OF THE CHILDREN

It is important that we should try to discover in what manner the society of the children reacts to the educational efforts of the parents. To some of them it makes a positive adjustment, others it dislikes because of the discrimination in status which they imply. It makes, in fact, an attempt to create in its play activities its own social life, with its own laws and cultural features.

It is possible to classify Chaga play activities into three groups. First, there is the playful exercise of the sensory and motor apparatus, resulting in the physical adaptation of the individual organism. Secondly, there is imitative play, consisting in an adaptation of adult life to the social needs and understanding of the children. Thirdly, there are competitive games, which test not only physical fitness but also intellectual and social qualities. These three groups follow one another in a rough time sequence, the first corresponding to infancy, the second to childhood, and the third to adolescence. Corresponding with this development there proceeds an increasing socialisation of the children's group, and its gradual separation from adult society.

While the play of physical adaptation is performed by infants in isolation, the mimicry type of play draws the child into a community of players who enact the daily round, the activities of the annual cycle, and scenes from individual life-histories and the different social classes. In calling these play activities imitative, we must be careful to describe what we mean by this term. Imitation among people having the same status in society must clearly be distinguished from imitation which cuts across boundaries of status, such as is seen in the native's craze for European clothes and the child's copying of the adult. In the latter case the mental outlook of the imitator differs from that of the imitated, and the copy performs a different function from that of the original. For instance, in considering the mimicry of married life the fact must not be forgotten that most children know of the marriage ceremony only by hearsay, as they are forbidden to attend weddings. Much of the subject-matter of imitation is in fact re-layed through the medium of speech only. This kind of imitation may therefore be described as "blind," *i.e.,* the children's performance is a free reconstruction of more or less imagined happenings.

It must also be noted that such imitative play is not a complete taking over of the example, but selective. Certain traits important or striking to the child are chosen from the adult pattern. This becomes apparent in the "imitation" of so-called "bride-lifting." This practice has long fallen into desuetude. The reasons which caused this exceptional custom to be resorted to were in most cases economic. With children out on the pasture the economic justification for "marriage by capture" obviously does not weigh. But it would also be an insufficient explanation to call their imitation of this custom a survival, a mere form without meaning. As a matter of fact, the "lifting" is to them a vital part of all play weddings, a symbol of marriage as they understand and practice it.

Having guarded against certain ambiguities arising from the use of the term "imitation", it must be admitted that the accuracy of the copying process increases as the child grows up and approaches adult status. Younger children insist on the meticulous repetition of isolated bits of behaviour, which are taken as representative of the corresponding adult activities. But this insistence becomes less and less pronounced with increasing conceptual specialisation in the minds of the children, which goes hand in hand with greater variation and realism in mimicry. This is the result of a mutually corrective process in which that child is accorded the approval of his associates who, by the standards of the play group, deviates least from the adult pattern.

The imitative play activities which copy family and tribal life also afford an opportunity for the exchange of experience regarding persons and institutions with which some children have little chance to become directly acquainted. The framework of social organisation in its practical working is learned through the boys' participation in organising the play group. This educates them to accept voluntarily a social system into which they would otherwise have to be forced when entering adult society. Besides, the element of secrecy which attaches to the copying of the more intimate scenes from the life of the parents and of the political

authorities draws the boys into a close social unit with a sense
of common interests and needs.

The play group on the pasture must be distinguished on the
one hand from the very much smaller group of infants who meet
in the yards and groves near the huts, and on the other hand
from the age-class, an institution with a ritual and a significance
which go beyond childish interests. The boys' group is altogether
independent; it is not established by a ceremony controlled by
adults, but is a spontaneous growth. While in the family and the
tribal age-class a strict, authoritarian order prevails, the boys'
group is an entirely democratic affair. Every boy enters it with
equal chances of rising to a leading position. The qualities which
decide his promotion are not the rank and wealth of his parents,
but intelligence, physical prowess, and social adaptability. It is
true that the chief's son is supposed to be treated with deference,
and he has strict injunctions to be affable to his playmates; but
his privileges count for little if he is a stupid or socially disagreeable fellow.

The methods by which the selection of the leaders in the boys'
group is carried out begin with practical jokes and tests of endurance for the younger members. The tests later assume the
form of competitive games, such as wrestling, fist-fights, bird-
shooting and battles with a hard green fruit the size of an orange,
exercises which resemble those which were part of the former
military training of the Chaga. Besides competitive games, the distribution of food (originally supplied by the mother) is a means
of obtaining at least temporary allegiance from others. Finally,
the leadership in certain games, etc., is decided by mere chance,
e.g., by drawing straws or lots.

The Chief of the Pasture, if he has risen to his post through
pluck and perseverance, often holds it for a considerable time.
He appoints his henchmen and orders the other boys about on
serious business. For instance, when during a heavy shower the
boys have retired to the hut which they have built for themselves,
he may command a boy to go out and look for the cattle, which
often bolt into the bush on such an occasion. He also has a
decisive voice in the choice and arrangement of the games and
play activities. However, it is inherent in the democratic nature
of the group that he may be superseded. His ascendancy may be
resented by a number of boys whom he has defeated, and jeal-

ousy may develop into open conflict, serious fights, and his final deposition.

In assessing the position and function of the boys' group within the general scheme of Chaga society, we realised that the traditional system of play activities offers the children opportunities for obtaining more or less correct notions about married life and the social organisation of the tribe. With the development of their own capabilities, this process assumes a more positive aspect and may well be described as an attempt by the children to create a society for themselves, keeping closely to the original from which they are still excluded. In a sense it is true to say that the children's society has its own culture, which on the one hand can be described as a system of instruments with which the children satisfy their needs, and on the other hand consists in the re-creation of the values possessed by the paternal generation. But the expressions "re-creation of values" and "children's society" must not mislead us. In its fundamental nature the society of the children has not developed far from its adult prototype. The reasons for this are obvious. The time and capacities at the children's disposal in their striving towards independence are too limited to allow of the creation of something absolutely original, if such a thing were possible. And yet, within the cultural tradition, the function of play as an autonomous means of self-education seems to be fairly well established, for the children's society achieves a set of distinctive cultural features which are absent in adult culture.

With regard to language it is a well-known fact that children have what has been called "age-dialects". But over and above these natural developmental stages, the children evolve special secret languages, which resemble our "Double Dutch," by transposing syllables, inserting infixes and saying words backwards.

In the economic substratum of culture, the boys' group attempts to be independent by stealing food either at home or from strangers, and by bird-shooting and buck-hunting expeditions. Moreover, as they approach adolescence, boys and girls are given their own gardens and a few chickens and goats as a reward for having helped their parents. As regards material objects, the boys use bows and arrows, which are not employed by the Chaga warriors, and the children's tops, small toboggans used on grassy slopes, and other toys have no equivalents in the adult culture.

Concerning magic, taboos which are binding on grown-up men are not observed by the boys on the pasture. Chaga men are not allowed to eat fowls, but the boys relish them. Again the strong, unchecked desires of play-life lead the children to invent their own magic. Girls use wish-magic to make their breasts grow, and I know of a boy who, to ensure the capture of his hiding playfellows, cut himself in the finger. Also with regard to law and order the children's society has its own distinctive features, handed down by tradition in the play groups. Thus girls have an ordeal for detecting nurses who eat the food of their charges, while boys more frequently use more forceful methods, such as bombardment with missiles, to discipline a social misfit.

From the educational point of view it is very important to realise that the fundamental sentiments of loyalty to social groups and the authorities, upon which life in all its various kinds of organisation depends, are not necessarily formed by teaching and the giving of instructions. They emerge naturally from the sentiments attaching to the "imitative" institutions of childhood which are created through play activities.

5 INSTRUCTION AND AFFECT IN
HOPI CULTURAL CONTINUITY

Dorothy Eggan

Although the Hopi Indians of the southwestern United States are one of the most studied indigenous peoples of North America, this is one of the very few accounts of their system of education. The Hopi have been remarkably resistant to prolonged external contact and have succeeded in maintaining their sense of cultural cohesion and continuity over several centuries of alien domination and assimilative pressures. The author, who writes with both anthropological and psychological problems in mind, shows clearly the important part played by education in establishing and maintaining a strong sense of cultural identification against the encroaching outside world. She also demonstrates how this educational program provides an effective means of social control in a small society that lacks any strong enforcing legal institutions.

EDUCATION and anthropology have proved in recent years that each has much of interest to say to the other (e.g. Mead 1931, 1943; Whiting and Child 1953; Spindler 1955), for both are concerned with the transmission of cultural heritage from one generation to another—and with the means by which that transmission is accomplished. And although anthropology has tended to be preoccupied with the processes of cultural *change,* and the conditions under which it takes place, rather than with cultural continuity, it would seem, as Herskovits has said, that cultural change can be best understood when considered in relation to cultural stability (Herskovits 1950:20).[1]

Reprinted from *Southwestern Journal of Anthropology* 12 (4), 1956: 347–70, with permission of Professor F. Eggan and of the editor, *Southwestern Journal of Anthropology.*
[1] The substance of this paper was originally presented to the Society for Social Research of the University of Chicago in 1943, and subsequently

Both education and anthropology are concerned with learned behavior, and the opinion that early learning is of vital significance for the later development of personality, and that emotional factors are important in the learning process, while sometimes implicit rather than explicit, is often found in anthropological literature, particularly in that dealing with "socialization," "ethos" (Redfield 1953), and "values." From Mead's consistent work, for instance, has come a clearer picture of the socialization process in a wide variety of cultures, including our own, and she examines early "identification" as one of the problems central to all of them (Mead 1953, particularly Part II, also Preface). Hallowell, too, speaking of the learning situation in which an individual must acquire a personality pattern, points out that "there are important affective components involved" (Hallowell 1953:610), and elsewhere he emphasizes a "need for further investigation of relations between learning process and affective experience" (Hallowell 1955:251). Kluckhohn, writing on values and value-orientation, says that "one of the severest limitations of the classical theory of learning is its neglect of attachments and attitudes in favor of reward and punishment" (Kluckhohn 1951:430). And DuBois states explicitly that, "Institutions which may be invested with high emotional value because of patterns in child training are not ones which can be lightly legislated out of existence" (DuBois 1941:281).

In fact, increasing interaction between anthropology and psychiatry (which has long held as established the connection between emotion, learning, and resistance to change in individuals) has in the last decade introduced a theme into anthropology which reminds one of Sapir's statement that "the more fully one

enlarged in 1954 at the request of Edward Bruner for his class in Anthropology and Education. Discussion with him has greatly clarified my thinking on the problems examined here. Some elimination and revision has been made in order to include references to recently published work and suggestions from Fred Eggan, David Aberle, Clyde Kluckhohn, David Riesman, and Milton Singer. But intimate association with the Hopi over a period of seventeen years has given me this perception of the Hopi world.

tries to understand a culture, the more it takes on the character-istics of a personality organization" (Sapir 1949:594).

Psychologists, while perhaps more cautious in their approach to these problems, since human emotional commitments—particu-larly as regards permanency—are difficult if not impossible to examine in the laboratory, emphasize their importance in the learning situation, and frequently express dissatisfaction with many existing methods and formulations in the psychology of personality. The shaping factors of emotion—learned as well as innate—are stressed by Asch in his *Social Psychology,* and focus particularly on man's "need to belong." He feels that the "psy-chology of man needs basic research and a fresh theoretical ap-proach" (Asch 1952:29). Allport speaks of past "addiction to machines, rats, or infants" in experimental psychology, and hopes for a "design for personality and social psychology" which will become "better tempered to our subject matter" as we "cease bor-rowing false notes—whether squeaks, squeals, or squalls . . ." and "read the score of human personality more accurately" (All-port 1951:168–69). And Murphy, starting with the biological foundations of human learning, particularly the individual form this "energy system" immediately assumes, examines man as psy-chologically structured by early canalizations in which personality is rooted, to which are added an organized symbol system and deeply ingrained habits of perception, and suggests that the struc-ture thus built is highly resistant to change. He says that, "The task of the psychology of personality today is to apply ruthlessly, and to the limit, every promising suggestion of today, but always with the spice of healthy skepticism," while recognizing "the fundamental limitations of the whole present system of concep-tions . . ." as a preparation for "rebirth of knowledge" (Murphy 1947, Parts I, II, III:926–27).

Anthropologists as well as psychologists are aware that any hypotheses in an area so complex must be regarded as tenuous, but since the situations cannot be taken into the laboratory, there is some value in taking the laboratory to the situation. Progress in these amorphous areas can only come about, as Redfield has said, by the mental instrument which he has called a "controlled conversation" (Redfield 1955:148)—this discussion, then, must be considered a conversation between the writer and others who have brought varied interests and techniques to the problem of resistance to cultural change.[2] It begins logically with a recent paper on "Cultural Transmission and Cultural Change" in which Bruner discusses two surveys (Social Science Research Council 1954; Keesing 1953; also Spiro 1955) of the literature on acculturation and adds to the hypotheses presented in them another which he finds relevant to the situation among the Mandan-Hidatsa Indians. As stated in his summary paragraph we find the proposition: "That which is learned and internalized in infancy and early childhood is most resistant to contact situations. The hypothesis directs our attention to the age in the individual life career at which each aspect of culture is transmitted, as well as to the full context of the learning situation and position of the agents of socialization in the larger social system" (Bruner 1956a: 197).

This proposition will be further extended by a consideration of the *emotional* commitment involved in the socialization process among the Hopi Indians; here the "conversation" will be directed to emotion in both teaching and learning, and will center around resistance to cultural change which has been remarkably consistent in Hopi society throughout recorded history *until the Second World War brought enforced and drastic changes.*[3] At that time the young men, although legitimately conscientious objectors, were drafted into the army. Leaving the isolation of their reservation, where physical violence between adults was rare, they were rapidly introduced to the stark brutality of modern warfare. In army camps alcoholic intoxication, an experience which was the antithesis of the quiet, controlled behavior normally demanded of adult Hopi on their reservation, frequently brought relief from tension and a sense of comradeship with fellow soldiers. Deprived of the young men's work in the fields, many older people and young women were in turn forced to earn a living in railroad and munition centers off the reservation. Thus the gaps in the Hopi

---

[2] DuBois 1955. Of particular interest in this problem is this paper of DuBois' and the discussion following it. See also Dozier's (1954) analysis of the interaction between the Hopi-Tewa and Hopi; compare Dozier 1955.
[3] An evaluation of these changes has not been reported for the Hopi, although John Connelly is working on the problem; see Adair and Vogt 1949 and Vogt 1951 for discussions of Navajo and Zuñi reactions to the war and postwar situation.

"communal walls" were, for the first time, large enough in numbers and long enough in time—and the experiences to which individuals had to adapt were revolutionary enough in character—so that the sturdy structure was damaged. It is emphasized, therefore, that in this discussion *Hopi* refers to those members of the tribe who had reached *adulthood* and were thoroughly committed to their own world view before 1941. Much of it would not apply as forcefully to the children of these people, and would be even less applicable to their grandchildren.

The major hypotheses suggested here, then, are:

(1) That the Hopi, as contrasted with ourselves, were experts in the use of *affect* in their educational system, and that this element continued to operate throughout the entire life span of each individual as a *reconditioning* factor (Herskovits 1950, esp. 325–26, 491, 627); and

(2) That this exercise of emotion in teaching and learning was an efficient means of social control which functioned in the absence of other forms of policing and restraint, and also in the maintenance of stability both in the personality structure of the individual and the structure of the society.

These hypotheses may be explored through a consideration of (a) the early and continued conditioning of the individual in the Hopi maternal extended family, which was on every level, an inculcation of *interdependence* as contrasted with our training for *independence;* and (b) an early and continuing emphasis on religious observances and beliefs (also emphasizing interdependence), the most important facet of which—for the purposes of this paper—was the central concept of the Hopi "good heart."[4]

If we can examine the educational system by which a Hopi acquired the personal entity which made him so consistently and

---

[4] The concept of the Hopi "good heart" as contrasted to a "bad heart," which is *Kahopi,* has been documented by every student of Hopi known to the writer, in references far too numerous to mention, beginning with Stephen (written in the 1890s but published in 1940) and Hough in 1915. But the clearest understanding of this and other Hopi concepts may be had in Whorf 1941, esp. pp. 30–32.

determinedly Hopi, we find that it was deliberate and systematic (Pettitt 1946; Hough 1915:218). Students of Hopi are unanimous on this point but perhaps it can be best illustrated by quoting one of my informants who had spent much time away from the reservation, including many years in a boarding school, and who was considered by herself and other Hopi to be an extremely "acculturated" individual. In 1938 when she made this statement she was about thirty years old and had brought her children back to the reservation to be "educated." Said she,

> It is very hard to know what to do. In the old days I might have had more babies for I should have married early. Probably some of them would have died. But my comfort would have been both in numbers and in knowing that all women lost babies. Now when I let my little son live on top [a conservative village on top of the mesa] with my mothers, I worry all the time. If he dies with dysentery I will feel like I killed him. Yet he *must* stay on top so the old people can teach him the *important* things. It is his only chance of becoming Hopi, for he would never be a *bahana* (White).

The education which she considered so vital included careful, deliberate instruction in kinship and community obligations, and in Hopi history as it is seen in mythology and as remembered by the old people during their own lifetimes. The Hopi taught youngsters fear as a means of personal and social control and for the purposes of personal and group protection; and they were taught techniques for the displacement of anxiety, as well as procedures which the adults believed would prolong life. Children were instructed in religious lore, in how to work and play, in sexual matters, even in how to deal with a *bahana*. Good manners were emphasized, for they were a part of the controlled, orderly conduct necessary to a Hopi good heart.

Constantly one heard during work or play, running through all activity like a connecting thread: "Listen to the old people— they are wise"; or, "Our old uncles taught us that way—it is the *right* way." Around the communal bowl, in the kiva, everywhere this instruction went on; stories, dream adventures, and actual experiences such as journeys away from the reservation were told and retold. And children, in the warmth and security of this intimate extended family and clan group, with no intruding outside experiences to modify the impact until they were forced to go to an alien school, learned what it meant to be a good Hopi from a wide variety of determined teachers who had very definite—and *mutually consistent*—ideas of what a good Hopi is. And they learned all of this in the Hopi language, which, as Whorf has made so clear, has no words with which to express many of our concepts, but which, working together with "a different set of cultural and environmental influences . . . interacted with Hopi linguistic patterns to mould them, to be moulded again by them, and so little by little to shape the world outlook" (Whorf 1941: 92).

Eventually these children disappeared into government schools for a time, and in the youth of most of these older Hopi it was a boarding school off the reservation where Indian children from various reservations were sent, often against their own and their parents' wishes.[5] Here White teachers were given the task of "civilizing" and "Christianizing" these wards of the government, but by that time a Hopi child's view of the world and his place in it was very strong. Moreover, trying to transpose our concepts into their language was often very nearly impossible for them, since only Hopi had been spoken at home. Examining Hopi memory of such a method of education we quote a male informant who said:

> I went to school about four years. . . . We worked like slaves for our meals and keep. . . . We didn't learn much. . . . I didn't understand and it was hard to learn. . . . At that time you do what you are told or you get punished. . . . You just wait till you can go home.

And a woman said:

> Policemen gathered us up like sheep. I was scared to death. My mother tried to hide me. I tried to stay away but the police always won. . . . Then we were sent to Sherman [in California]. . . . It was far away; we were afraid on the train. . . . I didn't like it when I couldn't learn and neither did the teachers. . . . They never punished me, I always got 100 in Deportment. . . . I was there three years. . . . I was so glad to get home that I cried and cried . . . , glad to have Hopi food again, and fun again.

---

[5] See Simmons 1942: 88–89 for an excellent description by Don Talayesva of the government's use of force in the educational policy of this period; and pp. 134, 178, 199, and 225 for some of the results of this policy. Cf. Aberle 1951 for an analysis of Talayesva's school years and his later reidentification with his people.

As children, the Hopi usually solved this dilemma of enforced education by means of a surface accommodation to the situation until such time as they were able to return to their own meaningful world. For, as Park has said, man can "make his manners a cloak and his face a mask, behind which he is able to preserve . . . inner freedom . . . and independence of thought, even when unable to maintain independence of action."[6] In other words, because the inner core of Hopi identification was already so strong, these children were able to *stay* in a White world, while still *living* in the Hopi world within themselves.[7] And while for some there was a measure of temptation in many of the things learned in White schools so that they "became friendly with whites and accepted their gifts" (Simmons 1942:88 and cf. 178, 180), the majority of these older Hopi acquired a White education simply as a "necessary accessory";[8] they incorporated parts of our material culture, and learned to deal with Whites astutely, but their values were largely unaffected.

If we now examine more closely the pattern of integration through which the Hopi erected a communal wall[9] around their children, we find in their kinship system the framework of the wall, but interwoven through it and contributing greatly to its strength was a never-ending composition which gave color and form, their religious ceremonies and beliefs.

Let us first contrast briefly the affect implicit in the way a Hopi born into this kinship system experienced relationships and the way in which Western children experience them. In the old days it was rare for a growing primary family to live outside the maternal residence. Normally each lived within it until the birth

---

[6] Park 1950:361. Cf. Kluckhohn 1951, who points out that values continue to influence even when they do not function realistically as providers of immediate goal reactions.

[7] Cf. D. Eggan 1955 on the use of the Hopi myth in dreams as a means of "identification."

[8] Bruner 1956b:612 indicates that his Mandan-Hidatsa informants were quite conscious of this "lizard-like" quality of protective coloration in White contacts.

[9] Stephen 1940:18 says that the Hopi "describe their fundamental organization as a people" by "designating their principal religious ceremonies as the concentric walls of a house." The concept is extended here to include the entire wall of "Hopiness" which they have built around their children.

of several children crowded them out. And in this household each child was eagerly welcomed, for infant mortality was high and the clan was always in need of reinforcement. Thus, in spite of the physical burden on the biological mother, which she sometimes resented, the first strong *clan* sanction which we see in contrast to our own, was the absolute need for and desire for many children. From birth the young of the household were attended, pampered, and disciplined, although very mildly for the first several years, by a wide variety of relatives in addition to the mother. These attentions came both from the household members and from visitors in it. In no way was a baby ever as dependent upon his physical mother as are children in our culture. He was even given the breast of a mother's mother or sister if he cried for food in his mother's absence. True a Hopi saying states that a baby is made "sad" if another baby steals his milk, but it has been my experience that these women may risk making their own babies sad temporarily if another child needs food.

Weaning, of course, when discussed in personality contexts means more than a transition from milk to solid food. It is also a gradual process of achieving independence from the comfort of the mother's body and care, of transferring affections to other persons, and of finding satisfactions within oneself and in the outside world. Most people learn to eat solid food; many of us are never weaned, which has unfortunate consequences in a society where *individual* effort and independence are stressed. The Hopi child, on the other hand, from the day of his birth was being weaned from his biological mother. Many arms gave him comfort, many faces smiled at him, and from a very early age he was given bits of food which were chewed by various members of the family and placed in his mouth. So, for a Hopi, the outside world in which he needed to find satisfaction was never far away. He was not put in a room by himself and told to go to sleep; every room was crowded by sleepers of all ages. He was in no way *forced to find satisfactions within himself;* rather these were provided for him, if possible, by his household and clan group. His weaning, then, was from the breast only, and as he was being weaned from the biological mother, he was at the same time in a situation which *increased* his emotional orientation toward the intimate in-group of the extended family—which was consistent with the interests of Hopi social structure. Thus, considering weaning in its wider implications, a Hopi was never "weaned"; it was not intended that he should be. For these numerous care-takers contributed greatly to a small Hopi's faith in his intimate world—and conversely without question to a feeling of strange-ness and *emotional insecurity* as adults in any world outside of this emotional sphere. The Hopi were often successful outside of the reservation, but they have shown a strong tendency to re-turn frequently to the maternal household. Few ever left it per-manently.

In addition to his extended family, while a Hopi belonged to one clan only, the clan into which he was born, he was a "child" of his father's clan, and this group took a lively interest in him. There were also numerous ceremonial and adoptive relation-ships which were close and warm, so that most of the persons in his familiar world had definite reciprocal relations with the child (Eggan 1950: ch. 2; Simmons 1942: chs. 3, 4). Since all of these "relatives" lived in his own small village, or in villages nearby, his emotional and physical "boundaries" coincided, were quite definitely delimited, and were explored and perceived at the same time. It cannot be too strongly emphasized that the kinship terms which a Hopi child learned in this intimate atmosphere were not mere verbalizations—as, for instance, where the term "cousin" among ourselves is sometimes applied to someone we have never seen and never will see. On the contrary, each term carried with it definite mutual responsibilities and patterns of be-havior, and, through these, definite emotional interaction as well. These affects were taught as proper responses, together with the terms which applied to each individual, as he entered the child's life. This process was deliberately and patiently, but unceas-ingly, worked at by every older individual in the child's surround-ings, so by the time a Hopi was grown kinship reaction patterns were so deeply ingrained in his thinking and feeling, and in his workaday life, that they were as much a part of him as sleeping and eating. He was not merely told that Hopi rules of behavior were right or wise; he lived them as he grew and *in his total en-vironment* (cf. Henry 1955) (as contrasted to our separation of teaching at home, in school, and in Sunday school) until he was simply not conscious that there was any other way to react. Note that I say *conscious!* The unconscious level of feeling, as seen in dreams and life-history materials, and in indirect behavior manifestations (jealousy and gossip), often presents quite a different picture. But while ambivalence toward specific persons among the Hopi—as with mankind everywhere—is a personal burden, the long reinforced conditioned reaction of *interdependence* on both the emotional and overt behavior level was highly uniform and persistent (Whorf 1941:87; also Aberle 1951:93–94, 119–23). Perhaps the strength of kinship conditioning toward interdependence which was conveyed in a large but intimate group, living in close physical contact, can be best illustrated by quoting from an informant:

My younger sister —— was born when I was about four or five, I guess. I used to watch my father's and mother's relatives fuss over her. She didn't look like much to me. I couldn't see why people wanted to go to so much trouble over a wrinkled little thing like that baby. I guess I didn't like babies as well as most girls did. . . . But I had to care for her pretty soon anyway. She got fat and was hard to carry around on my back, for I was pretty little myself. First I had to watch her and joggle the cradle board when she cried. She got too big and wiggled too much and then my mother said to me, "She is *your sister*—take her out in the plaza in your shawl."

She made my back ache. Once I left her and ran off to play with the others for a while. I intended to go right back, but I didn't go so soon, I guess. Someone found her. I got punished for this. My mothers' brother said: "You should not have a sister to help you out when you get older. What can a woman do without her sisters?[10] You are not one of us to leave your sister alone to die. If harm had come to her you would never have a clan, no relatives at all. No one would ever help you out or take care of you. Now you have another chance. You owe her more from now on. This is the worst thing that any of my sisters' children has ever done. You are going to eat by yourself until you are fit to be one of us." That is what he said. That is the way he talked on and on and on. When meal time came they put a plate of food beside me and said, "Here is your food; eat your food." It was a long time they did this way. It seemed a long time before they looked at me. They were all sad and quiet. They put a pan beside me at meal time and said nothing —nothing at all, not even to scold me.

My older sister carried —— now. I didn't try to go near her. But I looked at my sisters and thought, "I need you—I will help you if you will help me." I would rather have been beaten or smoked. I was so ashamed all the time. Wherever I went people got sad

---

[10] In a matrilineal household and clan, co-operation with one's "sisters" is a necessity for the maintenance of both the social structure and the communal unit.

[i,e., quiet]. After a while [in about ten days as her mother remembered it] they seemed to forget it and I ate with people again. During those awful days Tuvaye [a mother's sister] sometimes touched my head sadly, while I was being punished, I mean. Once or twice she gave me something to eat. But she didn't say much to me. Even she and my grandfather were ashamed and in sorrow over this awful thing I had done.

Sometimes now I dream I leave my children alone in the fields and I wake up in a cold sweat. Sometimes I dream I am alone in a desert place with no water and no one to help me. Then I think of this punishment when I dream this way. It was the worst thing I ever did. It was the worst thing that ever happened to me. No one ever mentioned it to me afterwards but —— [older male sibling], the mean one. I would hang my head with shame. Finally my father told him sharply that he would be punished if he ever mentioned this to me again. I was about six when this happened, I think.

This informant was about forty when she related this incident, but she cried, even then, as she talked.

Nor was withdrawal of support the only means of punishment. There were bogey Kachinas who "might kidnap" bad children, and who visited the mesas sometimes when children were uncoöperative; thus the "stranger" *joined effectively* with the clan in inducing the "ideal" Hopi behavior. But children *shared* this fear, as they also frequently shared other punishments. Dennis has called attention to the fact that a whole group of children often shared the punishment for the wrongdoing of one (Dennis 1941:263). This method may not endear an individual to his agemates, but it does reinforce the central theme of Hopi belief that each person in the group is responsible for what happens to all, however angry or jealous one may feel toward siblings.

Before we examine the religious composition of the Hopi "communal walls," we might contrast more explicitly the emotional implications of early Hopi conditioning to those experienced in our society. From the day of *our* birth the training toward *independence*—as contrasted to *interdependence*—starts. We sleep alone; we are immediately and increasingly in a world of comparative strangers. A variety of nurses, doctors, relatives, sitters, and teachers march through our lives in a never-ending procession. A few become friends, but *compared with a Hopi child's experiences,* the impersonality and lack of emotional relatedness to so many kinds of people with such widely different backgrounds is startling. Indeed the disparity of the relationships as such is so great that a continuity of emotional response is impossible, and so we learn to look for emotional satisfaction in change, which in itself becomes a value (Kluckhohn and Kluckhohn 1947:109). In addition, we grow up aware that there are many ways of life within the American class system; we know that there are many choices which we must make as to profession, behavior, moral code, even religion; and we know that the values of our parents' generation are not necessarily ours. If the permissive intimacy in the primary family in our society—from which both nature and circumstance demand a break in adulthood—is too strong, the individual cannot mature so that he can function efficiently in response to the always changing personalities in his life, and the always changing demands of the society (Riesman 1955; Mead 1948:518). He becomes a dependent neurotic "tentative between extreme polarities" (Erikson 1948:198; cf. Murphy 1947:714–33). But precisely because the permissive intimacy, as well as the punishing agencies, in a Hopi child's life were so far and so effectively extended in his formative years he became *interdependent* with a larger but still definitely delimited group, and tended always to be more comfortable and effective within it. His self-value quickly identified itself with the larger Hopi value (Hallowell 1955: ch. 4; Erikson 1948:198 fn.), and to the extent that he could continue throughout his life to identify with his group and function within it, he was secure in his place in the universe.

We have now sketched the situation which surrounded the young Hopi child in his first learning situations, and contrasted these with our own. For descriptive convenience this has been separated from religious instruction, but in the reality experience of the children—with the exception of formal initiation rites—no one facet of learning to be Hopi was separated from others. To understand the meaning his religion had for a Hopi one must first understand the harsh physical environment into which he was born. While it is agreed that it would not be possible to predict the character or the social structure of the Hopi from the circumstances of this physical environment (Redfield 1955:31–32; Titiev 1944:177–78; Whorf 1941:91; D. Eggan 1948; Thompson and Joseph 1944:133), it is self-evident that their organized social and ritual activities are largely a response to it. And such activities are at once a reflection of man's need to *be,* and his need to justify his existence to himself and others. If those who doubt that the forces of nature are powerful in shaping personality and culture were confined for one year on the Hopi reservation—even though their own economic dependence on "nature" would be negligible—they would still know by personal experience more convincing than scientific experiment the relentless pressure of the environment on their own reaction patterns. They would, for instance, stand, as all Hopis have forever stood, with aching eyes fastened on a blazing sky where thunderheads piled high in promise and were snatched away by "evil winds," and thus return to their homes knowing the tension, the acute bodily need for the "feel" of moisture. When rains do fall, there is the likelihood of a cloudburst which will ruin the fields. And there is a possibility of early frost which will destroy their crops, as well as the absolute certainty of sandstorms, rodents, and worms which will ruin many plants. These things on a less abstract level than "feeling" resolved themselves into a positive threat of famine and thirst which every Hopi knew had repeatedly ravaged his tribe. Is it possible that the effects of this silent battle between man and the elements left no mark on successive generations of individuals? It certainly was the reinforced concrete of Hopi social structure, since strongly conditioned interdependence was the only hope of survival.

Thus, the paramount problem for the Hopi was uncertain rain, and the outward expression of their deep need for divine aid was arranged in a cycle of ceremonies, the most impressive of which, at least among the exoteric rituals, were Kachina (Earle and Kennard 1938) dances. These were, for the observer, colorful pageants in which meticulously trained dancers performed from sunrise until sunset, with short intermissions for food and rest. Their bodies were ceremonially painted; brilliant costumes were worn, along with beautifully carved and painted masks which represented the particular gods who were taking part in the ceremony. The color, the singing and the drums which accompanied the dance, the graceful rhythm and intense concentration of the dancers, all combine into superb artistry which is an hypnotic and impressive form of prayer. Ideally, the Hopi preceded every important act with prayer, and with these older Hopi the ideal was apt to be fact. A bag of sacred cornmeal was part of their daily equipment.

In the religious context also, we must remember the intimate atmosphere which surrounded a Hopi child in the learning situation. Here children were taught that if *all* Hopi behaved properly —i.e. kept good hearts—the Kachinas would send rain. It was easy for the children to believe this because from earliest babyhood these beautiful creatures had danced before them as they lolled comfortably in convenient laps. There was a happy, holiday atmosphere throughout a village on dance days, but while each dance was being performed, the quiet of profound reverence. Lying in the mother's lap, a baby's hands were often struck together in the rhythm of the dance; as soon as he would walk his feet were likewise directed in such rhythm, and everybody praised a child and laughed affectionately and encouragingly as it tried to dance. As the children grew older, carved likenesses of these gods, as well as other presents, were given to them by the gods themselves. And as he grew in understanding, a child could not fail to realize that these dancers were part of a religious ceremony which was of utmost importance in his world—that the dancers were rain-bringing and thus life-giving gods.

When first initiation revealed that the gods were in reality men who danced in their stead, a *reorganization* of the emotions which had been directed toward them began, and there is much evidence in autobiographical materials of resentment, if not actual trauma, at this point. For some of them the initiation was a physical ordeal, but for those who entered this phase of their education by way of Powamu there was no whipping, although all initiates witnessed the whipping of those who were initiated into the Kachina cult.[11] However, the physical ordeal seems to be less fixed in adult memories than disillusion.

In Don Talyesva's account of initiation into Kachina we find:

> I had a great surprise. They were not spirits, but human beings. I recognized nearly every one of them and felt very unhappy because I had been told all my life that the Kachinas were Gods. I was

---

[11] F. Eggan 1950:47–50. Cf. Steward 1931:59 ff. The Powamu society is co-ordinate with the Kachina society and furnishes the "fathers" to the Kachinas on dance occasions. At first initiation parents may choose either of these societies for their children. It is reported that on First Mesa, Powamu initiates were whipped, but my Powamu informants from both Second and Third Mesas were not whipped.

especially shocked and angry when I saw my uncles, fathers, and own clanbrothers dancing as Kachinas. . . . [But] my fathers and uncles showed me ancestral masks and explained that long ago the Kachinas had come regularly to Oraibi and danced in the plaza. They explained that since the people had become so wicked . . . the Kachinas had stopped coming and sent their spirits to enter the masks on dance days. . . . I thought of the flogging and the initiation as a turning point in my life, and I felt ready at last to listen to my elders and live right (Simmons 1942:84–87).

One of our informants said in part:

I cried and cried into my sheepskin that night, feeling I had been made a fool of. How could I ever watch the Kachinas dance again? I hated my parents and thought I could never believe the old folks again, wondering if gods had ever danced for the Hopi as they now said and if people really lived after death. I hated to see the other children fooled and felt mad when they said I was a big girl now and should act like one. But I was afraid to tell the others the truth for they might whip me to death. I know now it was best and the *only way to teach* children, but it took me a long time to know that. I hope my children won't feel like that.

This informant was initiated into Powamu and not whipped. She was about thirty when she made this statement to the writer.

Another woman, from a different mesa, speaking of her initiation into the Kachina society, said to me:

The Kachinas brought us children presents. I was very little when I remember getting my first Kachina doll. I sat in my mother's lap and was "ashamed" [these people often use ashamed for shy or somewhat fearful], but she held out my hand for the doll. I grabbed it and hid in her lap for a long time because the Kachina looked too big to me and I was partly scared. But my mother told me to say "asqualie" [thank you] and I did. The music put me to sleep. I would wake up. The Kachinas would still be there. . . . I dreamed sometimes that the Kachinas were dancing and brought me lots of presents. . . .
When I was initiated into Kachina society I was scared. I heard people whisper about it. . . . Children shook their heads and said it was hard to keep from crying. . . . My mother always put her shawl over my head when the Kachinas left the plaza. When she took it off they would be gone. So I knew they were gods and had gone back to the San Francisco mountains. . . . My ceremonial mother came for me when it was time to go to the kiva [for initiation] and

she looked sad [i.e., serious]. She took most of the whipping on her own legs [a custom widely practiced among the Hopi]. But then I saw my father and my relatives were Kachinas. When they took their masks off this is what I saw. I was all mixed up. I was mad. I began to cry. I wondered how my father became a Kachina and if they [these men, including her father] would all go away when the Kachinas went back to the San Francisco mountains where the dead people live. Then when my father came home I cried again. I was mad at my parents and my ceremonial mother. "These people have made me silly," I said to myself, "and I thought they were supposed to like me so good." I said that to myself. But I was still crying, and the old people told me that only babies cry. They kept saying I would understand better when I got bigger. They said again that the Kachinas had to go away because the Hopi got bad hearts, and they [the Kachinas] couldn't stand quarreling, but they left their heads behind for the Hopis. I said why didn't they rot then like those skulls we found under that house? They said I was being bad and that I should have been whipped more. . . .

When children asked me what happened in the kiva I was afraid to tell them because something would happen to me. Anyway I felt smart because I knew more than those *little* children. It took me a long time to get over this sadness, though. Later I saw that the Kachinas were the most *important thing in life* and that children can't understand these things. . . . It takes a while to see how wise the old people really are. You learn they are always right in the end.

Before we try to find our way with the Hopi to an "understanding of these things" we must examine their concept of the good heart which functions both in their kinship system and religion to maintain the effectiveness of the "wall of Hopiness." Of greatest significance in all activities among these people, and particularly in their religious ceremonies, is the fact that everything of importance is done communally. Thus each individual who has reached maturity is responsible *to* and *for* the whole community. The Hopi speak of this process as "uniting our hearts," which in itself is a form of prayer. A slight mistake in a ceremony can ruin it and thus defeat the community prayer for rain; so too can a trace of "badness" in one's heart, although it may not be visible to the observer. Thus their religion teaches that *all* distress— from illness to crop failure—is the result of bad hearts, or possibly of witchcraft (here the simple "bad heart" must not be confused with a "Two-heart," *powaka,* witch), an extreme form of personal wickedness in which an individual sacrifices others, particularly his own relatives, to save himself (Titiev 1942; Aberle 1951:94).

This concept of a good heart in *conscious contradistinction* to a bad heart is of greatest importance not only in understanding Hopi philosophy but also in understanding their deep sense of cultural continuity and their resistance to fundamental change. A good heart is a positive thing, something which is never out of a Hopi's mind. It means a heart at peace with itself and one's fellows. There is no worry, unhappiness, envy, malice, nor any other disturbing emotion in a good heart. In this state, coöperation, whether in the extended household or in the fields and ceremonies, was selfless and easy. Unfortunately, such a conception of a good heart is also impossible of attainment. Yet if a Hopi did not keep a good heart he might fall ill and die, or the ceremonies—and thus the vital crops—might fail, for, as has been said, only those with good hearts were effective in prayer. Thus we see that the Hopi concept of a good heart included conformity to all rules of Hopi good conduct, both external and internal. To the extent that it was internalized—and all Hopi biographical material known to the writer suggests strongly that it was effectively internalized—it might reasonably be called a quite universal culturally patterned and culturally consistent Hopi "superego."[12]

There was, therefore, a constant probing of one's own heart, well illustrated by the anguished cry of a Hopi friend, "Dorothy, *did* my son die as the old folks said because my heart was not right? Do *you* believe this way, that if parents do not keep good hearts children will die?" And there was a constant examination of one's neighbors' hearts: "Movensie, it is those ———— clan people who ruined this ceremony! They have bad hearts and they quarrel too much. That bad wind came up and now we will get no rain." Conversation among the Hopi is rarely censored, and the children heard both of these women's remarks, *feeling,* you may be sure, the *absolute belief* which these "teachers" had in the *danger* which a bad heart carries for everyone in the group.

---

[12] See Piers and Singer 1953:6, where Dr. Piers defines "superego" as stemming from the internalization of the punishing, restrictive aspects of parental images, real or projected.

In such situations, since human beings can bear only a certain amount of guilt,[13] there is a great game of blame-shifting among the Hopi, and this in turn adds a further burden of unconscious guilt, for it is difficult to love properly a neighbor or even a sister who has a bad heart. However, in the absence of political organization, civil and criminal laws, and a formal method of punishment for adults, this consistent "tribal super-ego" has maintained, throughout known history, a record almost devoid of crime and violence within the group,[14] and it has conditioned and ever *reconditioned* a Hopi to feel secure only in being a Hopi.

For through the great strength of the emotional orientations conveyed within the kinship framework and the interwoven religious beliefs, young Hopi learned their world from dedicated teachers whose emotions were involved in teaching what they believed intensely, and this in turn engaged the children's emotions in learning. These experiences early and increasingly made explicit in a very personal way the values implicit in the distinction between a good heart and a bad heart. For public opinion, if intensely felt and openly expressed in a closely knit and mutually dependent group—as in the case of the child who left her baby sister alone—can be more effective potential punishment than the electric chair. It is perhaps easier to die quickly than to live in loneliness in a small community in the face of contempt from one's fellows, and particularly from one's clan from whence, as we have seen, comes most of one's physical and emotional security. Small wonder that the children who experience this constant pressure to conform to clan dictates and needs, and at the same time this constant reinforcement of clan solidarity against outsiders, are reluctant as adults to stray too far from the clan's protective familiarity or to defy its wishes.

---

[13] See Dr. Piers' definition of guilt and shame (Piers and Singer 1953: 5, 16). Hopi reactions are not classified here either in terms of guilt or of shame, since, as Singer points out on p. 52, an attempt to do so can confuse rather than clarify. In my opinion, both shame and guilt are operative in the Hopi "good heart," but it is suggested that the reader compare the material discussed here with the hypotheses in *Shame and Guilt*, particularly with Singer's conclusions in chapter 5.

[14] Cf. Hallowell 1955: ch. 4 on the positive role anxiety may play in a society.

There was much bickering and tension within the clan and
village, of course, and it was a source of constant uneasiness and
ambivalence among the Hopi.[15] But tension and bickering, as I
have indicated elsewhere, "are not exclusively Hopi"; the Hopi
see it constantly among the Whites on and off the reservation.
What they do *not* find elsewhere is the *emotional satisfaction* of
belonging intensely, to which they have been conditioned and
reconditioned. For, as Murphy says, "It is not only the 'desire to
be accepted' . . . that presses the ego into line. The basic psychology of perception is involved; the individual has learned to
see himself as a member of the group, and the self has true
'membership character,' structurally integrated with the perception of group life" (Murphy 1947:855; Asch 1952:334–35,
605). Actually the Hopi clan, even with its in-group tensions
and strife, but with all of the advantages emotional and physical it affords the individual, is one of the most successful and
meaningful "boarding schools" ever devised for citizenship training.

In this situation, where belonging was so important, and a good
heart so vital to the feeling of belonging, gossip is the potential
and actual "social cancer" of the Hopi tribe. It is devastating to
individual security and is often senselessly false and cruel, but in
a country where coöperation was the only hope of survival, it
was the *servant* as well as the policeman of the tribe. Not lightly
would any Hopi voluntarily acquire the title Kahopi (Brandt
1954:92)—*"not* Hopi," and therefore not good. Throughout the
Hopi life span the word kahopi, *kahopi,* KAHOPI was heard, until
it penetrated to the very core of one's mind. It was said softly and
gently at first to tiny offenders, through "Kahopi tiyo" or "Kahopi mana" to older children, still quietly but with stern intent,

---

[15] In a short paper it is impossible to discuss both sides of this question adequately, but these tensions, and a Hopi's final acceptance of them,
are discussed in D. Eggan 1948, particularly pp. 232–34. Cf. Thompson
and Joseph 1944: ch. 16, where Joseph speaks of fear born of the in-
ternally overdisciplined self in Hopi children, and its role both in adult
discord and social integration. See also Thompson 1945 for hypotheses
regarding the integration of ideal Hopi culture. Aberle (1951) discusses various tensions in Hopi society; see especially p. 94. All authors,
however, call attention to the compensations as well as the burdens in
Hopi society.

until the word sometimes assumed a crescendo of feeling as a whole clan or even a whole community might condemn an individual as *Kahopi.*

It is true that we, too, are told we should keep good hearts and love our neighbors as ourselves. But we are not told that, if we do not, our babies will die, *now, this year!* Some children are told that if they do not obey the various "commandments" they learn in different churches they will eventually burn in a lake of hell fire, but they usually know that many of their world doubt this. In contrast, Hopi children constantly *saw* babies die because a parent's heart was not right; they *saw* evil winds come up and crops fail for the same reason; they *saw* adults sicken and die because of bad thoughts or witchcraft (to which bad thoughts rendered a person more vulnerable). Thus they learned to *fear* the results of a bad heart whether it belonged to themselves or to others. There were witches, bogey Kachinas, and in objective reality famine and thirst to fear. Along with these fears were taught mechanisms for the displacement of anxiety, including the services of medicine men, confession and exorcism to get rid of bad thoughts, and coöperative nonaggression with one's fellows, even those who were known to be witches. But the best technique was that which included all the values in the positive process of keeping a good heart, and of "uniting our hearts" in family, clan, and fraternal society—in short, the best protection was to be *Hopi* rather than *Kahopi.*

It is clear throughout the literature on the Hopi, as well as from the quotations given in this discussion, that in finding their way toward the goal of "belonging" Hopi children at first initiation had to deal with religious disenchantment, resentment, and with ever increasing demands made by their elders for more mature behavior. These factors were undoubtedly important catalyzing agents in Hopi personality formation and should be examined from the standpoint of Benedict's formulations on discontinuity (Benedict 1938). Here we must remember that shock can operate either to destroy or to mobilize an organism's dormant potentialities. And if a child has been *consistently* conditioned to feel a part of his intimate world, and providing he still lives on in this same world, it seems reasonable to suppose that shock (unless it were so great as to completely disorganize personality, in which case the custom could not have persisted) would reinforce the individual's *need* to belong and thus would tend to reassemble many of his personality resources around this need.

If the world surrounding the Hopi child had changed from warmth to coldness, from all pleasure to all hardship, the discontinuity would have indeed been insupportable. But the new demands made on him, while more insistent, were not unfamiliar in *kind;* all adults, as well as his newly initiated age-mates, faced the same ones. He had shared the shock as he had long since learned to share all else; and he now shared the rewards of "feeling big." He had the satisfaction of increased status along with the burden of increasing responsibility, as the adults continued to teach him "the important things," and conformity gradually became a value in itself—even as we value nonconformity and change. It was both the means *and* the goal. Conformity surrounded the Hopi—child or adult—with everything he could hope to have or to be; outside it there was only the feeling tone of rejection. Since there were no bewildering choices presented (as is the case in our socialization process), the "maturation drive" (Piers and Singer 1953:15) could only function to produce an ego-ideal in accord with the cultural ideal,[16] however wide the discrepancy between ideal and reality on both levels.

And since the Kachinas played such a vital role in Hopi society throughout, we must consider specifically the way in which the altered faith expressed by informants gradually came about after the first initiation (cf. Aberle 1951:38–41). First, of course, was the need to find it, since in any environment one must have faith and hope. They also wanted to continue to believe in and to enjoy that which from earliest memory had induced a feeling of pleasure, excitement, and of solidarity within the group. A beginning was undoubtedly made in modifying resentment when the Kachinas whipped each other after first initiation; first, it was again sharing punishment, but this time not only with children but *with adults.* They had long known that suffering came from bad hearts; they also knew, as indicated above, that something must be done about bad hearts. The Kachinas whipped to cleanse the bad hearts implied by disobedience to the rules of

---

[16] Erikson 1948:198 fn.: "The child derives a vitalizing sense of reality from the awareness that his individual way of mastering experience (his ego-synthesis) is a successful variant of a group identity and is in accord with its space-time and life plan."

Hopi good conduct and then whipped each other for the same reason; thus there was logic in an initiation which was actually an extension of an already established conception of masked gods who rewarded good behavior with presents but withheld rain if hearts were not right, and who sometimes threatened bad children (cf. Goldfrank 1945:516–39).

Another reorganizing factor explicitly stated in the quotations was "feeling big." They had shared pain with adults, had learned secrets which forever separated them from the world of children, and they were now included in situations from which they had previously been excluded, as their elders continued to teach intensely what they believed intensely: that for them there was only one alternative—Hopi as against Kahopi.

Consistent repetition is a powerful conditioning agent and, as the youngsters watched each initiation, they relived their own, and by again sharing the experience gradually worked out much of the bitter residue from their own memories of it, while also rationalizing and weaving the group emotions ever stronger into their own emotional core—"It takes a while to see how wise the old people really are." An initiated boy, in participating in the Kachina dances, learned to identify again with the Kachinas whom he now impersonated. To put on a mask is to "become a Kachina," and to coöperate actively in bringing about the major goals of Hopi life. And a girl came to know more fully the importance of her clan in its supportive role. These experiences were even more sharply conditioned and directed toward adult life in the tribal initiation ceremonies, of which we have as yet only fragmentary knowledge. Of this one man said to me: "I will not discuss this thing with you only to say that no one can forget it. It is the most wonderful thing any man can have to remember. You know then that you are Hopi. It is one thing Whites cannot have, cannot take from us. It is our way of life given to us when the world began."

And since children are, for all mankind, a restatement of one's hopes to be, when these Hopi in turn became teachers (and in a sense they had always been teachers of the younger children in the household from an early age), they continued the process of reliving and rationalizing, or "working out" their experiences with an intensity which is rarely known in our society except, perhaps, on the psychoanalytic couch. But the Hopi had no psychiatrists to guide them—no books which, as Riesman says, "like an invisible monitor, helps liberate the reader from his group and its emotions, and allows the contemplation of alternative responses and the trying on of new emotions" (Riesman 1955:13). They had only the internalized "feeling measure" and "group measure" explicit in the concepts of Hopi versus Kahopi.

On the material level, the obvious advantages of, for instance, wagons versus backs were a temptation. And to the extent to which White influences at first penetrated to these older Hopi it was through this form of temptation. But outside experiences usually included some variation of hostility, scorn, or aggression, as well as a radically different moral code, and these were all viewed and reinterpreted through the Hopi-eye view of the world and in the Hopi language, so that a return to the familiarity of the Hopi world with its solidarity of world view and behavior patterns *was experienced as relief,* and increased the need to feel Hopi, *however great a burden "being Hopi" implied.*

In summary, the hypothesis here developed, that strong emotional conditioning during the learning process was an instrument in cultural continuity among the Hopi, is suggested as supplementary to that of early learning as being resistant to change. It further suggests that this conditioning was *constantly* as well as *consistently* instilled during the entire lifetime of an individual by a circular pattern of integration. For an individual was surrounded by a series of invisible, but none the less solid, barriers between himself and the outside world. To change him, influences had to breach the concentric walls of social process—as conveyed through the human entities which surrounded him and which were strengthened by his obligation to teach others—and then to recondition his early and ever increasing emotional involvement in Hopi religion, morals, and mutually dependent lineage and clan groups, as well as those attitudes toward White aggression which he shared with all Indians.

In 1938 one old Hopi, who in his youth had been taken away from his wife and children and kept in a boarding school for several years, said to me:

> I am full of curiosity; a great *bahana* [White] education would tell
> me many things I've wondered about like the stars and how a man's

insides work. But I am afraid of it because I've seen what it does to folks. . . . If I raise a family, clothe and feed them well, do my ceremonial duties faithfully, I have succeeded—what do you call success? . . . . [And again, while discussing fear in connection with a dream, his comment was] Well, yes, we are afraid of *powakas* [witches] but our medicine men can handle them. Neither your doctors nor your gods can control your governments so you have more to fear. Now you are dragging us into your quarrels. I pity you and I don't envy you. You have more goods than we have, but you don't have peace ever, *it is better to die in famine than in war.*

As the old man anticipated, enforced participation in modern warfare soon replaced instruction for Hopi citizenship, and the concentric walls were finally seriously breached. But for these older Hopi the walls still enclose "our way of life given to us when the world began."

6 A NEW GUINEA CHILDHOOD: FROM WEANING TILL THE EIGHTH YEAR IN WOGEO

H. Ian Hogbin

H. Ian Hogbin's many accounts of life in Wogeo, on the northern coast of New Guinea, provide a vivid picture of everyday life in a small, technically simple, and pre-literate Melanesian society. This chapter, on the earlier years of childhood, describes a pattern of informal education that is comparable to Raymond Firth's account of the Polynesian Tikopia in chapter 3. The whole process of education is integrated into the general development of the individual child. The aims and sanctions behind his education are the same as those that help his slow maturation into an adult of marriageable age; his technical and moral education are but two aspects of a single process.

THE FIRST three years of a native's life in Wogeo were described in my paper "A New Guinea Infancy" (Hogbin 1943). I now propose to carry the story a stage further and consider the next five years. This period has not been chosen arbitrarily; it begins, for boys, with the first stage of initiation, when the lobe of the ear is pierced, and is brought to a close by the second stage of initiation, when they are seized and carried to a sacred place, being fed, so it is said, to the spirit monsters, from whose bodies they subsequently emerge wearing clothing for the first time.

PLAY

Children continue with their play even when infancy is at an end and, until the eighth year is reached, are usually left to amuse themselves at home on about four days in every five.

Reprinted from *Oceania* 16 (4), 1946: 275–96, with permission of the author and of the editor, *Oceania*.

For a year or two boys and girls run about together, but the villages are small, and one seldom sees a gathering of more than half a dozen. Swimming is probably the most popular pastime, though such games as cat's cradles, wrestling, hide and seek, and football, using a round fruit instead of a ball, are also played. Imitating the activities of the elders is another favourite sport, but play marriages, common elsewhere in Melanesia, do not take place. Competitiveness is almost never in evidence, and if planning is necessary one or other of the elder boys, usually he who thought of the game first, makes the arrangements and gives the orders.

Grandmothers and unmarried girls are the usual guardians, but, if two or three women, all neighbours, have no convenient relative in their households, they sometimes accept this responsibility in rotation. They seldom take part in the game but remain close at hand with one eye on what is happening, ready to rebuke horseplay or murmur comfort if someone is hurt. Both the father and the mother, on their return from work in the evening, display a mild interest in how the day has been spent, and not infrequently their suggestions for new activities are accepted for the next day.

The Dap children generally played on the beach not far from my house, and the following account of what took place on three different occasions is taken practically *verbatim* from my note-books.

One day when I was watching them the old woman Gabwe had been entrusted with Gwa and Jaga, her grandson and grand-daughter respectively; Kalasika and Niabula, the young sons of two neighbours; and Wanai, the daughter of a third. As I came on the scene all five were splashing in the water and laughing gaily. Suddenly Gwa called out, "I am a shark!" and began biting Kalasika's toes. This led to a wrestling match, though after about ten minutes they were so exhausted that they had to lie down on the beach to recover breath. The rest at first sat watching, but Jaga soon became bored and climbed into Gabwe's arms where she went to sleep. After a time Wanai, too, walked away, but, in searching in the village for something to eat, she unearthed a piece of string and on her return persuaded Niabula to make cat's cradles with her. The other two boys had in the meantime gone back to the water, where they once more pretended to be sharks. Niabula joined them after an interval, but when they both chased him and gave him a ducking, he fled in terror to Gabwe, who scolded Gwa and told him that he would be punished if he did not moderate his boisterous behaviour. Wanai was now busily making mud pies and at this point begged Kalasika to build her an oven where these might be cooked. Gwa joined in the game, and, although no fire was kindled, the grubby mess was wrapped in leaves and put into the middle of a pile of stones. Wanai next made out that her water bottles were empty and told Niabula to fill them. "No, that's women's work," said Gwa. "We men don't touch such things. You go yourself." An argument would have developed had not Gabwe interposed and persuaded them all to sit down and play a hand game with little white stones.

On another occasion when Gabwe was minding Gwa and Jaga they were joined first by ten-year-old girl Keke, from the next house, and then by Nyem, one of the headman Marigum's wives, who was at home looking after her co-wife's daughter Jauon. The women seated themselves under a tree and, wanting an uninterrupted chat, told Keke to see that the two small children did not get into mischief. She played hide and seek with them for a time but was then persuaded by Gwa to teach him some new cat's cradles, at which she was particularly expert. Jaga and Jauon were much too energetic to sit still for long, however, and within a quarter of an hour they had walked off to a pile of wet charcoal and ashes. After covering themselves from head to foot, they pranced up to their nurses and danced round them, uttering blood-curdling yells. Shocked at the filth, the women told them to go down to the sea at once and wash. Keke followed guiltily and gave them a good scrubbing but later returned to Gwa and went on with her cat's cradles. That evening he proudly showed his father the two new figures which he had learnt, thereby earning congratulations on his skill.

An instance of the children's fascination with the doings of their elders occurred at a later date when young Tabulbul organized a food distribution in imitation of one which had taken place the previous day. He and his sister, Mwago, were spending the morning with their aunt, and Gabwe, as usual, was looking after Gwa, Niabula, and Wanai (Jaga had been taken on a visit to relatives in Mwarok village). The two groups soon joined forces, and Tabulbul, as the eldest, began telling the others what to do. He first set them collecting round pebbles, which, he stated, were coconuts. When sufficient had been accumulated, he de-

clared that he, Mwago, and Gwa were the Dap folk, and that
Wanai and Niabula were the inhabitants of Kinaba and Job
respectively, the two neighbouring villages. "Now let us fetch mats
for the display of our coconuts," he ordered, and forthwith began
to lay out a row of leaves and set the pebbles on top. Niabula
brought his pile along next, and Wanai added her quota at the
end. "The Kinaba villagers bring short measure, as we expected,"
Gwa muttered, repeating word for word what he had heard his
father saying. Then, seeing a butterfly, he ran off after it, crying
out that here was a pig to add to the other food. Tabulbul tried
to recall him with the reminder that pigs and coconuts are not
given away together, but he refused to listen and, having at last
caught it, proudly brought it along. "Let us carve it properly," he
said, and for the next quarter of an hour the pebbles were forgotten while the butterfly was solemnly disembowelled and cut into
joints. Mwago became so fascinated, in fact, that she ignored the
distribution entirely and spent the rest of the morning making an
oven and cooking her share of the "meat." The other four divided
the pebbles, and then Wanai went away to sit with Gabwe, leaving
the boys to have a swim by themselves.

Play continues to be of importance during late childhood, but,
as most children have by now developed a sense of responsibility,
an increasing amount of time is spent in learning the different
kinds of work traditionally associated with their sex.

The boys attach themselves to the father and do their best to
help him at garden work, fishing, and other tasks. As they cannot yet be trusted to look after themselves properly, however,
he is still forced to leave them at home if he expects the job in
hand to occupy his full attention. On such occasions they wander
off looking for entertainment with other lads who have also been
left behind. Sporting with the girls is forbidden, since association
with females is considered at this stage to be likely to stunt their
growth, but, to judge from the complete indifference of those I
knew best, the prohibition is probably unnecessary.

There are no regular gangs, for few villages can assemble more
than six small boys—Dap had only four—and even these are
seldom all at home together. The neighbouring settlements may
provide a couple more, but the average group seems always to
number about four or five. Swimming, wrestling, football, and
hide and seek still hold out attractions, but there are now a number of new amusements, including fishing, sailing model canoes,

shooting at birds with arrows, and fighting with spears from reeds. Headmen's sons now act as leaders, and, although others make suggestions, theirs is the final decision about what shall be done.

As in earlier years, a keen interest is taken in food distributions and similar ceremonial, and fish are often divided with great formality. Once the boys pass their eighth year, however, warnings are issued against imitating religious ritual, and one of the more familiar myths relates of how Wofa and his playmates were killed for this offence. Yet Sabwakai, the headman Marigum's youngest boy aged about eleven, one day persuaded a number of his contemporaries to hold a series of mock initiation ceremonies deep in the bush where no woman was likely to see. The men, on hearing what had occurred, were appalled at the sacrilege and gave them all a sound thrashing.

Youths in their early teens are usually too much caught up in adult concerns to have much time to spare for games with the children during the day, but one occasionally sees them hurling a ball about or racing model canoes. The evenings are devoted to recreation, nevertheless, and they either sit singing songs and playing the flute and hand-drum or else, on moonlit nights, join the smaller boys for a romp in the centre of the village.

The girls become conscious of their social liabilities at about the same time as the boys, in the eighth year, and from then onwards the majority make determined efforts to assist their mothers in every way possible. Their absorption into the life of the grown-ups is more rapid than is the case with their brothers, and during late childhood and early youth their play is confined almost entirely to the occasions when they are helping an older woman to mind the little ones. Small groups sometimes sit together over a cat's cradle, but one or other is soon called away to look after the baby, fill the water bottles, or fetch stones for the oven. Far from being a nuisance in the house or garden, where the women's work is mainly done, even the smallest girl is useful, and instead of being left to wander about with a playmate, she trails behind the mother almost everywhere.

THE COMMUNITY AND THE CHILD

In spite of their provision for its amusement, the adults consider that, once the child is weaned, it can be regarded as already in some degree a responsible being worthy of admission to a place in their own world. While this opinion is hasty, no doubt, when its backwardness is taken into consideration, one must bear in mind that infants have far more experience of everyday life than is customary for older children in our own society. The more important activities are carried out in their presence practically from birth and thus have few closed secrets even when the details of the different techniques, and the reasons for their employment, are as yet unknown. Many matters relating to sex, although not all of them, are freely discussed in front of the children, and by the third year they will almost certainly have been in the presence of death. Care is indeed taken to bring everyone, including the babies, to the bedside of dying relatives, who are induced, if possible, to speak a word or two in farewell. I was present when little Jauon, aged three, was taken to see her grandmother for what was thought to be perhaps the last time. "Alas, my little one, I am sorry to be leaving you," the old woman murmured. "I would like to have stayed and nursed you, and to have cooked food at your coming-of-age. I would have been content if I could have waited till then, for you could have comforted me with the dishes you had cooked. Alas, little one, that I should go so soon." Someone then carried the child outside and endeavoured to explain that she might never see her grandmother alive again. At that age she did not realize what was happening, but I have seen parents at funerals instructing youngsters not much older to do their share of weeping.

The child's change in status after weaning is illustrated by the new arrangements in the gardens, where special allotments are now set aside and referred to as its property. Wiawia, when showing me a patch of bush which he had just finished fencing, pointed out the two sections allocated to Gwa and Jaga. "This is the little girl's first garden," he explained. "She's just been weaned, you see, and now has her own plot. Yes, you're quite right: she's far too small to do any of the work. But her mother and I will say to her, 'This ground is yours,' and she'll soon understand. We shall put the seedlings aside and plant them next time we make a garden in a similar area. Then, when she and Gwa grow up, they'll be able to plant the descendants of these very plants."

The child also has a couple of young pigs assigned to it and, in the evenings, at feeding time, is encouraged to call them by name. Some parents even make pretence of consulting a youthful "owner" and asking permission before a beast is killed, and I have once or twice known men apologise for failure to contribute to a feast on the grounds that the only pig available belonged to a young son who had made it a special pet. Such explanations were criticized afterwards as flimsy or frivolous, but the fact that they were offered at all argues some recognition of the child's property rights.

Again, the presence of the children at dances is taken for granted, and on such occasions their decorations are almost as carefully arranged as those of their elders. The youngsters stand alongside the principal performers, imitating them as best they can, often, as is freely admitted, to the detriment of the general effect. No one ever seems to think of sending them away, unless, as I once saw happen, somebody trips over them and falls.

But perhaps the most striking proof of the grown-ups' acceptance of the child as already one of themselves is provided by their frequent long-winded explanations. Few orders are given without the wisdom of the course suggested being pointed out, and force is only applied after persuasion fails. Thus a small boy who picks up a knife is cautioned of the danger which he is running before being ordered to put it down, and the slap following an unheeded warning is administered not so much to punish disobedience as to discourage foolishness.

Similar explanations accompany moral training, and, when Gwa displayed some unwillingness to hand half a biscuit to a playmate, his grandmother gave him a long lecture in which she went into a multitude of details of what might happen if he became notorious for his meanness. His friend would talk about him behind his back, she averred, and he would have such a bad name that when he married and had a family—he was then between four and five!—no one would help him to make his gardens.

Attitudes appropriate to adults are also attributed to the children when they are still barely able to appreciate what is being said (an instance of this is quoted below). The parents readily agreed when questioned that remarks of this sort are deliberately aimed in the beginning at instructing their offspring in proper modes of conduct, but they speak with such conviction that I am tempted to think that they really believe what they are saying.

Finally, every child old enough to be trusted is expected to help its elders according to its capacity. Such assistance is taken for granted, and the grown-ups rely upon it to such an extent that I have twice known parents refuse permission when a daughter only seven years of age had been invited to visit another village at a time when they were engaged in some heavy undertaking. Boys and girls are always being sent on errands—to fetch fire from a neighbour, to find a forgotten handbag, to borrow tobacco, or to carry messages—and I often used to hear the adults, when making plans for the morrow, allocating light, but nevertheless essential, tasks to them.

As is to be expected, the youngsters in turn give every indication of regarding themselves as an integral part of the social organization. In their relations with me, for example, they identified themselves with their culture, and, on my asking them the reason for a particular line of behaviour, generally replied, with a sniff at my ignorance, "That is our custom, the custom of us people of Wogeo." Yet, once they realized I wished to be instructed in local usages, they often proved excellent informants. The little boys of Dap, for example, used to make a point on our walks together of indicating the different trees and shrubs and explaining that "we" make such and such from this one, "we" eat the fruit of that one, and so forth.

The argument between Gwa and Wanai regarding the filling of the water bottles by Niabula reveals an early consciousness of allegiance with the members of the child's own sex. Little Jaga already aligned herself with the women when barely out of her infancy, and, although still compelled to accept a ride on her mother's or grandmother's back for part of the journey, used to insist on carrying a small vegetable basket home from the garden, so that she, too, might "help with the men's dinner" (Hogbin 1938).

A remarkable instance of a child identifying himself with the grown-ups took place when a number of us were discussing the habits of the natives on the mainland. At one stage a man who had just returned from spending a number of years on a plantation informed us that the people of the village near by were accustomed to seeking intercourse at all times, even when the

women were menstruating. "Disgusting!" exclaimed a lad of
seven. "Why, our imbecile knows better than that." He was unlikely to have any sexual experience for the next decade, but no
one smiled or seemed to think him at all precocious.

Again, the judgments of the elders regarding conduct are repeated both in the children's own circle and in the wide sphere
of village life. A boy who has refused to share a choice morsel
of food is referred to behind his back, just as an adult would be,
as "the stingey person," and one found out in a petty theft is the
subject of derogatory remarks for days. Gwa, as has been mentioned, echoed his father's condemnation of the Kinaba residents
at the food distribution, and, on another occasion, when a serious
quarrel took place between the headman Marigum and his eldest
son, Tafalti, the small fry discussed the rights and wrongs of the
matter with profound concern (Hogbin 1940).

Adult notions of property are similarly absorbed. Gwa used to
point to his pigs with a proprietary air, and I once heard him
ordering his mother, in a lordly manner, to come and feed them.
She was much amused at the obvious imitation of his father, but
replied that she was too busy, and that he had better fetch a
coconut for them himself.

Another boy, Tabulbul, already referred to, was so well aware
of his claim to the land which had been cultivated by his father
that he left his widowed mother when only seven years old in order
to be near it. On her husband's death three years before she
had brought her young family from his village to Dap, where
her brother lived. "I am tired of walking between the two places,"
Tabulbul told me, "and have left Dap to stay with my father's
kinsmen. I can't look after my land properly if I live with my
mother."

EDUCATION

Yet, for all their ready adoption of the elders' point of view,
the upbringing of the young is not allowed to become a mere
haphazard process. The natives have a definite concept of education, for which they use the word *singara,* the primary meaning
of which is "steering." Children, they maintain, have to be
guided in order to achieve technical knowledge and a proper
sense of right and wrong. One of the chief disadvantages which

orphans have to overcome is lack of deliberate instruction—they are forced to pick up what they can from this house and that, to learn without being taught.

The guiding hand of the grown-ups is particularly in evidence when the boys decide to have a game with model canoes. Each lad makes a vessel for himself, and the party then adjourns to the shallow water off the beach. The men as a rule sit watching and afterwards give a detailed commentary on the different craft taking part. This one, they point out, was unwieldy because the outrigger booms were too long, that one went crab-fashion because the float was crooked, the sail of a third was too small to take full advantage of the wind, and a fourth would have been more stable had a few stones been put into the hull. The patience of one man when his little son, too unskilled as yet to carve a model out of wood, had fashioned a rough craft from half a coconut shell, was most touching. He treated the boy's efforts with the utmost seriousness, and his criticism could hardly have been more carefully phrased if the canoe had been a masterpiece of ingenuity. Suggestions are usually put to the proof at once and additional information sought if a prediction fails to come true.

Children are also encouraged to work side by side with their parents even when their efforts are likely to be a hindrance. Thus when Marigum was making a new canoe he allowed his youngest son, Sabwakai, to take an adze and chip at the dugout. On my enquiring whether the boy did not impede his progress, the father agreed that he would be able to work much faster alone. "But if I send the child away," he added, "how can I expect him to know anything? This time he was in the way, but I'm showing him, and when we have to make another canoe he'll be really useful."

The children are in most cases even more eager to learn than the elders are to teach. Sabwakai took up the adze on his own initiative and on another occasion asked permission to come along with his father to one of our conferences at my house. "By listening to what I tell you," the father explained to me with a smile, "he thinks he'll find out about the things he'll have to do when he's a man."

Moral training is also considered to be necessary, and, although I very much doubt whether parents are as disinterested as the statement would imply, they usually remark, when forced to administer a slap, "I beat you, but only that you may learn."

A distinction is drawn, however, between naughtiness which is the result of bad upbringing and that which arises from inherited temperamental defects. Faults arising from improper teaching are generally supposed to correct themselves when the child grows older and mixes with people outside the immediate family circle —though in practice I found that offences committed by grown-ups are not infrequently attributed to their early home environment. When his elder son Tafalti quarrelled with him, Marigum insisted, for example, that he had never been able to train him properly in childhood as a grandfather was always interfering and taking the boy's part.

Fundamental vices, on the other hand, are accepted as incurable, and children who are sufficiently unfortunate to be cursed with them are considered certain to remain a problem for life. An anatomical abnormality is thought to be the cause of this misfortune: the duct which is believed to lead from the outer ear to the lungs, the seat of understanding, is said to be so narrow that, although the superficial indications of perfect hearing may be present, few statements are fully comprehended. "I thought you were a boy like the rest but now begin to believe that you are one of those without ears," I used to hear the parents chide. "My jaw aches from talking, and my hand pains me from beating you, yet still you do not listen. Is it because you cannot? Were you born disobedient and mischievous?"

Sympathy is always expressed for the parents of children of this sort, but strong exception is taken to one whose offspring are unruly for the want of training and discipline. "He's a foolish fellow, the sort who makes us angry," said Waru of Gubale. "It isn't as though his son hadn't any ears, for I know he's a good lad. But he can't learn without help. If someone doesn't act as a father to him soon he'll turn out a ne'er-do-well."

Leaving aside its practical significance, education is looked upon, quite literally, as a sacred duty. The natives consider that their way of life, having been taken over direct from the heroes of old, the *nanarangs,* is the perfect ideal, and just as these beings taught the early ancestors the true refinements of behaviour and the latter in turn gave the inheritance to their children, so each generation is under the obligation of handing it intact to the next.

Such is the respect shown for the work of the culture heroes that I do not think I exaggerate in saying that the local opinion is that the culture owns the people rather than the reverse. In the course of centuries many changes must undoubtedly have occurred—axes and knives, for instance, are now regarded as vital necessities—but a premium is put upon conservatism, and I was frequently informed that changes cannot be tolerated because the heroes had forestalled all possible improvements. The elders are as much horrified as pained by the innovations of the present day, and even the wearing of European clothing calls forth the strongest criticism. I knew several men of the old school who, with shrill denunciations, refused to allow their daughters to wear dresses, and one who burnt a frock which had been given to his sister. Considerable moral disapprobation is also felt for such a comparatively minor matter as a breach of the rule that persons of different moieties must not strike one another. No new troubles have arisen, however, from infringements of the sexual code, a serious cause of dispute in other Pacific communities, for the natives were lax in such matters long before anyone went away to learn different habits on European plantations—indeed, so also were the culture heroes.

The reason most frequently advanced for the practice of adoption gives another illustration of the reverence for the cultural traditions (Hogbin 1935–36). A man must have someone to watch over his lands and perform the magic given to his forebears by the heroes, and, if unable to beget an heir, he must take over someone else's child and rear the boy as his own. Real distress is often expressed at the decline in population which has recently become noticeable in one or two villages, such as Mwarok. "Who will look after the land?" people ask. "Who will carry out the magic of the Mwarok heroes? We must let the people take some of our children."

Again, a man fearing that he may die before his sons reach maturity teaches his spells to relatives, sometimes even to women, who could not possibly use them, "so that the magic may not perish." "Our fathers gave the magic of the heroes to us," said Jaua, "and we must make certain that our sons receive it also." That this practice is inspired in part by genuine love for

the children and a desire to make adequate provision for their
future is proved by the promise which is extracted that the relatives shall in due course give the necessary instruction to the true
heirs, but this aspect of the question seldom receives explicit
recognition.

A parent who holds the culture in such little esteem as to be
unwilling to do his best to ensure that his children shall reach the
approved standards of conduct is considered to be guilty of what
amounts almost to blasphemy. "Did the heroes' youngsters fight
like that?" remarked Marigum one day in reproof when one of
the villagers had not interfered in a minor quarrel in which the
man's young son was involved. "I suppose you hadn't told the
boy that the hero children didn't fight their kinsfolk? Or is it
that you've been thinking that you know better than they did
how a family ought to be brought up? I suppose that's what it
was." Then, turning to me, he added, "Obin, haven't I often
told you that people nowadays are evil as well as stupid?" On
another occasion when he noticed that Wiawia was not correcting Gwa's childish pronunciation he uttered a similar protest.
"Don't you wish the boy to speak correctly?" he enquired. "Isn't
our language, which is the speech of the culture heroes themselves, good enough for you? I tell you that it's wrong to let
him go on talking like that."

The child's perversity is also an insult to the heroes, but ac-
cusations are seldom brought against it, the parents as a rule
being blamed instead. When the son of a neighbour showed unwillingness to run an errand for him, however, I heard Jaua
remark that hero children were obedient and that the boy had
better imitate them.

The culture is so highly valued, and its mastery by the members of the younger generation considered to be so urgent, that
the adults take great care to play as prominent a part as possible
in its transmission. Association with playmates of the same age
has a considerable effect on the child's mental growth, but it is
never entrusted to the care of youngsters only a little older than
itself for long periods, as has been recorded, for example, in
Samoa (Mead 1928). Further, if an adolescent girl has to look
after a small relative for an odd half hour, as sometimes happens,
she does not attempt to bully it into subservience but reasons and
argues with it as an adult would do. I one day watched Keke

when she was minding a neighbour's little boy, and, although he caused her a great deal of trouble by running into the sun, I noticed that she did not once lose her temper or try to restrain him by force. "See, it is pleasant to sit here in the cool," she kept saying. "The sun is hot, and your head is not yet strong like your father's. The heat doesn't hurt him but he'd be sitting under this tree here if he wasn't working." At last, finding that she was making no progress, she asked him to be good for her sake, pleading that she would be the one to be whipped if his parents returned and found him playing in the open. On other occasions I have been begged to intervene and use my powers of persuasion.

Most of the child's relatives play a part in training it, but the parents are normally the chief instructors, the father being mainly responsible for the son and the mother for the daughter. This association results in a good deal of copying, and I often used to hear children repeating their parent's pet phrases and characteristic intonations with remarkable accuracy. Adoption is common, and the natives have a saying, "Use your eyes to find out who begot a strange child and your ears to discover who is rearing it"—the implication being that it will resemble its real parents in appearance and its foster parents in speech and behaviour. The similarity is in a number of instances so striking that the child appears to have been invested with the personality of the adult.

TECHNICAL TRAINING

The various skills are acquired mainly through direct participation in everyday tasks. The child may watch the adults for a time and then, without any encouragement imitate them as best it can, but more usually a demonstration is given as soon as it displays a marked willingness to assist. The explanations are so detailed that the need for seeking additional information seldom arises, and "why" questions, the everlasting bane of parents in our own community, are rarely heard.

The initial impulse to engage in the activities of the elders arises spontaneously from play motives, and helping with gardening, fishing, and the rest seems for several years to be looked upon as a form of recreation. The child gives its services for the

most part willingly enough, however, even after the deeper significance of its efforts have impinged upon its consciousness.

Praise is probably the most effective spur to industry, and I
was constantly hearing zeal rewarded with approval. Yet the
adults are seldom more than half serious in their tributes, and,
although lazy children are sometimes compared to their disadvantage with those who have worked hard, a precocious youngster is never consciously set up as a model to the rest of the
village. Everyone is so firmly convinced that physical disaster
would result from an immature person working really hard that
attempts to create rivalry and competition so early are regarded
as out of place. At the same time, commendation is always welcomed by the children themselves, and they often boast loudly
of their attainments. The parents only interfere if playmates are
openly sneered at or slighted for their lack of ability.

An incident which I observed in Wiawia's garden well illustrates
the attitude to agriculture during early childhood. Gwa, awakened from a doze by my greeting, marched up to his father, who
was busy planting taro, and demanded a digging stick. A stout
bamboo was found, and the little boy stood alongside and began
making holes in the ground. Wiawia watched him for a time and
then interrupted his own labours to show him the best grip.
"There, put your fingers so," he said. "Hold the stick like that,
and you'll be able to dig deep and feel no pain in your back."
The boy seemed to be an apt pupil and worked diligently for
ten minutes or so, after which he ran off to join his young sister.
He showed her how to hold the stick, and the two of them then
made a garden of their own, using blades of grass instead of taro
shoots. At this age nothing held their continuous attention for
long, but for the time being they obviously believed in what they
were doing. "We mostly leave them at home with their grandmother, but they have to come here sometimes or they'd never
think about the taro," Wiawia explained. "They play at work, but
that is how they learn."

Karui, aged not quite eight, was already taking his labours
seriously, and I one day heard him asking his step-father to allow
him to plant some banana trees. The man stood behind him the
whole time, telling him when the holes were deep enough and
how far apart they ought to be, but did not handle either the
trees or the digging stick himself. At last, when the job was com-

pleted, he asked whether the boy could manage in future by himself. "Yes indeed; I know already," was the reply. "Good! You have done well," the step-father returned. "But you aren't a man yet and you'd better go now and sit down." That evening, when the party returned to the village, Karui began telling his friends of what he had done. "I planted the bananas alone, like a man," he said. "You fellows are still babies, but I now have an orchard of my own." "Enough!" his mother interposed. "You did well, but these boys will soon be planting bananas, too. Your tongue wags too much. Come and feed the pigs."

Clearing the bush seems to excite the children most, and they often ask how long it will be before a new cultivation has to be prepared. Games of hide and seek in the brushwood are admitted to account in part for their enthusiasm, but, in addition, it is said that they love handling knives and axes "as the men do." Worn-out blunted implements are given to them in early childhood, but as soon as they become proficient these are replaced by small tomahawks, and saplings are then set aside for them to cut down.

Instruction in climbing the tall almond trees is unnecessary, for, like European children, these boys go scrambling about in the branches when they are only four or five years old. At seven or eight they begin to accompany their fathers to the nut groves, though for a time they are dissuaded from attempting to reach too great a height. Some children, however, are as expert as their elders, and I often saw Sabwakai picking nuts on a limb nearly a hundred feet above the ground. Once he lost his nerve when out on a branch and began screaming for his father, who was in another tree not far away. Marigum called to him reassuringly—though he told me afterwards that "his belly turned over in anxiety"—and told him how to worm his way backwards to the trunk. A rescue was then effected with the aid of a rope. The old man sat comforting the boy for about an hour but finally suggested that they both go up together. "If you don't climb the tree now you may be frightened to-morrow," he added. "I'll follow close behind and tell you where to put your feet."

The walks to and from the cultivations give an excellent opportunity for indicating the different allotments into which the country is divided. "This piece of ground on the right here, from the stream to the big ficus tree yonder, is called Suaua," the parents explained. "Jaua makes his gardens there. Then on the left the ground is called Maeva all the way to the three heaps of rock by the side of the path. It belongs to Marigum." The child soon absorbs the information and when still quite small is able to answer the enquiries of visitors who sometimes pretend ignorance to test its knowledge.

Participation in fishing expeditions begins at about the age of four or five, when the father takes the boy out with him in a canoe. If he cries or is for some reason restless and troublesome—as Gwa was—a second trip may be postponed for several months, but this is on the whole unusual. At first the father only remains at sea about an hour, carefully choosing either a dull day or the late afternoon to avoid all risk of sunburn or headaches. The boy sits at the bow and is allowed to splash with a paddle until the fishing grounds are reached, but when the line is baited one end is fastened to the outrigger boom in case a fish should bite while he is not paying attention. As he becomes more experienced the methods of catching the different species are explained, and within a few years his haul is a valuable addition to the larder. Dangerous currents, tide rips, and hidden rocks are also pointed out and lessons given in steering and handling the canoe in a choppy sea.

A boy in his teens sometimes tries a younger brother out by persuading him to come for a short voyage and then leaping into the sea and swimming ashore from a distance of two or three hundred yards. As a rule both enjoy the sport thoroughly, though young Niabula was stricken with terror and made no effort to prevent himself from drifting away from the island. His brother in desperation at last put out in another craft and fetched him back.

The girls play at work just like the boys. Jaga had her little garden basket almost before she could carry herself properly, and I often saw her in the evenings marching off with the women to the spring with a small coconut water bottle slung over her shoulder. The procession also included Mwago, aged five, who was able to carry two bottles, and Keke, who, at ten, took nearly a full load. Keke was already of great assistance, too, in carrying home vegetables; her basket often held five or six pounds, and on one occasion she staggered in with nearly twelve. A relative informed me that she had wanted to fill it to the brim and had had to be restrained lest she should injure her back.

The first serious task entrusted to the little girls in the garden is scraping the earth from the tubers, but long before this I used to see them playing round with a digging stick. Mwago one day planted twenty new shoots, under her mother's supervision, an accomplishment of which she boasted several times to her companions. By the time they are ten or eleven many of them can safely be entrusted with their own small allotments. "This taro is from Keke's garden," her mother announced one evening as the food was handed round to a group of guests. "She dug it up this morning all by herself." On the conclusion of the meal, when the party moved outside, one of the visitors began telling a neighbour about the child's proficiency. "If she continues to be as busy as this," he concluded, "some man will soon be wanting her to marry him."

Housework begins with various odd jobs, such as putting the sliced food into the cooking pot, throwing away the rubbish, and sweeping the floor. The child's efforts are sometimes more bother than help, but the mother does not complain unless she is in a hurry. "I'll send her away presently and do it again myself," whispered Mwago's aunt to me as the child struggled valiantly with a broom as big as herself. But on the following afternoon the little girl sat weeping in a corner, because, as the aunt explained, she had been prevented from cracking any of the nuts for the evening meal. "She doesn't yet understand how to tap the shell properly, and when she works with us the kernels are all smashed," said the woman. "That doesn't matter if we are alone, but to-night we have visitors."

The earlier efforts at cooking have to be closely watched, but girls of about ten or twelve can usually, if necessary, prepare certain dishes unaided. Keke was so pleased when her first vegetable stew was pronounced satisfactory that she told the whole village and the next night insisted on making another pot for presentation to various relatives. A cousin of much the same age thereupon begged to be allowed to try her hand, and for the next week the two of them exchanged platters nearly every evening. Yet, though they both basked in the compliments which were showered on them, neither sought to prove that her own dishes were superior.

Having been so successful in this sphere, the two of them de-

cided that they were now old enough to make their own petti-
coats. Their mothers accordingly showed them how to prepare
the fibre, attach it to the belt, and cut it evenly into a series of
fringes, and within a few weeks the two of them were running
from house to house showing off their workmanship. The same
friendly spirit was still in evidence, and Keke actually waited till
the cousin's garment was completed before donning her own.

MORALS

In moral training the practical issues are stressed, the maxim
that friends are more helpful than enemies being quoted if behaviour seems likely to give offence. Any ethical reasons for ex-
ercising restraint are ignored, and the fact that honesty is the best
policy is the most cogent argument by far in its favour. Thus
the stock admonition if children begin meddling with other
people's belongings is simply, "That's his; he'll be cross if you
break it; better not touch it."

Again, no one ever tries to shame a child into conducting himself properly; the emphasis is laid rather on the injunction that he
should not cause embarrassment to others. When he becomes involved in a wordy argument, for example, and seems to be about
to insult his companions, he is told that if his remarks are going
to be unpalatable he had better keep them to himself. Warnings
are also issued against further humiliating a playmate who has
been reproved. "Continue with your game," the parents of the
other children whisper. "Don't let him see that you heard. He
will be angry with you for making him feel ashamed."

It is worth drawing attention to the contrast between this type
of educational practice and that of Malaita, another island with
which I am familiar. In Malaita the parents consciously strive to
inculcate feelings of personal responsibility; a child who interferes
with someone else's property is told not, "That's his; he'll be
cross if you break it; better not touch it," but "That isn't yours;
put it down," and one who has made fun of companions after a
rebuke has the enormity of his offence brought home to him by
some such remark as that he ought to go and hide his head
for having said such things.

It is no accident, I am sure, that in Malaita there is a word
which closely corresponds with our term "conscience," a concept

conspicuously absent from the Wogeo tongue. Wogeo behaviour is ruled not by a still small voice but by the notion of what other people's reactions are likely to be. If they are unlikely to be annoyed or there is a reasonable chance of them not being able to pin the guilt on a particular person, almost anything is permitted.

Inside the household a good deal of easy freedom obtains, and, although technically every single object is individually owned, husband and wife share their tools and all other possessions save clothing with the greatest goodwill. The child is allowed the same latitude, and, as most things for which it asks are handed over, without demur, it speaks of them as "our" rather than as "father's" or "mother's." Axes and knives, which until weaning are kept hidden, are withheld for a few months afterwards, but the parents are more occupied with the dangers of careless handling than with any notions of property. "That is a sharp thing which you have there, a thing which cuts," Wurun warned her small son, for example, when he began brandishing her gardening knife. "Look, turn it over and feel the edge. Isn't what I say true? That is what I use when I want to cut a liana—one blow, so, and the stem is in two pieces. That is how your fingers will be if you aren't careful—little pieces all over the floor. When you're older you shall have a knife of your own, but now, my little son, you are too small. Isn't that so? You know if you cut your fingers off you'll be angry with me for not taking the thing away. That's better. Put it into my basket."

The neighbour's property, on the other hand, is respected, and a person wishing to borrow from another, unless the two are closely related or great friends, always asks permission and apologises, for his intrusion. The children are accordingly cautioned not to touch things when paying calls for fear of arousing the host's resentment. Gwa, on being reproved for playing with a platter in the house of a neighbour, replied that he would be careful. "What about the oil that Karui upset in our fireplace yesterday," his father reminded him in a whisper, "Karui is a big boy, bigger than you, yet he let the bottle fall, and you know how cross we all felt. You wouldn't like the people here to say the same things about you that we said about him, would you? That's right. Put it down and sit still."

Visiting houses and gardens in the absence of the owners is

also deprecated, because, if afterwards something is found to be missing, suspicion inevitably rests upon those who were seen to have been in the vicinity.

About meanness, however, the people have somewhat stronger feelings: they stress that it is unwise but indicate that it is also rather disgraceful. The parents are accordingly at great pains to make the child generous, coaxing him at first but not hesitating, if necessary, to use blows. Liberality, they point out, ensures both a return of hospitality and an abundance of helpers, but the sweetness of charity for its own sake is never quite lost sight of. Kasule's advice to her seven-year-old son Tabulbul, with the moral aspect touched upon as a sort of afterthought, is characteristic. "Always take care to see that those who enter this house leave it with full bellies," she told him. "Learn to give away food now and continue giving after I am dead. If you do this people will never let you be hungry no matter how far you have to go. Besides, giving away food is good." At this point, an uncle interposed and reminded the boy that he must also think about enlisting aid in his cultivations. "If you're mean," he said, "no one —no, not one—will help you in your gardens." The anticipation of such difficulties by fifteen years or so did not strike him, or anyone else, as being funny.

Gifts are always handed to the children for presentation to relatives, and they are also expected to help in the entertainment of guests. The mother, when serving the meal, calls the younger member of the family to her side and sets a woven platter in its arms. "Take this to our kinsman over there and set it neatly at his feet," she whispers. "He is of our blood, and we must be careful to have something ready for him to eat." The father meantime smiles encouragement and grows expansive about the child's lofty motives. "See, our little daughter is sorry for those who travel far," he exclaims in a loud voice. "She says to herself, 'Let me care for this man's aching limbs by filling his belly.' No one is permitted to leave this house hungry if she is at hand." Bwa turned to me on one occasion as her little girl re-entered the house after taking a dish of food to her grandfather next door and remarked in a loud aside, "There, wasn't I telling you that Gaus is already a good grand-daughter? She is sorry for the old man and always makes me give him a meal even if we have to go short ourselves." "Nonsense," I replied—I knew Bwa and her husband very well—"she's much too small; and, besides, you know quite well that you always have plenty to spare." "That's true," Bwa answered; "but when Gaus has grown only a little bigger she'll be thinking of her grandfather first."

Endeavours are also made to have the child present something, no matter how small, to visitors of its own age. An incident which took place when Wiawia and Gwa were visiting relatives in Kinaba is in this connection instructive. On the appearance of the small son of the house with two bananas in his hand, the father told him to give one to Gwa. "One you may eat," he said, "but your cousin here is hungry." "Shan't," the boy replied firmly. "Come, my son," the father pleaded, "Gwa has walked across from Dap to see you. Would you let him go away hungry? Your talk is evil. Have I not taught you to look after your kinsfolk?" "These bananas are mine—grandfather gave them to me," the child maintained. Failing to persuade him, the father was forced to box his ears. "Greedy little pig," he said. "Give me one for Gwa and then go away. We don't want boys like you in the house." Turning to us, he went to the trouble of offering an apology: such conduct would be excused, he hoped, on the ground of youth. When Gwa on the return journey commented on how naughty the boy had been, Wiawia told him that he had better take care not to be called a greedy pig himself and talked about behind his back.

Parents insist, too, that a special delicacy received as a present must be shared with the bystanders, and my gift of a biscuit had sometimes to be broken into half a dozen pieces. Sabwa, the laziest man in Dap, who never had anything to spare, was regarded by everyone as a person of no account and provided a convenient horrible example. "Surely you don't want to be like him," the adults used to say if the children had not been sufficiently liberal. "If you keep things for yourself you'll be treated like him—not as a real person but as a ghost. Nobody will speak well of you."

The lesson is at times learned only too well, and more of the family supplies given away than can actually be spared. Gwa, for example, was most puzzled at being reprimanded for handing a bundle of tobacco leaves intended for household consumption to a group of men who were passing through the village on the way to a funeral—as he said, he was merely following instructions. His father told him that in future he had better confine his giving to his own property and wait and see what other people had to say before making free with theirs.

One little girl's too literal interpretation of her teaching gave rise to much laughter at her father's expense. On hearing some casual visitors chatting outside, he had come to the door of the house and apologised for having no betel-nut to offer them. "O yes you have, father," the child interrupted. "What about the bunch you put in the corner behind your bed? Have you forgotten? I saw you take it there when these men first came into the village."

Such incidents are, however, rare, and most children, if the risk of discovery is negligible, are not above hiding titbits until a favourable moment for eating them alone presents itself. Thus if I gave them two biscuits I found that they almost invariably popped one into their mouths before running to join their companions. In this they were no doubt following an example set by their elders. Although the various ingredients of the betel-nut mixture—areca nut, betel pepper, and lime—are handed round when plentiful with as much freedom as cigarettes were in our own community before the war, men whose supply has for some reason run short have no compunction in keeping back for private use the little that they have and in public cadging from their neighbours. The handbags in which personal possessions are carried are sometimes made with a whole series of compartments in order that a request for pepper or a nut can be accompanied by a tolerably convincing demonstration that nothing is left, and the fumbling which goes on if a newcomer asks has anyone present betel to spare is often reminiscent of a crowd of European women on a bus when each is trying not to have to pay the fares. At the same time, consistent begging is avoided by all right-thinking persons, and no one will tell a lie about his possessions if there is a reasonable chance of his being found out.

The attitude to emotional outbursts is equally practical; personal dignity is felt to be of infinitely less importance than the amity of the village, and parents are much concerned with directing the child's anger along harmless channels. Co-operation, which benefits everyone, would be impossible, they explain, without the appearance of goodwill, and free outlet for every minor grievance is therefore unwise. Yet no demand is made for the complete suppression of feelings, for the people believe that a permanent state of tension might then develop. The relevant maxim which is almost always quoted runs, "If you are angry, smash a pot; otherwise you'll be angry for a month."

Quarrelling is strickly forbidden, and the most easy-going parent always interferes at the first sign of violence. "What, you would strike a kinsman! That is wrong," he scolds as he drags the delinquents apart. "Kinsmen help one another: they never fight. Do you think that the boy you've hit will like you afterwards? And if he doesn't like you, what will he say when you ask for his help?" If really angry the children express their resentment with unrestrained passion and roll on the ground screaming and frothing at the mouth. Usually, however, they are led away in opposite directions, presented with an axe, and told to take out their rage on a tree. Most of the big timber close to the villages is as a result deeply scarred.

The elders do their best to comfort a child who is out of temper, but abandonment to the emotions is normally accepted with complacency; the culprit is hurting no one but himself. The treatment seems to be successful, for even when children sulk with one another for a week, they seldom attempt to renew the fight.

Such tantrums and weeping fits are liable to take place even in the boy's early teens if he is temporarily deserted, on account of some important undertaking, by a relative with whom he is particularly intimate, usually the father or grandfather. So intense may his misery be that hasty efforts are sometimes made at great inconvenience to bring the missing parent or grandparent back.

The female nature is supposed to be less violent than the male, and little girls are, in fact, far more self-controlled. "Tears from a girl!" the mother exclaims in mock astonishment if they weep or fly into a rage. "Why, perhaps she's a boy after all. She'll be growing a penis next." The reason for the rarity of such outbursts is clear: the girls' life of freedom ends so much earlier than that of their brothers and after about the eighth year, instead of associating with playmates, they accompany the women.

MORALS AND MYTHOLOGY

Myths provide an ultimate standard for judging—and justifying—conduct. The ancient culture heroes did not, however, in their divine wisdom, present men with a Decalogue for guidance; instead, some of them stole and were punished, others suffered for being mean, and others, again, brought misfortune upon themselves by bad temper, disobedience and unkindness.

Knowledge of the stories forms a part of everyone's equipment, and in the course of a few years the children hear dozens. Indeed, they often repeat them for their own entertainment, not infrequently developing remarkable dramatic talents in the process. Different voices are assumed for the various heroes and their actions cleverly imitated. (A favourite cycle gives the doings of Wonka and his two foolish brothers, Yabuk, who roared like a volcano when he spoke, and Magaj, who squeaked like a mouse.)

The more important myths are told with a good deal of solemnity, but the moral content is not specifically indicated, and recitals are never preceded by any such remark as, "Disobedience is wrong; listen to what happened to the hero who disobeyed his parents." Yet the point of an argument is sometimes underlined by a reference to the appropriate culture hero, and, in addition, oblique references, which are not unlike our own to such biblical characters as the Good Samaritan and the Painted Jezebel, are not infrequently used with the implication that a certain line of conduct is worthy either of praise or blame.

Myths are approached, nevertheless, in a realistic spirit. When they are told formally, it is true, the accent is on the moral content—a certain hero stole and was punished for it; thieving is therefore unwise. But after listening to fireside conversations I came to the conclusion that the actions of these beings are often used as sanctions for behaviour which is in fact anti-social. Thus a person who covets something belonging to a member of another village is as likely as not to ignore the hero's fate and to argue that, as stealing was apparently common in the past, there is no reason why he should not help himself. (I have mentioned in another publication how the myth telling of the dire consequences of the first adultery is now used not so much as justification for vengeance as an excuse for promiscuity (see Hogbin 1944a, 1944b).

A detailed account of the mythology would be out of place here, and I shall content myself with summarizing one or two of the tales very briefly.

The first relates of how two children were punished for thieving.

Kanak-Bokeboken ("crooked betel-pepper") and Bua-Bokeboken ("crooked areca nut"), having been left in the village to play, entered every house and took all the food, with which they stuffed their bellies to bursting point. After sleeping for a short space they decided to express their pleasure by decorating themselves and dancing. But when evening came on they grew frightened and hid in a tree. As they had feared, the grown-ups were most indignant, and the probable consequences of return appeared to be so unpleasant that they remained where they were. Days passed, and one boy, who had put on a tail of coconut leaves, turned into a bird-of-paradise, while the other, who was wearing a coronet of pandanus, became a cockatoo. They flew away to the mainland, never to return (birds-of-paradise and cockatoos are not found on Wogeo).

Another story tells of how a woman, becoming distressed by her son's constant disobedience, made him kill her. In her despair she had run away weeping into the forest, but when he at last found her she lied and told him that her tears were merely the result of a painful boil on her left breast. Taking his dagger, the boy proceeded to lance what looked like a small tumour. "Deeper, deeper," said his mother, and the weapon finally pierced her heart.

A number of folk tales teach similar lessons. A typical example gives an account of how a tree-climbing kangaroo paid his guests out for eating all his food. Having discovered that he could catch crabs easily by putting his tail into their holes and flicking it to the surface as soon as he felt a nip at the end, he decided to invite all his kangaroo friends and let them into the secret. They were so greedy, however, that nothing was left for the host, who accordingly followed them home and, after they had climbed into the branches for the night, scratched the trunks of all the trees. The natives of the neighbouring village, seeing the marks, set traps, and the kangaroos were all killed.

PUNISHMENT

Continued misbehaviour is met firstly by sarcasm or intimidation. The parents suggest that the child is, after all, not human but a ghost or that it must surely belong to another district; or it is told that it will receive no pork when the next pig is killed, that it will be banished to the forest, or that its naughtiness will be reported to the headman. In practice, however, it is never even put supperless to bed, and the adults are much too afraid of sorcerers to send it away from the village. The headman, if he hears his name mentioned, may deliver a short lecture, but discipline is felt to be a family affair, and he takes no steps to administer punishment. The children soon learn that they have little to fear, though the disapproving tone in which the elders speak generally has the effect of making them mend their ways. "He knows quite well that he'll have his share of pork," Wiawia told me after he had been scolding Gwa. "But he's also aware that I only threaten him when I'm vexed. As soon as I've let him see that I'm really cross he obeys me."

The spirits are supposed to take almost no interest in the doings of mortals, and the children are in consequence never terrorized by talk of supernatural intervention. Parents sometimes tell them half playfully that the forest spirits will take them away, and I heard references on several occasions to the bogey-man Karibua, who steals children when they refuse to go to sleep, but the lack of conviction is so very apparent that nobody takes much notice. I knew of only one child, Niabula, who was seriously frightened, and it is significant that his mother at once began to reassure him that there was no truth in what she had been saying. She and her husband later agreed that, as the boy was more than usually nervous, they had better refrain in future from letting the names of the spirits pass their lips.

Illness and death are supposed to follow if adequate precautions are neglected when a person has come into contact with the world of the sacred, but young children are carefully excluded from the religious life of the community and removed to a distance during the performance of important ceremonies. The men's house, where various sacred objects are stored, remains a potential danger, nevertheless, and they are repeatedly warned that entry is forbidden. "Come away, come away," the adults call urgently if they venture too close. "The men's house is for grown men only; to you it is death." The height of the building from the ground presents an obstacle to very small children, and I was acquainted with but one lad who followed his father inside. "Cover the masks," the man exclaimed in great agitation when he noticed the child at his side. Then, carrying him quickly outside, he patiently explained the terrible risk and probable consequences of future disobedience. No one could have doubted his real concern, and the boy was certainly aware that he was not being fobbed off with excuses.

Food cooked by women who are menstruating has also to be avoided, though not until after about the eighth year. Children are from this age onwards cautioned, too, against touching their mothers during her periods.

The adults' fear of black magic becomes so apparent after a death has occurred in suspicious circumstances that the children are inevitably impressed, and even the tiny tots are apprehensive. A wave of alarm sweeps through the village, and for the space of several days little else is discussed. Plans for visiting distant places are temporarily abandoned, and no one now stirs more than a few yards from the village without a companion for fear that he should come face to face with the sorcerer.

If the child's naughtiness continues unabated after it has been warned to stop, the parents next threaten it with violence. "I'll cut you into little pieces if you don't stop that noise at once," Karui's step-father shouted when the boy banged an empty tin a few yards from the house and pretended to sing. "Fetch that firestick from Waru immediately or I'll smash your head in as if it were a coconut," Sabuk yelled to Manoua on another occasion. Gwa was sometimes told, too, that he would be whipped till the blood flowed down like rain. Yet when driven at last to action the elders are usually satisfied with boxing the child's ears, cuffing it on the back of the head, or belabouring it once or twice round the shoulders—never on the buttocks—with a stick. They strike only when, tried beyond endurance, they momentarily lose control of themselves, but everyone maintains the fiction of being inspired by the loftiest motives. "We hit the children only to teach them," they insist, and I have actually heard a man claim, as he banged his son on the head, "Alas, I don't want to hit you, but you won't learn otherwise." The bystanders preserve the illusion by reiterating, "Teach him, teach him," or "Good; slap him to make him do as you say in future."[1]

---

[1] The contrast with Malaita is again interesting: there the adults frankly admit that they whip the child when angered. As the blow is administered, moreover, instead of pretending an interest in education, they usually made some reference to "payment for disobedience."

Punishment is usually inflicted by the parents, but uncles, aunts, and other relatives have few scruples if the child is particularly troublesome. The fact that they help to feed it is held to give them the right of correction, and objections are only raised if the blows are unduly hard.

Wogeo women are almost as heavy-handed as the men and would certainly not subscribe to the theory that discipline is the prerogative of the father. Children in consequence are never subjected to the torture of awaiting a thrashing in the evening after his return. Execution is, indeed, immediately, and, if no steps are taken to implement a threat at the moment of its utterance, it is invariably forgotten.

The injury to personal dignity is resented most, and the lighter taps are followed by floods of tears, even after teen age has been reached, when force is very rarely resorted to. The child's hands are held if it attempts to hit back, and after a time it usually retires by itself to some quiet corner or else visits a relative. Those of especially violent disposition may hurl stones, however, and Sabwakai once made a cut at least two inches long in his mother's cheek. Frightened by what he had done, he made no attempt to escape when his father gave him a good hiding. When on another occasion a little girl snatched a knife and attacked her mother, her father quickly seized her arm and urged her to cut down a tree if she felt angry.

After the lapse of an hour or two an attempt is made to regain the child's confidence. The parent puts an arm lovingly around its shoulders and either offers it a delicacy or invites it to accompany him to the beach or to the cultivations. The overtures are at first resisted or ignored, but he perseveres with further acts of kindness, until in the end relations are back on the old footing.

7 THE STRUCTURE OF THE SOCIALIZATION PROCESS IN PAPAGO INDIAN SOCIETY

Thomas Rhys Williams

In this chapter, Thomas Rhys Williams discusses the structure of the total program of education among the Papago, a small North American people of the southwest United States. Unlike the Hopi of the same region, who have maintained a strong sense of cultural isolation and identity, the Papago would appear to have been affected to a greater degree by the impact of the outside world. Nonetheless, their system of education has remained central to their efforts to maintain their identity and internal social order. The author presents six principles on which their process of education is based, and places this particular educational system within a wider comparative and theoretical framework.

THE PHRASE process of socialization[1] is used most often by students of human behavior to denote the techniques by which desired social behavior is elicited from a child as he matures in a human group.[2] A review of the extensive literature reveals that two distinct types of investigations have been carried on under the heading of "research in socialization."[3] The first,

Reprinted from *Social Forces* 36 (3), March 1958: 251–56, with permission of the author and of the editor, *Social Forces*.

[1] This research was made possible by a pre-doctoral fellowship of the Wenner-Gren Foundation for Anthropological Research, Inc. The study was conducted during residence from January–June 1956 in the Gu Achi district of the Papago reservation. Preliminary research on this topic was undertaken in this area in the spring and summer of 1954.

[2] Child 1954; K. Davis 1949.

[3] For references to the literature of socialization see the text discussions and bibliographic citations in Child 1954; Haring 1956; Orlansky 1949; Kluckhohn and Murray 1953; Whiting and Child 1953; Heinicke and

involving the largest number of projects, has been concerned with the effects of the process of socialization on adult behavior. The second type of research has been focused largely on the nature of the process.

The first type of research can be said to have been carried on under the general assumption that certain regularities exist in the human socialization process that engender particular types of adult behavior. As a consequence, most research of this type has been concerned with attempts at delineation of exact causal relationships between specific features of the process and particular aspects of adult behavior.[4] Investigators who have undertaken the second type of study generally have been more cautious in making an *a priori* assumption that specific features of the process invariably lead to certain kinds of adult behavior. Studies of this type have been concerned primarily with description of the total process of socialization as a unique set of functionally interrelated social events. Few of these studies have attempted to define specific causal relationships between the process and adult behavior, although most have stated that there is evidence of the existence of some type of causal relationship between the process of socialization and the behavior of adult individuals.[5]

It is commonly agreed upon by research workers in the area of socialization that there now can be little question about the position that most patterns of adult social behavior are learned as a consequence of the process of socialization.[6] There is, in addition,

Whiting 1953; Honigmann 1954; Sargent and Smith 1949; A. Davis 1949; Kluckhohn 1954; Slotkin 1951; Mead 1946.

[4] For examples of this kind of research see Goldman 1948–50; Goldman-Eisler 1951; C. A. Barnes 1952; Blum 1949. See also the reviews of such research in Fenichel 1945; Blum 1953; Orlansky 1949; Child 1954. For a variety of this type of research, which has concentrated upon comparative analyses of specific causal connections between particular events in the process of socialization and general types of adult character in different societies, see Kardiner 1939, 1940; Benedict 1934, 1946a, 1946b; Mead 1935; La Barre 1945, 1946; Gorer 1948, 1950; Gorer and Rickman 1949. See also the recent reviews of national character in Mead 1953; Inkeles and Levinson 1954.

[5] Mead 1928, 1930; Thompson and Joseph 1944; Whiting 1941; DuBois 1944; Leighton and Kluckhohn 1947; Joseph, Spicer, and Chesky 1949.

[6] Honigmann 1954:172–73; Child 1954:688–89. See also the text discussion of Whiting and Child 1953:16–38.

a growing consensus rejecting the assumption that a specific event in the process of socialization causes a particular adult behavior.[7] This agreement is based upon data which demonstrate that there is little empirical support for such an assumption. It now appears that definite causal connections between the process of socialization and adult behavior are most likely to be found in a series of structurally interrelated events that extend through the time of socialization.[8]

The fundamental task of a science is the precise description of the phenomena it seeks to subject to causal analysis. The history of the use of the method of science in the study of human behavior shows that meticulous description and classification of the grosser, directly observable phenomena will gradually narrow the limits of the unknown to the point where the intangibles of causal relations no longer continue to defy formulation and examination. So also in the study of the human socialization process, continued and careful use of this method should further reveal the broad limits within which the intangibles of causal relationships operate.[9]

With these data as a background the writer recently described

---

[7] Kluckhohn 1954:949; Orlansky 1949; Slotkin 1951; Hsu 1952.

[8] Gillin 1951:123; Leighton and Kluckhohn 1947:85; Underwood and Honigmann 1947; Goldfrank 1945; Sewell 1952.

[9] It should be noted that contemporary claims for having isolated any type of universal causal relationship between the socialization process and adult behavior must take account of two facts: (1) There is an amazing paucity of descriptive data about the socialization process; a review of the literature of research in socialization and the listings of the Yale University Human Relations Area Files show that not more than one hundred of the more than two thousand societies have had their total process descriptively recorded (Whiting and Child 1953 list seventy-five studies which these authors feel give acceptable descriptive data on the socialization process); (2) there are less than a dozen societies that have been partially described over a period of time by more than one observer. There appears to be only one systematic attempt to describe the process of socialization in a single society by the use of a number of trained, independently working observers. This research, carried on under the title of the "Harvard Ramah Navaho Project," has shown much promise of providing basic data about causal relationships in this society. See C. Kluckhohn 1949. Mead's recent restudy of the Manus socialization process is the only published study that the writer would consider comparable to the Ramah Navaho work. See M. Mead 1956.

and analyzed the events that constitute the process of socialization among the Papago, a native North American Indian society (Williams 1957). This research is the first of a projected series of studies whose aim is to determine, if possible, some specific causal relations between the process of socialization and patterns of adult behavior in this group. The discussion which follows is a brief summary of the nature and functional interrelations of the social events that make up the structure of the Papago socialization process.

The Papago, about ten thousand in number, live by cattle ranching and floodwater farming on a two and three quarter million acre Federal reservation eighty miles west of Tucson, Arizona. The reservation is the center of a physiographic zone known as the Sonoran desert. The area is characterized by less than five inches annual rainfall and daily temperatures that for seven months of the year range well over 100° F. It may be said to be one of the few truly inhospitable areas of the United States regularly inhabited by man. Archeological and historical records point to the Papago as probable occupants of this land for more than two thousand years (Haury 1950).

Although they have had sporadic contacts with Euro-American peoples for nearly three hundred years, the basic ways of aboriginal Papago life have remained essentially intact; only in the past half century have they begun to adopt many of the white man's tools and a few of his customs. However, these changes have not seemed to alter the core of old Papago ways.[10]

_____

[10] T. R. Williams 1954. Descriptions of Papago life by trained observers are to be found in Underhill 1939, 1940, 1946; Joseph, Spicer, and Chesky 1949. Underhill's works are attempts to "reconstruct" aboriginal customs from the memories of her oldest informants. The text by Joseph, Spicer, and Chesky is the only source providing a general survey of contemporary Papago behavior. A brief descriptive section of this text has been the sole reference on the Papago socialization process (Joseph, Spicer, and Chesky 1949:115–67). No attempt was made in the course of the writer's research to follow these data; the present study was undertaken without any field reference to this publication. A discussion and comparison of the two descriptions may be found in Williams 1957. The two sets of observations appear to be mutually verifying with respect to the main structural features of the process of socialization in Papago society; such verification would appear to increase reliable knowledge of the limits within which causal relations may operate in the Papago socialization process.

There are six major structural features of the process of socialization in Papago society.[11] These may be enumerated as follows; (a) the pattern of reward and punishment, (b) the pattern of social deference, (c) the pattern of joint sharing of family work, (d) the pattern of supernatural sanctions as controls of disruptive and physically dangerous behavior, (e) the pattern of similarity of expected social behavior for adults and children, and (f) the pattern of treatment of the child as a person.

Outstanding among these is the pattern of reward and punishment used by adults to elicit desired social behavior from the maturing child. This pattern appears to rest on three interrelated ideas; a child who cannot talk, cannot understand; a child who cannot understand, cannot learn appropriate social behavior; children will learn appropriate social behavior when they are ready and capable of so doing. Social situations in which these ideas are expressed are to be seen daily in the society. It is possible to draw several conclusions from data describing these situations.

The first is that there are few specific, overt techniques of using punishment as a motivation for the child to learn appropriate social behavior. Parents and parent-surrogates rarely harshly warn or scold children. They almost never physically threaten or punish them. Until puberty the child is indulged with respect to the greater part of his behavior. He is permitted the greatest freedom of social action under five years of age and is rarely paddled, hit, pushed or slapped for nonconformance to group standards. After five years of age the same general pattern prevails, with rare physical punishment for failure to meet social norms. However, the child of five and older is expected to begin gradually to meet certain standards with regard to regular control of bowel and bladder functions and in physical care of himself.

---

[11] The term structure is used here in the analytic sense. In this usage it is best defined as the arrangement and interrelation of parts as dominated by the general character of the conceptual whole. In the discussion to follow, the whole to be considered is the process of socialization. The parts making up that whole are the patterns of social behavior that are concerned with the elicitation of culturally standardized behavior in the maturing child. These patterns may be said to be functionally interrelated in that they exist as the result of the operation of this structure through time. For an elaboration of this position see M. J. Levy 1952; R. K. Merton 1949. See also the review of structural-functional analysis by R. Firth 1956.

If there are repeated failures at meeting these few standards the older child will receive a parental lecture. On infrequent occasions of marked failure, he may become the object of mild family teasing. He is rarely punished physically for such failures.

Conversely, there are few specific, overt techniques of providing reward as a motivation for exhibiting approved social behavior. A child seldom is praised directly by adults for learning physical skills and displaying social achievements. Children apparently learn expected social behavior largely by imitation based on observation of adults and older siblings. They rarely are shown how to perform a task or to master a social skill. Adults do not attempt to demonstrate to a child the specific means of acquiring any skill that is a part of expected behavior. When a child does accomplish something for the first time, he generally is not given direct verbal praise or material recompense by adults or older siblings. The major form of overt praise in childhood is the granting at puberty of some adult personal freedom and social recognition for the assumption of adult work tasks. Before this time adults provide only unspoken approval for the child that tries to act according to his impression of adult standards. This approval can be recognized indirectly in expressions of the parents to each other and to other adults to the effect that "he's growing up to be a good Papago." Such indirect approval appears always to take a positive form because of the three ideas expressed above. Hence, if a child fails prior to puberty to exhibit some of the adult approved behavior forms, parents and other adults are not too concerned and say, "he is only a child."

A second conclusion about the pattern of reward and punishment is that the general absence of physical and verbal punishment in childhood appears to be related to the presence of a close affective relationship between the parents, parent-surrogates and the child. These relationships would seem to be the basic motivation for the child eventually to exhibit desired social behavior. He notices early in life the differences between his social actions and those of the adults with whom he is identified emotionally. Although he receives no direct praise for his efforts the child attempts, through his play and in his efforts to seek out adult work tasks, to be like those with whom he has the close affective ties. When given, the first reprimands for repeated failure to exhibit expected social behavior come from adults with close affective ties with the child. Such reprimands do not threaten withdrawal of these ties. They generally take the form of reminding the child that the adult is disappointed in his repeated failures in not recognizing "the way to do things." Such a reprimand will not take the form of sharp ridicule used with nonconforming adults. Thus, the full force of the major form of adult discipline is not brought to bear on the child until after puberty, when he has assumed most of the rights and duties of adulthood.

A second structural feature of the process of socialization is the pattern of deference to all seniors in age, regardless of the seniors' sex, social ranking, or degree of relationship. This idea is vital to the success of life in the desert, for it is the primary basis of group coöperation. In learning this pattern, the child appears to learn the control of many of his urges for self-gratification. Like most Papago social behavior, it is learned by observation and imitation. It is learned early in the child's life for it forms quite noticeably the basis for his extra-familial relationships in his first play groups and contacts with adult nonrelatives. He observes early the constant deference his parents accord to their seniors in the household and village. He begins to adopt this same form of deference by four years of age; children of this age are noticeably silent in the presence of adult seniors, speaking only when spoken to. By seven years of age children constantly exhibit deference to all seniors and manifest most of the personal traits identified with this pattern by the adults. With persons who are his seniors by many years the child is humble, unobtrusive and reserved in speech and action. His social relations with play group members who are his seniors are marked by these same traits, but in a lesser degree.

The pattern of deference is unquestioned by the child for he observes that there are no exceptions to it and that the powers and privileges of seniority are based on an idea of fairness that usually leads to the consideration of his interests and desires. He soon learns that the privileges and powers of seniority rarely are abused because of the public ridicule and gossip directed to persons who misuse them. The child comes to value this idea, for with his maturity his own seniority grows and he is treated more and more as an adult by his juniors. As a consequence, he seldom abuses the advantage of social deference from his younger siblings or other children.

A third structural feature of the process of socialization is the pattern of joint sharing of family work. This pattern also stresses the subordination of self-gratification to close coöperation within the group. The assignment of small tasks is made early for all children. They observe that work is performed by all persons who are capable and that there are few adult exemptions from its undertaking. As the child matures, he is given more responsible tasks and is rewarded for quiet assumption of a share of the family work by an increasing recognition of his social maturity. Coöperative work thus acquires value as a means to attainment of adult privileges.

With the assumption of an increasingly larger share of family work, the child eventually finds it necessary to give up his playtime. This apparently causes little difficulty; the desire to indulge in play seems easily overcome. This stems from the fact that much of children's play is devoted to imitations of adult work activity. Hence, they generally welcome the transition from play to work because it signals the beginning of recognition of social maturity.

A fourth structural feature is the pattern of supernatural sanctions in the control of social behavior that would disrupt closely interdependent group life. Personal physical aggression and open displays of temper are almost entirely controlled in children by the supernatural sanction of the mysterious illness and eventual death that may come to the individual who strikes, pushes, or touches another in anger. A child is made aware of this sanction by hearing adults repeat it many times in folk tales. The effectiveness of the sanction in channeling the child's resentment of thwarting by others is quite evident in the general absence of physical quarrels or open expression of violent anger in play groups and in his personal relations with his family, household and nonrelatives.

A similar sanction exists for the control of behavior by children that would be physically dangerous. The desert environment of the Papago is filled with species of fauna and physiographic features that are extremely hazardous for young children. The supernatural sanction of illness and eventual death that comes to the person who handles animals or goes near dangerous locations is repeated often to the child in folk tales. As the child conforms and no harm comes to him he finds reinforcement for strict adherence to the prohibitions of both of these sanctions.

A fifth structural feature is to be found in the social expression of the idea that children cannot be held responsible for their social behavior until they have learned to act like adults. This idea is expressed most directly in the fact that no separate rules of behavior exist solely for children. The adult social behavior forms are the only ones to be learned by the child. Hence, there is only one set of appropriate behavior forms for the child to exhibit; when adults begin to expect conformance to a pattern of social behavior, it is the adult standard and not one unique for children. The demands made upon the older child for work, non-violence, deferences, etc., are identical in form, function and meaning with those made upon adult members of the group. As a consequence, there is no period of transition for the child from one set of expected behavior to another.

The sixth structural feature is the pattern of the general treatment of the child as a distinct person by his parents, their surrogates and his older siblings and playfellows. A young child is felt to be the same as other persons; he is someone with a set of ideas and desires that ideally ought to be considered in most choices of action that directly affect him. The child is consulted as to his wishes on matters which adults feel an adult person would have the right to decide. These decisions range from choice of colors in new clothing and foods to be eaten to participation in ceremonial activity.

This pattern of giving the child wide freedom in personal choices of social action is in accordance with the adult social deference pattern idea that consent of a junior is required by a senior in actions affecting the junior person; this same idea is the basic rationale of the adults for the treatment of the child as a distinct social person. Consideration of the child as a person does not vary as he matures, it is essentially the same through the whole of the process of socialization. As a consequence of this pattern, children are thrown almost entirely on their own judgments as to proper action in specific social situations. The choices made are accepted by adults without comment until after puberty, when the child is supposed to know "what people do."

These six patterns may be regarded as the main components

of the Papago socialization process. Together, they impart to this process its characteristic uniqueness and represent the structure of the culturally derived ideas that constitute the major orientation points for adults in their elicitation of desired social behavior in the maturing child. This structure is felt to be the most likely locus for further research, for it appears to be the broad outline within which the factors of causality between the process of socialization and patterns of adult behavior probably will be found to be operative.

At the present level of research no conclusions concerning causality can be offered. However, it can be pointed out that the Papago socialization process, in marked contrast to those of many other societies, is unencumbered by many deliberate attempts to use overt and specific techniques to lead children to exhibit behavior that is held by this group to be customary and acceptable.[12]

---

[12] A comparison of the structure of the Papago socialization process with those reported in other societies may be made by reference to the citations listed in Whiting and Child 1953; Haring 1956; Honigmann 1954. It should be noted that the Papago socialization process can be placed at the permissive end of the continuum "permissive-restrictive," and that the Papago adult may be generally characterized as "easy-going." These data would quite logically, under psychoanalytic rubrics, lead to the generalization that "permissive socialization leads to permissive adults . . ." were it not for empirical evidence that several societies with quite similar structures of socialization have completely different "types" of adult behavior, while several societies that have completely different structures of socialization have quite identical types of adult behavior patterns. See Kluckhohn 1954:472–85, 951.

8 EDUCATION FOR CITIZENSHIP
AMONG THE NUPE

S. F. Nadel

*This chapter is from a famous account of a central Nigerian
kingdom, Nupe, published in 1942; the research was carried out
in a colonial situation which is referred to several times. The
Nupe are Muslims and are organized into a feudal-like state
whose king, the* etsu *Nupe, lives in the capital city of Bida.
Notions of social rank, hierarchy, and aristocracy are central to
Nupe ideas about society. The author shows how these notions
are embedded in the process of education, part of which is formally Muslim and part of which is associated with membership
in age-associations. Here we see an educational program that is
partly specialized: The Muslim teachers are specialists and represent the outside world and its superior power and authority,
while the age-associations are concerned more with everyday
education in moral and social matters. The author describes not
only the educational process, but also the role of Muslim teachers
and of the associations in the total Nupe social organization. Besides their overtly educational roles, both have other, wider roles,
and the interplay between them is of great significance in understanding Nupe education.*

AS EDUCATION in the widest sense must be described all efforts, organized or otherwise, which tend to impart to individuals habitual forms of acting and thinking. Understood in
this sense, every social institution involves educational activities
by means of which individuals are led to acquire the behaviour-
patterns that make up the institution. Thus our description of
economic life has involved the description of certain educational

Reprinted from *A Black Byzantium*, London, Oxford University Press for
the International African Institute, 1942: 388–402, with permission of the
publisher.

techniques—the training in productive methods, the imparting of educational knowledge, or of concepts of property and wealth. But most societies also operate with more formalized methods of education, specific educational institutions which make it their business to train the rising generation in forms of acting and thinking regarded as essential by the society. We shall deal in this chapter with these formalized educational institutions, of which there are two in Nupe: the institution of the Koran school, concerned with Mohammedan religious teaching, and the institution of age-grade associations. The shortest definition of an educational institution is by the 'type' which it is meant to produce. In this sense we can say that Mohammedan religious education produces the Mallam, the Mohammedan scholar, and the age-grade associations the *zoon politikon* as understood in Nupe. We shall see that in certain respects both types of education can be identified with motives and aims underlying the political system, and thus with institutions devoted to what I have called in the heading of this chapter 'Education for Citizenship'.

MALLAM SCHOOLS

There are many degrees and varieties of Mohammedan learning. The title 'Mallam'—*mân* in Nupe—which one encounters so often among the Nupe, is by no means a safe guide. For the man who has gone through a few years' study of the Koran, having learned by heart a few *sura;* the sand-diviner or charm-seller who writes out verses from the Koran and sells them as amulets; the man who has acquired real learning and scholarship, and who can read and write in Arabic and possibly in Hausa— they all are called Mallam. Though the title is used indiscriminately, no Nupe ignores the essential difference between scholarship and the thin veneer of semi-learning. The Nupe distinguish two grades of learning: the lower grade is the study of the Koran (*kurani*), which consists mostly in the memorizing of prayers and whole pages and chapters from the Koran; the higher grade is called *kpikpe,* knowledge, or *litafi* (Hausa), book, and consists in the study of Arabic and the careful reading of the Koran and the better-known commentaries. The most advanced scholars would study, in addition to these books, also the historical records of the Nigerian Emirates which have been compiled (in Hausa, written in Arabic script) by scholars of former days. Only a student of 'knowledge' can claim to be a 'real' Mallam. While there are hundreds of Mallams of the lower grade, there are few real scholars, and they are well known and highly esteemed. These scholars will occupy that most influential position which a Mohammedan culture accords to the men of learning.[1] Their advice will be sought by friends and strangers, in matters spiritual or profane.[2] The important political and religious offices of judge, scribe, and Imam at the town mosque are open to them. Some become attached to a noble household as 'private chaplain'. Royal princes and noblemen will seek their friendship, give them their daughters in marriage without bride-price, regarding marriage with a Mallam as *sádaka,* pious alms. Such is, the Nupe say, the *cinwa katū,* the Greatness of Learning. To some extent, however, the high reputation of the learned profession is reflected also in the persons of lesser erudition. Learning is, after all, relative. And a Mallam of very inferior scholarship judged by Bida standards, may be revered as a fount of knowledge in a small half-pagan village. These Mallams in the villages are frequently supported by the people and receive annual gifts of crops as *dzanká,* tithe.

The Mallams are, above all, teachers. They teach both children and adults, the former the Koran and the latter 'knowledge'. Every Mallam may, besides, be called in to perform a marriage ceremony or to officiate at a funeral—services for which they are remunerated according to their status and reputation. A few are well-to-do and own land, which is worked by their sons and pupils or, in some cases, by wage-labour. But most Mallams practise, in addition to teaching, some other occupation, which may or may not be associated with their scholarly profession, to supplement the meagre income of a Koran teacher. Some write out and illuminate pages of the Koran, or copy Arabic manuscripts, for sale. You can buy a sheet of this sort, very beautifully illuminated, for 5*d.* on the Bida market; more ambitious scribes would

---

[1] Bida learning has a great reputation even outside Nupe; Mallams from Bida have been given important posts in other countries, and several Bida Koran teachers have established flourishing schools in Ilorin.

[2] One aspect of this spiritual advice is divining, which plays an important part even in such political activities as the election of a high officer of state or the preparation for war.

sell a whole copy of the Koran and receive for it—the work of five months—£1. Students of 'knowledge' eagerly buy these copies and use them in their studies. Other Mallams, again, embroider gowns, make straw hats or saddle-cloths, or do tailoring.

The size and standard of the Koran schools varies as widely as the status and standard of learning of the Mallams. You find 'schools' with two little boys for pupils, and these close relations of the teacher; and you find others—the schools of famous Bida scholars—the classrooms of which (as a rule the *katamba* in the Mallam's house) are crowded with pupils. The teachers are very jealous of the reputation of their school. When I was a regular visitor to Bida Koran schools the Mallam of one which I had not yet visited came to me complaining that I had left out his school, and quoted as reference a Bida Mallam of very high standing who was a special friend of mine. In the large Koran schools the Mallam himself teaches only the adult students of 'knowledge', while the elementary teaching is carried out by his sons or certain advanced pupils. Certain progressive Bida Mallams include the teaching of Hausa and elementary arithmetic in their syllabus, and many adults, traders and other native business men, attend their classes to acquire knowledge so invaluable to their trade.[3] In certain Bida schools you will find young girls being taught together with boys. They come from the families of the nobility, which, conscientious Mohammedans, insist on elementary religious instruction being extended also to women. Girls, however, are only taught the Koran, and do not study 'knowledge'.

Adult students, specially those who study the Koran or 'knowledge' for their edification, following another profession besides, visit the house of the teacher only for their lessons, which take place in the evenings, once or twice a week, or even at longer intervals, according to the leisure which their occupation allows them.[4] Young pupils who live in the neighbourhood attend their

---

[3] The Education Department in Bida has arranged special evening classes for these enterprising Koran school teachers, and gives them also certain practical assistance, for example, by supplying them with blackboards. This scheme of adult education is of considerable value in the spreading of elementary education among that section of the population which has not had the advantage of education in the Government schools.

[4] Students in a Koran school in Kacha, who were canoe-men by profession, attended the school whenever they returned to Kacha from their voyages,

classes daily while living with their family. Pupils whose family live some distance away will stay in the house of the teacher as members of his household.

The teacher of the Koran may not demand special payment for the tuition; according to Mohammedan principles religious instruction must be free—*ebo albarka,* 'for the sake of blessing'. The wealthy Mallam, in fact, scorns all such payments as contrary to the spirit of religion. The poorer Mallam depends on what the family of the pupil offers him as *sádaka,* alms: a penny or twopence every two months, or a bundle of grain (worth 9*d.* or 1*s.*) once a year. Even these small gifts are very irregular; in the school of a Bida Mallam of good reputation, whose pupils numbered thirteen, half of the parents had sent nothing for over a year. Sometimes it happens that a boy's father dies while the boy is still studying, and his relations are unwilling to pay for his education. In this case the Mallam will continue to teach the orphan, let him live in his house and give him food and clothing, again *ebo albarka* only. Koran teachers in the country are worse off than their colleagues in Bida. In Kacha a Mallam who taught Hausa and arithmetic in addition to the Koran and 'knowledge', and who had eight young and fifteen adult students, received no payment from his students except an occasional gift of kola-nuts. If he asked for money, the students would indignantly threaten to leave and to seek another teacher. But both poor and wealthy Mallams receive a final gift from the parents of the student who has completed his studies, either money (in Bida), between 5*s.* and 10*s.,* or (in the village) grain or a goat. The teachers can also obtain a certain indirect remuneration by letting their pupils work for them. Schoolwork does not take up the whole day, nor every day in the week. In their spare time the boys will help in the house or on the farm, or sometimes in the handicrafts which their teachers practise.

The students of 'knowledge' pay nothing for the tuition. But they have studied the Koran with the same Mallam under whom they are now studying 'knowledge'; and they will send their children again to his school, or to the school of his sons. Thus reputations are built up and firm links established between families of Koran teachers and families which patronize their school.

---

interrupting their classes for weeks and months at a time when they were out on a canoe expedition.

There are Mallam families in Bida which have been teaching three generations of the same families. For the sons of famous Mallams will follow the profession of their father. Many also intermarry with other Mallam families. They carry on the reputation for scholarship won by their fathers and families, and thus help to build up the dynasties of Mallams, of which there are many in Bida and Nupe.

As teaching implies so meagre and irregular an income one might ask how it happens that certain Mallams become well-to-do, and even join the wealthy landowning class. These Mallams do not come from the families of the hereditary or office nobility. Although many men of this class study the Koran and 'knowledge', and proudly call themselves Mallams, they do not adopt the teaching profession, but remain amateurs, noble *dilettanti*. Sometimes a Mallam who in the past attained one of the official positions open to Mohammedan scholars has laid the foundation of the wealth of the family. Another has benefited from the close association as the 'guide, philosopher, and friend' of an influential personage—a clientship of more exalted order—and received land and wealth through the help of his patron. It is, for example, customary for all marriage services in the royal family—a most lucrative office—to be held by the Mallam who is attached to the house of the *Shaba;* or at all funeral services of the royal house of the *Liman,* the head of the Mohammedan clergy, will officiate. However, wealthy Mallams are rare. Most Mohammedan scholars are poor, or at least unable to maintain themselves by their religious and educational work alone. But poverty is no impediment to scholarly reputation; nor does it detract from the honour of the profession. In fact, ordinary people will never call in a titled or even wealthy Mallam to perform a marriage or funeral service; they invariably prefer a Mallam of the *tálaka* class. A 'great Mallam is too weighty', they explain; they want a man whom they can offer a small *sádaka* as fee.

Among the Mallams of the town a certain loose economic co-operation exists, which comes into play at all such ceremonial occasions. At large marriage ceremonies or funerals several Mallams may be called in to assist the Mallam who is officiating. They will also divide part of the money which they receive for their services among their other colleagues in the same town quarter. Or the family which celebrates the ceremony will send *sádaka* to all the Mallams in the neighbourhood. This practice of communal benefits does not involve any closer or more formalized co-operation among the Mallams. The wide diversity between them with regard to social status, wealth, and standard of learning forbids any more strongly pronounced appreciation of their commonness beyond that fluid unity embodied in the fact that they all work with their brains, and represent, in a society of peasants, craftsmen, and traders, the intelligentsia. This will become even clearer when we examine the motley rising generation of Mallams.

Koran teaching begins as a rule in early youth, when the child is 6 or even 5 years old. The teaching of the Koran itself is reckoned to take five to ten years. Some pupils learn quicker than others, and in one school I found a boy of 13 already studying 'knowledge', while one of 17 was still worrying his way through the Koran. But on the whole this elementary stage is considered mere routine work which most students can master in the given time. The teaching of 'knowledge', on the other hand, depends entirely on talent and individual inclination. Pupils may be eager enough to try, but will give up later when they discover that 'they have no head for it' (a literal translation of the Nupe phrase). Nor can the time taken by these higher studies be fixed precisely. Ten to fifteen years is an average estimate—at least, after fifteen years' study one is reckoned to have become 'fully a Mallam'. But only prospective teachers will take this advanced course systematically, and continue their study year after year. The *dilettanti* pursue their studies much more irregularly and leisurely, and students of 35 or more may often be seen in the schools of the teachers of 'knowledge'.

The Mallam schools receive pupils from every class and every walk of life. I have compiled some figures to illustrate the social origin of the pupils of Bida Koran schools:

Father's profession	Mallams	Traders	Farmers	Guild-crafts-men	Individual crafts-men	Nobility	Clerks, messengers, &tc.	Total
Studying:								
Koran	49	16	30	6	20	22	8	151
'Knowledge'	28	4	2	..	20	8	10	72

That the sons of Mallams are in a majority is not surprising, nor that individual craftsmen and members of the nobility should come next in number. Of the twenty-eight sons of Mallams who were studying 'knowledge' six were going to adopt a different profession (of messengers, clerks, labourers, or servants to Europeans). Of the forty-four other students of 'knowledge' sixteen were going to become Koran teachers either in Bida or in the villages. These sixteen prospective Mallams included, incidentally, the two farmers' sons. None of the sons of guild-craftsmen took up teaching as a profession: a proof of the strong organization of these 'closed professions'. The large number of farmers who send their boys to Bida Koran schools may appear surprising; and even more so that a certain number of them should take up the study of the Koran professionally (for among the boys who are at present studying the Koran a few are likely to become Koran teachers). One example may serve: a boy of 13, the only son of a farmer, was studying to become a Mallam. He was well aware that at the death of his father the land would be lost to his family. Nevertheless he would not return to farm-work. His father had made him a Mallam, and that was all there was to it. Again and again, in similar cases, I was told: 'We are no longer strong enough to work on the land', or 'After all, is the profession of a Mallam not as good as that of a farmer?' There is no evidence, incidentally, that physical disability, an ailment which might impair their working capacity, is a reason for sending boys to Mallam schools. The choice of the Mallam profession is, in the full sense of the word, a free choice of profession.[5]

The Mallam schools both in Bida and in the peasant districts are steadily increasing. The Nigerian Census mentions over 1,000 Koran schools in Niger Province, most of which are found in Nupe Emirate. I have estimated that Bida town possesses over

---

[5] I had wondered whether there was any relation between the professional choice and the size of the family, whether perhaps in large families a son would be more likely to study for Mallam than in small families, where every member would be needed for farm-work. Then again, I thought it possible that in these days of the breaking-up of the family-unit orphans would be placed more readily in Mallam schools. Neither correlation, however, is true—as is shown in these figures: of 32 students of farming stock 9 were only sons, 10 were one of two sons, 9 had brothers who also studied the Koran, and 4 were orphans.

100 Koran schools, with over 1,000 pupils (out of a population
of 24,000, with 5,000 male children). Kacha has fifteen Koran
schools, Kutigi, a much more primitive and semi-pagan village,
six, of which two already give higher instruction. This spreading
of Mohammedan education leaves no doubt that parents increasingly desire their children to receive the benefits of Mohammedan
learning. We have to accept this as a general trend in modern
Nupe society, not so much towards true education—which few
of the boys will ever attain—as towards the higher social status—
the status of a leisured-class intelligentsia—which the position of
a Mallam, rightly or wrongly, suggests.

Earlier in this book I have referred to the profession of Mallams as one of the mechanisms of social mobility. I have also
called Mohammedan education, by means of which the religion
and, indirectly, the whole spiritual background of the ruling
classes is diffused throughout the country, one of the 'binding
forces' of the Nupe state. Here we have found concrete evidence
to support these statements. Let me summarize the main conclusions which we can draw from the present discussion. First,
the profession of Mallams comprises contrasts of wealth and
rank, which occur nowhere else in the framework of a single
profession. The only common feature is that of a life without
manual work, and of a certain social status raised above that of
the ordinary commoner. Secondly, the Mallam profession is the
only profession which we discovered in Nupe which is not ruled
by the motive of material gains. On the contrary, people will
sacrifice even the security of work on the land for the meagre
and insecure income that goes with the rise in status and the
attainment of the life of the leisured class.

AGE-GRADE ASSOCIATIONS

The Nupe name for age-grade association is *ena gbarúfuži,*
lit. 'society' or 'association of the young men'.[6] Although nearly
every Nupe boy or young man belongs to one or the other age-
grade association, the age-grades are not a compulsory organization. No coercion is used to induce individuals to join the associa-

---

[6] Informants who have picked up a few words of pidgin-English translated
ena as 'company'.

tion, but failure to do so would be regarded as unusual, and under certain circumstances even suspicious. The constitution of the *ena gbarúfuži* is based essentially on the agreement of a group of individuals who, with clear knowledge of the purpose and the rules of the organization, form themselves into an age-grade association. Sociologically, then, our translation of *ena* as association is fully justified.

The description of the age-grade system of Nupe is compli-cated by the large number of variations that occur. There exist, above all, certain essential differences between the age-grade as-sociation in Bida and in the village; we shall, in fact, have to contrast the two throughout this discussion. The rules governing the internal organization of the age-grades are elastic: much more so in Bida than in the village. In the village association, too, minor differences occur, sometimes even between certain lo-cal associations in the same village. Thus, the age-factor itself is not rigidly defined, and the entrance age and age-limits of the different grades vary widely. Nor is the duration of the single age-grade fixed universally or permanently. In the village we find a more rigid arrangement: in Kutigi, for example, all age-grades last six years, in Jebba four years. In Bida the term of the age-grade association varies from four to ten years, and the duration may vary in different grades, in accordance with the wishes of the members.

In the village each grade is represented by one *ena* only, and age-grade associations ascend as a rule *en bloc* from grade to grade. Changes in the membership, so far as they occur, as the *ena* advances to higher grades, take the form of a slight decrease caused by death or emigration. In Bida each grade is represented by a number of associations, and prospective members have the choice of alternative associations. The rules of membership are more flexible in Bida. One may skip a grade—'rest', as the people say—one may start in a higher instead of the bottom grade, or one may leave the association before it advances to the highest grade, even before its term comes to an end. In two villages age-grade associations of which I examined the membership, which was 17 and 18 in the highest grade, had remained almost unchanged through the three grades of which the age-grade asso-ciation is composed. In Bida there is much coming and going. In two *ena,* for example, the highest grade of which numbered 26 and 30 members, respectively, only 7 and 15, respectively, had gone through all three grades, 16 and 10 through two grades, and 3 and 5 had joined the highest grade without having passed through the lower grades.

The most common and, in the eyes of the people, normal type of age-grade association comprises three grades, which are numbered from the top downward: the senior grade is called First Grade, the middle grade, Second, and the junior grade, Third Grade or *ena dzakangíži,* Children's Grade. We shall deal, in what follows, with this most typical three-grade organization. The average age in the senior grade is 20 to 30, in the second 15 to 20, and in the junior grade 10 to 15. The age-limit for membership is about 30. It is interesting to note that the fact of marriage is of no significance—the highest grade comprises both married and unmarried men. The sign that a man is past the age of membership of 'young men societies' is the appearance of the external symptom of manhood, a beard—*za na de nŭkpayi na da ena be à,* 'a man who has a beard no longer joins the association'. In certain small communities the age-grade system may be limited to the two higher grades; in other communities a fourth, junior, grade is added, called *ena wawagíži,* Association of the Small Children. This lowest grade is not taken seriously: it is regarded as mere *dzodzo,* play—of the children-playing-at-adults type—and shares with the other grades only their superficial external characteristics. The junior, third, grade is also in some measure regarded as less serious and significant than the higher grades, and as essentially a preparatory stage. Certain important activities of the higher grades are, as we shall see, of necessity excluded, or reduced to insignificant proportions, in associations which are composed of young boys. In one respect, however, the junior age-grade makes its own specific contribution to the age-grade system; it is the only one which has its counterpart also in the other sex. The highest age-grade, too, possesses certain specific features, in the form of certain age-grade ranks which are not bestowed on members of junior groups.

As *ena* membership is defined by age, and not by generation, it happens occasionally that, in large families, the young men of different generations but of approximately equal age belong to the same *ena,* and that young men of the same generation are members of different age-grade associations. The following genealogical diagram will illustrate a typical case. The letters S, M, and J indicate membership of the senior, middle, and junior agegrade, respectively; FH means family head, and a cross a deceased family member.

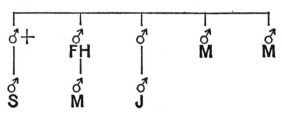

The separation from family and homelife is indeed one of the most characteristic features of the *ena gbarúfuži*. The people attach considerable weight to the fact that the bonds and forms of obligation which are implied in the *ena* are of an entirely different, and specific, nature. Even small boys, the youngest members of the junior *ena,* will tell you with an air of importance that the *ena* has nothing to do with family, home, or parents. The father? 'Yes, we tell him, and we ask him sometimes to help out with money or food for a feast which we arrange. But he has no say in our *ena.*' Fathers will confirm this. In Kutigi parents were quite surprised, and laughed uproariously, when I told them about the titles which had just been distributed in a newly started junior grade; the boys had gone with the times and introduced titles which did not exist in the days of their fathers' *ena*. But for my information the parents would have remained unaware of these changes, which were regarded as a purely 'internal' matter of the age-grade association.

Let us now see how an age-grade association starts its life. We will begin with the Bida *ena*. Here the procedure is the same both in the foundation of a new *ena* and in its promotion to a higher grade. A number of boys or young men who have become well acquainted with one another in various walks of life, possibly when participating in a previous *ena,* decide to form themselves into an age-grade association. They meet in the house of one of them, a group of only six or seven members at first, and discuss how many more members they can muster. Each of the founders of the prospective *ena* then enlists other friends and acquaintances of the same age, till eventually the membership reaches the required number, twenty or twenty-five. The first thing now is to find a 'captain' and a 'president' for the new association, or, in native terminology, an *Etsu* and *Ndakotsu* (lit. Grandfather of the *Etsu*). The *Etsu* is a member of the age-group itself, as a rule one of the original founders, who is elected by the group.[7] The *Ndakotsu* must be of senior age: in the junior grades he will be a member of the next higher grade, and in the senior grade an adult who has 'passed', *go ga,* i.e. already gone through all the grades. Under their *Etsu* the members of the prospective *ena* approach a certain young man whom they regard as a suitable candidate, and request him to accept the position of president in the new association. Every member of the Nupe age-grades is assigned a certain rank which defines his place on the miniature social scale of the age-grade association for the duration of the *ena.* It is the first official duty of the newly elected *Ndakotsu* and *Etsu* to call a general meeting in the house of the *Ndakotsu* at which the distribution of these *ena* ranks is to take place. The elastic rules which govern duration and membership of the Bida *ena* imply also that no fixed rules can be laid down with regard to the time when associations usually start or 'change over' to higher grades. Moreover, in these associations in which only a small nucleus of members may remain faithful to the *ena* throughout its three grades long waits are likely to occur between the termination of one *ena* and the founding of a new association of a higher grade.

In the village the procedure governing the foundation and promotion of the *ena,* although the same in principle, differs in certain significant features from that obtaining in Bida. To begin with, the time when age-grade associations are started and promoted to higher grades is fixed permanently: it falls towards the end of the dry season, an arrangement which gives the new association time to be fairly launched when the agricultural season begins, and ready to undertake the tasks which, in a farming community, fall to the age-grade associations. The enrolment of members for the new *ena* is much less selective and arbitrary. In a small community where most boys of approximately the same age know each other, and normally meet in work or play, there is no need to canvass the new *ena* among friends and acquaintances. Nor is there any special search for captain and president of the

---

[7] Sometimes the captain of the second grade bears a different title, *Sokyara.*

new association. The village associations have, in fact, their *Nda-kotsu* and *Etsu* appointed for them in advance. Shortly before the existing associations are dissolved previous to their reorganization on a higher grade, the outgoing presidents of the different grades appoint, as a last official act of their term of office, one of the members of their group as '*Ndakotsu*-elect' of the next junior group, i.e. the group which, in the new term, will take the place of the outgoing group. The *Ndakotsu*-elect will then take charge of the organization or reorganization of the new *ena,* and also of the appointment of a captain for the new association.

In these age-grade associations which rise *en bloc* to higher grades there is no gap between the termination of the old and the foundation of the new *ena.* The association which is about to be dissolved and promoted stages a last public appearance in a great feast, with music and dancing, to which all friends and relations are invited. A few days later the members of the *ena* meet again for the preliminary discussion in the house of the new *Ndakotsu,* for the distribution of the age-grade ranks which will be assigned to them in the new *ena.* When all ranks have been satisfactorily allotted the group arranges another large festivity, which is to announce publicly its reorganization and to inaugurate the new term. I had the good fortune to be in Kutigi in 1936, the year when the six years' term of the local *ena* came to an end and the general 'change-over' took place. It fell in the middle of March; the last public meeting of the old association was on the 7th of March, the session in the house of the *Ndakotsu* took place five days later, and the inaugurative meeting of the group in its new form as a senior grade on the 2nd of April.

Now, what are the qualifications for the position of a *Ndakotsu* and *Etsu,* and according to what principles are the *ena* ranks distributed? For the election of the *Ndakotsu* a well-established social position, good reputation, intelligence, and also a pleasant nature and, if possible, an open hand, are regarded as essential qualifications. A satisfactory financial position is essential because the *Ndakotsu* will be expected to entertain and to organize parties—and to do it in style. Most of these conditions also apply to the election of the group captain. The members of a newly founded Bida *ena* explained to me: 'We made Mohamadu our *Etsu* because he is a nice fellow. We all like him. He has good connexions; you see he is invited to the court; besides, he has plenty of money, and both his father and his mother are rich. He is also ready to spend it when we have a feast and want drummers and dancers.' On the other hand, a very ambitious young man who had been *Etsu* of an *ena* (of the second grade) and who hoped to be made *Etsu* again in a new, senior, association whose captain was resigning shortly, complained to me that his chances were slight, for he had not much money and could not afford the expenses which he would be expected to meet. It is implied in the nature of these qualifications that the *Etsu* is not always the oldest member in the group. In one *ena* which I analysed the *Etsu* was 20 when the *ena* started, and there were three members older than he. But as a rule he is of higher social position, and often better educated, than the rest of the members. Thus in a Bida *ena* which consisted almost entirely of tailors and embroiderers the captain was a weaver, the son of the Bida guild-head. In another group of a similar composition the captain was an expert cap-maker, who made the expensive, fashionable embroidered caps. And in a group the members of which came mostly from the classes of the nobility, the captain was the son of a late Emir. It has become the fashion for captains of Bida age-grade associations to adopt an additional, allegoric or symbolic, title, which would also give the *ena* its name. Bida associations compete with each other in the invention of high-sounding names, which should evince the refinement and select-ness of the *ena*. Thus one *Etsu* was known as *Etsu Yimani,* 'King Faith', as the *ena* over which he presided prided itself of the piety of its members; another captain called himself *Etsu Hankuri,* 'King Forgiveness', for more or less the same reason; a third *Etsu Turu,* 'King of the Europeans', a title which was meant to bear witness to the fact that this *ena* was organized on 'European lines' (to be explained presently).

The financial qualifications and those of status are of less importance in the village, where inequality of wealth and status are much less strongly marked, although even in the village *ena* the captain may be of a somewhat higher social position than the rest of the members, e.g. the son or brother of a village elder of high rank. The symbolic names of age-grade associations are absent in the village, where age-grade associations are neither as numerous as in Bida nor as interested in advertising their refine-ment and selectness.

The allotment of ranks in a newly founded association of the youngest grade is largely a formality—although the popularity and influence of the young boys among their age-mates will to some extent be taken into account. We have seen that these junior age-grades are generally regarded as representing a preparatory stage rather than a fully fledged *ena*. In the higher grades the distribution of ranks becomes much more serious. Change of rank during the lifetime of the *ena* occurs only when a member dies or withdraws prematurely, especially if he was holding one of the higher *ena* ranks, which must be represented. But when the *ena* terminates and the members form themselves into a new group, a complete reshuffle takes place. As the different grades use largely the same rank-system this redistribution of ranks at the end of an *ena* makes conspicuous the promotion, non-promotion, or degradation—as the case may be. These changes in the holding of *ena* ranks reflect faithfully the success or failure of individual members in the previous association, the capability shown in the performance of group activities, and the popularity enjoyed among comrades and superiors. The eager competition notwithstanding, the task of distributing ranks justly and to everybody's satisfaction does not, as a rule, take very long. I have seen these discussions carried through in one or two afternoons. But then, the general discussion is only a last, formal, step. Mostly, the two leaders of the group have decided the distribution at least of the more important ranks long before the first general meeting. The *Ndakotsu* of a prospective village *ena,* for example, knew a few months before the group was actually called into being exactly whom he was going to invest with the three highest ranks. As a rule the authority of captain and president is sufficiently strong to carry the vote. But instances of disagreement and long fruitless discussions also occur, both in town and village, and sometimes a compromise has to be effected by introducing a special title (with the word *Tsowa* before any rank, equivalent to 'vice-' or 'sub-'), which will satisfy a refractory member without upsetting the arrangement at large. Severe degradation, on the other hand, is rare, as it can be easily circumvented in these associations which are not compulsory, and cannot force members to accept their status. This is a typical instance: A very ambitious and vain young man of Bida who had held high ranks in previous *ena,* but was given a very low rank in a senior grade, resented this treatment as unjust; he could, however, do nothing except to show his disdain by disinteresting himself in the association, and staying away from all their meetings. Actually he never told me of his shameful treatment when we discussed his association with the *ena;* I learned of it only by chance when, examining a certain association, I came across his name on the list of members.

The village *ena* comprises one rank which can be won only in strict competition. This rank carries the title *Sode,* and is bestowed on the best farmer of the group. Sometimes there is also a second farmer's rank, won in the same way for which, rather incongruously, the title *Maiyaki,* 'Minister of War', has been chosen. These ranks are taken only in the highest and middle grade, and are won in open competition at the first of the more important *egbe* occasions of the season, frequently at the *egbe* performed on the farms of the village chief. Traditionally, the title *Sode* ranked next to that of group captain in importance and precedence. To-day it has been degraded to a lower place on the scale of ranks. Of course, neither the title nor the particular qualification for which it is bestowed is recognized in Bida. The rank of *Sode* is also the only rank that may change hands (at least in theory) during the term of the *ena.* Although this happens very rarely (I have not met with any actual instance), all people agree that if at one of the occasions of collective farm-work an appointed *Sode* proved himself to be inferior in skill to another member of the *ena,* he would have to surrender his title.

Age-grade ranks are largely copied from the political rank-system obtaining in the community to which the *ena* belongs. It is not a very exact copy—although the *ena* tends to arrange its ranks according to the order of precedence which they follow in the political hierarchy. In Bida the distinctions between the different classes of political ranks are not observed, and military and civil ranks, office titles and titles of the royal nobility, are bestowed indiscriminately. The village *ena* remains more faithful to the rank-system of the community, and would, for example, adopt its typical, possibly uncommon, titles of elders. But as the membership of the *ena*—especially of the junior grades—may be considerably larger than the number of titled village elders, ranks from outside the traditional rank-system may have to be introduced, preferably from the rank-system of the capital. The younger generation is indeed always ready and eager to adopt such innovations. Rank-systems of heterogeneous nature, and rather arbitrary precedence are the result. However, we must not forget that the rank-systems of many villages are themselves similarly heterogeneous and arbitrary, including Bida titles among its traditional village ranks.

The system of precedence involved in *ena* ranks and grades is taken very seriously, and the rigid rules of etiquette which govern it are enacted with all solemnity. Much of the *ena* business takes place, as we shall see, within the single *ena;* but when members of different grades meet—for example, at family feasts in the house of a member, or at collective farm-work—submissive or condescending behaviour marks their relation towards each other. Members of a junior grade will never dance when members of senior grades are present, except with their special permission and at their request; in collective farm-work the junior grades work at the back of the team, at less important and less conspicuous tasks. Age-grade etiquette is even more emphatic within the individual association. At communal meals the 'subalterns' will wait till their superiors have eaten; at *ena* feasts subaltern and senior ranks will never dance at the same time; when greeting a superior, the age-grade member of lower rank will squat down and bend his head, exactly as prescribed for intercourse between superiors and inferiors in the social scale of 'real life'.

In the village *ena* it is only in general terms that the ranks indicate social position on the rank-scale of the association. In the town *ena* the ranks are sometimes chosen so as to indicate and do justice to the special gifts, or the special social position outside the *ena,* which characterize individual members. In this the organization of the town *ena* reflects the more highly differentiated social structure of urban society. Thus a Bida *ena,* composed largely of illiterate members, assigned to a young man who had been educated in the Government Middle School the title *Naïbi,* a rank of the Mohammedan clergy which can be held only by scholars. The rank-list of another *ena* included the rank *Borotí,* lit. Head of the Bororó, its holder being the son of the late Emir's 'regent-delegate' for the Bororó Fulani. Some Bida age-grade ranks indicate a certain official capacity held by a member in the *ena*. Thus I found a rank *Dzufā* (lit. pocket) bestowed on a young man who acted as 'purser' of the group. All purchases and payments for *ena* purposes were made through him; when, for example, a member decided to give a party for the group he would place his money contribution in the hands of the *Etsu,* who would then hand it over to the 'purser' as the member responsible for financial arrangements. In one *ena* I found the rather curious rank *Mataushe* (Hausa, lit. 'the man who rubs', i.e. 'masseur'), by which name a certain slave or body-servant of the Nupe king was known whose special duty it was to massage the feet of his master. In like manner it was the duty of this 'office holder' in the age-grade association to massage the feet of his *Etsu* at meetings of the group when his master felt tired.

One group of ranks typical of the Bida *ena* deserves special attention, namely the ranks which are organized on 'European lines' and copy, not ranks and offices of Nupe society, but ranks, offices, and even names of Europeans with whom the Nupe had come into contact. Such titles are often amusing and even puzzling. In one *ena* the head of the group was not called *Etsu* but *Gomna Ture,* European Governor. Other ranks in the same *ena* were *Kantoma* (Station Magistrate), *Joji* (District Officer), *Likita* (Doctor); there was also the rank *Dupienne,* derived from the name of Mr. Dupigny, a former Resident of Niger Province, a rank *Borti* (Major Burton), *Mallam Smi* (Mr. Smith, a former Superintendent of Education), and *Jamsi Dogo* (lit. Long James, a title which referred to a former clerk in the Divisional Office); it was, not unnaturally, the lowest title on the rank-list. Another *ena* organized on modern lines was divided into two sections, a 'native' and a 'European' section, the former consisting of Nupe titles, the latter of Europeanized names and ranks, such as *Gomna, Joji, Likita, Rezdet* (Resident), *Kantoma, Misisi* (Mrs.), *Hafissa* (Officer), and *Karamin Joji* (Assistant District Officer). In the normal business of the *ena* these two sections behaved differently, and were bound by different rules of etiquette, native and 'European', which meant that the members of the 'European section' had to greet each other in European fashion, by lifting their caps, and had to eat at a table with fork and spoon. I could not help laughing when these rules were explained to me; but the head of the group pointed out, rather indignantly, that this was the most natural thing in the world; after all, 'a Governor does not eat with his hands'.

The seriousness with which these distinctions of ranks are observed, the realism with which this playing at society *à la Européenne* is enacted, forbids us to treat it merely as a childish and meaningless make-believe. Psychologically, it has the significance of a substitute for thrills and achievements which normal life cannot offer. The inclusion of titles and forms of conduct copied from the British officials in the country is part of that 'realism' which marks age-grade etiquette and precedence: it does justice to the new political order of the society, and partly also to the fact that high social position in present-day native society implies intimacy with the Administration and high British officials. If it were asked why the Bida *ena* chose as symbols for social gradation ranks and offices so far removed from their ordinary life, I should point out that there is less difference than one might assume between the two models which the *ena* could choose—the model of European and the model of native society. To the average Bida man the highest ranks and offices of his own society are no less remote and inaccessible than the office of a District Officer or Governor. We must add that the choice of a particular rank-system for the *ena* is in no way determined by the social stratum from which it is recruited. Bida age-grade associations of *tálaka* and *saraki* alike adopt the highest ranks both of traditional and British society. Only for a small minority—the few *ena* of the ruling class—may these ranks and offices, and the whole exalted social life which they depict, one day become reality. For the large majority they represent an infinitely remote, imaginary social existence.

Here we are led to the wider problem of the relation between the world of pretence built up in the age-grade association and the values of 'real', that is, adult, social life. It can best be approached through a comparison of village and town *ena*. In the village association the social life enacted in the *ena,* and its prototype in adult life, stand in the relation of potentiality and reality. The prototypes of *ena* ranks are all (at least theoretically) within the reach of the individual members. Every one of the young men who have gone through the *ena* may find when he reaches the suitable age that elimination by death or illness of senior relatives has singled him out for the position of a family head, and thus for a *nūsa* rank. Indeed, the promotion which accompanied his age-grade career will serve as an important qualification in the bestowal of the real rank by chiefs and elders. In certain respects all *ena* ranks of the senior grade retain their validity outside the *ena*, and after its expiry. The code of age-grade etiquette expires with the age-grade association. Not so the symbols of age-grade achievement: a man will be called by his rank rather than his name years after the *ena* has come to an end, often even for life—especially if he had held a very high rank. Men who have once been elected as *Etsu* or *Ndakotsu*, even when they are not, or not yet, appointed to a *nūsa* rank, will occupy a position of some distinction in their native village. Not only are they addressed and known by their *ena* titles, but village elders will pay attention to their opinion, and will entrust them with responsible tasks—in the organization of a ceremony, or of important collective work carried on outside the framework of the age-grade association. *Ena* ranks will never be confused with the political ranks of the village; they remain *tici nya ena,* ranks of the age-grade association. But although still only models of the 'real thing', they are 'real' in the sense that they indicate the varying qualification of individuals for access to the final social advancement. In the village *ena,* then, and similarly in the few age-grade associations in Bida which are recruited from the ruling classes, the *ena* rank-system anticipates a future social status; it introduces social concepts, and practises forms of conduct the effectiveness of which will be proved in adult life.

None of this is true of the average Bida association. Although here, again, the ranks attained in the senior grade accompany a man through life, they can claim no significance beyond that accorded to them by the rules of the game. A game indeed it is. These ranks let you enjoy fictitious contacts with a world of rank and power which you can never hope to enter in reality. Their upward trend, their incentive of competition, imply, not preparation or anticipation, but pretence, imitation—'substitution'.

Let us examine now the composition of the age-grade associations with regard to the social groups and strata which they absorb. In small villages a single age-grade association includes the youths of the whole village, and may even go beyond it, including the 'dependencies' of the village, the small *tunga* settlements, or linking a number of *tunga* settlements with one an-

other. In the scattered hamlets round Bida the boys and young
men of three to four hamlets join in a common *ena*. In very
large villages (e.g. Kutigi) the age-grade is subdivided into a
number of associations, each embracing one large, or two or three
small, neighbouring, village *efu*. The age-grade itself, however,
stretches across the whole village community, and the different
associations conform to the same pattern with regard to the length
of the term, and the time and year of the 'change-over' from
grade to grade. In Bida the subdivision goes much farther, and
we find a large number of disconnected associations, which are
no longer co-ordinated or conform to a common pattern. I estimate the number of age-grade associations in Bida at 200. The
individual *ena* is, again, bound up with locality, and includes
boys and young men from the same part of the town. But here
two new factors enter: social differentiation, and divided political
allegiance. The very fact that the Bida *ena* finds its members
among friends and close acquaintances already expresses the
tendency to make it socially homogeneous, and to limit its membership to individuals from the same social stratum, or the same
professional group. *Sarakiži* and *talakaži* never mix in the same
ena. Nor do prosperous traders or Mallams join the same *ena*
as peasants or small craftsmen; nor does, finally, the youth of
the craft-guilds intermingle—glass-workers, blacksmiths, weavers,
all have their separate age-grade associations. The limitation with
regard to locality and close acquaintances is less rigid in the
highest grades than in the junior grades. For as in the course of
years the membership decreases, some members having died,
others having left the *ena* or perhaps the town, it sometimes
becomes necessary to open the membership of the highest grade
to people from other parts of the town. Yet no *ena* would accept
members from beyond the boundary of the town *ekpā*. The
political solidarity of the three dynastic divisions of the town is
thus reflected in, and even, as we shall see, actively supported
by, the age-grade associations of the capital.

Here once more we gain insight into the social significance
of the Nupe age-grade association: it underlines and fosters
the solidarity of the existing social groupings. This means something different in the village and in the town. In the former it
refers to the village community at large, and we find the age-
grade associations stretching across it, and across the large kin-

ship units and 'houses' into which the village society is divided. We can liken the age-grade system to a horizontal plane cutting across the separate structures of the extended families, with their wide base, tapering off to the apex of the one official representative of the family group, the titled elder. The age-grade association must thus counteract all possible separatist tendencies of individual kinship groups and sustain the large-scale integration on which the existence of the village as a social unit depends. In large villages this integrative scheme is in some measure narrowed down, owing to the size of the groups that can be absorbed effectively in a single age-grade association. It assumes, in fact, a somewhat different aspect, in uniting the extended kinship units within themselves—in the form of the large *efu* group —that is, in holding together the widely expanded structure which is to support the apex of a common official representative.

In the town the existing social grouping is created and held together by political and class interests. Here again, the age-grade association fosters the unity of a group which is to submit, in 'real' life, to a common head. But he no longer represents the 'apex' of an organically grown structure; as the *ena* is largely the product of a free, voluntary association, the group loyalty which it fosters is towards the freely chosen leader of a local political faction.

The integrative tendencies in the *ena* are expressed in every one of the typical age-grade activities. In the village they revolve round the three centres of social life; work, recreation, religion. In the Bida *ena* the first is reduced to insignificant dimensions; the second is raised to almost paramount importance; the third remains on the whole unchanged, being only transferred to a different plane—Mohammedan religion.

I have already spoken of the role which the *ena* plays in organizing collective farm-work in the village. We need only add that these activities concern the higher age-grades more than the junior groups, the members of which are not yet skilled farmers. It is commonly agreed that every young man who has gone through the three grades leaves the *ena* a fully trained farmer. Not everyone can become a *Sode;* but the success of the team counts for much. Here the *Ndakotsu* will prove his capability as organizer. He will put his pride into making his team the most efficient—all means being counted as fair. An old man,

still known as *Ndakotsu,* told me how he used to help his group
of workers to defeat all the other teams by means of a charm
which 'made their hoes go twice as fast'.

Under recreational aims we must understand both recreation
in the narrow sense—age-grade feasts and 'parties'—and the
conventional festivities with which the Nupe celebrate kinship
events: naming ceremonies, weddings, and funerals. The recreational activities in the narrow sense concern the individual association; in the celebration of kinship events to which all young
men who are related to the family are invited, members of different grades frequently join. The *Ndakotsu, Etsu,* and also the
members of higher rank are expected to entertain the group in
their houses at fairly regular intervals. There will be food, drinks,
kola-nuts, and often drummers and dancers. In Bida the members of the *ena* meet at least once a month at such parties.
Smaller festivities are attended only by the *ena* members themselves; to the larger meetings, especially those which mark the
beginning and end of the *ena* term, friends and relations of both
sexes are also invited. At one of the festivities with which the
inauguration of the new age-grade term was celebrated in Kutigi
I counted well over a hundred guests.

Let me take you to such an age-grade feast in Bida. It is
held in the courtyard of the house. It starts in the afternoon
or evening and lasts far into the night. The guests sit and squat
in a closely packed circle, leaving a small space in the centre
for drummers and dancers. On one side the host is sitting together with *Etsu* and *Ndakotsu;* as a rule they only sit and
watch the performance; but the guests are ready at every moment
to exchange the role of spectators for that of performers. There
exist special *ena gbarúfuži* dances, performed at these occasions:
they consist of a slow, graceful forward-and-backward movement
of a row of dancers, five or six young men, who dance side
by side, the arms stretched out and the body bent slightly
forward, setting their feet in small, measured, steps. Group follows
group in the dancing arena. Individual dancers leap into the
'arena', and perform a short solo or *pas de deux* of leaps and
cart-wheels which, when executed skilfully, will be greeted with
applause or, when less successful, with good-natured laughter
and banter. There are special drum-signals for every higher *ena*
rank which are sounded when the young men take the scene

and join in the dance. Rich age-grade associations, or certain
high rank-holders in the association, even have special dances
and songs composed for them, which are played, not only at
these meetings of the *ena,* but also whenever the *ena* members
appear elsewhere at a public gathering. Drummers and woman
dancer would walk up to the young man, and the dancer would
recite the song which she composed in his honour.

> Moonlight makes all things good to look at.
> The *maba* bids the townsfolk farewell for the night.
> Give us of thy knowledge,
> Ibrahim Ganleyi,
> Thou grandson of wealth.[8]

Drum-signals and songs are not the only symbols of age-grade
status. At every such festivity one of the drummers or some
self-appointed 'master of ceremonies' will assume the role of
an announcer. He is called *maba;* announcer and jester in one,
he must be witty and have the gift of the gab. He collects
the small gifts of money which guests make to drummers and
dancers; he announces the name and rank of the donor and recites
the virtues of his ancestors and famous relations (impressiveness
counting more than truthfulness), adding such praises or witti-
cisms as seem appropriate to the rank of the donor and the
amount of the gift. We see again how closely Bida age-grade
etiquette follows its model—the Nupe nobility; it copies every
detail of its symbols of status and wealth, even such features
as the specific interpretation of dignity forbidding persons of
high rank to join in the common dance.

It is easily understood that in the village, along with the model,
the copy must be absent also. At the gatherings of the village
ena professional dancers and musicians are rarely summoned.
There is no *maba* and no extolling the feats and virtues of
celebrated ancestors. Age-grades and age-grade ranks 'own' their

---

[8] This song, which was composed by the *zaworo* group of dancers in the
honour of the young man called Ibrahim Ganleyi, was recorded at an age-
grade feast in the house of a well-known Bida Mallam. It begins in the
fashion of all Nupe songs with the quotation of a well-known proverb. The
term *maba* which occurs in the second line is explained in the description
that follows.

special drum-signals and dances; but they are associated with
the group, and not with certain individuals who can afford to
pay for the distinction.

The religious events in which age-grade associations participate
concern all grades. In the pagan ceremony especially the different
grades are allotted different tasks, which imply in varying measure
admission to the esoteric ritual activities. The main religious
ceremony of pagan Nupe, the *gunnu,* makes the *ena* members
the protagonists of its ritual drama and dances. Another ceremony,
which occurs only in the Benu sub-tribe of Kutigi, Enagi, and
Dabbā, the *gani* even dramatizes the age-grade structure itself,
its system of ranks, and the promotion from grade to grade.
The *gani* assigns different ceremonial duties to the different grades,
and involves certain symbolic tests of manhood of progressive
severity which the different age-grades, one after the other, must
undergo. The ceremony can, in fact, be regarded as a ritual
of age-grade initiation. However, I must leave the description
of this ceremony, closely associated though it is with the conception of age-grades, for a future occasion.

Let us turn to the Mohammedan religious ceremonies. At the
celebration of the *Sallah* the age-grade associations play a much
less specific role. They arrange a small festivity in the house of
their group captains on the eve of the *Sallah,* at which—as in all
houses of Bida and Mohammedan Nupe on that evening—a ram
is killed and eaten. On the following morning the various *ena*
of the town meet in the market to join the thousands of people
who will follow the royal procession to the mosque and round
the town walls, and gather later in front of the Emir's house,
listening to drummers and musicians, and watching the display of
the horsemen and the coming and going of the royal guests.

The celebration of the Mohammedan New Year, on the other
hand, called *navū* in Nupe (lit. torches), represents the climax
of the public appearances of the Bida *ena.* The *navū* is essentially
a festival of youth. Its ritual acts, which appear to express,
symbolically, the death and renewal of the year, are carried
out by the young folk of Bida. On the eve of the New Year,
at sunset, all the age-grade associations meet in the houses of
their captains, and then march to the market of their town
quarter, where all the associations of the *ekpā* forgather. They
carry burning torches of grass in their hands, and are clad in

simple, scanty garments. Three long processions, one in each *ekpã,* move slowly through the streets of Bida, down to the arm of the river flowing through that part of the town. The boys sing and dance while they walk, and throw their torches high up in the air, catching them as they fall. Arrived at the river, they take off their garments, and, clad only in a loin-cloth, wade into the water. There is no atmosphere of ritual or ceremony about it; they splash and play in the water, dance, wrestle, sing, and laugh at the clumsiness of those who drop and extinguish their torches. All the time the torch-play goes on; they play with the torches like balls, throwing and catching them. It is a dangerous game: I saw many lucky escapes, and quite a few incidents not so lucky.

Girls and young women, too, go to the river to bathe on the *navũ,* and the sexual attraction adds its stimulus to the general excitement. The *navũ* is, in fact, the only occasion on which I have seen the Nupe indulge in open, undisguised, sexual play. Torches are thrown into the water to light up the spot where girls are bathing naked; boys accost girls in the water, and couples disappear in the dark of the river-banks. But the *navũ* is in more than one respect a period of licence. Indeed, more important than this amorous play is the licence which was extended till about fifteen years ago to all acts of violence and assault that might occur on *navũ* night. And such liberty of action was not limited to acts of violence committed unwittingly, in the course of the torch throwing and playful fighting. The torch processions invariably led to serious organized fights between the three *ena* groups from the three divisions of the town. On their way back from the river one *ena* would ambush another, and try to invade its 'territory'. A fierce fight would ensue, lasting the whole night, fought with torches, sticks, stones, and even formerly (as my older informants maintained) with swords and guns. Serious wounds and loss of eyesight were a common feature of these 'battles of youth', which were fought with all the violence of heated party feuds. For party feuds they were— inspired by the political rivalry that is embodied in the threefold dynastic division of the kingdom. Let us reflect that the *navũ* provides the only occasion at which all the scattered age-grade groups of Bida are united in common action. The unity which they achieve is typical of Bida society—a unity based on partisan-

ship and political factions. The acts of violence committed in
the *navū* fights led the Administration to intervene, and the
fights were forbidden under *Etsu* Bello. Yet the memory is still
vividly alive. Younger and older men who have once participated
in a fight still proudly recount their feats which helped their
side to win. But even young boys, novices at the *navū*, are
aware of the traditional significance of the ceremony. At the
navū of 1936 schoolboys from the Middle School had been
encouraged by their teachers to send, for the first time, an
official contingent to the *navū* procession and to take their place
among the age-grade groups. The boys did not anticipate a
'proper' *navū;* for, as they explained to the director of the school,
if they were to behave according to traditional standards, 'the
yan doka (police) would get nasty'.

Certain important activities and obligations embodied in the
age-grade association outlive the lifetime of the *ena* and accompany the individual through his whole adult life. The celebration of kinship events with the co-operation of age-grade
associations is a first instance. All members of an *ena* are required
to appear at the kinship feasts celebrated in the house of one of
the *ena* members, and this duty applies both to comrades and
ex-comrades. When a man celebrates the naming ceremony of a
new-born child, or the wedding of himself or a close relative,
or when he buries his father or elder brother, he will expect
all his old comrades to come, to bring their congratulations or
condolences, and to join the family guests. The Nupe greatly
appreciate kinship festivities on an imposing scale, with a large—
and generous—attendance. Age-grade loyalty is thus enlisted to
make the festivities a success and to add to the prestige of the
host. The readiness of the ex-members of an *ena* to fulfill these
social obligations towards an old comrade depends, however, on
the rank which he had held in the *ena,* and on the popularity
which he enjoyed among his fellow members. If the age-grade
association is thus designed to contribute to the social prestige
of its ex-members in adult life, this dependence on the goodwill
of one's comrades must, in anticipation, act as an important
controlling influence upon behaviour in the age-grade association
itself.

There exists also a certain clearly formulated code of conduct
which lays down the rules of behaviour for *ena* members, and

which is again valid for life. These rules demand friendliness towards one another, and avoidance of all quarrels; mutual assistance in work (though not with regard to loans); respect towards one's superiors in the group; and respect also for the sanctity of marriage among all fellow members. The significance of this last rule, which applies to brides as well as wives, in age-grade associations the lifetime of which comprises the years when the adolescents first awake to the reality of sex, when they court and finally marry, need not be emphasized especially. Yet only in the village can the rule be regarded as tending to eliminate quarrels and feuds which must disrupt the community. In Bida it is in effect abetting matrimonial laxity outside the small group to which this code applies. The narrow political and class loyalty of the Bida *ena* has thus its counterpart in the no less narrow *esprit de corps* with its qualified respect for matrimonial rights.

In the case of a breach of the age-grade code the culprit is summoned before the *Etsu* and *Ndakotsu*, who have the right to punish him. A first, light offence may entail only a warning. Repeated offences will be punished more severely. If a young man shows himself lazy in *egbe* work or reluctant to fulfil the obligations of collective farm-work, it is regarded as sufficient punishment to order him to work in the back row, among the youngest and most inexperienced *ena* members. In the case of more serious offences the penalty may take the form of social ostracism: the *Etsu* and *Ndakotsu* would rule that no member of the *ena* must attend festivities in the house of the offender. This sentence, I was told, soon brings the culprit to heel; he will kneel down in front of the *Etsu* and ask him for forgiveness, protesting that he would henceforth mend his ways. In certain age-grade associations, especially in Bida, fines are inflicted in the case of grave offences against the *ena* code. Expulsion is never practised, not even as a penalty of the gravest of all age-grade offences—misconduct with the bride or wife of a comrade. However, my inquiries into the occurrence of this offence were invariably answered with a blunt denial. Whether or not it was founded on fact I have no means of deciding. Quite possibly the *esprit de corps* of the *ena* forbade admission of so shameful a charge. The rather too sweeping denial with which my questions

were met makes it appear not unlikely: 'We are like brothers,'
many of my informants said, 'who would steal a brother's wife?'

In one respect, at least, this statement is undoubtedly an exag-
geration. Age-grade comrades are not 'like brothers'. The intimate
relation between age-grade comrades which this simile suggests is
not true to facts. The relationship existing between friends, on
the other hand, is often likened to the relationship between
brothers, and does in certain respects resemble it. But age-grade
comradeship as all informants agreed, is sharply distinguished
from friendship, and the mutual obligations of friendship in no
way coincide with those implied in *ena* membership. The subject
is worth pursuing.

A man (or woman) will never have more than one friend.
The friend may come from a different locality, a different profession, even a different tribe. I have seen friendship between a
Nupe and a Yoruba in Jebba, and between a Kutigi farmer
and a *konú* weaver, between a Bida tailor and a peasant from
Patigi. Only social class remains an effective barrier even in
friendship. Unlike age-grade comrades, friends will help each
other with money. Friends may also exchange their children, that
is, adopt each other's children, and marry them to their own
children—as is also done by men who stand to each other in the
relationship of classificatory brothers. This practice has the aim,
as the people say, 'to increase friendship'. The essential difference
between age-grade fellowship and friendship is thus clear: if the
former fashions sentiments of 'belonging together' on the basis of
similarities in outlook and interest, i.e. similarities involved in
common locality, tribal origin, common occupation, the latter
unites individuals *qua* individuals, in a union which is essentially
new, and initiates rather than follows existing bonds and sentiments.

It remains to discuss the *ena nyentsugízi,* the age-grade associations of the girls, and the relation between the parallel age-
grades of the sexes. I have said already that the girl's *ena*
is limited to the youngest age-grade. As explanation of this
different organization among the girls the people argue there
can be no senior grades among girls, since the approximate age
limit of the junior grade, 15 to 16 years, coincides with marriageable age. Unlike boys, the girls can no longer carry on in the
ena once they are betrothed or married; their duties towards

husband and family cannot be reconciled with age-grade activities. This explanation is borne out by the characteristic relations that unite the parallel *ena* of boys and girls. They both take exactly the same titles; and a boy and a girl who bear the same title enter a special, close, relationship: the boy calls the girl *nna,* mother, and the girl the boy *nda,* father. Girls' and boys' groups meet at the various feasts which age-grade associations arrange. It is the duty of the girls to prepare food and beer, the money being contributed by the boys, and to serve it at the *ena* feast. The *Etsu* of the boy's *ena* presents the girls with kola-nuts. The girls will sing and dance, and the boys will watch, and then, in their turn, the boys will perform before the audience of the girls. They all behave with utmost dignity, and even severity: the *ena* is quite obviously not the place for flirts and amorous play of the kind one can observe between boys and girls who meet in the street or market. The symbolism of the names by which girls and boys address each other—names which are never used by lovers or by husband and wife—emphasizes the 'respectable', non-sexual, nature of this relationship, even to the extent of excluding any reference to legitimate sex relations—marriage. It is supposed to happen occasionally that boys and girls who were brought together in the *ena* marry afterwards. I have not come across an actual case. The relationship between them, while the *ena* lasts, is definitely meant to be in the nature of comradeship, and must never lead to sexual relations. Yet once the girl is married, it may be difficult to maintain this aloofness. The danger of jealousy on the part of the husband, and possibly the temptation of carrying comradeship with the other sex to a more intimate relationship, forbid a continuation of the girls' *ena.* So much for the interpretation of the *ena nyentsugízi* on the lines of the Nupe argument.

But if for women the age-grade career comes to an end with marriage, while for men marriage represents neither a limit nor even a conspicuous grade in the age-grade career, this reflects also the different sociological significance that marriage has for women and men. For women, it is the end of one life and the beginning of another. It means change of home and family bonds, and initiation into new aims and duties. For men, marriage—a first marriage—does not even coincide with the periodical readjustments in the labour-unit, i.e. the release from the *efakó* group which, as we have seen, takes place as a rule when a man has two wives or grown-up children. The social career of the men—achievement of economic independence, promotion to office, and responsible position in the community—only begins to fulfil itself long after their first marriage; that of the women is meant to enter its last phase in marriage. Indeed when the woman claims the right of an independent, continued, social career, she must buy it with the sacrifice of the marriage union.

As regards the institution of the parallel age-grades its practical value seems to be that it prepares the ground for the first experiences of sex relations. Or rather, it aims at circumventing, and dulling, this unsettling first experience. Enabling the sexes to meet in the critical age, between 13 and 16, as it were on neutral ground, openly and respectably, it tends to remove some of the secrecy and unhealthy curiosity that is part of the mental transition from the self-contained existence of early youth to the new awareness of the polarity of sex. Our study of adult sex morality has left no doubt about the restricted effectiveness of this native 'co-educational' scheme. It must fail because it is, like all faulty education, in the nature of a palliative. It breaks the adolescent, we might say, gently, to the moral code of adulthood, but it adopts this code in all its dangerous narrowness and its rigid exclusion of amorous experiments and pre-marital sex relations. If age-grade discipline paves the way for adult sex morality, it does so also with respect to its repressions and inhibitions, and that final sweeping reaction against conventional morality which we could study in the adult life of the Nupe people.

To summarize. The age-grade associations include the adolescent male (and to lesser extent female) population of Nupe from early youth up to the threshold of adulthood. The most vital years in individual development are thus brought under the influence of this institution. We have studied the decisive part which it plays in moulding the personality of its members and in defining their attitude towards tasks and problems which they are to face in adult life. The essence of the institution of age-grades is, then, preparation—a twofold preparation. Its first aspect is the fashioning in the framework of the age-grades of sentiments of solidarity which are to bind the group at large.

This involves an important theoretical problem which has

greatly engaged the attention of modern sociologists and social psychologists, namely, the possibility of transferring co-operation and solidarity achieved in one context of social life to other social contexts.[9] Our data allow us to make the following observation on this point: co-operation and solidarity fashioned in the age-grades appear capable of being transferred to other social contexts because of two conditions which they satisfy. Co-operation and solidarity are not left to grow at random and, as it were, unconsciously; rather they are of a specific, *ad hoc,* type; they clearly formulate their purpose and operate in the sphere of distinct awareness. Moreover, age-grade co-operation is actuated in circumstances of psychologically impressive nature, i.e. in the context of religious experiences. But age-grade integration also admits its own limitation in that it avoids attempting to bridge over the deepest existing social gulfs, of local community and social class.

The second aspect of the preparation embodied in the age-grade system is the training of the adolescent, through discipline and certain concrete activities, in the tasks and duties which await him in adult life, and in the values and incentives which he will have to make his own. In the village this preparation represents a first step towards a final social career; in Bida it mostly implants in the mind of the adolescent values and incentives, as it were, *in abstracto,* without promising equally their fulfilment in later life. It teaches people who will never share in directing the fate of their country to appreciate, and make their own, the motives and values which govern the conduct of those who do. It imparts, if not claims to responsible citizenship, yet its spirit.

THE MEANING OF NUPE LIFE

If we compare Nupe religious teaching with the teaching implied in the age-grade system we find that the two educational institutions supplement each other in many respects and that, between them, they take in the whole field of 'education for citizen-

---

[9] Cf. F. C. Bartlett 1939:43:'A specially interesting question is: if cooperation is established in one respect, when and how far does this help individual members of the groups concerned to cooperate in other respects?'

ship'. The Mallam school offers promotion to one social plane; the age-grade association practises promotion in the framework of a complex scale of steps and grades. The promotion afforded by religious education is 'real', in the sense that it involves social privileges in adult life; that practised in the age-grades is fictitious, even vicarious, and concerns mental readiness rather than concrete achievements. Religious education, finally, creates a loosely organized professional group and at the same time fosters a much wider psychological unity, which embraces the whole of Nupe society, across tribal and class boundaries. The age-grades create an intensive solidarity, but only in a very narrow framework, and give tribal and class boundaries a wide berth. Common to both religious education and the age-grades is the social upward trend, the motive of rise and promotion. This upward trend appears indeed as the paramount motive in Nupe cultural life. If it is possible to reduce a whole culture to a single formula, to a fundamental unitary *ethos,* we find it in this *leitmotif* of Nupe education. No aspect of culture affords closer access to the paramount cultural motives and values. For education not only teaches openly the specific aims and conceptions of life accepted by the society, but reveals them also indirectly, in the motives and conceptions which it utilizes to call forth the desired response.

9 THE SOCIAL CYCLE AND INITIATION AMONG THE MENDE

Kenneth Little

*One of the more famous educational institutions found in tradi-
tional societies is the "bush school" of the so-called "secret
societies" of western Africa (it is not the membership of these
societies that is secret, but rather their programs of education and
initiation for new members). Most accounts of them, however, are
merely sensational and inaccurate, and there are very few first-
hand descriptions. The following chapter, based on anthropological fieldwork among the Mende people of Sierra Leone, in
west Africa, puts the initiation schools, for both boys and girls,
into their full social setting: that of orderly preparation for and
recognition of adulthood and of the transmission of the society's
cultural values from one generation to another.*

A CONVENIENT way of understanding the general structure of
Mende society is to consider the life of the ordinary individual. Each age has its special rôle. There are also *rites de
passage* of varying degrees of significance, at birth itself, at
puberty, at the birth of the first child, at widowhood, and at
death.

INFANCY

Broadly speaking, each important change of status is marked
by a certain amount of training and ritual preparation which
varies according to the sex of the individual. In the earliest
stages, however, there is little distinction between the sexes, either
in training or in their relation to the rest of the community. The

Reprinted from *The Mende of Sierra Leone,* London, Routledge and Kegan
Paul, 1951, pages 113–30, with permission of the author and of the publisher.

arrival of a female child is greeted by the women with greater delight than that of a boy. They say that girls do not forget their mothers in time of need as boys do, and they prefer to train a girl. There is a cry of '*hooyo*' when a boy is born.[1]

A boy or a girl is named according to whether they are the first or a subsequent surviving child; for example, the first girl will be known as Boi. The children who follow her will be named after various ancestors or after important members of the descent group of either parent.[2] Boys are named four, and girls three, days after birth. The woman whose name a girl-child is to bear takes her out in the early morning, faces the sun, spits on the child's face, and says, 'Resemble me in all my ways and deeds, because you are named after me.'[3] The boy's naming is done either by the father, the father's brother, or mother's brother. The boy is known as an infant as *heilopui,* a girl as *nyalui.* Though both may enjoy the considerable affection of the parents, their social significance is very small. Should the infant die, there is no formal and ritual 'crying' for it. The corpse is simply wrapped up in leaves and buried under a banana tree, or in some other place where it is customary to deposit rubbish. The mother sits on the heap of earth that has been dug away and pushes it backwards into the grave.[4]

CHILDHOOD

Children are suckled at the breast until they are about three years old. In addition to their mother's milk, they are fed from the earliest age on pap made out of yam or cassada, and some-

---

[1] This is to inform the menfolk that a future member of the Poro has arrived. "*Hooyo*" is generally used as a cry by initiates of this society.

[2] A boy who is given an ancestral name may be addressed by the term "grandfather" by his relatives to avoid the disrespect of using the ancestor's actual name. If he has his own father's name, the father's brothers will refer to him as "father's namesake."

[3] Names are also given according to the circumstances of the birth. If the mother has lost a previous child, the next arrival may be named in Mende, *Gilo,* in the case of a girl, and *Gibas,* in the case of a boy; meaning, "let this one be saved."

[4] This is done as a way of avoiding the witch spirit which is assumed to have brought about the child's death by entering its body.

times on palm-oil and rice. In general, there is little supervision
of what they eat. They are given food quite irregularly, at the
breast when they cry for it, or when other members of the
household sit down for their own meal. Quite often, food is
forced on them until the stomach is 'hard'. If the mother is ill,
the child is suckled by any female member of the household
who has milk, e.g. by another wife of its father, or by its
grandmother. Children at this early age are carried around on
the mother's back tied to it by a *lappa*. If a girl is the daughter of
a chief, or of people living in a 'civilized' manner, she may be
put into a cotton frock, even as a baby. Usually, however,
children are allowed to crawl, and later, to walk about quite
naked, except for a string with a charm attached to it round
the waist, until they are about six years old. They are usually
washed from head to toe at least once a day, and taught to
relieve themselves in the bush. A girl-child remains in and about
the compound and under the care of other women and older
children of the household, until about six years old. The children
learn to address all adults as 'mother' and 'grandmother', etc.,
according to age, sex, and social status.

Almost from the time she starts to walk a girl-child imitates
the habits of the older children and women in carrying a bowl or
piece of cloth on the head; or she may lend an occasional hand at
pounding the rice. She goes down to the farm with her mother
and helps her to tidy up the field after weeding, or she carries up
water to the men. A boy is more frequently with his father by this
age. He eats with him and starts to imitate the men folk in their
daily activities and in their way of talking.

PUBERTY

A child's proper period of training begins at about the age of
six. A girl may undergo a mock initiation into the Sande society;
in which case she follows the Sande women about in their 'extra-
mural' activities, such as dancing; or she is sent away to relatives
to be 'minded'. The boy, too, may be sent away to a relative,
because the Mende fear that their children will be 'spoiled', if
they remain too long at home. If a girl has already been 'given'
as wife to a chief, she leaves her mother and lives in his compound under the care and instruction of his head wife. If their

parents are educated, or ambitious for them in modern terms, both boys and girls may be sent to live with some person of well-known housewifely qualities; or may be put into the charge of a Creole family in Freetown, usually with the idea of their attending school at the same time. Boys, and a smaller number of girls, are also sent direct into available Mission and Native Administration schools in the Protectorate, soon after this age. The boy who remains at home is circumcized at about the age of 10, and then begins to take some small responsibility in farming matters. He collects firewood for the house and traps small animals for the household pot.

Western education for a boy is approved, nowadays, to an increasing extent, but it is regarded with mixed feelings in the case of a girl. The disadvantage from the point of view of people living tribally is that the girl will probably become lost to them 'socially'. She may contract marriage with a Creole, or a native *pu-mui*,[5] thus foregoing bridewealth; she may be difficult to control on account of her new ideas and habits, and may speak disparagingly of the way her parents dress and behave. On the other hand, there is the possibility of her making a good marriage with a chief, a wealthy trader, or some one in government clerical employment, and being better able, thereby, to help her relatives financially than if she remained on the farm. Generally speaking, most notable persons, such as chiefs, like to have at least one of their daughters 'educated', partly because it adds considerably to prestige to have such a girl about the place. It also helps the making of suitable unions of a dynastic kind. The daughter selected usually becomes the favourite of her father, if she is not so already. She is not expected to go to the farm, and is granted favours and privileges which her sisters do not share.

A girl who is being 'minded' remains with her guardian until she is old enough to complete her initiation in Sande.[6] In the meantime she acts as a personal maid and servant to her guardian. She prepares her bath-water, accompanies her to market, carries her loads, runs messages for her, and does a large part of the household chores. Generally, she is taught how to prepare and

---

[5] *Pu-mui*=white man, i.e. a person who follows European ways, and hence one who would not observe the native custom over marriage.

[6] The popular name by which the Sande society is known is "Bundu."

cook rice and other dishes and, sometimes, how to sew and do crochet work. She is also taught to defer to her elders. She lives entirely as a member of the household concerned and is subject to the same discipline and treatment as other younger members of it. Her guardians are responsible to the local community for her conduct and to her parents for her safe-keeping. Here is a typical nine-year-old girl's day:

A.M.

7.30– 7.45	Awakened and washed her face, arms, and legs.
7.45– 8.00	Greeted the elders and took out pans.
8.00– 8.30	Swept out the veranda and helped to clean up the kitchen, and washed pots and other utensils.
8.30– 9.00	Went out to market to buy food (cassada, etc.).
9.00–11.15	Helped the older women to wash clothes.
11.15–11.45	Helped the oldest member of the household (who is a petty trader) at her stall.

P.M.

11.45–12.5	Ate her midday meal.
12.5 – 2.30	Was given punishment and forced to sit at the stall.
2.30– 4.00	Still at the stall.
4.00– 6.00	Fetched water from a stream outside the town.
6.00– 7.30	Helped in the preparation of the evening meal.
7.30– 8.00	Cleaned pans.
8.00– 9.00	Ate her evening meal.
9.00–10.00	Cleaned the kitchen, put away cooking utensils, and had a bath.
10.00–10.30	Listened to story-telling on the veranda. Went to bed.

Initiation into Sande is at the age of fourteen or fifteen. This, and, for a boy, Poro initiation, is perhaps the most important period in the life of the ordinary Mende person. By this time, a girl may already have been betrothed as a wife and, as such, is receiving periodical presents from her husband. During this stage, she is known as *Sande nya*. She keeps the name she was given at birth until the actual initiation, when she usually takes a fresh name, either of her own choice or to commemorate the circumstances of her career in the society bush. The first girl to be initiated in a particular session is known as *Kema*. The same considerations apply in the case of boys, whom it is a considerable insult thereafter to address other than by their Poro names. Sometimes, however, a Mende girl takes the name of the woman 'minding' her in compliment to the latter. Or, if boys and girls attend a Mission school, they may be baptized and given an English name, the effect of which is to mark them out as Christian and literate persons. Though some prefer to keep their native names, most of those who have attended school, or have been brought into contact with Creole influence, show a strong desire to imitate certain ways of any Creole friends they have. They copy their style of dress, and the girls emulate the fashion of brushing out instead of plaiting the hair, as is the native style.[7] Both sexes learn and use Creole forms of verbal expression[8] in ordinary conversation, and the girls generally make a good deal of effort to be thought *'Creole nyapoisia'*—Creole girls.

This tendency has entered even into the Sande itself. At the end of their period of seclusion, the initiated girls make their customary and ceremonial return to ordinary life. They enter the town in procession wearing their newest clothes, which are not native-style *lappas* and head-ties, but European frocks and high-heeled shoes. Every girl, who can, carries an umbrella.

INITIATION AND THE BUSH SCHOOL

A child's real training begins at initiation, and so the institution is worth studying. Let us consider first the boys who pass through the rites and syllabus of the Poro.

Preparation of the Poro camp. A full Poro session lasts from November, throughout the dry season, until May, and during this period several sets of initiates may be taken. New initiates do not

---

[7] For the sociological implications of all these points see the final chapter of this book. The practice of 'hair-straightening' is followed generally by Negro Americans in the United States, as well as by Negro people in other parts of the New World who have been influenced by the social and æsthetic values of Western culture.

[8] The claim has been made that this Creole medium of communication contains sufficient grammatical structure and vocabulary of its own to merit description as a language. The proponents of this view distinguish, however, between 'Creole', or *Krio,* as specifically developed in the Colony and the 'pidgin' English used by native speakers throughout the length of the West African Coast.

remain in the bush for more than a few weeks, as a rule, and in the case of schoolboys the time may be even shorter. Formerly, individuals might attend in the bush for a course of instruction which lasted several years, but the tendency now, apparently, is to restrict proceedings to little more than the bare requirements of initiation itself. A boy usually enters at puberty, though even younger lads may be taken, and there is nothing to prevent an adult person joining at the same time. The session is inaugurated by the senior members offering a sacrifice in the bush, in order to obtain the favour of the (Poro) spirits. Then a present is taken to the Paramount Chief, requesting his approval and patronage for the forthcoming session. The bush close to the permanent and sacred premises of the society is cleared as a temporary camp (the *kpanduinga*), and huts are put up to accommodate the initiates. There are no rites in connection with this operation and the camp can be moved about quite freely; but so long as the Poro is in session the ground in question is strictly out of bounds to non-members. Women who may be in the neighbourhood must give warning of their approach by clapping their hands. A road is then cut from this place to the town. Tall poles, connected to each other by ropes to which moss is tied, are erected along it, and at the spot where this passage joins the main road, the Poro sign, known as *ndimomoi,* is placed. In the meantime, the parents of the candidates have been preparing food for them.

Entry into the school. On the eve of the session, Poro members meet in their house (*ngafa welei*) in town. It serves as a temporary residence and meeting place, and is a small round house with a mat screening the entrance in place of a door. The Poro men go round the town saying: 'We will dance tonight'. Then the Poro spirit himself is heard leaving the bush. He enters the town, making harsh nasal sounds, like someone groaning. His followers go from house to house taking out those who are to be initiated. The latter are escorted to the bush, and on arriving at the mat which hides its entrance from the road, they are met by an official. He puts a number of questions to which the appropriate answer is always 'Yes'. 'Could you carry water in a basket?', 'Could you uproot a full-grown palm tree with your bare hands?', etc. The officials then make as if to pull the candidate inside. The latter resists, but is drawn in at the third attempt. In the meantime, a great deal of drumming and noise is going on inside. It increases as he enters, and he is welcomed with shouts. He hands over his initiation fee, which consisted traditionally of a leaf of tobacco but is paid, nowadays, in cash, often amounting to as much as several pounds.

The boys, who are now standing in a ring, are greeted by the cry: *'Sokoti.'* They reply: *'Numo.'* This is repeated three times. One of the first sights they see is an official with the spirit's pipe in his hand. This individual does not wear any distinctive costume, but on the various occasions during the initiation period, when the spirit visits the town, he is its impersonator. The pipe is made out of cow horn, or is a curved stick with a hole in it. The pointed end has been pierced, covered with lizard skin, and a hole, through which the performer blows, has been cut through the skin. One horn of this kind is used in connection with initiation, and another kind is used by older members. The harsh nasal sound mentioned above is produced by this instrument. The effect is as if a wooden megaphone has been used. By stationing a number of men in different parts of the bush, each of whom speaks, in turn, through his horn, the effect is created of the spirit 'flying about the bush', as it is explained to non-members.

The marking ceremony. Every boy must be circumcized before he is initiated, but circumcision plays no part in the initiation rite itself. If necessary, the former operation is carried out on the spot before the marks of membership are given. The boys are then given certain marks on their backs, according to the order in which they enter the bush. The first boy is known as *ndoinje;* the second as *lavalie;* the third as *petuja;* and the last as *gbonu.* Each boy is seized in turn by a number of the men. He is stripped naked and his clothes kept to wipe away the blood which flows from the cuts. Then he is thrown roughly on to the ground, and the appropriate marks are made, either by a hook, which raises the skin, or by a razor. If he shows fright, or tries to run away, his head is pushed into a hole which has already been dug for the purpose. During the operation, the 'spirit' plays loudly on his pipe and there is a clapping of hands, which drowns the noise of the boys' cries and prevents them being overheard by passers-by, especially women and children.

The initiation rite and the whole time spent in the bush which follows it symbolize the change of status. The young initiate is supposed to be 'swallowed' by the (Poro) spirit when he enters, and separation from his parents and kinsfolk signifies his death. The marks on his back are evidence of the spirit's teeth. At the end of his time, he is 'delivered' by the spirit and 'reborn'. Thus, the period in the bush marks his transition from boyhood to manhood, and as a result of the experience he emerges a fully fledged member of Mende society. The training he receives is symbolical as well as practical. It inculcates him with the deeper implications as well as the rules of the part he has to play as a man. It aims at teaching him self-discipline, and to rely on himself. He learns how to work co-operatively and to take orders from others.

The training. While in the bush, the boys wear a garment of red netting. They must sleep in the camp, but are allowed out during the daytime, when not undergoing instruction, after the initial ceremony. They carry pipes about with them and utter wild cries to give warning of their approach. As a practical example of their training, the boys are allowed no modern equipment. Their material requirements, including part of their food, must be provided by themselves. They start by lighting a fire when darkness falls, and for the first night special songs are sung and no one is allowed to sleep. The next morning, the work is shared out, after the boys have been sorted out for training in terms of groups of the same size. The first boy who entered delegates the tasks. The second helps to make the spirit's pipes. The third is to sweep out the camp every morning. The fourth is to boil water for the elders any time it is required.

The boys are expected to bear hardship without complaint and to grow accustomed to it. They sleep at night on a bed of sticks under covering clothes which have been soaked in water, and they remain out of doors, if it rains. The singing and drumming lasts until one or two o'clock in the morning and the boys are awakened again at dawn. They are expected to get up and sing any time they are called. According to some accounts, training in hardihood also includes a certain amount of punishment play which is administered by the elders. Impossible requests are made jokingly to the boys as an excuse for inflicting pain on them and no crying is allowed. Sometimes, too, it is alleged, the boys are encouraged to steal food from neighbouring

farms during the night-time, and to bring the spoils to the *Sowa*
(head official) in the morning. The accusation of cruelty is
generally denied, but other Poro members admit that a certain
amount of stealing is carried out by the boys. They claim that
it is severely punished, if detected, and is usually the result of
some of the boys, whose parents are poor, going short of supplies
from their homes. Occasionally, boys whose relatives cannot afford
the fees demanded, work their way by doing jobs during the
daytime on neighbouring farms. The money they earn goes to
the officials.

In general, the training provided varies according to the length
of time the boys are able to remain in the bush. It may include a
certain amount of native law and custom, exemplified by the holding of mock courts and trials, in which the boys enact the rôles of
their elders. Boys who can afford to stay for a length of time learn
a good deal about native crafts as well as the ordinary duties of a
grown man, such as 'brushing' and other farming operations, and
cleaning roads. Individual specialists at making raffia clothes,
basketry, nets, etc., sometimes go into the bush with the boys and
help them to become proficient in the particular craft they choose.
Bridge-building, the making and setting of traps for animals and
fish, are also taught. On the social side, the boys learn drumming
and to sing the special Poro songs. They practise somersaults and
acrobatics, and altogether their experiences produce a strong sense
of comradeship.[9]

The parents of the boys are expected to 'feed' the spirit, so long
as their sons are in the bush. They give rice to an old member
who carries it over to the camp. The basin is brought back
clean, having been wiped with raffia. The spirit is supposed to
have licked it clean. Another trick, performed to show the spirit's
mysterious power, is the building of his house, the *ngafa-welei*.
Some time in advance, the initiates erect a light structure of
sticks and daub it over with mud. A canopy for a roof is made

---

[9] The drumming and dancing of the Poro boys can be heard throughout
the dry season in such songs as the following: *Oh, gbenjiwaa leinga-oh!*
(The large pot is cooking-oh!); *Gbengben nyɛkɛ ndoli nya ngotua kpu
kɔwoma!* (The enticing waists of the women have sent me crazy!); *Pɔi
lapo a gongo mɛɛ ganu ma, gomgo a fee!* (When the Poro boy meets grass
in a corner, he passes it by as quickly as a squirrel!, i.e. he does not clean
it out).

and thatch is cleverly tied to it. The walls are whitewashed and the house is ready. Then the spirit goes down to the town and announces that his own house has been burned; he proposes to build a new one within an hour. At the appointed time, the 'pre-fabricated' house is carried out to a conspicuous place and is planted over a pit, wherein the spirit sits, playing on his pipe. Non-members are then invited to come out and see the house and to wonder at this example of the spirit's skill.

The initiation rites. The process of initiation is completed by means of three separate ceremonies, known respectively as *Nda-hitie, Kpowa-mbei,* and *Kpia.* The opening rite is prefaced by a visit of the spirit to the town. He is accompanied by both old and new members. They dance there and return to the bush where the ceremony is performed, and the first 'warning' is given to the boys. The contributions of food which have been provided by the parents are brought forward, i.e. rice, fowls, and one bottle of palm-oil per head. A fowl is seized, its head placed on a large stone and severed by another stone. It is then thrown to the members. All the fowls are killed in a similar way. While the head is being severed, an official says, 'Sokoti', to which the expected reply is given. This is repeated over each fowl in turn, and the ceremony is a warning to the boys to expect the same kind of treatment, if they divulge any Poro secrets to a non-member. Everyone agrees to accept and abide by the warning. Food is then cooked and eaten, and when the feast is over the crowd returns to the camp.

This marks the first ceremonial stage in the boys' initiation, and a similar rite is enacted about a week later. This is *Kpowa-mbei,* the literal meaning of which is 'non-members' rice'. The people in the town cook rice, and this time the smaller boys collect it from outside the bush. The spirit pays another visit to the town, and nets are spread over the house to catch him. He sounds his pipe to indicate his presence there, and immediately afterwards a second pipe is heard from the bush, suggesting that he has flown away. His interpreter leaves quietly in the crowd. The Poro group then returns to the sacred bush, and the ceremony proceeds.

The completion, or 'pulling' of the Poro (*Kpia*), is prefaced by a rite known as *Ngafa gohu lewe lei* (hitting the spirit's belly). The spirit is said to be reluctant to deliver the boys he has eaten and to whom he is expected to give birth, one by one. Force has therefore to be used upon him, and members strike him in the stomach.

The day before this is a busy one. Further contributions of food are collected. Everything used by the boys during their novitiate must be destroyed, so as not to be seen by the women. Their clothes and rags are packed into a large hamper, which will represent the spirit's belly. As night approaches, old members flock in from all sides, and at about 9 P.M. a large dance is staged in the town. At first, only the Poro spirit and the men take part, but after a while the spirit goes to rest in his house and women freely join in the dance, which goes on until daybreak.

For the initiates, however, this is a night of fear. They have been warned to keep awake lest they dream of the spirit. This would cause them to die in their sleep, and the idea is impressed upon them throughout the day. Their parents send them kola-nuts to sustain them, and a large quantity of rice is eaten in order to ward off sleep. Then, at about 4 A.M., the *ngafa gohu lewe lei* begins. Like a woman in labour the spirit groans and sighs mournfully. His interpreter explains that the spirit is giving birth. The women clap their hands and the men reproach him for detaining their children so long. They threaten to beat him out of the town, unless he delivers them immediately, and pretend to be angry with him. Then, the hamper is dragged about while others belabour it with clubs. At each blow given, the spirit moans and leans against various objects, such as banana and paw-paw trees. Anything he rests against is pulled down by the men with large wooden hooks. Roads are blocked with branches of trees and a good deal of damage may be done to plantations around the town.

At dawn, however, the spirit takes a road out of the town and stops playing. He is said, according to one version, to have flown off into the depth of the forest to feed on the giant crabs of the forest lakes and will be away for a year. Before going, he asks for a new name to be given to him. Sometimes nets are spread around the bush the next morning to show the way he has climbed off into the sky.

As soon as the spirit is gone, the boys are hurried into the *kameihun* (the sacred part of the Poro bush) and everything in the temporary camp, including its huts, is burned on the spot. This means that the 'pulling' of the Poro—the happiest and long awaited day in the life of the initiates—has begun in earnest. Each boy is now told the final secrets he has to learn about the society, and he takes his final vow of secrecy. The boys are lined up in a semi-circle at the stones in the *palihun* (the deepest part of the bush) round the *Sowa,* or head official, and the *Maɔle.* (The *Maɔle* is the only woman official of the Poro and serves the boys as a matron.) Moss and thread are wound round the boys' toes, so that they are all tied together in a continuous chain. On their heads they wear caps of moss and leaves of the umbrella tree.

The *Maɔle* stands in the middle, facing the sacred stones. She invokes the spirits of the society on their behalf, and prays that each new member may be as strongly attached to the society as the thread and moss which now bind them together. She asks that they may be productive of many children when they have wives. Prayers to the ancestral spirits on this occasion are addressed to former leaders of the society, not, of course, to the ancestors of the individual offering them. The method of communication, how-ever, is the same as the general one, i.e. the ancestors are called in order of seniority, beginning with the oldest and finishing with the one who has died most recently. The prayers conclude with a general supplication. Thus: 'Father Siaffa, let it reach you; let it reach to Kanga; let it reach (lit. "be laid down") to the head, the great one (i.e. God). This is what *Leve* (an old name for God) brought down (showed us to do) long ago. These children, whom we are "pulling" from the Poro today, let nothing harm them; let them not fall from palm trees; make their bodies strong; give them wisdom to look after their children; let them hold themselves in a good way; let them show themselves to be men!'

As the *Maɔle* speaks, she dips a white fowl into a medicine, composed of leaves and water, and sprinkles the boys with it. Each boy holds out his tongue, in turn, and the *Maɔle* places some grains of rice on it in order to test his future. Holding up the fowl, she says: 'If this boy has ill-fortune before him, do not pick the grains.' (N.B. The fowl used has been starved of food since the previous evening.)

The chicken is then killed, as in the previous ceremonies, by severing its neck with a stone, and the boys are sprinkled with its blood. At the order to rise, they jump up joyfully, and cut away and throw behind them the moss and thread which bound them. They are now full members of the society; but their heads must be shaved bare of boyish hair. While this is being done, the *Maɔbɔlɛ* prepares the ceremonial meal. When it is ready, the *Sowa* rolls the rice, chicken flesh, and palm-oil prepared into lumps, placing each piece on the *Maɔbɔlɛ*'s foot. Then, one by one the initiates bend down with their hands behind their backs to take the food. She raises her foot three times to the boy's mouth, saying, *'Sokoti'*, to which he replies, *'Numo'*. At the fourth time, he picks up the lump of food with his mouth and while he chews it the ceremony of swearing him in takes place. He is told that he will be choked by the rice if he reveals any society secrets.

When this is over, the initiates are given a general ablution with the remaining medicine before being taken to a stream for bathing. Each boy is seized in turn, one man holding his feet and another his neck, and he is lowered into the water. A fowl is demanded from the boy's father and he is kept there until it arrives. This is repeated four times and then the boy is given his new set of clothes. The boys dress in these and wear a head-tie over their shaven heads. The latter signifies that their heads have been broken by the spirit and are in process of healing. A further aspect of their re-birth is the new name they acquire and which is a mark of their entrance into manhood.

Completion of the Poro school. When everyone is ready, the boys then march in procession to the town under a large country cloth. Their bodies have been smeared with burned palm-oil to give them a particularly fresh appearance. Parents, kinsfolk, and well-wishers come out to meet them, and the boys are led to the town *barri,* which has been specially prepared to lodge them. Gifts are brought out to them, and they remain there for four days, feasting heartily. Before they are finally discharged on the fourth day, as many pots of palm-wine as there are boys are taken into the *kameihun* for the farewell. The wine is supposed to be exclusively for the *Sowa* and *Maɔbɔlɛ,* but thirsty elders also flock in for refreshment. As the *Maɔbɔlɛ* takes up a pot of wine, the initiate who has contributed it, comes forward and kneels, facing the stones. The *Maɔbɔlɛ* prays for him, a small libation is poured on to the ground, and the *Sowa* pulls off the head-tie. The initiation of the new member is now entirely complete, and when all have been finally dealt with in this way, the Poro session itself is declared over.

In former times, should any of the boys die during the session, it was the custom to bury them secretly in the bush, and the parents were not informed officially until the session was over. Then, one of the Poro elders would go round to the mother's house and break a pot in front of her, saying: 'Of the pots you asked us to build, we are sorry to say that yours was broken.' There would be no 'crying' for the lad—the usual mourning custom—'because the mourners might breathe in some kind of disease'. Nowadays, any such deaths are reported and officially investigated.

INITIATION IN THE SANDE

In the case of Sande initiation a shorter description must suffice. Like the Poro society, the Sande is under the control of a number of senior officials, consisting of older women, who have attained the higher grade. These senior women are distinguished by the white head-tie they wear in public, and they are known as *Sowoisia* (pl. of *Sowo*). It is a status that must be achieved: that is to say, no initiate can proceed to the higher rank without undergoing a further period of training. This applies even to the daughter of a Sande leader, though as the latter's heiress she has the advantage of the various secret medicines. The principal official is the *Majo*.

The Sande is convened for initiation purposes about the same time as the Poro, but in a less formal way. Individual Sande women make themselves responsible for the institution and develop what might be described as a personal connection with various households and compounds within the local community. This means, in effect, that there may be as many as five separate Sande 'schools' within the same town. Occasionally, a fresh Sande group is started by some woman who is popular in the town. She must, of course, possess the necessary seniority and qualifications for the task. Quite often, the prelude is a dream in which the woman concerned learns of the whereabouts of certain important herbs and thus receives a 'call' to the work.

These individual Sande groups compete with each other, to some extent, for public patronage. Some enjoy a better reputation for the training they offer than others. The head woman, or *Majo,* of each has other senior women helping her with the 'curriculum', and the number of girls taken depends both on local support and the number of staff available for the purpose.[10] The total enrolment, however, is rarely more than thirty and, sometimes, is no more than half a dozen.

A girl, and even an adult woman, is admitted into the initiation school at any age. A girl who is as yet uninitiated is known as *gboa.* Age is estimated according to size, and after the girls have been divided up in this way they live in separate compartments of the bush. In addition to the initiates and women in charge, the ordinary session or 'school' includes a number of 'first grade' members who have re-entered the bush in order to take a higher degree and to qualify for the extra privileges that go with it. The session is convened by means of a circular sent round in the form of a small piece of tobacco—*sokolo.* This is a token of the head woman's hand in delivering any important messages. Fees, which may take the form of money, cloth, or other commodities, are also due at this time.

The aim of the Sande is much the same as that of the Poro school. It is to educate for the accepted pattern of life; and its methods, also, are symbolical in part. The girls are taught to be hard working and modest in their behaviour, particularly towards older people, and omissions in this respect are severely punished. As part of the training, their duties are to attend the senior members, fetching water and warming baths for them, etc. The girls themselves are allowed only cold water. They are expected to arise early in the morning, at the second crowing, and to greet all women of the higher ranks with a song, before proceeding on the domestic and other duties of the day. While in the bush, they are smeared heavily with clay and wear it on their faces and bodies for some time afterwards. This is a form of beauty treatment.

The period of seclusion may last up to 3 months, but nowadays it is usually much shorter. Prior to the final ceremony itself, the girls are allowed to move about in public, but under the supervision of one of their elders. The most important ceremonies are

---

[10] As this and succeeding paragraphs indicate, there is a fairly close similarity between the Sande school and the European type of 'finishing school'.

performed, in fact, immediately on entry. The first girl to be initiated is announced, and completion of the rite is celebrated by loud and joyful singing and the beating of drums, there being a special song for this moment. The *Majo* then sends back a piece of tobacco to the girl's parents as an official certification. The first girl, who is known henceforward as Kema, acts as head over the other girls for the remainder of the session.

During this early period of confinement great care is taken to keep the girls out of the sight of the rest of the community, and of men, in particular. Water and other necessities are brought into the bush by one of the older women until the wound, caused by excision of the clitoris, has healed. As the other ceremonies follow, the ban is gradually relaxed; but the girls must take a cloth out with them to conceal their heads if they meet anyone on the public road. Gradually, they appear more and more in public and pay an official visit to the chief and other big men, dressed in woollen embroidered jackets and woollen coloured caps. From the latter they receive small 'dashes' for their dancing.

In the meantime, the women taking higher grades have also completed their own appropriate ceremonies. The day on which the newly graduated members return to daily life is one of great rejoicing, which parents and relatives and all concerned share and celebrate. This also marks the final transition of the girls into full womanhood. They move in procession from their temporary camp, headed by the officials. The whole row of girls is covered by a canopy of large, good-quality country cloths which are held high over them by parents and older members of the society. In the old days, the girls would have been profusely decorated with jewelry and smothered in oil to make their skin glisten. Nowadays, as already mentioned, it is a point of honour for a mother to turn out her daughter in the latest modern style. Alongside the procession dance various 'spirits' of the society impersonated by officials wearing masks. When the town is reached the girls remain for a time in the town *barri* receiving the gifts which their friends and suitors bring them. Afterwards, each girl goes to her mother's house where a large chair has been placed like a throne for her, and there she sits in state for a time in all her finery.

The recreational activities of the Sande school are even more

extensive than those of the Poro. Songs and dances learned in
the bush are repeated and sung on all major occasions in the
social and ceremonial life of the people. This largely explains,
no doubt, the popularity of the institution itself. It is clear that
a very marked spirit of comradeship among the women is engendered and passed on through its medium. Nor should the
economic side be overlooked. Senior Sande women rely for a
substantial part of their personal income on the perquisites gained
from initiates and from fees and fines rendered by other individuals requiring the offices of the society. Moreover, the fact
that a girl's initiation is important to the whole community means
that the families concerned have a special incentive to earn
extra money. Cash is required to secure the material necessaries,
including food and cloth, which are essential if her relatives'
prestige is to be upheld.

The net result of the latter point is that the expense of sending
a girl through Sande is relatively large, and this in turn affects
the question of bridewealth. Alldridge (1901) says that in 1901
the entrance fee was a bushel of rice, a fowl, a gallon of palm-
oil, a barrel of rum, and a 'head' of money at £3. This would
suggest that the cost in those days was at least as high as it is
today. Expenditure varies, of course, from district to district
and is probably much greater in the larger towns where the
social requirements are higher and where food, which is home-
grown elsewhere, has to be purchased. There is also considerable
variation in outlay on the part of parents, relatives, and prospective husbands. The items to be considered, in addition to food
and clothes, include bush equipment, such as mats, enamel ware,
etc., as well as subscriptions to the *Majo* and other officials.
A rough estimate of the total budget, which was taken from one
of the more rural areas, amounted to some £4 7s.[11] An estimate

---

[11] Detailed particulars, in terms of the individual ceremonies, were as follows:

Mbele gbia hani (this is the initiation fee which is handed over to the
officials for looking after the girl). It included 5s. to the Sande 'spirit'; 1s.
to the *Ligbe,* another official, and one mat at 3d.

Sowo vewui ('rice for the head official'). This consisted of a daily ration
of 4d. of rice; 2d. of palm-oil; 3d. of fish 2d. of condiments. It is cooked
for each girl entering the bush and is regarded also as a small pot for the

made in a more urban part of the country amounted to some £7.

But the Sande differs somewhat from the Poro in being fairly adaptive to the march of time. The traditional costume is indeed worn in the bush, but the girls return to ordinary life dressed in the most up-to-date Creole fashions. Nor does the Sande scruple to advertise itself and the services it offers. The mock initiation of small girls of four or five years old with the object of getting them 'interested' is an instance of this. In general, there is a readiness to keep up with the times, even to the extent of compromising with traditional rites which are repugnant to modern ideas. It is claimed, for example, that the practice of excising the clitoris in initiation has been replaced by a small incision. It is equally significant that in certain areas of Mendeland, the Sande leaders have been willing to include educational experimentation in the customary programme. Under the supervision of a Government Medical Officer, girls, already trained in modern methods of mothercraft and hygiene, have been allowed to take part in the training in the Sande bush (see Margai 1948).

Sowo. On this basis, over a period of two months, it would amount to £2 15*s.*

Ndegbe lewe, or *Kpowa gowo wuilei* ('the gathering of the herbs'). The food costing about 1*s.* goes in this case to the officials.

Ndahitie ('quite fit'). This is the principal ceremony. After it has been performed, the girls are said to have graduated, and they can be seen in public. The cost of food in this case amounted to some 7*s.*, and in addition there was a small present for the *Sowo*.

Gumihun. This is performed outside the town and behind the houses where the girls spend the night prior to the final washing. One bottle of English wine was provided at 4*s.* 6*d.*, and there were various small presents for the Sande officials.

Bush equipment consisted of one second-hand cloth, two second-hand head-ties, and one new mat at a cost of some 9*s.*

10 THE AIMS AND METHODS OF SOCIALIZATION IN SILWA

Hamed Ammar

The previous chapters have dealt with education in traditionally pre-literate societies. This chapter is concerned with education in a community in a large literate society that is part of a world religious system: a Muslim village of Upper Egypt. It is taken from the author's book Growing Up in an Egyptian Village *(1966), and summarizes much of the detail presented in its earlier chapters that cannot be included in the present collection. The author discusses both the formal and informal content and methods of this education, and also its underlying principles, the most important of which is to instill an attitude of obedience and respect for ordered authority, to one's elders and parents, to the rules of one's culture, and, in this strongly Muslim society, to God.*

IN THIS CHAPTER it is intended to outline the procedures and methods that are adopted in this community to inculcate the norms that transform the child, who is relatively peripheral, into the adult who is the central link in village social life. The transition can be considered, as Fortes puts it, as one 'from an economically passive burden into a producer, from a biological unit into a social personality, irretrievably cast in the habits, disposition, and notions characteristic of his culture' (1938:6). Fortes has also provided the writer with certain insight in evaluating the learning process as a by-product of the cultural routine, a phenomenon which obtains in the village community. It is obvious that in Silwa the education of children is not surrounded, as in some primitive societies, with ceremonies of initiation, elaborate ritual, or narration of totemic myths. Learning accrues mainly

Reprinted from *Growing Up in an Egyptian Village: Silwa, Province of Aswan,* New York, Octagon Books, 1966, Chapter 6, with permission of the author and the publisher.

through children's observing, imitating and assisting their adults in their everyday activities. For the villagers express the educational process through emphasizing life and time as the most important educational agencies which mould and influence the character, and provide the experience. The difference between an adult and a child is, on the whole, quantitative rather than qualitative. The former knows and thus conforms to the cultural norms, while the latter does not. The commonly used word is not the classical word 'tifl' (infant) but another word which is also classical but literally means 'ignorant' (jahil)—and thus identifies ignorance with childhood. It is because of this ignorance of expected skills, norms and attitudes that the children are considered inferior to the adult, and the younger as subservient to the elder.

Here socialization is to include its two aspects of technical training and cultural or regulatory training. In Chapter I it was shown how a boy or a girl is progressively introduced to the economic pursuits of adults, and what skills were expected of them at successive stages of their growth. It was also emphasized how the child was expected to take over from his father or his elder brother (or mother or elder sister) those tasks which he or she is capable of doing. The child must work for his family as a necessary requisite to enjoying their protection. This is made explicit to children by parents who, on seeing their negligent children enjoying their food, would rebuke them by saying, 'Yes, you only know how to eat and drink', or 'You know how to increase the size of your buttocks'. There is nothing to add here concerning technical training, and further reference will be made in connection with its relation to cultural training. The lack of mastery in skills required from boys at a particular age is attributed to inefficient training by the parents. Once in the fields I heard a father blaming his son for his inability to get the right fodder for the cow by saying, 'The fault is not yours; it is the fault of him who has brought you up'.

The process of growing up is envisaged as a way of disciplining the child to conform to the adults' standards, and to comply with what their elders expect them to do, thus acquiring the qualities of being polite—'muaddab'. In adult eyes, the period of childhood is a nuisance, and childhood activities, especially play, are a waste of time. The 'giving of adab' to children is

the guarantee of the survival of the social structure, with its
patrilineal bias and respect relationships, especially filial piety,
which is sanctioned by the Koranic injunctions. To become
'muaddab' is the ideal set up by parents for their children, and
the adherence to which is constantly impressed upon them. The
ideal, although emphasizing subservience and obedience of the
children to their parents, is actually extended to include the
whole range of children's activities for which their elders are
responsible. The adult sense of keenness to bring their children
to realize this ideal can be traced in parents' prayers that God
might not make their children disobedient or cause them shame.
One of the most effective insults to a boy or a girl is the provoking
remark that he or she has no people to discipline him or her.
'She is a divorced girl' or 'unrestrained'; or for a boy, 'he is a
pushing boy' (literally 'ascending'). Such comments are addressed to young persons who show no respect to people of
their parents' age or who transgress the limits of behaviour
expected from their age or sex group, e.g. a boy walking through
a gathering of men, a married man insulting his father, a girl
shouting from the roof of the house while fetching fuel, or a girl
caught entering the guest house.[1]

The acquiring of the procedures of 'adab', which incorporate
the prescribed standards of behaviour, has also a religious sanction
behind it from the prophetic tradition. It is related that the
Prophet said, 'God has disciplined me, and has perfected my
discipline'. The word 'muaddab' is applied to a child who def-
aecates outside the house at the age of three or four, and goes
further and further away from the house as he grows older.
After the age of ten, for instance, he is not considered 'muaddab'
unless he covers his genitals while urinating. A boy of fourteen to
sixteen would be 'muaddab' if he played in the evenings only,
and still better, if he did not play games at all. Boys and girls become 'muaddab' if they do not mix in play after the age of eleven
or twelve. After the age of twelve, a girl would be considered
'muaddab' if she drops her glance and keeps clear of male
gatherings, and when she becomes older, covers part of her face
if she is passing by a group of men. A boy is 'muaddab' if he
recognizes that he should sit in the back row on going to the

[1] Use of the guest house is restricted to males.

mosque. As Mahmoud put it, a disciplined boy or girl is one who knows when and where to sit and stand, where and when to put his or her feet and thus become 'Ibn halal' (literally 'heir to the permissible'). Ali, on the other hand, expressed the importance of 'giving adab' to children by saying that it is believed that one of the signs of the end of this world will be when discipline and modesty (adab wa haya) disappear from the acts and deeds of the people.

The keynote to the educational process is the eagerness of the adults to create a docile attitude in their children and thus make them acquire filial piety.[2] The children readily accept the authority of their seniors, whether in work or play, and they endeavour to avoid their anger. This ready acceptance of the authority of those older than the child is epitomized in the axiom: 'He who is one day older than you, is in fact wiser by one year', which is a common saying often repeated by adolescent boys and girls. A child of twelve told me that it was always better to avoid the outbursts of one's elders: one of their curses might receive a hearing from God.

The ideal norm of 'adab' is a value which also has its religious sanction, as a pious son (ibn salih) is synonymous with 'muaddab'. Such a value does not only include the child's economic services and his observance of the expected social behaviour, but also implies a pattern of reciprocity between child and family. A father who neglects the care of his 'polite' children may be frequently exposed to illness, failure of crop, or death of cattle. Moreover, a family that infringes on the moral and religious code may consequently have sickly children. This connection between the moral values and the welfare of the family could be illustrated by the children's swearing by their parents' life and honour.[3] One also hears from the villagers that a loss of a son, or a camel, or sudden illness, is caused by the dealing of the inflicted person in usury, his swearing untruthfully by the name of Allah or his children, his giving false evidence in court, or spreading malicious

---

[2] M. Fortes maintains that filial piety, in patrilineal societies, is a value counteracting the suppressed antagonism between father and son, and mother and daughter. Fortes 1949:347.

[3] A father may swear "by the neck" of his son, where life is supposed to be located.

gossip. It is clear that the welfare of the family members, children as well as adults, is contingent on some basic reciprocal relations fused with moral and religious sanctions.

Besides learning from their parents and elders, children also learn through their association with slightly older boys and girls (by three or four years but certainly not more than five or six years) who usually assume the role of leadership or teachers in work or play. As in Tale society, every pupil becomes, in some situation, a teacher for others.

It must be noted, however, that the behaviour pattern and motivation in the learning situation where adults are involved are different from those of the age-group learning situation. In the former, subservience, respect, and fear are expected, while in the latter rivalry and reciprocity on equal terms are the norms. If the child does not come up to adult expectation, it is because 'it deliberately twists its neck which should be straightened by a slap'. Discipline and compulsion are the means for enforcing conformity and 'adab' on children by their elders. On the other hand, amongst the age groups, mocking, ridiculing, and scoffing at those who do not reach the expected level of maturity are the pressures exerted by their peers. In this connection, nicknames are frequently used by children to single out the ones who are laggards in their social maturity, partly a continuation of the sibling rivalry pattern of motivation.

The two following examples indicate some of the ways in which boys deal with each other. A boy of fifteen who did not appear weak found it rather difficult for some time to fill the panniers of his camel with fertilizer, and other boys had to help him. Failing to perform the task expected from boys of his age, his fellows decided to put a girl's headcloth round his head-cap, by taking off his turban. Then he was tied to the panniers and the other boys led the half-laden camel to the field. This method, occasionally resorted to by such boys, is supposed to awaken the sense of shame in those who are not sufficiently keen on doing what is expected of them. The other example is that of a fight of a boy of about ten years old with other boys because he 'broke wind' while they were playing. When asked, he denied the fact, and they went on smelling each other. When they discovered that he was the culprit, they started building him a grave in which they buried a stone as a symbol for the boy,

shouting 'the farter is here, the farter is here'. They also be-
wailed him as adults would bewail a deceased person, by saying,
'There is no God but Allah, and Mohammed is his Prophet'.
Indeed, lack of control and modesty after the age of ten can be a
source of ridicule for children about this age.

Moreover, if restraint and docility are the keynotes of child
behaviour towards adults, a free and impulsive life reigns amongst
children themselves. Their own problems must be kept to themselves and not communicated whenever possible to their adults,
who are not expected to enquire about children's activities. For
children, it is gossip that a child would go and tell his parents
what other boys and girls have been saying or doing. If two
boys or more start quarrelling with each other, they should fight
the issue out for themselves. The laying of complaints by children
before their elders about quarrels with other children is greatly
discouraged, and when complaints are taken up by fussy parents,
they might keep the whole neighbourhood wrangling for some
time. In this case, boys who have been sneaking are referred to
by other boys as 'women', or in the case of girls are branded
as 'loose' or 'prostitutes'. Parents' advice to their children is,
'Hit back him who hits you'.

Thus, before adolescence, a boy, not only through overhearing
the gossip of his elders, but also through his age-group norms,
becomes aware of the significance of gossip as a means of social
control. He is perhaps the cause of gossip or included in it, and
this would expose him to shaming or avoidance by other children.
The boy's friends might not speak to him and this would make
him stand exposed and isolated.

Thus, it is obvious that though any signs of children's aggression
towards adults is tabooed and punishable, their expression of
hostility towards their age-mates is given full play. Rivalry and
competition are mainly directed both in the adult and in the
child world towards equals. Rivalry between generations seldom
occurs, as it is mainly horizontal and not vertical.

The cultural axiom is for the adult to give and for the young
to receive: to accept aid in kind or money from one's elders is
permissible, while the reverse would be humiliating, or at least
embarrassing, unless prescribed by kinship obligations, such as
aid rendered by the son to his father in old age.

There is a vivid contrast between the lively, free, and rough behaviour of children in their groups and their shy and diffident manners when they are attending grown-ups, while eating or during any celebration in the house. On being punished or rebuked by his elders, the child is expected to obey, while if he shows any submissiveness, if wronged by his 'pals', he would be punished by his parents and would be asked to retaliate for himself. A boy was called Abdu the Batil (the coward) by his pals, a name for which he seemed to have no outward resentment. On asking the boy about how he got this nickname, he told me that his father had applied the name to him and told the other boys with whom he associated to call him so, as his father was annoyed by his constant appeals to his parents to protect him from other children.

After reviewing the general atmosphere of the two educative spheres in the child's life, it is appropriate to discuss the means by which some social norms are impressed on him. As mentioned earlier, one of the cardinal virtues of a disciplined child is his respect for his elders. Till the age of four or five, this respect expresses itself in the young boy, on being introduced to a gathering in the house, touching the older person's hands with his lips and forehead. When the child grows older, this is replaced by a handshake followed immediately by his withdrawal from the adult gathering. The sign of respect by kissing the older person's hand with one's lips and forehead, although it ceases to apply amongst village people themselves, would still be practised by older boys and adults towards strangers visiting the house. Moreover, this is always the sign of respect for a son meeting his father after a long absence, as well as the greeting of adults for religious men and those who are believed to be endowed with 'baraka'—holiness.

Whilst in the first five or six years the child's respect for its parents and elders is inculcated mainly through physical gestures and intimacy, the respect later on is expected in terms of a decrease in word intimacy and physical proximity. Moreover, certain manners must be observed, such as walking behind the father or an elder and not abreast of him, standing up or at least sitting properly on the ground on his approach, dismounting from donkey-back on seeing the father in a formal gathering, and so on. Whether in attending to the hand-washing of guests, the distribution of tea amongst them, or in shaking hands with them, a fairly definite order of precedence is observed by the child and even by adults themselves. On the whole, with the progress of the child in age, details of etiquette are gradually enforced upon him. It is also interesting to note in this respect that a father when taking his son of four or five years to the field, would make him ride behind him and not in front, and one cannot argue that this is merely a matter of convenience as fathers who take their sons in front of them are considered to be spoiling them.

It is important here to distinguish between two categories of behaviour with regard to respect relationships, and this distinction is mainly related to whether there are any outsiders or public onlookers. The child, for instance, is allowed a certain amount of latitude in conforming to the external tokens of respect to its parents in the intimate circle of the family, for example, to sit on the bed while the father is sitting on the ground, to make himself a nuisance with the mother, or to hit back when she scolds him. Yet this is severely disapproved of and punished if there is a visitor in the house, or if done outside the house. This is the root of the absolute bonds of kinship behaviour on formal occasions. No plea could absolve the person from not fulfilling his obligations towards his relatives on public occasions such as mourning or exchange of gifts on ceremonial occasions. The failure to fulfil such obligations, as the villagers put it, 'makes a special history for the person'. The distinction between formal and informal behaviour gradually recedes as the child grows older and he is supposed to approach progressively for all occasions the formal expectations of behaviour.[4]

The general pattern of behaviour between the child and its elders is thus largely one of dominance, submission couched in the term 'filial piety'. The filial sentiment, however, is not taught to or expressed by the child in any sentimental phrases. It was a great joke amongst the children in one neighbourhood to repeat statements of an urban child whom they heard saying 'I love my father, I love my mother'. Such open expressions of filial senti-

---

[4] R. Firth distinguishes between formal and informal behavior. In the latter there are more individual differences and variations; while the former is enjoined upon each member of the society and the observances and fulfillment of formal behavior are regarded as the sure test for the harmonious functioning of society. Firth 1936:173.

ment are considered by the children as one of the ways in which Cairo people spoil their sons and daughters. Children's respect for and devotion to parents must be absolute and unconditional and do not have to be verbalized. Yet, on the other hand, the appeal to please the mother or father is usually invoked to persuade the child to behave properly or to perform certain duties. 'Fetch fuel for mother so that she can say that her daughter is good.' 'Wear this garment so that uncle's people will say they have a good boy.' While the affection of blood relatives is used to stimulate and motivate the child, he is not expected to express his sentiment towards them directly.

During early childhood, kinship terms are learnt, and by the age of five, the children I spoke to were quite capable of telling the categories of paternal uncle and aunt, maternal uncle and aunt, cousins and nephews and nieces. As anthropologists have repeatedly pointed out, the child does not start off in life with a full set of kinship terms, but gradually, and not without difficulty, fits itself into the framework provided for it by its elders (Firth 1936:272). During its development, contacts and associations, a child begins to know what type of behaviour and sentiment is expected from him towards different relatives. In terms of behaviour the above-mentioned children distinguished between those closely-related children with whom they could play freely, more co-operatively, and possibly with more superficial wrangling, and those with whom they could not play in the same way; between those from whom they could demand a piece of bread or a bit of onion, and those from whom they could not; between those who could, without suspecting malicious intentions, accept their curses and those who would resent such curses. They also knew that their close relatives are those by whom they can be protected or punished, and whom they fear and love, and to whose houses they can stray, accepting food without fear of being punished by the parents. One of the children told me that his mother punished him for going with another boy to the latter's house. She rebuked him by saying that those who offered him food would call him a son of beggars, and that it would have been quite different had he gone to his grandfather's people. Children who stray quite often into houses which are not those of close relatives, are sometimes dubbed by their elders as paupers ('fakeers', who roam about and knock at the gate of Allah).

Such an excuse is given by the elders to avoid the sense of shame that their children might bring to them. In this way a child is made to learn the difference between the easy flow of mutual obligations between close relatives and the strain of accepting hospitality from distant people which is considered almost as a debt. On such occasions, one also sees the importance of parental obligations towards their children, whose hunger would reflect on their parental duties and prestige.[5]

In this way the child experiences the processes of kinship, entering gradually widening circles of people with concomitant responsibilities and meanings. About the age of seven, for instance, kinship sentiment means running errands for close relatives, borrowing things, helping in carrying presents and gifts for them, and so forth. A child runs errands for his paternal and maternal uncles and grandfathers whether they live with the father or not, whether they are on good terms or not. Beyond these categories of kinship, the child is not compelled to run errands for other relatives who are not in harmony with his parents, on pain of punishment. Through the disciplinary powers of the uncle and the parent's family in general, the child finds himself more drawn towards his mother's people whom he usually goes to visit with his mother, because, as mentioned earlier, he finds them less censorious than paternal relatives. These visits to the maternal relatives are more frequent in the case of adolescent boys who can enjoy a relaxing and more genial relationship in their leisure time at night. As they grow older, kinship for boys and girls means help and assistance on ceremonial events of the extended family and the clan. It is significant to notice that children use only eight terms of address: father, mother, grandfather, grandmother, paternal and maternal uncle and aunt. The last four categories of uncle and aunt are only used when those addressed are married; otherwise they are addressed merely by their first names. In Silwa, unlike many other rural areas in the province of Kena, boys and girls tend, on the whole, to drop these four categories of kinship address after their marriage and usually call their uncles and aunts by their first names. It seems that after marriage boys and girls attain a certain amount of social

---

[5] For such a connection between hunger and prestige, see Richards 1932: 43–44.

independence, and thus they do not address uncles and aunts by
kinship titles in the same way as they do not address the latter
if they are not married, or if the age difference is slight. The
recognition of blood relation, however, is usually used as a test
for young children by their elders: one might hear an elder
questioning a younger, 'Who is your uncle? Who is your cousin?
Where do they live? Whom do you prefer?' and so on. The
adolescents have a few puzzles depending on kinship terms, and
division of inheritance, the solution of which lies in the understanding of a linguistic twist, or a pun.

The child's recognition of the importance of his family and
his identification with it is acquired at a very early stage of his
development. The child usually talks in the first person plural,
by saying 'our donkey, our camel'. In fact, it is preferable to use
the plural pronoun rather than the singular, as it is considered
to be modest and less presumptuous. This identification with the
family is also evidenced by the fact that in children's swearing,
and in that of the adults for that matter, the curse is directed
towards the father, the mother, the family, or to one's origin
(seed). It is very seldom indeed that a curse refers directly to
the child or the person addressed. When children are praised
by visitors, such praise is couched in terms such as 'you are the
son of poeple who are like princes', and this type of praise
is more common than that related to the good qualities of the
child himself. In this way, the identification with, and submergence
into, the family is impressed upon the child. It is not surprising
that on asking many young children about their names, their
immediate answer was 'I am the son of so-and-so'. If the identity
of the children is enquired about by the villagers, the question
is normally formulated as 'Whose son are you?' It is noticeable
that identification there goes with a sense of pride in one's family
which causes wrangling and quarrelling amongst children as well
as adults. The following conversation is typical of children's alter-
cations in this connection. One child said: 'My father is better
than yours; he never worked for someone else, and his turban
has always been white. My people (our in Arabic) are all
leaders (Arab sheikhs)'. The other boy retorted: 'All your people
are liars and deceivers. We offer a larger tray of food for
guests and on funeral occasions than yours. Your cow is "rotting"

and its bones are sticking out from starvation. What is the use of just talking?'[6]

At an early age the child acquires the sense of property and becomes interested in possessions. Many uncles, or grandparents, for example, give presents to the children. Such a practice also forms the basis of one of the cardinal interests of children in animals. On my entering a house, a child insisted on showing me his goat, which his grandfather had sent him as a gift on the occasion of his circumcision. Sometimes parents may allocate a young calf or sheep to a boy, and in the case of a girl, a mother might keep a certain chicken or duck.[7] This is regarded as the child's own property, 'ala zimmatuh' or 'ala bakhtu', to be kept 'for his sake and luck', and consequently, at least theoretically, the parents do not dispose of the animal except for his or her benefit, e.g. to clothe him or her, or to buy things for him or her, or in the case of killing the animal or the chicken, the child would get the lion's share of the meat. In practice, however, under the pressure of hardship, the parents would more often sell the animal or give it away for their own account.

It is not difficult to see that the main objective of child training is to cultivate a docile and yielding disposition in the child as the main characteristic of a 'muaddab'. For the attainment of such a goal, the motive of fear is very much worked upon in the training of children by their elders during the period of childhood. Parents usually resort to making the child conform to their wishes by frightening it with an imaginary creature called 'silowa'. There is hardly any young child who does not fear this chimera which is supposed to eat children, especially at night. It is held by children that 'silowa' is a huge, ferocious animal that eats its young after suckling them for some time. Boys and girls between the ages of four and seven are often heard talking about the 'silowa' roaming through the village at night on its way from the hills to its nightly drink from the Nile. The 'ghool' is another imaginary beast, with a huge and hairy body,

---

[6] A. Tannous remarked that in the village community of Lebanon, swearing in mild cases refers to strictly personal characteristics, whereas in intense conflicts, more violent terms, usually involving the family, are used. See Tannous 1942.

[7] Such a chicken is usually marked by a thread tied round its leg or by cutting one of its claws.

to whose attacks the children are exposed during their sleep. Other ferocious animals, such as dogs and wolves, are also invoked by mothers to induce the child to come home early or to accept food.[8]

Some of the children's games concern themselves with the establishment of a hierarchy in the order of fears. A child would move his fingers in front of another child's eyes, challenging him, by asking: 'Whom do you fear more, your father or God?' If the child blinks, then that indicates that he fears his father more than God. This is sometimes asked of a younger child wtihout attempting to make him blink, merely to test his knowledge. The same puzzle is also posed in a slightly different manner. An older boy would ask a younger boy the question: 'There is a very small boy in the market whom nobody can see, do you fear him or me more?' The proper answer is expected to be 'him' as the invisible small boy in the market is supposed to signify God. In this type of guessing game, it is obvious that the children learn that fear is the symptom of recognizing the dominance of the supernatural authority of God over that of the worldly authority of the father. Moreover, children test each other through the expression of fear as to whose authority they first submit, the paternal or the maternal uncle.

The fear of sacred objects is also inculcated during the period of childhood. The child is made to believe in their blessings as well as their dangers. He is taken to a saint's tomb or wears a Koranic charm when he is ill. At the same time he is warned against urinating near a saint's tomb or running about in the cemetery for fear of incurring the saint's wrath. The same double attitude is inculcated in him with regard to bread, milk, treading on written paper, passing over ashes from the burning of a charm made by someone else, or stepping over someone's legs. Durkheim has pointed out that the sacred objects are invariably thought of

---

[8] E. S. Stevens writes: "The Silowa occupies much the same role in Iraki legend as the witch or ogress in Western fairy tales. She is a water spirit, for she dwells in the river or in caves near running streams. Her body is covered with long hair, her breasts are pendent, reaching her knees, and when she wishes to suckle her children, whom she carries on her back, she throws her breasts over her shoulder. . . . She is fond of human flesh . . . she has a partiality for human lovers" (Stevens 1931:xvi). The classical word for "Silowa" is "Silah," pl. "Saali."

as possessing the power of sanctity and danger simultaneously. Psycho-analysts have traced this cultural phenomenon to the emergence into the field of consciousness of the dual role of the mother, and the ambivalent attitude connected with it. This probably mirrors the process whereby 'good objects' such as the mother or her milk turn into 'bad objects' such as the denying and frustrating mother and faeces (Devereux 1949:115).

Parents also scare their children by threatening them with dangerous creatures like scorpions and snakes. They scold them by saying: 'May you be bitten by a scorpion or a snake.' Apart from the fact that such scolding may be taken as a warning against the danger of such creatures, it is considered as a frightening threat to the children. Some children told me that they would prefer their parents swearing at them by the snake rather than by the scorpion. They told me that the reason for their hatred of the scorpion is that it was a wicked creature, which stings ruthlessly and indiscriminately, whereas the snake bites only when it is provoked. An older lad present remarked that the scorpion is the enemy of Moslems. He related that once upon a time a snake curled round a man's leg and yet nothing dangerous happened to the man; then a scorpion passed by and bit both the snake and the man, and caused their deaths. In the same gathering of boys, one of them told me that he actually saw the 'silowa' passing by him while he was sleeping near the harvest. He went on to say that after it had quenched its thirst, it gave a terrifying sound before going to its dwelling in the hills.

During childhood the instilling of fear is one of the expedients that parents constantly use to repress their children and make them docile. Yet I noticed that older boys, as well as adults, were highly ashamed of admitting fear of anything; to be courageous like a lion is the sign of a daring male, while for a girl, timidity is not a defective trait. One might suggest, in the light of Bateson and Mead's findings in Bali, that the horrifying mythical images of 'silowa' and 'ghool' are a cultural projection of the ambivalent feeling towards the parents, the 'silowa' symbolizing the mother, and the 'ghool' representing the father. Parents are thus represented as being both loving and affectionate as well as frightening and devouring. Children also tell the story of the enticing man who comes to them while asleep, wakes them up, offers them dates, and leads them to an unknown world in the mountains. During the journey he reiterates that the child's mother is in front of him, and whenever the child asks about his mother he is always told that she is waiting at a short distance ahead. Thus the enticing man, by taking the children away from their homes, devours them when he feels secure.

Fear responses were quite striking during the Rorschach testing of the children as revealed by the frequent occurrence of responses such as 'silowa', 'ghool', 'scorpion', 'snake', 'wolf', 'fire', and 'blood', many of which do not actually match the blots chosen.

Moreover in the dreams of both boys and girls, the manifestations of fear, repression, and anxiety cannot escape one's notice, however one interprets these dreams. In boys' dreams, one comes across images of a child afraid of the village barber cutting off his head, the ground on which the boy is lying sinking down, a boy being chased by older people, another boy being stung by a scorpion and his family wailing for him, and so on. Girls' dreams reveal the images of being in danger of drowning in the canal, black jinns with frightening eyes following them, men beating them, and so on.

Children also show fear of certain places believed to be inhabited by evil spirits, for example, deserted or ruined houses, deserted wells, spots where a murder was committed, some certain areas round the cemetery, a spot where a train ran down a person or an animal. It is believed by children and many adults that the person who meets a violent end will reappear as a violent ghost—'sul' or 'marid'—haunting people at night and causing them harm by frightening them with its fiery eyes. A boy of twelve told me of this horrified feeling, when on an errand at night the 'sul' followed him, throwing stones at him, but it disappeared suddenly when the boy passed by a gathering of people on his way, as the 'sul' only appears to a person walking alone at night. Children are also warned against talking to or looking at their shadows, especially on moonlit nights, as this might lead them to insanity. The girls are warned against looking too much at their shadows at night or at their reflection in the mirror for fear of the same malady. To avoid evil spirits, however, children are told to recite the 'Fatiha' or any part of the Koran on passing near the haunted places. Charms are also held to protect children from such dangers.

In discussing these sources and manifestations of fear, especially those connected with the supernatural world, one cannot ignore the psycho-analytical interpretation which considers spirits and demons as projections of repressed aggressive tendencies against beloved persons. The writer is inclined to explain children's fears and their genuine belief in the existence of ogresses and bogies in the village as a projection of repressed hostile attitudes towards their parents or other members of the family (Freud 1950:87, 140).[9]

In this connection, one is tempted to ask the question: to what extent does the incentive of fear as a motive, so much emphasized in the village, affect the undercurrent trends of the social relationship between the villagers? The tension and suspicion discerned in the interpersonal relationships epitomized in the saying that 'every man has an enemy' could be related to the excess in resorting to both fear and rivalry motives in the bringing up of children. The favourite legendary figure of 'Jiha' is liked by both children and adults, because of his trickery and cunning that always enables him to take revenge. It could also be suggested that this anxiety and fear through which children are stimulated is partially responsible for the adult defence mechanism of rigidity and caution. However, one of the well-known characteristics of the Egyptian fellah is his stubbornness, obstinacy and tenacity, which sometimes take the form of an obsession.

Connected with producing fear in the children is the violent and bad-tempered manner in which adults administer punishment to them. Punishment, however, may be in the form of fulminations or curses, or it may be corporal. As mentioned earlier, a father may curse his son by saying 'Curse on your father; a curse on your people; a curse on your origin (seed)', and so on. It seems that such curses have their effect on the children. A child of about nine years old told me that the curse of his parents, especially that of his mother, when she uncovers her head, is a thing which he tries to avoid; one cannot enter Paradise if one

---

[9] For a reference to the striking feelings of ambivalence of children towards their parents in primitive society, see M. Fortes 1951, where he says that as the parents in primitive societies are responsible for the passing on of cultural traditions, relations of children towards their parents tend to be ambivalent. There is commonly a feeling of hostility underlying the affection and gratitude of children felt towards their parents.

invokes one's parents' anger, and their blessings increase one's span of life. Punishment can also take the form of denouncing the boy as a girl, or condemning him as a homosexual, and also through depriving him of his food or his share of meat. On certain occasions, if the child shows reluctance to comply with, or to conform to, its elders' commands, they impugn one of its senses by expressing their disapproval or reproach in phrases such as, 'Aren't you listening?' 'Haven't you got eyes to see?' 'Are you blind?' 'Don't you smell?' 'Don't you feel?' 'Haven't you got blood?' Such phrases imply that the child should have done the accepted thing without being prompted, because he has only to make use of one of his senses. It is occasionally pointed out to the child that his jaw which uttered the words, or his hand that committed the offence, or his ears that heard the unpermissible, should be punished.

Corporal punishment is not uncommon either by beating, striking, whipping or slapping. Such punishment is inflicted upon the child normally after he has committed a serious misdemeanour, such as talking back at his parents while being rebuked, throwing stones at his mother, causing trouble with the neighbours' children, or on complaints being made against him by an older person. The child's ambivalent attitude towards its parents or uncles expresses itself in its appeal for their mercy when it is thrashed by one of them. He makes a screaming appeal, by crying out: 'O father, O father, by the name of the Prophet, O father', even if the father himself happens to be the one who is thrashing him.

The mother invariably gets the worst of the child's temper, aggression and disobedience, and consequently she is apt to administer punishment more frequently than the father. She is the parent with whom the child comes into active contact in terms of give and take. The child feels her punishing powers as he breaks things, loiters on being sent on an errand, loses money which he was given to buy things from the shop, or when he makes himself a nuisance when visitors are in the house, and similar other misdemeanours. Having more contacts with children's problems of upbringing, the mother tends to be the target of their ambivalence; they wrangle and quarrel with her, are rude to her, run outside the house and throw stones at the door or climb the wall and swear at her. On the other hand, children feel that the mother is their most reliable source of care and affection, and that she is more accessible and amenable than the father. In this capacity she is the one usually approached for expressing their wishes or asked to mediate between them and the father. Mothers themselves recognize that their treatment of children is different from that of the father. This is epitomized in the mothers' popular saying to their children in persuading them to obey them: 'On the death of my father I eat dates; on the death of my mother I eat hot coal.' In this way the mother tries to win from her offspring assistance and service as she is not invested with the same power of authority as the father. On the other hand, withdrawal from the father, keeping away from his bed while he is asleep, and keeping quiet while he is about the house, is told and retold to children by the mother or older siblings for fear of punishment. The father's authority cannot be flouted; and a change in the tone of his voice must be seriously considered. Although his punishment might be less frequent than that of the mother, yet it is certainly more severely administered. While the former pinches the ear, or the thigh, and seldom slaps, the latter normally slaps and thrashes with a rope or a cane.

It is also worth noting here that very little chance is given to the child to justify his misdemeanour, and hardly any effort is made to persuade him to avoid falling into the same error. Moreover, in administering punishment, there is no consistency or regularity; for the same offence the child might be beaten harshly, or his offence allowed to pass unnoticed. This depends, of course, on the parents' mood, or on their feeling towards the child at that particular time.

Such methods for disciplining the child normally lead to the child's attempts to tell lies or go for things in a roundabout way to evade punishment. He would swear that he has not committed a fault and that it is someone else who is responsible for it, or that he was forced by older or stronger boys to do it.[10] Deceptive tricks are frequently adopted in games when, for in-

---

[10] It is interesting to note that in the Kuttab (Koran school), Kuttab sheikh enquires from one of the boys about his misdemeanour and the other boys volunteer without being asked to give evidence concerning the boy's offence. With this also goes constant attempts of children to correct each other's behaviour or ways of learning or attention.

stance, a boy tries to frighten another boy by saying that the latter's father is approaching with a stick and thus seek to compel him to leave the game. An older boy, in trying to deceive younger children, would run in front of them shouting in terror, 'The Silowa is coming, the Silowa is coming', and the young boys would disperse. One boy might tell a group of boys an untrue story, and if the teller succeeds in making his listeners 'swallow' it he would vaunt his triumph over them by saying, 'I've been telling lies. I've cut your ears off—Kaddabt 'alaikum, gattat wadanaikum.'

It does not require any emphasis here to point out that the effects of these techniques of fear as forcing children to resort to lies and deception are reflected later in the prevailing atmosphere of adult life which is charged with suspicion, secrecy and apprehension. Fear, moreover, is an efficient lever for the maintenance of social cohesion in the pattern of father-son relationship, and hence it is not surprising to find the common saying that 'fear is a blissful thing' (al khof baraka).

The popular sayings connected with the administering of punishment are also varied and inconsistent, perhaps to maintain a balance and to avoid excess. On the one hand one hears phrases such as 'If you don't beat the child, nothing good would come out of him', 'The stick is for the disobedient', 'Those who do not feel, the stick would make them feel'. On the other hand, there are other sayings such as 'The stick makes the boy dumb'. 'The threat would have no effect on those who do not obey spontaneously'. It is considered, however, that childhood is the most appropriate period for punishing and disciplining the child. It is said that the child during this time is like the maize plant in its second irrigation (this irrigation is considered to be important for the plant's growth and is preceded by the pulling out of the grass and other weeds). The concentration of punishment at this period is justified on the grounds that the boy or the girl at this stage is neither too young nor too old to learn. The only form of corporal punishment administered to adolescents on some rare occasions is slapping.

However, the administering of punishment by parents to children is checked from being unduly excessive by other relatives, neighbours or other adults who happen to be present. Mediation (literally separation—'hajazat') as institutionalized in the 'Arab council' is an important force in the legal and social functioning of the community. It is practised by children themselves and even mock fights are sometimes played by them to enjoy the wranglings of conciliation similar to those amongst the adults. Some children told me that on seeing their parents quarrelling, they immediately go out of the house to invite one of their close relatives for mediation. Adults are also expected to stop children's fights if they happen to be passing by, and even punish the disputants.

It is appropriate here to evaluate the period of childhood in Silwa, in comparison with their period of infancy. With the exception of observing sex and religious norms, childhood in Silwa is the period through which a boy or a girl experiences a great number of the pressures of socialization. Some modern anthropologists have pointed out the importance of discontinuities or inconsistencies in child-rearing practices as relevant cultural data especially in connection with personality organization (Benedict 1938). Esther Goldfrank, for instance, postulates four categories of societies with regard to the continuity or discontinuity of disciplinary policy between infancy and childhood:

(1) Societies where infant and later disciplines are weak.
(2) Societies where infant and later disciplines are severe.
(3) Societies where infant disciplines are severe and later disciplines are weak.
(4) Societies where infant disciplines are weak, and later disciplines are severe.

Goldfrank continues to say: 'From the standpoint of logic these categories pose no problems. However, difficulties may arise when an attempt is made to assign specific societies to any one of them, for permissiveness and pressure are present at all stages of development' (Goldfrank 1945:517). The writer feels that the child-rearing practices compared with infant practices could be classified, without much debate or appearance of subjectivity, into the fourth category of societies where infant disciplines are weak, permissive, and protective, while the later disciplines are prompt, strict, and on the whole, severe.

It has been shown in Chapter IV on infancy how the angelic children are treated permissively and with very few controls until they start to respond orally to the external world. Perhaps the only forbidden fruit in the mother's paradise for the child is the biting of her breast while he is suckling, which normally results in her withdrawal of the breast from him, and might be accompanied by some angry words or a push. On the other hand, we have noticed how the period of childhood is seized upon to discipline the child, and make him conform as well as know his position in the adult world.

In this connection, a question of a psychological nature could be asked. How does the child bridge the gap or adjust himself between the early permissive training and the stern childhood discipline without a complete disintegration of his personality? In answer to such a question, certain points must be remembered. The child receives the pressures of socialization, and forgoes his mother's blessings at a stage when he is capable of using his newly-developed interest, such as walking and talking, in his contacts with other children. The social arrangement of the extended family could be also considered as a factor in making up for the mother's deprivation. The rough and aggressive games are an outlet for the strain of socialization during childhood. The gap is also bridged through the integration of the child into the work of the adults. From the economic point of view, the child is continuously conditioned to participate in farm work as a responsible member. Through work in the fields, which is meaningful for the child and indispensable to his family, the child is incorporated in the family circle, and is recognized as a valuable member in it, and this contributes in no small way to the satisfaction of the individual's psychological need for social recognition.[11] These are some of the forces the writer regards as maintaining some sort of healthy effect in the growing up of children in Silwa; otherwise the strain of childhood would have been unbearable in a predominantly authoritarian community where the child is regarded as its father's possession. Erich Fromm would consider such a community as thwarting the child's legitimate strivings for freedom, independence, and self-fulfilment.

[11] C. M. Fleming 1948:47–48. See also Abram Kardiner (1939), where he emphasizes the emotional meaning of work: "There is, first, the intrinsic gratification in work as a form of mastery. This must be credited with being a basic gratification. The satisfactions derived from it are common to all forms of mastery. They give the individual a feeling of effectiveness and control" (p. 50).

He maintains that the social arrangement of an authoritarian patriarchal society, frustrating man's wishes to self-realization, tends to create in him a destructive passion, which in turn must be suppressed by external or internal force (Fromm 1948:153–58).

If one thinks of the disciplinary policies of childhood in terms of a straight line, at one end of which is the easy-going discipline of some primitive societies, and at the other end the harsh discipline of a society like the Japanese, it is apparent that the type of discipline to be found in Silwa is closer to that of the Japanese society than to that of those primitive societies.

The period of childhood is considered by the adult as an unimportant stage which should be quickly passed over. The writer seldom noticed grown-ups talking about their childhood, and his informants found it very difficult, even unbecoming, to recall their childhood days. The villagers' attitude towards children is indeed a mixed one, regarding them both as supernumerary entities as well as a sub-adult. A child is an economic asset as well as a social nuisance. It was shown in Chapter I how the child is continuously expected to take over from the adult the tasks which it is capable of performing as a part of its acquisition of discipline—'adab'. On the level of social action, however, it is supposed to be insignificant and to have no opinion of its own. On the whole, a son or a daughter, whether young or old, cannot replace the parent in performing formal social obligations; for example, taking gifts to circumcision and wedding ceremonies or entertaining a guest, unless there are extenuating circumstances which justify it. The child's world is always connected with the female world rather than the grown-up male world. In the ceremonial celebrations, children are usually mixed with women more than with men. If children happened to be in a male gathering, they must keep to their place, and be able to withdraw at the earliest opportunity to play on their own, or to join the female crowd. At this level of social action, the unity of the social sphere between children and grown-ups tends to break. Although the child's life is directed towards aims, responsibilities, and values similar to those of the adults, he is debarred from adult circles, and adult activities; and grown-ups do not expect their children to express any opinion on matters which are outside their domain. Although they are expected to orientate themselves to the same sphere of life, children are not given any significant role in the social life of the village, apart from their economic role. Until the age of twelve the children are not expected to go to the mosque to say their prayers, and if they go they are allowed to sit in the back row only, and never in the front or the middle. Women and girls, however, do not go to the mosque at all in Silwa, and are not expected to do so. There is no religious sanction for this, however; Islam has enjoined mosque prayers on both sexes. Compared with the Tale child, the social sphere of the Silwa child is more restricted in many respects. In the former society, the social sphere of adults and children is differentiated only in terms of relative capacity. 'Nothing in the universe of adult behaviour is hidden from children, or barred to them. They are actively and responsibly part of the social structure, of the economic system, the ritual and ideological system' (Fortes 1938:9). In Silwa, however, although children may know about the happenings and events of the adult world in the social sphere, they are not expected to take an active part, or to show interest in them, unless they are asked to do so. On some occasions the writer heard children who, on enquiring about the guests coming to the house, or the nature of the gifts taken to relatives, or where father was going, were silenced and asked to 'mind their own business'.

Moreover, the process of 'growing-up' is believed to be affected by the character traits of the parents and close relatives on both the patrilineal and matrilineal side. The belief is that the virtues and vices of the parents and their family line are transmitted, through heredity, to their offspring. Especially in the case of outstanding physical features or social characteristics, their presence is invariably accounted for by inheritance from ancestors; if not directly inherited from the parents, they could be traced to the grandfather or to the great-grandfather. Trends of character, whether of meanness, hospitality, piety, wickedness, aggression or docility, seem to run in the families. A person who deviates from what is known about his family is referred to as 'a mistake' or 'a slip', whether in praise or blame depending on the context. One hears sayings and phrases to the effect that 'so-and-so by nature is good or bad'; 'his roots are rotten'; 'nature prevails over nurture (attaba yaghlib attatbu)'; 'people are of different metals; those who were good in the pre-Islamic period, will be equally

good in Islam (annas maadin), Khiyaruhum fi al-Jahiliya, khiyaruhum fi al-Islam'.

It must be pointed out here that the process of socialization
which is strongly felt during childhood and adolescence is not
only conducted through the agency of the family, both conjugal
and extended, but also through age and sex groups. The family
does not directly play as great a part in the educative process in
Silwa as in towns or cities of Egypt. An equally if not more
important part is played by other children, adults other than the
parents, play-groups, gossip gatherings, groups of girls going to
fill their jars, or groups of boys fetching fertilizer, situations of
hand-washing, tea-serving, ceremonies and celebrations, and by
hundreds of other life situations which go to communicate the
heritage of the village life to the growing child. In Silwa, like
the Midwestern Highlands of Guatemala, 'the heritage of the
group is communicated in situations much less clearly defined
than institutions . . . (through) that multitude of daily situations
in which by word or gesture, some part of the tradition is communicated from one individual to another' (Redfield 1943:644).
The literary and written aspects of the village Islamic culture
are left to a few literary people who teach or recite the Holy
Book and enlighten the other villagers on religious matters; while
theoretical religious knowledge is the concern of a few, all are
concerned with the ritual aspects of religion such as prayers and
fasting.

Moreover, the slow rate of social change in the village has
hardly affected the aims and methods of socialization. Children
are reared approximately in the same way as their parents
and are expected to imbibe the same cultural assumptions, and
follow the same path. A qualification must be added here. Growing
up in a folk homogeneous society does not necessarily mean a
smooth, painless or unhampered process. But however traumatic
or frustrating the life experience is, it can nevertheless be presented to each growing individual as viable, and to that extent,
bearable (Mead 1947:633). Intensive case studies would certainly reveal the various problems of social adjustment, and show
the compensatory mechanisms of those who fail to measure up
to the ritual assumptions and requirements.

11 EDUCATION AND CULTURAL
DYNAMICS: DAHOMEY
AND THE NEW WORLD

Melville J. Herskovits

*The long-range transmission of culture is a process that has
interested many people. In this chapter, Melville J. Herskovits
discusses not only cultural continuity from one generation to
the next within an ongoing society, but an unusual situation
involving the physical displacement of the culture-bearers and
their transmission of the original culture to their descendants who
form a subgroup in another society. The author first considers the
traditional educational system in the West African kingdom of
Dahomey, and then the transmission of elements of that culture
among the slaves and ex-slaves of Dahomean origin in the New
World. The retention of many of the meaningful components of
their original culture by these people has been significant for their
continuing sense of identity within a wider and usually hostile
society.*

I

THE ROLE of the educative process in maintaining cultural
stability is today too well recognized to require renewed emphasis. The understanding that this experience far transcends the
limits of any formal scheme of training the young has brought
with it the conception that education is a conditioning process
which begins with birth and does not end until the death of
an individual. From this broad point of view, every experience
is educational. Even if the concept is restricted to formal methods
of introducing the young to their culture, the range of situations

Reprinted from *American Journal of Sociology* 48, 1943:737–49, with
permission of Mrs. Frances Herskovits and of the editor, *American Journal
of Sociology.*

under which the ends of instruction are achieved is far more inclusive than any institutional framework could hope to cover.

This approach, however, emphasizes the stabilizing force of education, and thus tends to minimize the aspect of change. Yet it is a truism to students of culture that one of the most difficult paradoxes inherent in their materials is contained in the fact that while a body of traditions is conservative, maintaining its identity often over centuries, no living culture exists that is not in a constant state of change. In the study of cultural dynamics, therefore, it is essential, not only to determine the resistance to cultural change as against relative rate of change in societies existing under various conditions and for various aspects of given cultures, but also to analyze the mechanisms which have made for stability or have encouraged change in as many historic situations as possible.

It is here that students of education in primtive societies have made their most slender contribution. The tendency to stress the conservative aspect of education is understandable in the light of the relatively great stability of small, isolated, nonliterate "primitive" societies when these are compared with the enormous industrialized aggregates that carry the historic cultures. Statements which content themselves with pointing out that there are situations which cause a given individual to rebel against an incest taboo, let us say, or that cause a person of unstable psychological makeup to have visions which give religious patterns new turns, contribute but little to an understanding either of how new elements are taken up and retained, or of how they are worked into tribal educative schemes and thus made a part of a cultural heritage.

Negro peoples of Africa and the New World, in their institutionalized forms of behavior and in the sanctions that underlie this behavior, run the gamut from full-blown aboriginal customs to patterns which, especially in the United States, reflect a high degree of acculturation to the sanctions and institutions of the Europeans with whom, in the New World, they have been in contact. Such materials are particularly germane, since by implication, at least, the usual assumption made by students concerning the stabilizing role of education has here given way almost completely to a position holding that the opposite result was achieved. Especially is this true in the United States, where those concerned with the understanding of Negro life seem to have ignored almost completely the possibility that the stabilizing element in education, as concerns aboriginal patterns, may have retained its strength in the new situations which confronted the Negroes in this country.

The common assumption that the attitudes, modes of behavior, accepted values in life, and other fundamental parts of the non-material cultural equipment of the Negro slaves were given over in contact with the whites tends to turn its back on the educative drive to retain earlier patterns.

But it is difficult to have one's educational cake and eat it. When it is recognized that children in Africa were taught so well that they, like all human beings, in acquiring automatic responses to given situations and in reacting in terms of these accepted modes of procedure, gave continuity to their cultures, can it be assumed that these same conditionings readily and completely gave way in a new social climate? Can emphasis be shifted thus easily from acceptance of custom to rejection, from accommodation to reaccommodation, from stability to change?

The problem can be solved only in terms of data drawn from the nature of present-day institutions of these folk, and of an examination of the ways in which they are inculcated in the young. It is proposed here, therefore, to outline something of the educational process operative in one West African society, Dahomey, which all records indicate contributed heavily to the peopling of Negro America. Some consideration can be given to certain aspects of Negro behavior in the United States which seem to reflect something of the same traditions that are found in this West African society, and the means whereby these have been preserved and are handed down. It will be borne in mind, in reading this discussion, that limitations of space make brevity necessary; and that much relevant material from West Indian and South American societies which would fill in this sketch cannot be included. Nonetheless, enough data can be given to raise the question whether or not it is acceptable, either logically or methodologically, to assume that the stabilizing factor of education in African society disappeared as promptly and as completely under conditions of New World slavery as is indicated in current hypotheses regarding the failure of Negroes to carry over any part of their aboriginal heritage into the present-day American scene.

II

The culture of Dahomey, French West Africa, has been relatively untouched by the circumstances of French political control since the conquest of the kingdom in 1894. Except in certain obvious areas, life goes on much in the way it went on in the autonomous kingdom. Slavery is no longer practiced; the cowrie shell has been replaced by French currency; a railway runs from the principal port of the colony into the interior; one on occasion sees sewing machines. Yet, in many parts of the territory of the kingdom, descendants of those who were slaves still give half their time to working in fields owned by members of the families which owned their forebears; the cowrie shell has by no means disappeared from the market; the railroad is an inactive factor in the lives of the vast majority of the people; sewing machines, in accordance with the aboriginal patterns governing this type of work, are operated by men and not women. Thus, once the student probes beneath surface details of this kind, their superficiality becomes apparent. In Dahomey, and, as we are realistically coming to understand, elsewhere in Africa, training in aboriginal modes of behavior is a mechanism which is permitting the people to hold fast to traditionally sanctioned custom; and this, more than any other single factor, is preventing the breakdown in morale that has been the experience of so many other peoples who have made contact with European civilization.

This culture of Dahomey is a complex entity, "primitive" only in a technical sense of not having a written language. As has been shown (Herskovits 1938) this culture comprises involved economic institutions and mechanisms and numerous social structures based on relationship and nonrelationship groupings. It was marked in the days of its autonomy by a well-organized political structure that ruled the considerable population with firmness and efficiency. The theological sanctions of its religious system make up a sophisticated concept of the universe, and the supporting structure of ritualism occupies the time of many specialists and impresses by the richness of its resources. Its graphic and plastic arts take on many forms. One pattern is particularly worthy of mention as significant in aiding this people to maintain so involved a civilization without the aid of writing—the explicit recognition of all institutions. The proper verbal label can be found for each detail of this culture, and the number of individuals who easily and freely use the correct terminology in the routine of life, to say nothing of those who can give it on request, is striking.

The desire for children is a convention that drives deep in Dahomean culture. This can be traced to economic as well as psychological sanctions, since, on the economic level, children constitute a kind of insurance. In the case of the man, sons will help him till his fields and aid him in many other ways, while a man's son-in-law will likewise owe him certain duties year by year. As for a woman with offspring, she can be assured of support in time of need and when old age sets in.

The tendency to draw distinctions, to categorize, and to name is nowhere better evidenced in this culture than in the conventions which govern the naming of children. The very fact that the existence of these differences is recognized implies differing attitudes toward such children; and their reactions to this offer suggestive leads in future research toward an understanding of the shaping of personality by social convention. A person assumes various names at given critical periods of his life, but his most important designations are those given at birth. The child born with a caul or with feet foremost; the child born to members of various cult groups; or the one who survives after a series of still-born forerunners—all these are given particular kinds of names which inevitably set attitudes and aid in conditioning behavior. Extra fingers or toes place children under the protection of one of the powerful members of the Sky pantheon; and persons bearing the names indicative of this are believed to be predestined for riches, since polydactylism is held to be a sign of good luck. A four-fingered child belongs to the feared river spirits, whose priests and the diviners are consulted to determine whether it will bring riches or poverty to its parents and whether it is to be "returned" to the spirits that gave it. In this case it is exposed on the river bank, unless it "refuses to accept the verdict" by wailing, in which case it must be taken back and reared, though with what attitudes on the part of the parents can be imagined. Children having other anomalous traits, such as macrocephaly, likewise belong to this category. Twins are, in a sense, the darlings of this culture. The effect of the twin cult on twins, and even more importantly on the child born after twins, in influencing the development of children in this category must be considerable, for on such individuals are lavished all forms of special attention.

Existence in a polygamous household, or even in a monogamous establishment governed by patterns based on plural marriage, dominates the early life and training of the child. In accordance with these patterns, a wife has a dwelling of her own within her husband's compound, where she lives with her children. The common husband likewise has his own dwelling, and here each of his wives in turn cohabits with him out of this routine until her child has been born and weaned. The difference in early experience, particularly in terms of unconscious conditioning or of later attitudes in terms of relative closeness to father and mother, as contrasted to what obtains in those cultures where, for example, a man and woman and their children inhabit the same hut continuously, the child often sharing the same sleeping-place as its parents, is obvious. Particularly in postinfantile and preadolescent years, such matters as the relative lack of opportunity of witnessing the sex act, which as we know can have such far-reaching effects in shaping the personality of the growing child, is here a factor of some significance.

The closeness of contact between mother and child in the earliest years, outstanding in the Dahomean system of child-training, is as striking as it is important, since for the first year of life the child is almost literally never away from its mother. She busies herself about the compound, with her child always in sight, lying on a cloth under the eaves of her house, shaded from the sun. If the child becomes restless, she will put it astride her back in a cloth which she ties in front, proceeding then to go about her tasks regardless of whether the child is awake or asleep, pounding meal in a mortar, or washing clothes, or cooking, while the head of the child rolls this way and that as the mother moves. If she is the favorite of a wealthy husband, she may be permitted to do lighter tasks inside the compound for a year after the birth of her child; but in the case of one in less favored circumstances, she resumes her economic obligations after a period of three or four months, working in the fields, or trudging along the roads obtaining goods to sell in the market, or making pots, with the child always astride her back, or near by.

During the first months or life little food other than its mother's milk is given the infant, though after four or five months other foods are introduced into its diet. As among many primitive folk there are no regular feeding times, the breast being presented whenever the child cries for it, or, in any event, every few hours. As soon as other foods are given the infant, however, the Dahomean tradition of discipline comes into play, and the child is fed forcibly until it learns to eat whatever food is presented to it. Dahomean mothers are busy women and have no time to pander to fastidious tastes of their children. Their methods are direct and effective. As the child lies or sits in its mother's lap, she supports its chin on the palm of her left hand while she presses its nostrils together with the index and second fingers of the same hand, thus forcing the mouth open if the child is to breathe. When this occurs, food is placed in the mouth with the right hand. Methods of weaning are equally efficient; the mother sprays her breasts with some evil-tasting, sour substance, and in most cases the desired effect is obtained with all promptness.

It is not to be thought that the child's early existence is characterized by any lack of affection, however; for Dahomeans are extremely fond of their young, and both fathers and mothers have no hesitation in manifesting their regard. The variation in methods of training between gentleness and brutality may be indicated by considering the way in which children are taught to walk, as against the way in which sphincter control is inculcated. When a child is about a year old, it is put in charge of a young relative, who holds the baby by its hand and encourages its first efforts. When it has learned to take a few short steps, four small bells of a special type made for the purpose, strung on a cord, are tied about each foot. The child, hearing the pleasant tinkling sound made at each step, is encouraged to continue its efforts, and the delighted shrieks of small children testify to the efficacy of this device.

Training in the control of excretory functions varies from continuous teaching to a type of conditioning experience that might well, in sensitive children, result in traumatic shock. As a mother carries about her infant, she senses when it is restless; and when it must perform its functions, she places it on the ground.

In ordinary cases the training process is completed in an easy fashion after about two years, but some children do not respond to this training and manifest enuresis at the age of four or five years, soiling the mats on which they sleep. In such a case the child is first beaten; then, if this does not achieve the desired result, a mixture of ashes and water is poured over the head of the offender, who is then driven into the street, where all the children run after it, shouting over and over again the words of a song especially reserved for the purpose, "Urine everywhere." Or, in the coastal area, such a child is thrown into the lagoon. If, after a second immersion, the habit is not stopped, a live frog is attached to the child's waist, which frightens it into a cure.

Between infancy and puberty, two major educational strands can be traced in the experience of the developing child. One of these comprehends the overt training he receives, particularly in those occupational techniques that must be mastered if the individual is to take his proper place in society. In this category also is included training in proper behavior toward the living and the dead and some knowledge of religious and ceremonial custom. The other strand is constituted by continuing exposure to the psychological atmosphere of the household in which he lives and which determines the attitudes he will later take toward others, especially those belonging to his own relationship group, with whom he will in the course of normal events associate throughout his adult life.

The training gained through observation and experience of the manner of life of his elders is predominant under the first category. As in African societies generally, children are encouraged to do things done by adults and are intrusted with tasks that would seem to the Euro-American observer far beyond their years. A child of two and a half is to be seen carrying its mother's stool to the market place, or balancing an empty calabash or dish on its head. A year or two later, he is able to handle a sharp bush-knife, or cutlass, with facility. On days when work in the forges is forbidden by supernatural precept, the boys of the ironworking sib take over, an infant of three or four operating the bellows for his preadolescent brother in the same manner as this brother performs the identical task for his father, while the preadolescent hammers out red-hot iron on the anvil to make a small blade for the miniature hoe he is constructing. A little girl, when three or four years old, goes to market with her mother, performs her allotted tasks about the house, helps weed the fields, or carries clay for pots. Boys likewise participate, the son of a farmer helping his father work in the field, the offspring of a clothworker cutting out crude patterns and stitching these designs to remnants of materials left by his father, the child of a weaver learning the intricacies of threading a loom by operating a simple one. Patterns of economic co-operation are similarly inculcated at an early age. Le Herisse tells how, in the early days of the French occupation, small boys were individually employed to bring water to the Residency. Difficulties ensued, however, and were not resolved until the boys formed a group, appointed a responsible head, and received orders "through channels."

On this institutional level, also, the child may be said to absorb noneconomic aspects of life just as effortlessly. In the main, the ceremonials that affect him directly between the first two crisis periods of his life, birth and puberty, are few in number. The many rites that mark the birth of an infant, its introduction to society, and the return of its mother to full participation in the daily round probably occur too early to affect his behavior or personality structure. As he grows older, however, observing these rites when performed in his compound for younger siblings, he soon senses the realization of the need for supernatural sanctions in all situations, a pattern that is emphasized by his contact with the larger ceremonial round of his village. Children are ubiquitous at religious rites; nor does the Dahomean pattern of proper behavior before the gods require children, as in our culture, to be small replicas of their elders. Sanctimoniousness is entirely absent, and children play as they will during the long daylight hours when rites are performed, effortlessly absorbing the drum rhythms and melodic patterns of song, imitating dances as they wish, or, finally, as night wears on, returning to their parents to fall asleep in their places. The childhood freedom during such rites operates to induce a feeling-tone in later life toward the gods that is not unrelated to the deep interest with which the Dahomean, like most West Africans contemplates the supernatural and the almost matter-of-fact attitude he takes in his relationship to deified ancestors and other gods.

On occasion, however, ceremonial life does take the child at first hand. Children who have been vowed to the gods by their parents may be called at an early age. In such cases, unless divination shows a willingness on the part of the deity to postpone the long and expensive initiatory rites, the child will be received in the cult-center by the priests for induction into the group of initiates together with its adolescent or adult members. On one occasion the participation of an infant barely able to walk was witnessed. The child was carried on the back of a priestess throughout the long twenty-eight-day ritual, and the case illuminates the effectiveness of the conditioning process. For, though no attempt was made to teach so young a child the proper dance steps before the end of the period when it had learned to toddle, this child on one occasion danced in perfect form and rhythm the basic steps of the Sky-gods to whom she was vowed.

There are a few ceremonies performed by the children during this period, such as when a first deciduous tooth works out of the gum. When this occurs, the child assembles its playmates, who dance about in a circle, clapping their hands and singing such rhymes as:

> He who has lost a tooth,
> Cannot eat salt:
> Come, give me palm-oil
> To eat with my cake.
>
> I don't want the teeth of a pig,
> They're big!
> I want the teeth of a goat,
> They're small!

Training is also effectuated by the evening gatherings of the children of a compound to tell stories. Here the child is introduced to the sanctions underlying approved modes of behavior by means of the morals drawn from the tales. These are of the familiar Uncle Remus animal type where the principal character is the trickster, sometimes, but not always, getting the better of his more powerful but less able fellows. The child thus absorbs sanctioned reactions toward the situations of later life, learning the need for proper reserve in dealing with one's fellow-men and that too great frankness in discussing one's affairs or the naïve taking at face value of another's expressed motives often leads to disaster.

The manner in which these stories are told helps to inculcate in the child the competitive drive which, as a counterpart of the co-operative patterns of Dahomean life, are of such great moment here as everywhere in West Africa. This setting has not a little of the picturesque, and the warmth of human relations involved in the situation is of some significance. The children gather in the evening, usually at the home of one of the old people of the compound. They may perhaps first listen to stories told by their elders, but eventually one of them takes charge and, as leader, conducts the rest of the session. This develops into a contest in which each child must demonstrate his story-telling ability. Riddling is an integral part of the pattern, and the losers are assigned by the leader a certain number of tales to be told the group. Each child strives to fulfil his task, so as not to expose himself to ridicule. The educational role of these stories is recognized by the Dahomeans, one of whom, sophisticated in French culture, directly compared them to the books from which European children learn their lessons.

The second strand in the experiences of these years is more important in shaping personality structure than in teaching the child to carry on the institutionalized cultural patterns. As in the case of infants, the fact of living within a polygamous compound is paramount in this context. As far as is known, no detailed study of this situation has ever been made, which is regrettable. For, despite the methodological difficulties inherent in such an analysis, the restraints imposed by these situations and the blockages to the attainment of goals are to the highest degree suggestive for an understanding of numerous problems in the culture-personality equation as this manifests itself in polygamous cultures. Factors of sexual rivalry, of jockeying for position, of attaining preference for a child, make for intrigue that goes on against a background of shifting alliances between co-wives which reveals the inner drama of such groupings. The atmosphere of such a compound cannot but affect the growing child, not only in his immediate relations with his mother, his father, his mother's co-wives and their children, but in the way in which it shapes attitudes and typical reactions in later life.

In large Dahomean compounds rivalries between wives are intense. There are in this culture thirteen different categories of marriage, which can be grouped under two large headings— those in which the control of the children is in the hands of the father, and those in which the mother retains control over her offspring. In institutional terms this means that for the first group a man has made certain ceremonial payments and accepted certain continuing obligations toward his fathers-in-law, who have approved the marriages. In the second category these obligations are not undertaken. Wives married in the same category have a fellow-feeling, and help one another when quarrels arise between co-wives. To what extent these quarrels result from the constant jockeying for position vis-à-vis the common spouse, or from the inadequacy of sexual satisfactions, or are the result of the clash of irreconcilable personalities in constant close contact, cannot be said. That all three probably enter would seem to be justified from a priori consideration of the setting. Certainly gossip and argument run rife; and the depth to which feeling goes is indicated by the songs sung by a co-wife against another with whom she has quarreled, as she works at her mortar in the courtyard of their common habitation:

> Woman, thy soul is misshapen
> In haste was it made, in haste;
> So fleshless a face speaks, telling
> Thy soul was formed without care.
> The ancestral clay for thy making
> Was molded in haste, in haste.
> A thing of no beauty art thou
> Thy face unsuited for a face,
> Thy feet unsuited for feet.

In Dahomean society, where ambition runs high, the chief objective of a plural wife is that one of her children succeed his father. This means that it is important that her sons make a good appearance. Though children are whipped when guilty of misdeeds, such misdeeds are, wherever possible, kept from the ears of the child's father, and the punishment, at least for minor infractions, is carried out at the home of the mother's sister or at her parents' home.

The fundamental factor in the child's situation, however, is that while he shares his father with the children of other women, who in a very real sense constitute obstacles in his life-career, he shares his mother with his "very own" brothers and sisters. This attitude is reflected when the inheritance of an estate is involved. For it is a truism in Dahomey that, though a man's heirs quarrel without end over the distribution of his wealth, for "real" brothers and sisters to dispute concerning a mother's estate is unheard of. Personal relationships follow similar lines. Though a man may be proud of his father's exploits and feel affection for him, the warmest regard of a child is reserved for his mother, who is, to all intents and purposes, the effective parent.

Space does not allow the discussion of other educational devices which come into play in late preadolescence and during puberty. It is not without significance, however, that the stages in a boy's and girl's life are carefully noted and named, so that even a young individual's place in society is objectified. Important but too involved to permit them to be recounted here are the techniques of sex education. Particularly as regards the girls, one here finds the closest approximation to formal schooling that exists in Dahomey; though the fact that in early puberty groups of boys build and live in houses of their own, electing their own leaders and carrying on much in the fashion of adults, is also regarded by Dahomeans as educational. Especially important are the recognized mechanisms for sexual experimentation, while perhaps not less significant is the withdrawal of nubile girls from contact with boys who might cause them to become pregnant. This creates a situation which leads either to further training of young men in sex through illicit relations with older women, or to indulgence in homosexual experience, which is sanctioned for this period. The attainment of adult status, marked for the girl by the cutting of designs in her skin which later develop into cicatrized aids to beauty, is also to be noted. In the case of boys the experience of circumcision, marked at its termination by ceremonial intercourse with an old woman to "cool the heat of the knife," is likewise important in helping make a Dahomean the kind of person he is to be as an adult.

It is thus apparent that there are numerous mechanisms which operate to shape the personality structure of the individual, at the same time fitting him into his place in the community by training him to carry on its institutions in the manner approved by his society. The degree of variation in individual reactions to the learning process is not easy to determine. On the whole, however, the product can be characterized as one which accepts the stratified forms of social structure that mark the culture, manifesting at the same time ambition to attain prestige in recognized ways, and having a drive to take advantage of such avenues of social mobility as may present themselves. At the same time, the individual is trained to co-operate with his fellows and, as a result of the overt characterization of the ways of life, to have an objectively manifested affection for and pride in his people and the institutions by which they live. He shows reserve in his dealings with others, but in certain situations, particularly when dealing with those who stand in the relation of institutionalized friendship to him or with members of his own cult group or association, he manifests a warmth of regard and a willingness to aid in difficulties that compensate for these other characteristics. Certainly, whatever the stability of such a psychological type, the effectiveness of the training given in carrying on the institutional aspects of Dahomean life from generation to generation have been demonstrated by perpetuating this culture for many generations and by performing well the task of adequately adjusting those who live in accordance with its sanctions.

III

We may now turn to a brief consideration of the problem of determining the role, in the New World, of the educational process in making for the retention or disappearance of habit-patterns and of institutionalized forms of behavior, such as have been described in the preceding section. That students of the Negro tend, with few exceptions, to posit the disappearance of African modes of behavior among Negroes of this country is not so significant as it might seem on first glance, since this conclusion has been reached on the basis of little or no acquaintance with the African background. The historical processes held to have brought about this presumed great loss of aboriginal endowment are rarely investigated realistically, a fact the more remarkable when it is considered that so radical a change in the cultural habits of so many people, achieved in such a short time, would, if true, be unique in the experience of man.

This is not the place to adduce evidence as to the validity of the common assumptions, for an analysis of such matters can be presented only in extended form (cf. Herskovits 1941). What is important for the major point under discussion is acceptance of a hypothesis involving an almost complete breakdown of pre-American forms and techniques of education as a method of transmitting aboriginal beliefs and modes of behavior. Yet such a position would seem to involve a reconstruction of the setting of slave life that is unjustified historically or logically. Can it be held, for example, that the slave mother took no part in teaching her infant to walk? That perhaps somewhat later she imparted no instruction in behavior habits, in attitudes toward elders, in etiquette? Can it be seriously maintained that no instruction in terms of any moral code was given? That the young were not taught ways and means of meeting the hardships of their life? Must it not be recognized that, however sparse the slave culture may have been, it had to be taught, and the teaching had in the main to be done by parents? And, granting the obvious affirmative answers to these questions, can it be maintained that in all this the values and traditions of African life must have been completely ignored by those concerned with training their young?

We may envisage the situation of an African-born slave, mating and having offspring. It is impossible to assume that an educational experience of the type that has been indicated in the preceding section, so strong that it has made possible the continuation of a complex civilization over many generations, should have been completely lost in all its aspects on those brought to this country. A certain dilution in African behavior resulting from his new setting would be expected, yet it is difficult to see how it would have been possible for a slave to bring up his children without inculcating in them something of the values of life and the modes of behavior that he had in Africa been taught to regard as right and proper. Some of this teaching, in all likelihood, would, indeed, be without any direction and would involve no more than unconscious imitation by the children of habits that themselves lodge below the level of consciousness in the adult—motor behavior of various kinds, such as postures, modes of walking, the use of the hands while talking, characteristic facial expressions, and the like.

The imitation of speech habits would lie on almost the same level. Controversies concerning the derivation of American Negro speech appear almost pointless in the light of an understanding of the manner in which languages are learned. Certainly, in the light of our knowledge of educational psychology, it would be difficult to maintain that African speech habits were so completely given over by adults through more or less casual acquaintance with white people that nothing of the earlier modes of expression remained to be taught to their children. The matter bristles with further difficulties if the assumption is followed through to its customary conclusion. For in this case it would appear that not only did Africans lose their own forms of expression on contact with the whites, but in that same contact they only received and never gave.

A further point must be made. In most analyses of the carry-over of Africanisms in the United States, the Negro is regarded as a passive element in the situation. In a sense this is merely a restatement of the assertion that the educational processes—education in the larger sense—that went on in slave cabins are completely overlooked. No competent student of culture could take the position that the Negroes were not affected, and deeply affected, by the new setting in which they found themselves. But few students of the Negro have recognized that, in the New World, Negro culture or white culture is not to be regarded as a unit and that, if we look at the Negroes not as a passive but as an active element in the developing situation, our perspective will be false if we do not recognize the different interests which these people have traditionally held in various aspects of their own culture, interests which carried over as they gained competence in handling the culture of their masters. In African societies, as in all cultures, certain aspects of life are of greater concern to a given people than others. This means, further, that in every culture interests tend to center on certain activities. These take the form of conscious drives which, directed toward a certain segment of the entire body of tradition, determine that area of the culture wherein the greatest elaboration is achieved in a given period of a people's history. For Negro studies, the significance of this principle lies in the fact that, under the stresses of contact with a foreign body of tradition, these interests tended to be maintained with the greatest possible tenacity and were emphasized in the teaching of the young.

If, then, we assess the acculturative situation of the Negro in the United States in the light of his differing interest in the several phases of his traditions and in terms of varied opportunities for the retention of Africanisms in the several aspects of culture, we find a certain coincidence between the two which significantly indicates a means whereby the carry-over of earlier traits not only could have been achieved but must in many cases have been consciously striven after. When we consider the operation of the slave system, it is apparent that African technology, economic life, and political organization had but relatively slight chance of survival. Utensils, clothing, and food were supplied by the masters, and it is but natural that these should have been of the type most convenient to procure, least expensive to provide, and, other things being equal, most like those to which the slaveowners were accustomed. The extension of African political institutions was also prevented by the total setting of slavery, so that only in the most secret fashion could African legal tradition find expression or African political talent be made effective.

On the other hand, in the fields of religion and magic and certain nonmaterial aspects of aesthetic life, retention by the slaves of African customs was not only possible but, in some cases, held to be desirable by the masters. One cannot read the literature of the slave period without being impressed by the number and strength of the complaints made by leaders of church groups at the lack of religious instruction given the slaves. It is difficult to suppose that the outstanding interest of the African in the supernatural, mentioned in the preceding section, could have been completely set aside by the slaves themselves. It would seem to be more logical, as well as to be better history, to argue that the slaves carried on as best they might, in secret if necessary, thus continuing earlier patterns in sufficient vitality so that when eventually they were exposed to Christianity they developed the aberrant types of religious behavior that to this day differentiate the ritual of Negro churches from that of their white counterparts. Again, the attitudes of the masters toward song and dance and folk tales varied throughout the New World from hostility and suspicion through indifference to actual encouragement. It was recognized by all slaveowners that recreation was necessary and desirable if morale was to be maintained among the slaves. African types of dancing and singing were permitted as long as they did not interfere with work or were performed on holidays; at such times, according to numerous accounts, they were enjoyed by the masters who watched them.

The field of social organization stands intermediate between technology and religion with respect to retention of Africanisms in the face of slavery. The plantation system rendered the survival of the African compound impossible, though it by no means completely suppressed various approximations of certain forms of African family life. The marriage tie was naturally rendered unstable, yet even in the United States it is far from certain that the existence of many permanent matings among the slaves has not been lost sight of in the dramatic appeal of the large numbers of enforced separations. Certain obligations of parents to children, and of children to parents, were carried over with all the drives of their emotional content intact, particularly as concerns the relationship between a child and its mother. The vivid sense of the power of the dead, and the related feeling that the ancestors are always near by to be called on by their living descendants, tended to give a kind of strength to family ties among Negroes that persists even today. And it was but natural that these attitudes and beliefs concerning kinship should have been taught to oncoming generations without undue interference by the masters, as long as they led to no action that would impede the smooth functioning of the plantation.

Traditions underlying nonrelationship groupings of various kinds likewise survived the slave regime, especially the spirit behind the numerous types of African co-operative societies which was kept alive by the very form of group labor employed on the plantations. The feeling of the importance of helpfulness inherent in this tradition must, as a matter of fact, have contributed directly toward the adjustment of the African to his new situation, for without some formula of mutual self-help he could scarcely have supported the vicissitudes of slave existence. That this formula did survive is to be seen, moreover, in the manner in which African types of co-operative agricultural organizations sprang up in the Sea Islands immediately following emancipation, and how insurance societies, a phenomenon common to West Africa, likewise came into being. To be mentioned here also is the great number of Negro lodges in the United States today. For, though these follow in their outward form conventional white patterns, they are by no means the same as their white counterparts in inner sanction or as concerns their objectives. To explain facts of this kind, however, it is necessary once again to turn to the role of instruction, which gave to generation after

generation a sense of the importance of leadership that characterizes all African social institutions. Analysis on this basis must
conclude that here, rather than by the lash of the overseer, was
inculcated the principle of order and regularity induced by a
discipline exerted through responsible headship.

To analyze the educational devices that tended to retain African
elements does not mean that the problem may be neglected of
how the European patterns of behavior manifested by Negroes
today, and their non-African sanctions, were established. We
must also consider those positive measures which, in adults, made
for acceptance of the masters' way of life and were thus taught
to the children, while it is likewise essential to bear in mind
the negative forces that, without conscious direction, tended to
discourage the retention of aboriginal customs. The difference
between these two may be illustrated by an example. As has
been pointed out, the economic workings of the plantation system
inhibited African material culture and technological capacities.
Ironworking, wood-carving, basketry, and the like simply had
no place in the new scene, and hence such techniques almost
everywhere died out of sheer inanition. On the other end, proselytizing among the slaves by Christian missionaries constituted a
positive drive. There is, for example, no logical reason why the
African world view might not otherwise have been continued to
the same degree that African motor habits in dancing were
retained. Changes would undoubtedly have appeared of themselves, as they have in the dance, since some measure of innovation must result from contact stimulus. Yet, in the case of the
African world view, efforts directed toward affecting change
caused a premium to be placed by the whites on the overt
acceptance of Christian beliefs and practices and thus accelerated
the disappearance of African religion in recognizable form.

Recognizing that more intimate contact between Negroes and
whites in the United States has brought about greater accommodation on the part of the Negroes here to white institutions than
elsewhere in the New World, the question as to the Africanisms
that have been retained may be raised. In the main these take
the form of less tangible manifestations: those that are of the kind
that, as has been pointed out, would be transmitted to a considerable extent on the unconscious level, in the intimacy of the
household. Aside from certain curios in the cultural cupboard,

few recognizable overt African institutions are to be found except for some instances in such isolated regions as the Gullah Islands or the Mississippi Delta. Beliefs like those concerning the supernatural powers of children born with a caul or with some other unusual characteristic, or certain forms of hair-braiding of children and old women, or certain dance steps, or the fact that the coiled basketry in the Sea Islands is always done in clockwise direction are of this nature. Elements in Negro funeral rites similarly persist. These range from reinterpretation of the West African custom of having partial and definitive burials in terms of the delayed funeral of this country to the part played by secret societies (lodges) in preparing the corpse, or the custom of passing a child over the body of a deceased parent.

It is not materials of this order, however, that are the most significant for an understanding of the effective role of education in permitting the carry-over of cultural values, even under conditions of most severe stress. It is more revealing to attempt to account in these terms for certain aspects of Negro social organization peculiar to this group. Thus it has been often remarked that family types found among Negroes are aberrant when contrasted to the present forms of the family among majority groups in this country. The importance of the mother as against the father, the role of the grandmother, the meticulous care with which relationships are traced, and above all, the fact that illegitimacy in the legal sense has little meaning as a sociological force in communities are some of these traits. It is rarely recognized, if at all, that a tradition stemming from the relationships within the African polygamous household might account for some of this. As has been seen, in Africa the child is closer to its mother than to its father; and this tradition can be thought of as having been reinterpreted and re-worked in the light of the American scene in terms of families where the relationship between mother and children has continued to be stronger than that between father and children. As concerns family structure accommodated to a pattern of monogamy, this results in a grouping wherein the man, in many instances, tends to play a secondary role. But the attitudes on which such a structure is based are attitudes that are the result of the continuation, through teaching within the family, of a point of view that is far more easily thought of as originating in Africa than on the slave plantation. This latter

situation, viewed in these terms, can again be regarded merely
as something which reinforced earlier custom.

The very manner in which the Negro children in rural communities are trained shows again the carry-over of an earlier
custom. Whipping is far more prevalent among Negroes than
among whites, as is evidenced by the comments of many observers. But, as has been seen, whipping is an outstanding African
mode of correction of children; this has been retained and, in all
probability, reinforced by the corrective patterns of slavery.
Other educational devices that derive from Africa may likewise
be mentioned. Teaching of techniques of various kinds on the
informal level is widespread, and the greater self-reliance of
young Negro children in rural communities as against those of
white families is well recognized. The manner in which a child
has impressed on him, through constant contact, the types of accepted behavior at religious rituals, and the absence of sanctimoniousness at these rituals in Negro churches, where children
are free to go about as they will, are similar carry-overs of
African educational methods.

Even more important than such traits are the attitudes of suspended judgement, of reserve in contact with others, of keeping
one's own counsel, that so characterize the Negroes of this country,
not only in their relations with whites, but with members of
their own group as well. It may be asserted that this is merely a
survival of the protective coloration developed by any oppressed
minority, and there is no desire in this discussion to minimize the
extent to which reactions of this kind are essential if an under-
privileged group is to survive. It is striking, however, that in
Africa itself, where the people are free and where the relationships
between individuals are those of any normal community, the
same tendency toward reserve rather than frankness, toward
keeping counsel rather than revealing one's affairs, characterizes
the point of view of all classes. The continuation of an approach
toward life of this kind, so widespread among such a large
group of people, is not a matter of chance; it has obviously
been passed on, by precept and example, from older to younger
members of the group as generation has succeeded generation in
this country.

Another survival, only to be accounted for by teaching in the
Negro slave cabin and in the Negro home after emancipation, is

the great importance of proper modes of behavior. Here, again, the simplistic explanation, that this is merely a reflection of the discipline of the plantation, or copying manners observed in the Great House, is popular. Yet the etiquette of the whites who lived in the Great House, though this may have been copied, was not observed by most Negroes, who were field hands; more often the whites who could be closely observed by the slaves were the small planters, the crudity of whose modes of behavior has been remarked by traveler after traveler in the antebellum South. It is not easy, either, to see how the codes of behavior exacted of the slaves in the fields by their overseers were such as to inculcate the soft graciousness that so outstandingly characterizes the Negro's behavior. "Mind your manners" is a phrase so well known that it has become a part of the stereotype of the Negro "mammy"; and materials are not lacking which show that within the slave community the need to be well-mannered was impressed on children in such a way as to insure proper behavior on their part. Slave autobiographies again and again testify to the respectful behavior exacted of the young slave toward his elders, and the punishment he received if he did not fulfil this expectation. But the importance of proper recognition of status, respect for elders, and the like is very great in West Africa itself; and it is here that one must look when considering points of origin.

The exploration of techniques of teaching and effective results of instruction in terms of the perpetuation of Africanisms of this less apparent type might go on indefinitely, if considerations of space permitted. The point to be made here, however, is the need for students concerned with assessing the role of education in shaping human institutions and human personalities to recognize that undue stress must not be laid on the function of education either as a stabilizing element in culture or as one making for change. Each situation must be analyzed in terms of its historical past, and of the sanctions underlying the institutions involved. The essential problem is to discover what are the situations under which one aspect or the other will predominate and to recognize that predominance of change does not rule out retention, or that predominance of retention does not imply complete stability.

12 EDUCATION IN AFRICA: ITS PATTERN AND ROLE IN SOCIAL CHANGE

Margaret Read

This essay is by an English anthropologist who carried out field research among the Ngoni of Malawi, in central Africa, on whom she has published both a general study (1956) and a book on their system of education (1968). The paper was written with the educational problems of the former British colonial territories in mind, the principal of which was how to introduce Western education to people who were still essentially "traditional" in their ways of thinking about the world in which they found themselves. It provides a useful introduction to the study of the aims, place, and methods of Western-oriented educational programs in newly literate and developing societies, and of the reactions to these programs on the part of the peoples of the territories themselves.

IN ORDER to give this section on education some integration and validity, arbitrary limits have been set on the territories covered. They include all territories from the Sahara to the Zambezi River, and from the Atlantic Ocean to the Nile Basin. By excluding North Africa, Egypt, the Sudan, Eritrea, Ethiopia, Somaliland, Southern Rhodesia, and the Union of South Africa, the remaining territories, with the exception of Liberia, are all at present non-self-governing or trusteeship territories with a political relationship to some metropolitan country in Europe.

In the general assessment of education within these set limits a historical perspective is essential, and here we find that the existing data are very uneven in respect to coverage and precision and that the needed research has not yet been done except in

Reprinted from *The Annals of the American Academy of Political and Social Science* 298, March 1955:170–79, with permission of the author and of the American Academy of Political and Social Science.

isolated studies. This historical view is the more important considering the rapidity of modern change, especially in territories, such as the Gold Coast, where political changes herald great expansions of educational facilities.

The relation of descriptive material to analytical studies raises another set of problems in presenting this article. Since 1945 in spite of certain large-scale surveys of education in particular areas, there have been very few "compilation studies" of the extensive amount of material appearing in periodicals and in annual and special reports. There are three major problems for the student in this field. One is the difficulty of relating educational plans as they appear on paper to actual achievement in practice. Another is the lack of "bench marks" for estimating advance in educational facilities and in school enrollment and attendance. The third is the absence of accepted criteria for assessing educational progress, using that term in a wide and comprehensive sense.

TRADITIONAL TRAINING

Modern studies of socialization, especially among preliterate peoples, have drawn attention to the provision for training in behavior and in technical skills which has been described sometimes as a traditional educational system. The use of these terms and the attempt to equate tribal training in Africa with a modern school system have led to considerable confusion among Europeans, and to resentment among African peoples on two counts: one the ignoring of the training given by them to their children and the other the reiteration by educational writers that tribal training should have a place in the school system without taking any steps to achieve it or to integrate it. One of the sharpest clashes between Europeans and Africans arises from a misunderstanding by the European of the significance of traditional interpersonal behavior as taught by tribal elders; and one of the major reasons for the increasing fragmentation of African society in urban and industrial centers is the abandonment by African parents and elders of all attempts to train their children on traditional lines.

The patterns of socialization among African peoples have received on the whole very little attention from social anthropolo-

gists. Among the studies which have been made two distinct
patterns emerge: those among the small communities, organized
on a clan or restricted tribal basis, such as the Tallensi of the
Northern Territories of the Gold Coast, as described by Professor
Meyer Fortes (1938); and those among the large tribal units
or military states, where there was a centralized political authority
and a hierarchical social status system. The age-set systems of the
East African peoples are found both in smaller tribal groups
and in larger centralized ones, and were sometimes, but not always, related to cattle keeping and to training for warfare.

The life of the small communities, such as the Tallensi, was
centered in the struggle for livelihood and in the intricate pattern
of kinship relationships. We find therefore an emphasis on the
importance of children to the family groups, demonstrated in the
indulgence shown during the early years of childhood, followed
by the desire of children to grow up as quickly as possible and
take part in adult activities, both social and economic. This stress
on children being "little adults" was in sharp contrast to the
recognized age sets in East Africa, where after the infant and
wholly dependent stage was passed, boys and girls, according
to their age, had recognized and progressive positions and responsibilities in the life of their community and later of the tribe
as a whole. The emphasis in most of the training in the age
sets was on obedience, endurance, and co-operation in a recognized unit. Training in both the larger and the smaller communities emphasized correct behavior to equals, superiors, and inferiors,
and the acquiring of the necessary technical skills for craft work,
cultivation, cattle keeping, or warfare.

When the former training of children and young people in
African societies is compared with the modern school systems
now operating, certain features of the traditional patterns appear
to have been abandoned, notably those which showed the close
correlation between the training of personality and character and
the integration and cohesion of family, clan, and tribal units.
Three of these elements were absent in the early forms of schooling
as introduced in Africa, and though their significance has been
progressively realized, the attempts to incorporate them into the
modern school system have been spasmodic and not altogether
successful.

Physical development and social recognition

The first was the close correlation in African tribal society between physical development and social recognition. The so-called age sets were organized not so much by age in years as by recognized physical changes—the appearance of second teeth, prepuberty changes, the actual onset of puberty, the birth of the first child, and so on. The emphasis in the majority of African societies on fertility and on the capacity to beget and bear children was the keynote of the initiation rites where they were on an organized tribal basis. This emphasis included instruction given during these rites, and privately, before and at puberty, in sexual intercourse, sex hygiene, and sexual behavior in general. This instruction, which was associated with general social behavior and the responsibilities of young adults, was given at or about the period of the most important physical change for boys and girls. Their normal activities ceased while they were withdrawn from ordinary life to undergo this training, and they returned to their community as individuals charged with new knowledge and new responsibilities. The age at which children went to school, the prevalence of mission boarding schools, and features of the initiation rites which were dangerous to health and objectionable on Christian moral grounds caused the missionaries to clash with this traditional training. The result was that it was largely abandoned by Christians, and at the same time the essential sex teaching and training in social behavior were omitted.

Enlargement of social and political horizons

The second element in the traditional training which was squeezed out by modern schools was the gradual enlarging of the social and political horizons of the children. The learning of genealogies of the families and clans, as among the Ashanti and the Baganda, the recognition of social groupings in hierarchical tribal settings and of their reciprocal relationships, the hearing of tribal "history" in praise songs and legends told at tribal gatherings—these were forms of direct learning which had no place in schools but had set times and places in a traditional situation. In more specific behavior patterns the organization of age villages, as among the Nyakusa (Wilson 1951), of boys' dormitories in

villages and of competitive dance groups between village and
village as among the Ngoni, and of attendance at tribal law
courts where codes and norms of behavior were in review—all
these gave young Africans a training in citizenship which was
related to their own society.

Artistic expression

The third element for which the early schools, and to a great
extent the schools of today, made no place was those aesthetic
activities which had for African peoples a deep emotional content.
Music of all kinds, vocal and instrumental, tribal dancing, the
telling of hero stories and folklore, tribal expression in dress,
house decoration, carving and painting of ritual and common
objects, dramatic recitations and miming—these touched the roots
of African emotional life.

ROLE OF TRADERS AND MISSIONARIES

It is generally accepted that in all the African territories south
of the Sahara missionary societies were responsible for opening
schools wherever they established their stations. It is not always
realized that the commercial company, especially in West Africa,
played a significant part in what the Portuguese first and the
French and Belgians later called "the mission of civilization"
(Read 1953). European thought in the seventeenth and eight-
eenth centuries saw no incompatibility between establishing
"forts" to regulate the slave trade and educating a very limited
number of Africans to assist them in their enterprises. This education implied as a rule conversion to Christianity, and in this respect the early trading companies anticipated the work of the
missions.

Some of the chief gaps in the history of education in Africa
are gradually being filled by historians, by missionary writers
reviewing their work for centenary celebrations, by research students carrying out investigations in a limited field on material in
the Records Office, in local archives, in the archives of mission
houses, and in the Vatican library. The results of this research,
as illustrated in Dr. Roland Oliver's book, *The Missionary Factor
in East Africa* (1952), and in recent unpublished theses on
West Africa in the University of London, show how varied were

the beginnings of educational work in all the African territories. The common element, in trading posts and in all kinds of mission stations, was the need for intermediaries between the foreign traders and missionaries and the people. The emphasis in the majority of missionary enterprises, apart from their primary task of conversion to Christianity, was on the importance of training teachers, evangelists, clerks, and artisans who would assist them in establishing their mission stations and by taking over the routine duties enable the missionaries to extend their work.

Another result of recent research has been to establish the intention of the early missionaries to emphasize the training of Africans in agriculture and elementary technical skills such as building and carpentry. There has been widespread criticism over the last half century that mission schools gave too literary and academic an education, and unfitted boys for working on the land. Investigations of missionary records have shown that in many cases mission boards and the missionaries themselves intended to emphasize the practical vocational aspects of education. The eventual emphasis on literary skills was largely due to pressure from the Africans themselves because that was what they wanted from the schools; and also, at a later stage, to standards of academic attainment set up by systems of inspection and examination.

Present mission schools

The contemporary picture in the African territories today is that of a widespread network of mission schools at all levels, from the "bush" or village school up to the full secondary school and teacher training college. The widest development of mission schools has occurred in the Belgian Congo and in British territories, with the exception in the latter of Northern Nigeria, where the treaties made with the Muslim emirs at the beginning of the century precluded the opening of Christian schools among the Muslim peoples. A common feature in the Belgian Congo and in British territories has been the use of the vernacular languages in the lowest classes of the primary schools. The study of these languages, and their reduction to writing, was one of the outstanding contributions of the pioneer missionaries. While they attacked and rejected much of the African cultural background in their attempts to abolish "heathen practices," these early missionaries did signal service to the African peoples and to the future of African studies by recording and transcribing the vernacular languages and by giving the African peoples the New and Old Testaments in their own language.

In the British territories the missions depended for their educational, and indeed for all their work at first, on contributions from the home churches, and on the gifts, often in kind, from African peoples and the almost universal payment of fees by the pupils in schools. As the governments in the territories assumed full responsibility for all the administrative services, they established a system of grants-in-aid for mission schools, dependent on the standards attained and the reports of inspectors appointed and paid by the government. The present methods of financing schools, in Liberia as well as in all the non-self-governing territories, have developed from the history of mission schools over the last fifty to sixty years. In addition to the government schools, which now exist in all territories, there are assisted and non-assisted schools, conducted primarily by missions but also by plantations and other industrial undertakings.

In the Belgian Congo a distinction is made between "national" missions based in Belgium and "foreign" missions based in other countries. After 1948 the foreign missions were offered equal subsidies for their schools if those in charge were equally qualified —that is, if they had taken courses in French language and literature and had studied the Belgian educational system and Belgian history and culture. In British territories there is a supposition that non-British missionaries will be able to use and teach English in their schools. In the past it has not been stringently enforced, but the tightening up of the grants-in-aid system indicates that this requirement will in the future be necessary for continued financial support.

DIVERGENT EDUCATIONAL SYSTEMS TODAY

The new edition of Lord Hailey's *African Survey* (1957) has a section on education which incorporates the situation as recorded in the most recent surveys and studies. Two recent comprehensive surveys have been made, one on the Belgian Congo by Dr. J. Vanhove (1953) and the other on the British territories in East and Central Africa and in West Africa, carried out by two educational missions (Nuffield Foundation 1952). No studies of contemporary educational systems comparable in scope and integration have been made in the French or Portuguese areas or in Liberia, though some significant effects of education on social change have been recorded in recent French sociological studies. It is clear from the information available, whether integrated in a survey or scattered throughout reports and articles, that Africans in these territories have educational opportunities which differ widely in type and extent, and that the systems also show divergences in the philosophy and intentions behind the facilities offered. This is true also in the ten British African territories, which have no uniformity in their educational systems. Since it is impracticable to describe the existing system in any detail, a selection has been made of four of the most salient features of the present day found to a greater or lesser degree in all the territories and relevant to the effects of education on social change.

Integration with metropolitan systems

This feature affects the non-self-governing territories only and is directly connected with the general political relationship between the African territory and the metropolitan country. Thus there are variations in the administration and planning of education, as illustrated in the Gold Coast with its almost complete autonomy and in French West Africa with its close integration with metropolitan France. This relationship, however, cannot be summarily dismissed as one of virtual autonomy or integration. It has to be analyzed into several component factors: the responsibility for policy making and implementation; the financing of education; the determining of educational standards and of the equivalence of certificates and degrees; and the varying educational opportunities offered to different racial groups in multiracial states such as the Belgian Congo and Kenya. In the British territories, though there is in London an Advisory Committee on Education in the colonies, which assists in recruiting and training expatriate teachers and in giving specialist help in the territories which ask for its co-operation, the full onus of policy making lies with the ten respective governments, and they are also responsible for the financial implementation of their policies. They have looked, however, since 1940 for additional financial help, especially in capital expenditure, from the Colonial Development and Welfare Fund, grants being allocated on the basis of long-term and shorter-term planning. In educational standards, local autonomy exists up to the end of the secondary school period, when external examinations are taken, based on the Cambridge School Certificate. A West African Examinations Board has now been set up which will conduct examinations within these territories at the secondary school level. In the French territories the postwar educational system in France has been taken as the model, and the colonial teaching and inspectorate service are unified with that of France.[1] The responsibility for policy making and finance lies with the Director of Education in each of the two French territories, and all diplomas and certificates awarded by him are valid throughout the French Union. Contributions to colonial education are made from the French Development Fund. In the Belgian Congo, though there is recognition of the dual nature of the Congo population and of the essential link with the French language and with Belgian cultural institutions, policy is determined in the Congo and education is financed from Congo sources.

Degree of educational uniformity and methods of control

Two factors have influenced the development of education in all these territories, including Liberia. One is the multiplicity of mission schools which preceded but now exist alongside the state schools. The other is the marked divergence between education in the towns and the coastal areas generally and in the hinterland away from the main routes of communication. Nowhere is there any uniformity in educational facilities between the towns and the up-country areas; nor is there anywhere, in spite of all attempts at control, much effective equivalence in the kind of education given in mission and state schools, especially at the lowest levels. Throughout the African territories the methods of control of educational facilities and standards at different levels follow the same pattern: the inspection of schools through a central inspectorate; an examination system, which varies in its application to primary, secondary, and technical schools; the

---

[1] French North Africa is not considered here. The units in French Africa referred to are the Federations of French West and French Equatorial Africa.

standards of academic attainment required for entry into post-school training or into direct employment; and the control of the training of teachers and of their conditions of service. Systems of inspection based on a central government department of education are a universal method of control. It has been the experience in most British territories that where mission or government supervisory services to assist teachers were set up, following the recommendations of the Phelps Stokes Commission in the 1920's, the effectiveness of the inspecting staff has been much increased. In addition the appointment of education advisers to the Protestant and Roman Catholic missions in a territory, paid for by state funds, has made for better co-operation in carrying out policies. In the French territories the leaving certificate of the primary schools is equivalent to the French "certificat d'études" and is universally recognized for entry into employment and into vocational training. In British territories where the school nomenclature varies greatly, and especially in those areas where educational standards are rising rapidly, the entry into employment from the schools is being raised continuously.

The situation created by the coexistence of schools under government and voluntary agencies is nowhere seen more clearly than in the recruitment and training of teachers. The history of mission education and the recent educational surveys have shown that the expansion of school facilities and the maintenance of standards in the teaching profession are very difficult to reconcile. In all the territories "untrained" teachers are found in large numbers and are regarded by the education authorities as their major problem, professionally and administratively. Governments exercise some control through the grants-in-aid system where it is based upon the qualifications of the teaching staff in a school. Professional standards are maintained through the recognition given to teachers trained in normal colleges. Thus the diploma awarded in the nine Écoles Normales in French territories is valid throughout the French Union, but this high standard of teaching when applied to staffing primary schools makes them too expensive to establish universally.

Appearance of educational ladder

In the names of the kinds of schools provided there is no uniform practice, not only between the different regions but between the British territories also. The universal term "primary school," for example, means the first eight years in Liberia; in the Belgian Congo it is a four year course divided after the first two years into an ordinary and a selective course; in French West Africa there is one type of primary school lasting five years for Africans and Europeans; in French Equatorial Africa there is a village junior primary of four years and a regional or urban full primary of six years; in the hinterland of several British territories there is an unrecognized preprimary or "bush school" course, and a full primary one of six years, or a four year junior primary and a further four years called senior primary or middle school. The demand for secondary education, both academic and technical, which far exceeds the facilities available, poses the problem of selection in an acute form, and this in its turn is closely connected with the language medium used in the primary and middle schools. In all territories the medium in the secondary schools is the European language of the metropolitan country, though in the Belgian Congo and in most British territories courses at the secondary level can be offered in African languages. Where the primary schools, as in the state schools of French West Africa, use only French as the medium of instruction, the problems of selection can be solved by competitive examinations. In many other territories the basic instruction is given in the primary schools in a vernacular language, with a European language introduced either early in the curriculum or at a later stage. Here selection for the secondary school poses problems of testing intelligence as well as attainment, in order not to exclude able children who may have been handicapped by language difficulties.

Universal primary schooling

Compulsory education may exist as a policy on paper, but it can only be made effective where there are school facilities provided for every child. Several territories, Belgian, French, and British, have compulsory ordinances which can be put into effect in restricted areas, but it is clear that no considerable area of any territory has all its school-age population enrolled in school. The best documented study of the expansion of educational facilities is found in the Gold Coast publications, beginning with the report dealing mainly with reorganization in the years 1937–41 and following through with the Ten Year Plan of 1947, the Accelerated Development Plan of 1951, and the report on progress in education in 1954 (Gold Coast Government 1942, 1947, 1951, 1954). These documents illustrate clearly the two major problems in educational expansion in Africa: the provision of finance and the provision of teachers. They also illustrate the determination of a territory on the verge of self-government to provide universal schooling facilities in all but the most remote section of its territory.

HIGHER EDUCATION AND AFRICAN ADVANCE

From French and British West Africa before World War II an increasing number of Africans were going to the metropolitan countries to take university degrees and higher professional training in law and medicine. Some of these men went at their own expense, others secured state scholarships. French policy continued and increased after 1945 the system of scholarships. British policy did the same, but also set up university colleges, one in East Africa, two in West Africa, and most recently one in Central Africa. These university colleges had a dual purpose: to give increased facilities for Africans to get degrees and higher professional training; and to equip a number of them to fill administrative and professional posts in their own countries. In 1950 an Institute of Advanced Studies was opened at Dakar, already an important research center, to give diplomas in arts, science, medicine, and law, with the intention that it should become the university of French Africa. In 1954 university courses were begun at Kisantu in the Belgian Congo under the auspices of the University of Louvain. In 1951 a new university college was opened in Liberia, based on the higher college founded in 1862.

In most African territories therefore there now exist institutions for higher education of a university grade. There is a clear intention to integrate the standards of work and the degrees given with university standards in the metropolitan country and thus to ensure that Africans have equivalent qualifications for senior administrative posts and that they are eligible for research grants. The pursuit of research in the human and physical sciences and in fields such as history, law, and language is taken for granted in the university colleges. In addition there are three social science research institutes in British East, West, and Central Africa; in the Belgian Congo research institutes in medicine and agriculture have long been at work, and the Institute for Scientific Research in Central Africa is actively engaged in an extensive program of research in the natural, biological, and social sciences in the Congo. In Dakar l'Institut Français d'Afrique Noire has established a world-wide reputation for its published and projected research.

EDUCATION AND SOCIAL CHANGE

There is general agreement, based on abundant evidence of a political and economic character, that the spread of modern education has been one of the most powerful forces in African social change. Yet there have been very few studies, either historical or contemporary, which focus in a limited area on the sociological changes resulting from modern education, such as the one by K. A. Busia on Sekondi (1950). It is clear that the impact of schools, over a historical period, has had very different results in the coastal areas and the hinterland, where in some remote parts it is still possible to study the effects of the first impact of the new schools on a preliterate people. Hence though the generalizations which follow, based on data drawn from material in other fields, can be regarded as valid in respect of the main social changes due to education, they are less illuminating as guides to future planning than they would be if they were supported by detailed sociological studies for given areas.

Occupational mobility

As we saw at the opening of this article, one of the first purposes of the early schools was to train Africans to serve European enterprises, commercial, missionary, administrative. From that time on, the traditional and relatively standardized forms of livelihood and employment underwent progressive changes. Warfare, cultivation, herding stock, fishing, trading, craft work were the main occupations in tribal life. The demands of European enterprise, for which boys were taught and trained, introduced a money economy as well as new skills. This led to two main forms of mobility. One was a change over from following the local traditional and family form of livelihood—a change which implied individual choice, new rewards, new skills. The other was the movement of individuals and groups from remote areas to centers of employment, inaugurating the modern phenomenon of migrant labor. Sociological research has shown clearly that one effect of the spread of schools is to increase emigration from rural areas, and it was pointed out in the British educational survey of East and Central Africa that "the flight from farming" was causing great concern about the maintenance of the basic food supplies.

Urbanization

The growth of towns for administrative, commercial, and industrial purposes caused a demand for increased facilities for schools and also for some educational solutions for the problems of seasonal unemployment, slum conditions, and juvenile delinquency. The contrasts here between the Copper Belt towns in the Belgian Congo and in Northern Rhodesia are illuminating. The Belgian policy of permanent urbanization, as contrasted with that of mainly migrant labor in Northern Rhodesia, led to the use of school facilities and of adult informal education to meet the new situation for the Africans. It provided also a ladder of advancement in technical training which created a new skilled artisan class which was at home in and enjoyed industrial employment and urban amenities.

Rural community life

The combination of migrant labor, cash crops, and a money economy has probably caused more changes in social life in the villages than the village schools themselves. Since many of these schools were part of the missionary enterprise, the religious and ethical teaching given has had significant effects, especially on the outlook and status of women. The postwar work in community development and adult literacy has not only given women the skills of reading and writing but has created amenities such as water supplies, better roads, co-operative stores, maternity homes, dispensaries, giving village women more leisure, more security, and less isolation. In many parts of Africa women's clubs and societies have been started or have received a new impetus where they never existed before, and women are emerging from a purely domestic and physically arduous life to take part in community affairs, to express their women's point of view, and to organize themselves for further advance.

This changed outlook among rural women is part of a wider change in the status and authority patterns in village life. Wherever local government on modern lines is being introduced, younger educated men and women are taking responsibility and the traditional status and authority of the older age group is being challenged. In many rural areas the division between Christian and non-Christian in the community is on the basis of age, since the younger group have been to school and have been baptized, and show signs of challenging traditional authority where it seems to them to oppose social and economic advance.

Part of the change in outlook in rural areas is also due to the gradual penetration of informal education through the media of radio, films, and newspapers. The spread of the small household receiving set known as the "saucepan specials" in Northern Rhodesia, coupled with the publication of *The African Listener,* directly connects literacy with listening in. The popularity of the new vernacular journals is another instance of the desire to use a new-found skill; and the development of African film units in several territories is related to the growing interest in locally made, as distinct from foreign, films.

Intergroup and interpersonal relations

Social change can be measured in concrete terms, such as new types of houses, clothing, and amusements; supplies of water and electricity; and circulation of newspapers and sale of radio sets. Though most of these developments are a result of education, many of them can be enjoyed by the illiterate and are a result of general economic improvements. It is modern education, however, which is mainly responsible for the new middle classes in the towns, and for the vigorous women's groups in towns and rural areas. It is responsible too for the gradual splitting up of the former large joint families and patriarchal households, and for efforts on the part of younger educated women to bring up their children on more modern lines. These new group and personal relations create tensions within the existing society and in some areas, such as the big towns, by undermining the stability of family and household groups create new forms of insecurity.

13 CULTURE AND EDUCATION IN THE MIDWESTERN HIGHLANDS OF GUATEMALA

Robert Redfield

Some of the problems mentioned in Chapter 12 are brought up again in this account of modern education in a non-colonial society, Guatemala. Rural Guatemalan society consists of two main groups, the Indian and the Ladino. Indian culture is transmitted by the learning of moral values through myth and folktale, and by other non-pedagogical means. The Ladinos lack the necessary traditional institutions to transmit their culture in the same ways; they must depend instead on informal means. The schools set up by the government are regulatory agencies that are external to both cultures, and they play little role in anything but purely technical training. As schools in any wider sense, therefore, they are not effective and the peoples of both groups do not consider them as an integral part of the process of growing up. The main point made is that education is part of a total social process, and not merely a pedagogical system.

W̱HEN EDUCATION is considered as it occurs in a modern society, we think first of the school. In a primitive society there are neither schools nor pedagogues; yet we speak of the "education" of the primitive child. In so doing we are, of course, recognizing a conception of education much wider than the domain of the school; we are thinking of it as "the process of cultural transmission and renewal"—a process present in all societies and, indeed, indistinguishable from that process by which societies persist and change.

When we describe education in such school-less and bookless societies, we are likely to fix attention upon other institutions

Reprinted from *American Journal of Sociology* 48, 1943:640–48, with permission of Mrs. Margaret Park Redfield and of the editor, *American Journal of Sociology.*

which obviously and formally express and communicate the local tradition. Such are ceremony, myth, tribal and familial symbols and stories, initiation ceremonies, and men's houses. In these we recognize a certain fixity and emphasis of major elements of culture, and we see that in their perpetuation and repetition these elements receive restatement and are communicated to the young. Indeed, we have come to think of primitive societies as providing a well-organized and self-consistent system of institutions by which children are brought up to think and act as did their fathers. In such societies we connect education with traditional forms expressive of a rich content. In comparison with the educational effect of a katchina dance upon a Hopi child, a chapter in a civics textbook seems pretty thin, educationally speaking.

To the invitation to give an account of the educational process, I respond from a point of view of certain rural communities in the midwestern highlands of Guatemala which are neither modern nor primitive but in many respects intermediate between a simple tribe and a modern city. Educational institutions among these rural mountain-dwellers do not quite conform to either the primitive or civilized type. These people have schools, but the schools are of small importance. They have ceremonies and legends, but these forms do not have so much content as one might suppose. In these Guatemalan societies schooling is far from accomplishing what our educational experts claim generally for schools. On the other hand, ceremony and myth do not come up to the standard set by many primitive societies. In this part of the world there are no central and powerful educational institutions around which an essay can conveniently be written.

The situation is not without value, however, for students of the cultural process. In recognizing in this part of Guatemala the limited educational influence of schools, on the one hand, and of traditional forms on the other, one is brought to see aspects of education which underlie all formal institutions. People in Guatemala do get educated (in the sense that the heritage is transmitted) with adjustments to meet changing circumstances, even though many of them never go to school and even though there are no great puberty ceremonies, with revelations of the sacred *alcheringa* and narrations of totemic myths, such as occur among Australian aborigines. In this paper I shall make some observations on certain features of these highlands societies in so far as the educational process is concerned; and I shall, in particular, call attention to aspects of that process which are probably to be encountered in every society. I call attention to them because education is ordinarily studied without much reference to them.

As I look at the school in the little village where I once was resident, it appears to me to play a greater part in changing the culture of the people than in handing it on from one generation to the next, although its influence in the direction of change is indirect. Nearly all the time in the school is given to learning to read and to write and to calculate. Some children acquire a fair command of these arts; others do not. The arts of literacy have many practical uses, and their possession carries some prestige. They improve the opportunities for gainful employment, and their possession disposes the individual to seek his fortune in the town or in the city. In some cases success in school leads to higher education in the city and so to participation in urban civilization.

The majority of people of this community are Indians; a minority are a Spanish-speaking people of mixed ancestry known as Ladinos. The cultures of the two groups are identical in many areas of experience; in others they are still notably different. Where both kinds of people live in the same settlement, both attend the same school. The school makes more change for the Indian than for the Ladino, because through association with the Ladinos in the school he learns Spanish and in not a few cases is disposed to put off Indian dress, to live in the manner of the Ladinos, and so to become a Ladino. There is here no obstacle of prejudice or law to prevent this not infrequent occurrence. The school is one important institution, therefore, through which the Indian societies tend to lose members to the Ladino society and so ultimately to disappear.

As such an instrument of acculturation and culture change, the school is only one among a number of effective institutions. The penitentiary deserves mention, for, although its liberalizing influence is less widely distributed than in the case of the school, not a few individuals profit by this form of widened experience and return to the village with a new song, a new trade, and a less parochial view of life. The common custom of bringing up other people's children is also effective, as when the child is an

Indian brought up in a Ladino household. Of such individuals it may later be said that "that Ladino is really an Indian," but the ethnic origin of the individual carries little or no social disadvantage and is quickly forgotten.

Considered as an institution helping to preserve the local culture, the role of the school is small. I venture the assertion that the abolition of schools in these highlands would leave the culture much as it is. Except for the texts of prayers recited on many occasions, little of the rural Ladino heritage depends on literacy. And, furthermore, it is only necessary that a few individuals in each society be literate so as to preserve access to written or printed sources. Indeed, for generations the Indian cultures in the more isolated societies have got along with a semi-professionalization of literacy. A few individuals in each village or group of villages were trained to read the Mass; the central government sent from the city a literate person to deal with the written communications of formal government. The more pagan religious ritual was, and still is, stored, unwritten, in the memories of a small number of professionals. Their knowledge is highly specialized and is little understood by the layman.

The village school in this area devotes little time to instruction other than the purely technical; and the little "cultural" instruction which it gives has small support in other branches of the village life. Some instruction is given in Guatemalan history and geography. What is taught is not reinforced by books in the homes, because there are almost no books in the homes. Nor is the instruction closely related to the content of oral tradition. The knowledge that Columbus discovered America is perpetuated in the school and is possessed by most Ladinos as an item of information, but few people whom I interrogated were able to tell me that that discovery was the event commemorated by the little celebration which the government orders to occur each year in the village municipal building on October 12. (Of course the more sophisticated townsman understands the meaning of the occasion.) At any rate, Columbus is no tribal or village legendary hero.

As not a great deal is accomplished by formal instruction in the school, one might suppose the lack to be made up by a great deal of deliberate inculcation and discipline in the home. At least with regard to the rural Ladino society, I am sure that this is not the case. Children are taught to do what they are expected to do chiefly as an aspect of coming to perform the tasks of adults. Moments of instruction are not segregated from moments of action. Boys are taught to farm and girls to cook as they help their elders do these things. Along with instruction in the practical arts, parents comment on conduct, saying what is "good" and what is "bad." The word *pecado* is applied to innumerable interdicted acts, from those which are regarded as mildly unlucky to those to which some real moral opprobrium attaches. Some parents will select a serious and special moment in which to convey sex instruction, and sometimes other subjects will be somewhat formally inculcated; but on the whole I should say that instruction in the home is casual and unsystematized.

Certainly it is not characteristic of this Ladino culture that the young gather around the knees of the old to listen reverently to a solemn exposition of the holy traditions and sacred memories of the people. Indeed, in this society, as in our own, it is hard to find the holy traditions, let alone to get anyone to listen while they are expounded. Most instruction that occurs in the home or outside it is connected with the practical arts of life.

It seems to me interesting that, while few of these Ladinos are today teaching their children the prayers of their Catholic tradition, they do take pains to teach them the traditional forms of address and salutation, which in these cultures are complicated and elaborate. It is characteristic of this people that requests and other communications are not abruptly and directly presented but are wrapped in highly conventional preliminary and terminal utterances; also, in general, among them polite language is regarded as seemly conduct.

It also seems to me that this formal language is a way in which people preserve their personal lives from too easy invasion and that it is therefore a useful art. It is, moreover, one which every man must practice for himself. The case is different with the prayers. Apparently it is not thought sufficiently important that every child have formal language in which to talk with God. It is, however, thought important that the prayers be recited by someone on the occasions of novenas for the saints and following a death. But all that is necessary is that one or a few persons be available to recite the prayers. It would not greatly surprise me if in these villages the reciting of Catholic prayers became

a paid profession, as are now the reciting of a Mass by priest
or layman, the teaching of the spoken text of a dance-drama,
or the playing of the little flageolet which accompanies processions
bearing images of the saints.

This observation about the teaching of prayers and of mannerly
speech may be generalized into two wider characterizations of
these Guatemalan cultures. The point of view on life is practical
and secular rather than religious or mystical; and formal activity is more than usually large, it seems to me, in proportion to
the content of symbolic meaning which underlies it. This statement I am disposed to make about both the Indian and the
Ladino cultures, although there are differences of degree or kind
in these respects between the two.

For the rural Ladinos it may be safely asserted that religious
pageantry and mythology do not play a large part in the education of the individual. The Christian epic is known very incom-
pletely; it exists in the form of many unco-ordinated fragments
of lore, and it is not vividly presented in any coherent or impressive way. These country people read very little sacred literature; they very rarely hear sermons; and there is no important
traditional ceremony or drama in which it might be expressed.
An exception in part must be made for the ninefold repetition at
Christmas time of the journey of Mary and Joseph and for the
little enactment of the birth of the child. The effigies of and
stories about Christ, and in less degree and importance of and
about the saints, do constitute a body of lore in which significant
traditional conceptions are perpetuated. But these ceremonials
occupy a very small part of the time and interests of the Ladinos,
and the element of mere entertainment in them is very large.

For the Indian, more is to be said as to the contribution of
ceremony and myth to the educational and cultural process. The
cult of the saints is more elaborate, and ritual observances are
more extensive. Justification for the statement that the culture
of the Ladinos is more shallow or less integrated than that of
the Indians is in part to be found, it seems to me, in the fact that
most stories told among Ladinos—and they like to tell and to
hear stories—deal chiefly with fairies, witches, talking animals,
and the adventures of picaresque personages, and that these
stories are not regarded as true and are not thought of as describing the world in which the individual lives. They are recognized

as fanciful creations that serve to entertain. The Indian, on the other hand, is disposed to regard the stories which he tells as true. Taken as a whole, the Indian's stories deal with men and animals and supernatural beings that he believes to exist about him, and their telling helps to define and redefine the conventional world in which the Indian lives.

A story well known in the Indian village of San Antonio tells how St. Anthony was once a man who dwelt in that village as other men, and how, counseled by his friend, Christ, whom he sought to rescue when our Lord's enemies were after him, he took the form of a saint so as to help the village where he lived and worked. The story offers an explanation for the origin of every significant element of costume and accouterment in the effigy of St. Anthony as customarily fashioned and as it exists in the village church; and it explains and justifies by reference to the saint's divine will many of the elements in the cult now customary: the marimba, the masked dancers, the fireworks, incense, and candles. Indeed, except that the content of the story is of Old World origin, the story in feeling and form is quite like many origin or hero myths that are told among non-Europeanized Indians.

A study of the educational process among these Indians would certainly have to take into account the existence of these stories and the circumstances under which they are told. It is plain that their telling helps to communicate and perpetuate the tradition of the group. It is significant that in the Indian villages every man passes through a series of public services; that in the course of many of these employments he spends long hours sitting in company with his age-mates and his elders, and that the elders at such times tell stories and relate episodes. The Ladino society is almost entirely without such an institution.

The existence of such a story as the one about St. Anthony is another evidence of the power within a culture to make itself, if such an expression may be employed. We may be sure that no priest set out to teach just this story to the Indians of the village. The story has grown in the course of generations of speculation upon an effigy and a ritual already sanctified and mysterious. Indeed, we catch glimpses of this process today when we hear of Indians who have found new explanations for some element of decorative design in church, or when an ethnologist's informant begins to offer speculations of his own.

Yet I am struck with the fact that even in the case of the Indian cultures there is more form than content in their collective life. In this same village of San Antonio there is performed every year in Holy Week a series of ceremonies occupying several days. It is generally understood that these ceremonies are a representation of the Passion of our Lord, and a general air of gravity attends them. But in my notes is a list of elements of the ritual for which none of my informants has been able to offer any explanation at all. Structures are erected and taken down, and effigies are used to which no meaning is assigned other than mere custom. One could fill many hundreds of pages with a detailed account of the goings and comings, the processions, the handing-over of effigies, the ritual drinking and bowing and the like, which custom provides must be carried on each year in one of these Indian villages among the groups of men in whose custody rest the images of the saints. On the other hand, even making liberal allowance for the relative difficulty of getting trustworthy information on the meanings of these acts, I feel sure that little could be said about the symbolic connections these acts have with the content of tradition. Yet, even in so far as these rituals have no symbolic meaning, they do maintain traditional ways within which behavior is regulated, and, therefore, they have their place in a broad investigation of the educational process in these communities.

The relatively formal or external aspect of much of the Guatemalan cultures is conspicuously illustrated in the dance-dramas. These are performed by Indians at most Indian festivals and very infrequently are performed by Ladinos at Ladino festivals. The observer sees a score of men dressed in brilliant and fantastic costumes, carrying highly specialized objects in their hands, and dancing, gesturing, and reciting long lines of set speech. The performance might be an enactment of some centrally important holy myth. It is, as a matter of fact, nothing of the sort. There are about a dozen dance-dramas known in Guatemala. Most of these have spoken text. Specialists possess these texts and at festival time are hired to teach groups of Indians to speak them and to perform the accompanying dances. The texts are in oratorical Spanish, and it is rare that an Indian understands well what he is saying. The general theme of the drama is known: if the dance called "The Conquest" is danced, the combat between Alvarado, the Spanish invader, and the pagan Indians is understood. But the tradition means little to the dancers; they will just as well enact Cortes' triumph over Montezuma, if that dance is cheaper to put on or provides a better show. The dance is performed, indeed, because a group of men is willing to put money and time into doing something lively for the festival. It may be compared to putting on a minstrel show in another culture, or hiring a merry-go-round. The comparison is not quite fair, but it suggests the truth.

In these societies of which I write, then, the educational process is not greatly dependent upon institutions organized for pedagogical purposes or upon organized and deliberate instruction within the family or other primary group. The ceremonial and other expressive customs which we find in every society are significant educationally here in Guatemala, too; but at least this one observer finds that, compared with some other societies, there is a great amount of formal machinery for the regulation of activities without corresponding symbolic content. To a marked extent the transmission of culture takes place within a complex of regulations: the traditional machinery of government and of ritual observances, the superimposed police control of the Guatemalan national government, the general traditional emphasis upon forms of utterance and conduct.

Nevertheless, an investigation of the educational process in these communities would be far from complete if it were to consider only institutions, pedagogic or ceremonial, as elements in that process. Here, as elsewhere, the heritage of the group is communicated and modified in situations much less clearly defined than any of which mention has so far been made in this paper. I refer to that multitude of daily situations in which, by word and gesture, some part of the tradition is communicated from one individual to another without the presence of any formal institution and without any deliberate inculcation. This class of situations corresponds in a general way with what Spencer called the "primary forms of social control."

Let us imagine that we are standing unseen outside a house in the village where I am living. Within the house some Ladino women are praying a novena, and outside it six men and two boys stand around a little fire and talk. Someone compares the heaping-up of pine cones made ready for this fire to the heaping-up of twigs by Indians at certain places on hilltops where, by Indian custom, the traveler strokes away the fatigue from his legs with a twig and then adds the twig to a growing pile. As soon as the comparison has been made, one man of those beside the fire expresses derision at this Indian belief, which is well known to all present. Others briefly indicate similar disbelief in the custom. Another man then makes a remark to the effect that what does in fact serve to relieve tired legs is to rub rum on the ankle-bones. A younger man—apparently unfamiliar with this remedy—asks how this can be effective, and the older man explains that the rum heats the nerves that run near the ankle-bone and that the heat passes up the body along the nerves and so restores strength. The explanation is accepted; the apparent physiological mechanism provides a warrant for accepting the worth of rum as a remedy.

After a short period of silence, conversation begins about snakes, one man having recently killed a large snake. A young boy, apparently wishing to make an effective contribution to a conversation in which he has as yet played no part, remarks that the coral snake joins itself together when cut apart. The man who laughed at the Indian belief about tired legs scornfully denies the truth of the statement about coral snakes. Another older man in the group comes to the support of the boy and in a tentative way supports the truth of the belief as to coral snakes. A younger man says that it is not true, because he cut apart such a snake without unusual result. The skeptical man appeals to the company; another witness offers testimony unfavorable to the belief. The boy has not spoken again; the other man who ventured to support him withdraws from the argument. But this man wishes, it seems, to restore his damaged prestige. With more confidence he offers the statement that some animals *can* do unusual things: the monkey, when shot by a gun, takes a leaf from the tree in which he is sitting and with it plugs the wound. The smaller of the two boys, who has not yet spoken, adds that the jaguar can do this also. Discussion breaks out, several persons speaking at once; the trend of the remarks is to the effect that, although undoubtedly the monkey can do as described, the jaguar is unable to do so. The quick statements of opinion break out almost simultaneously, and very quickly thereafter the matter is dropped. The bystander recognizes that there is substantial consensus on the points raised; the boy is apparently convinced.

We may safely assume that in such a situation as this the states of mind of the participants in the conversation with reference to the points at issue differ from one another less at the conclusion of the conversation than they did at the beginning. The matter is not ended for any one of them, of course; subsequent experiences and conversations about fatigue, snakes, and monkeys will again modify their conceptions, or at least redeclare them. We may suppose also that the outcome of this particular conversation—an apparent consensus in favor of rum and against twigs, supporting the belief about monkeys and unfavorable to the beliefs about coral snakes and jaguars—will not be duplicated exactly in the next conversation that occurs among similar men on these subjects. We are not so simple as to suppose that by attending to this little talk we have discovered "the belief" of the Ladinos on these points. The personalities of the influential men, the accidents of recent experiences had with monkeys or snakes, and, indeed, probably also the general tone of the moment, which may or may not have been favorable to the serious reception of a marvelous story, are among the factors that have entered into the situation. They have brought about, not a conclusive conviction, but a sort of temporary resting-place of more or less common understanding. We may think of the outcome of such little exchanges of viewpoint as the component of many forces. Because each man's state of mind at the time of the conversation is itself the component of many such forces, most of which have been exerted within the same community of long-intercommunicating men and women, it is likely to be not greatly different from that of his neighbors. Still, there are always individual differences; and it is largely in such little happenings as that which took place around the pine-cone fire that these differences are made influential and that they come to be adjusted one to another.

The episode may be recognized as one of that multitude by which the heritage is transmitted. It was a tiny event in the education of the people. Some part of the heritage with reference to the treatment of fatigue and with reference to the behavior of certain animals passed from older people to younger people—and, indeed, it passed also from younger people to older people, for oral education is a stream that flows through all contemporaries, whatever their ages.

At the same time it was a small event in which the culture of the group underwent a change. Some old people in the community tell me that when they were young they heard about the ability of the coral snake to join itself together and did not doubt its truth.

Perhaps the boy who advanced the belief received his first knowledge of it from such a grandfather. After this evening around the pine-cone fire he will treat grandfather's remarks with a new grain of skepticism. Some of the men who took part in this conversation have traveled and have lived in the city among men whose tradition disposed them more readily to laugh at the story of the coral snake, and the effects of such experiences were also registered in the outcome of the evening's conversation. The result of these various influences was to shift, though ever so slightly, the center of gravity of the community beliefs on these points.

Furthermore, the trifling occurrence was also an event in the transmission of tradition from one group to another. No Indian took part in the conversation, but one man, who was born an Indian but had lived long among Ladinos, stood silent in the dark edges of the group. As an ethnologist who has talked with Indians, I know that the belief about getting rid of fatigue by brushing the legs with twigs is by them generally accepted, and great credence is given to beliefs as to the ability of injured animals to treat themselves. Now there has impinged upon that silent Indian a set of forces tending to shift the center of his belief; and now, when he takes part in a similar discussion among Indians, he is more likely to be on the skeptical side of the center of consensus than if he had not been here this evening. It is largely by the accumulating effect of innumerable such occurrences that the culture of the Indians and that of the Ladinos are becoming more and more alike.

We are not to suppose that it is always the Indian who is disposed to change his mind so that it becomes more like that of the Ladino. For certain reasons the predominating trend tends to substitute Ladino tradition for that of the Indians. But the

Ladino has in four hundred years taken on a great deal from the Indians—the techniques of maize-farming and the use of the sweat bath, to mention just two elements—and he still learns from the Indian. The episode around the pine-cone fire could be matched by an episode in which Indians, showing Ladinos the nicked ears of wild animals, by this evidence tended to persuade the Ladinos that these animals were indeed under the domestication of a supernatural protector inhabiting the woods.

It is a fair guess that in any society the process of education depends more on such events as represented in the conversation I have reported than it does upon all the formal pedagogical devices which exist in the society. In the speech and gestures which take place in the home, in the play and work groups, and wherever people talk naturally about matters that are interesting to them, the tradition is reasserted and redefined. In these situations the culture is not merely spoken about; it is acted out; it happens before the eyes and even through the persons of children, who by this means, in large degree, are educated. This basic part of the educational process takes place in every society and probably to such an extent that societies are greatly alike in this respect. Upon the flow of such experience are erected those more clearly defined institutions of the folk traditions, as well as the deliberate enterprises of pedagogy and propaganda. As to these, societies will be found greatly to differ.

Comparing these particular Guatemalan societies with—let us say, that of the French-Canadian villages—I should say that here education is more secular and more casual. These Guatemalan societies seem to me relatively meager with respect to organized moral convictions and sacred traditions. What the Indians tell me about the times of their grandfathers suggests strongly that the Indian societies have lost in ceremonial richness, as I suspect they have lost in the moral value and the integration of their local traditions. Because I have observed the influence of priests in other communities in maintaining a sacred tradition and in explaining symbolic significance of traditional rituals, I think it likely that, if, indeed, these societies have been becoming more casual and more secular, the lessened influence of the Catholic priests has been one factor in this change. The Guatemala of today is well regulated by secular government in the interests of public order and hygiene. My guess—which is to

be tested by historical investigation—is that secular external regulation (important probably even in pre-Columbian times) has
grown in later years, while that control dependent upon moral
conviction and instruction and upon local tradition has declined.
The school, for these rural people, is another form of external
regulation rather than an expression of local tradition.

Whatever study of the history of this part of rural Guatemala
may in fact show, the present situation in these societies suggests
the question of whether a rich culture is compatible with a society
in which the mechanisms for education consist chiefly of formal
regulations and of casual conversation. The comparison between
Indian and Ladino societies—alike though they are in their generally secular character—indicates a correspondence between certain characteristics of culture and certain characteristics of education. The Indian beliefs and tales have relation to current life,
and more of them have moral content or depth than is the case
with Ladino beliefs and tales. And, second, in the Indian societies
there is a social-political-religious organization—a system of progressive public services through which all males pass—that is
largely native to the community, that is a force in social control,
and that involves relatively sacred things. This organization is
largely lacking in the Ladino societies. These differences may be
stated in terms of differences in the educational institutions of the
two peoples: To a greater degree than is the case with the Ladinos, the Indians hear and tell stories that express and justify
traditional beliefs; and by passing through the hierarchy of services the individual learns the ritual that is the inner and relatively
sacred side of the formal civic organization. Emphasizing characteristics of those Guatemalan societies which are more evident in
the case of the Ladinos than of the Indians, this paper concludes,
then, with the suggestion that an education which is made up, on
the one side, of practical regulation and instruction without reference to tradition and, on the other, has nothing much more com-
pulsive and expressive in which to exert its influence than the
casual contacts of everyday life is not likely to educate with
reference to any greatly significant moral values.

14 EDUCATION IN A NEW NATION.
THE VILLAGE SCHOOL IN UPPER BURMA

Manning Nash

This chapter makes some of the same points as were made in Chapter 13. The author discusses the role of the system of education in Burma, at both the level of the university and that of the local school in two northern Burmese villages. The school has been introduced as a central institution for the development of modernization, an essentially economic and political process. But it cannot act as such effectively because the necessary changes in the local social system at the village level have not yet taken place. The school thus acts instead as a conservative agent, since the roles of teacher and pupil are not yet separated from traditional social values and culture: Teachers take on traditional roles and do not understand the part they should play in the modernization of contemporary Burma. This problem is found throughout the world, in both "developing" countries and also in our own; the case study provided in this chapter is an excellent example of the underlying processes at work that can mar the effectiveness of a program that may be perfect in pedagogical terms but that is not geared to the social roles and aspirations of the people concerned in it.

IF THE industrial nations are agitated by questions of education for what and for whom, the newly developing nations of Asia and Africa have a clear and broad mandate for their systems of education. In Burma the object of education is not in doubt: Education is to serve as one of the means of social transformation from a raw material producing society where the bulk of the people had a narrow, peasant, traditional view to a diversified,

Reprinted from *International Journal of Comparative Sociology* 2 (2), September 1961: 135–43, with permission of the author and of the editor, *International Journal of Comparative Sociology*.

somewhat industrialized society able to absorb and use the most modern of scientific knowledge: it is to build a modern nation of responsible citizens. Every Burman has the right to education and the government is dedicated to provide the maximum opportunities for all. The objectives are clear, the ideology not a matter of debate, but the task imposed on educational agencies is enormous. Against the historical background of education in Burma and the functioning of schools at the village level, where 85 per cent of the Burmans live, it is possible to form some assessment of the forces that shape an educational organization in a new nation, resolved to enter the modern world in the form of a socialist democracy.

In this paper, I concentrate on the village level school, not because anthropologists are committed to a worm's eye view of society, but rather because the same kinds of variables are in play at the village level as in the national society, and because the national picture is well summarized in Tinker (1959: 191–222). Also I have first hand material gathered from a year's field work in Upper Burma[1] of the sort of intimate detail which pins down and humanizes the larger historical forces shaping the educational establishment of Burma.

Burma's school system grew from religious roots. Prior to British conquest and annexation, monastic education was virtually the only kind available. All Burmese boys and many girls went to the *phongyi kyaung* to learn the elements of reading and writing, and some of the lore of Buddhism. Beyond these schools were higher ones concentrating on deeper and subtler aspects of Buddhist teaching. Education was in the hand of the monks, *phongyis,* oriented to religious subjects, dependent on traditional material, and given over to emphasis on memorization, rote learning, instilling a great respect for received knowledge.

With the coming of the British and some American Mission schools, new dimensions were added to the educational system. A university, Rangoon, was founded and a system of primary, middle and high schools, leading up to it were instituted. At the

[1] Field work was conducted from August 1960 to June 1961 under a grant from the National Science Foundation. Travel and survey work was aided by funds from the Committee for the Comparative Study of New Nations, University of Chicago. The remarks in this paper do not extend to the hill peoples of Burma, nor do I know their applicability to the Delta area.

same time the monastic system of village education continued, as it does to this day.

The colonial secular education was formed by the prevailing notions of education in the early 1900's and by the needs of British Burma. Though there is not much rancour in present day Burma about the colonial legacy, it is the consensus of the educated and governing segments that education under the British was, in the words of Prime Minister U Nu, designed "to produce salaried servants in their imperialistic machine".[2] As early as the 1920's the university manifested the syndrome of that malaise which continues to plague it. First as a government agency it was subjected to ministerial pressures and political influences. Being in the political orbit, the tactic of the strike became a favorite weapon at the university. Students at Rangoon are notorious for agitation, high volatility, and the presenting of demands to the faculty, administration, and government.

Sheer numbers, the problem of finding room for students, has always plagued the university. Since students stay around virtually as long as they like, irrespective of academic performance, and new ones must be admitted, the student body mushrooms beyond the capacity of personnel and physical plant. There has always been a continual pressure on standards. And they were lowered again in 1960, leading to the resignation of the vice chancellor.

The University at Rangoon is still caught in the political turmoil, the student strike and agitation, and the continual pressure on academic standards. It is over-developed on the Arts faculty side. In pre-independence days this was explained by the structure of opportunities available to graduates: the civil service. And now that is still the chief opportunity for a young graduate, and the aim of most of the student body.

At Mandalay, the college has been raised to the status of University. With the aid of outside funds (Ford Foundation) there was the hope of building on fresh foundations a university of good, modern, diversified curricula. Without the historical legacy of serving as political agitation center for independence, with a small student body, without the barnacles of the past, Mandalay offered an opportunity to set an example of what could be done with higher education in a newly developing nation.

---

[2] U Nu. Convocation Address at Rangoon University, 22nd December, 1951.

But the experiment is in temporary suspension. The vice chancellor was suspended, later relieved, and a new man appointed in 1961. Headless, the university sat back and waited for new leadership. It has problems of staffing now, and there is some controversy over the Burmanization of the faculty. To tide it over the early days, Indian, American, and British lecturers were employed. There is currently a drive to give preference to Burmans, and sometimes this leads to problems of whether the best academic man does get the open post. It is too soon to judge the Mandalay experience. How resistant it will prove to the malaise that afflicts its sister, senior institution, only time will show.

The pre-war system of Burma was split by two axes: age (into primary, middle, and high schools) and language (vernacular, Anglo-vernacular, and English schools), and administered by many different authorities. Primary education was chiefly in the hands of private headmasters, who could be "recognized" and get government aid. A couple of hundred monastic schools agreed to the syllabus of the Education department, and about half of the high schools were in the hands of Christian missionaries (Tinker 1959:192). At any rate, most Burmans continued to get a rather traditional education, with few in the stream leading toward the university and the modern world. Pre-war Burma, in educational philosophy for higher education at least, shared the prevalent belief that education was for an elite, though talent, not wealth or family, was the key to entry to the schooling that marked one as a member of the elite.

World War II and the Japanese occupation and a decade of civil war following independence virtually destroyed the educational system of Burma. The physical plant, the training of teachers, the provision of books and laboratories, all had virtually to be begun from scratch. Only the new goals and demands on education and the increase in the student numbers sorely taxed the abilities of Burma to provide them. The following tables[3] indicate the rates of growth in the educational system.

In 1960–61 in Burma's 30,000 village tracts, only about 10,000 of them have primary schools and some neither *kyaung* nor government schools. Most Burmans still get their education through

[3] H. Tinker 1959:197.

SCHOOLS AND TEACHERS

| | State | | | | Recognized | | | |
	High	Middle	Primary	Teachers	High	Middle	Primary	Teachers
1952	108	72	3,335	9,318	10	5	7	200
1953	148	227	5,507	16,652	9	6	21	227
1954	202	347	8,888	21,679	?	?	?	?
1955	220	405	8,951	27,997	?	?	?	?

PUPILS

| | State | | | Recognized | | |
	High	Middle	Primary	High	Middle	Primary
1952	10,670	35,103	392,398	1,595	1,404	3,975
1953	16,628	54,960	633,707	948	1,914	2,361
1954	23,169	80,426	771,525	?	?	?
1955	42,600	103,600	10,196,000	?	?	?

the monastic school, though a third of eligible children do have a crack at a Primary secular school. Education in Burma cannot be made compulsory. There are just not the facilities to handle all the children. Even if the physical plant were available, qualified teachers are not (especially in upper teaching levels) and books and other aids are scarce.

Against the background of the hope of Burmese education and constraints in personnel and plant, I shall examine two village schools: a primary school in a wet rice village; and a mixed monastic and secular school in a dry crop village. The intention is to show how the schools work and what the students get out of them, and in passing to illustrate the enormous complications that underlie the oft voiced contention "that education transforms society".

About 40 miles south and west of Mandalay, in the Sagaing district, lies the village of Nondwin. Nondwin is a representative mixed cropping dry zone community. I chose to study it because it was ordinary, demographically, culturally, economically, and so far as data went, historically. The community makes its living by cultivating cotton, sesamum, beans, pulses, maize, and a few garden crops. Apart from a tailor, kettle maker, pig breeder, school teacher and cotton broker, everyone makes his living through agriculture. It is a peasant village set in a grove of trees, with its houses scattered along a dusty trail which is the village's main street. There are in the village proper, no public buildings, only the houses and the sheds, and the storehouses for rice, cotton and sesamum. About a mile or two outside of the village are two phongyi kyaungs. There are the resident monks who serve the village. In one of the kyaungs is the village primary school. The school is conducted on the same premises as the phongyi kyaung, and the young monastic scholars and the secular students mix and take classes together. The kyaung where the *koyin* (novices) and the *kyaungtha* (students) take classes is a wooden structure raised on high stilts. The classroom is on the concrete floor below the building itself. It is open to the four winds. A score of wooden desks spaced out facing a blackboard is the physical layout. In the main classroom several grades (or standards as they are called in Burma, following British usage) are grouped together. Only the younger, first standard students, are kept apart in another open classroom. In the school are 70 students, 15 girls and 55 boys. In the kyaung, under the phongyi are 21 koyin, 18 of whom get only religious education, the other three younger boys take some work with the primary school teacher. In the other kyaung, to the west of the village are 15 students taught only by the monks. The whole school population of Nondwin is thus 106 students. With a population of 553, this is nearly everybody who is in fact eligible to go to school, even though education is not compulsory.

Education, for the Nondwin boy or girl virtually stops at the fourth standard. In the last two years, only four students, (2 boys and 2 girls) have gone beyond the fourth standard.

The differences between the phongyi kyaung and the state primary school lie chiefly in the content, not the method of education. The state primary school besides reading and writing, teaches some history, arithmetic, geography, and general science. The phongyi kyaung teaches only reading and writing, a bit of Pali (the language of the Buddhist scriptures) and some bits of Buddhist cosmology and the life of the Buddha. The only point of friction between the curricula lies in geography. The state school teaches about the globe and uses mercator maps. The kyaung imparts the traditional four island, many levelled world of Hindu cosmology. The children learn both and believe but one, the Buddhist.

In way of teaching the schools are virtually identical (except that phongyis still beat recalcitrant students and civil teachers have suspended that practice). The teacher's role is one of great respect, and the gap between him and the student is marked by a great gulf. In traditional Buddhist belief the things most worthy of honor are the Buddha, the Sangha (the monkhood), the Dhamma (the teaching), the parents, and the teacher. At many ceremonials these five honorable things are remembered, and children are always hearing about the debt incurred to the teacher. The teacher is the repository of knowledge. He knows, and he leads the student forward into knowledge. The student used to, and in monastic schools still does, perform many services for his teachers. He carries things for him, brings him tea, may do odd jobs around the teacher's house, and even bring to the teacher problems of deep personal concern. Addressing a teacher a student always uses the respectful *hsaya* (master) or if the teacher is old and venerable, *hysayagyi* (great, or large master). The student is always addressed by name, prefixed by *ma* (for a woman) or *maung* (for a man) both indicating junior status. This role definition of teacher influences the way of teaching. Couple this with the prevalent belief that knowledge is a fixed, or nearly fixed thing, to be transmitted from a respected elder to a subordinate junior and one gets the framework of Burmese teaching.

The teaching is rote learning. The teacher writes something on the blackboard. The students read it aloud in unison. Their job is to get it letter perfect. Questions are asked of them, asking them only to repeat what the teacher has given. The only questions students ask are questions of clarification of the material, if they do not understand it or hear. They would never challenge it, or say they had heard differently, or that they know differently. For a Burmese pupil to question his hsaya is nearly unthinkable. If the hsaya says it, it is right, and I must learn it that way, is the thinking of a student. From the first standard to the university this lack of questioning, challenging, curiosity is a feature of Burmese education.

The role of teacher is just one of a number of senior and respect roles, which *vis à vis* the junior alter, questioning and doubt are barred. Burmese village education is not designed to open the mind, to train it for further exploration, to give it tools for the analysis of new experience. The method of teaching is fitted to stuff the mind, to train the memory, and to fix a respect for what is known. Students are rewarded for feats of memory, for long letter perfect recitations, for knowing answers to standard questions.

Such a method of teaching, and the definition of the teacher-student relationship, putting aside for the moment content, is much more suited to social continuity than it is to social change and innovation. The village educational system is a means of cultural transmission, not cultural change. Both the phongyi kyaung and the state school, as they now operate, contribute to the maintenance of traditional culture. This is the self-imposed role of the phongyi kyaung, but at variance with what the state system is supposed to be doing. But it fits the rest of Burmese village society. Education does not stop at the school exit, but, of course, goes on in the home, in the play group, in the whole round of social interaction in fact. And in these other educational places the same features are observed: learning flows from re-spected elder to aweful junior, with a premium for rote learning. The educational system of the village is not detached enough from the rest of the institutional complex to have its own dynamic, standards, or ethics. It is but a further extension of a society teaching its young to be well built-in members.

Although education, in the abstract, is one of the most highly valued things in Burmese life, support for schools and teachers is meagre at the local level. In Nondwin, books are few, benches and desks in short supply, and even a simple building for the school is lacking. The teacher has tried to get the people of Nondwin to make contributions to buy or build these things. They have turned a deaf ear. They say there is a national government to provide these things; it is not their worry. They have no social sense about government projects, and will not voluntarily donate time or money toward them. Village Burmans donate money and time chiefly to religious ends. They would not be without a phongyi kyaung, and they would not see a monk in need of any of the requisite articles, but a school and its equipment leaves them unmoved. The sense of *civitas,* in which the pedagogical aspect is the means of making citizens is replaced in the community of Nondwin by the more basic process of enculturation, the induction of the young into the conventional understanding of the society. The fundamental sense that education is but a way of refining and deepening what everyone knows, or should know, is a barrier to the development of local interest and initiative in providing educational facilities. As the villager says, education only requires wise teachers and patient, plodding students. Only the teacher really requires books, and buildings are not essential.

The concern of villagers in communities of Upper Burma like Nondwin is a mixture of the mundane business of making a living, getting along with relatives and neighbours, earning respect and honour, and the religious activity of laying up *kutho* (merit) so that a favourable rebirth may come in the next life. If education does not bear on these concerns, it does not mean much to the village Burman. Education as a consumption good, as a thing in itself, is not in village purview. Education should lead to success in the economic sphere—and that's why village boys go beyond the fourth standard, to be clerks, teachers, or civil servants—it should conduce to the accumulation of kutho, and that's why the kyaung schools or the sangha is chosen. And it should lead to a display of refinement of common knowledge, for that is the way that the educated get respect. An education oriental to handling nature, changing the world, raising doubts, or making explorations is not for the villager, and not worth his time and resources. It is on these grounds that girls get less education than do boys, that attendance is spotty, and that every household or religious task has priority over education. For the villager, local education results in a barely functional literacy, an ability to read the occasional newspaper, consult the sacred writings, and sign his name when the government requires it.

In Nondwin, the teacher, and his sister who is his assistant, are not native to the village. They come from a nearby village. This, may in part, account for their inability to raise local support for the school equipment, but it cannot account for their bad luck with the national authorities. The village teacher is the lowest rung of the educational hierarchy. He must go through the channels of headmaster, supervisor, inspector, etc., to make any sort of demand. The ministry of education is beseiged by demands and cannot accede or even pay attention to most of them. The teachers do form an organization and meet in the district headquarters at Sagaing. Here they discuss problems of teaching in the villages, air their grievances before superiors, and hear the government answers and plans. But the village school teacher is like the villager, he feels powerless before the authority and might of the government. His only mode of coping with it is that of compliance in the official context. If he wants to make himself felt, he must join a political party and bring political pressures to bear through the teachers' organizations. The teacher, much more than the villager, is aware of the basic fact that educational decisions are really political events. For the personnel of the educational system, local education is at once too much and too little politicized. Too much so, because the parties, not the educational experts decide the direction of Burmese education, and too little so, because the teachers are not well enough organized, or important enough in the political arena to make themselves felt.

A brief comparison with the rice farming community of Yadaw, just about seven miles south of Mandalay, underwrites and amplifies some of the contentions offered above. Yadaw has a single state primary school, situated near the center of the village. There are two phongyi kyaungs near the village, but they receive only koyin. All the schooling for children of Yadaw is through the secular state school. Children can attend from the first to the fourth standard in Yadaw's school. Like Nondwin, the school and the educational method is made up of the same kinds of elements. Within Upper Burma, one does not move from distinct local culture to distinct local culture, rather one sees the same elements, the same patterns, slightly re-arranged and differently combined to fit the local ecology, economy, demography, and historical circumstance. So Yadaw exhibits that teacher-pupil relationship which characterized Nondwin. It has that same element of *anade,* a complex idea, of feeling reluctance or shame, if a junior should ask unseemly questions of a senior, or the impossibility of a pupil contradicting his hsaya. And the teaching stresses the same mechanical learning procedures and offers the same rewards for memorization. It is a dreary sight to see the pupils bending over their slates and all reciting in unison the words or figures the teacher has put on the blackboard. The school is also an embedded institution with no autonomy and no direction of its own. The local people do not control it, barely support, and expect it to give their children only minimal skills.

In the four standards of Yadaw there are 110 children on the rolls. The first standard has 82 students, and the fourth has only 10. In the first standard are 36 boys and 46 girls, in the fourth, 8 boys and 2 girls. This numerical and sex skewing rests chiefly on economic grounds. Yadaw is a poor village. Many of its people have barely enough land to even meet the modest needs of the Burmese peasant. And rice growing is a labour intensive business for several months of the year. Education competes with child labour in the fields, and at the age of the fourth standard (about 10 or 11) a child is a useful field hand. Girls can help their mothers as well as work in the fields, so they drop out more drastically than do boys. Even in the lower standards attendance is spasmodic. For the four months of data I have on Yadaw, daily school attendance averaged about 80 of the 110 on the rolls. Regular attendance is a problem the school teachers of Yadaw have been unable to solve.

The school is scheduled to have three teachers. In fact there is only one. There is a teacher shortage at the village level, and it is easy to understand why. This teacher is a native of Yadaw, she has family, friends and neighbours here. It is for her a second income (her husband is also a village teacher in another village). She has only a seventh standard education plus a year training course in elementary teaching back in the 1930's. For her, teaching in Yadaw is a reasonable, useful, and not unexciting life. For the young graduate from a teacher training school, life in a poor village is repellent. Being assigned to a village is almost a sentence to isolation, boredom, and frustration for a young graduate. And the salaries of beginning teachers do not compensate for these evils. It takes great devotion and idealism for a rural teacher to stick out his job.

What Yadaw indicates is the pressure of poverty upon the Burmese village educational system. Poverty has the expected effects: reduced attendance, skewing toward the early years, predominance of the economically less useful over the more useful in school. Poverty does not shape the Burmese village school, it is not the root of its difficulties; it merely exacerbates them. The point is here laboured because there is a prevalent belief that money and means would solve all the ills of local education. What increased funds would do, more likely, is merely to shift schools like Yadaw's toward the full achievement of the Burmese pattern as exemplified in Nondwin and other villages.

In Upper Burma, I surveyed some 36 villages, and in most visited the school or phongyi kyaung. These other brief glimpses of local education have only served to corroborate the fuller picture of Nondwin and Yadaw. For example, in the town of Ondaw where a government middle school is operating, a class in English was visited. The teacher asked some of the students to speak to me and show what they were learning. A boy stood up and in response to my question of how old are you, said in flawless English: "I am thirteen years old, sir." I asked a smaller boy, and he replied, "I am thirteen years old, sir." I turned to a little girl, "I am thirteen years old, sir" she said a bit less expertly. The teacher beamed. "They are learning their English" he proudly said. No more vivid demonstration of the rote, routine, memorising character of local education could be imagined.

This sketch of village schools as viewed through two typical Upper Burma communities indicates the magnitude of the task the Government of Burma has set itself in the education fields. If education is to serve as one of the means of social transformation, the local societies and cultures which carry on the schools must first change. The local definitions of education, the role of teacher and pupil, the way the school is built into the community, the conception of knowledge, the image of an educated person—all these militate against the school and education playing the role of innovator, of transformer, of catalyst for the birth of the modern world in Burma's villages.

The problem of education in a new nation with development aspirations is a political problem and a matter of social and cultural change. The higher echelons of education—the universities and advanced training schools—are inevitably involved in the political arena. Getting them organized as institutions for the transmission, conservation, and innovation of knowledge rests on the prior solution of the political problems agitating the new nation. On the local level change in the economic, religious, and interpersonal relations are an antecedent to change in the educational system. From Burma's village schools the broad contention may be hazarded that in newly developing nations the local schools tend to be conservative agents transmitting by means that reinforce local tendencies toward stability. It is a function of economic and social development to make the school and the educational system a locus and agent of social change, not the other way round. Education serves as a means of social change when the school and its personnel are in some part detached from, and even opposed to, the prevailing cultural norms and social arrangements. Education becomes a force for change through the process of social change, and in new nations like Burma the solution of political and economic problems are likely to bring in their wake modifications in the educational system. These aphoristic-like conclusions are offered partly as a goad to a recasting of thought on the role of education in non-Western societies, and partly as admonishment to the holder of the unexamined article of faith that education is the royal road to change and development.

15 EDUCATION AS AN INTERFACE INSTITUTION IN RURAL MEXICO AND THE AMERICAN INNER CITY

Robert Hunt and Eva Hunt

The last three chapters have shown how education is an integral part of the entire process of social change and development. This chapter presents a relevant analysis of two kinds of educational programs in two different social situations—rural Mexico and the modern American city. In rural Mexico there is a great distinction between the Mestizo and Indian populations, and the schools set up for Indians fail to lessen the gap. In the American inner city the distinction between the middle-class and lower-class segments is likewise perpetuated by the kind of schooling offered and the relationship between the backgrounds and roles of teachers and pupils.

The Multiple Society: Mexico

THE EDUCATIONAL institutions of rural Mexico share many of the problems which beset education in the American inner cities. Comparison of the two systems will, hopefully, provide some insight for thinking about the American public schools.[1]

Southern Mexico, a multiple society with plural cultures, is composed of two social segments, the closed corporate Indian villages, and Mestizos, who represent the national culture. Each of these segments, with its own culture, social structure, value

Reprinted from *Midway* 8 (2), May 1967:99–109, with permission of the authors and of the editor, *Midway*.

[1] The field work upon which this paper in part rests took place in Mexico during 1963–64 and was generously supported by the National Science Foundation, grant GS 87, which we gratefully acknowledge. We are heavily indebted to the comparative literature, and the specialist will note our great reliance upon the work of Eric Wolf and Morris Siegel.

system, and life-style, regards the other as immoral, and they try to avoid each other as much as possible. But the two segments still must interact in order to survive. This interaction is handled largely by interface institutions which include the impersonal market, the school system, government departments, and political parties, among others. The people working in these institutions, such as merchants, political bosses, bureaucrats, and teachers, are brokers who tend to monopolize most of the interaction between the two segments.

The Indian can best be described as a subsistence peasant who cultivates food crops to feed his family. While he may occasionally hire some labor for help, this is rare. The Indians do not, by and large, produce cash crops, although they may earn cash by selling small amounts of surplus food products. Their major mechanism for obtaining cash is by selling their labor to Mestizos, who grow cash crops for the national and international markets. The value system of the Indian can be described as one fostering an economic homogeneity. The Indian surplus is not invested in ways which will increase productivity but instead is funneled into consumption activities for the whole village, which both raises the moral prestige of those individuals who can afford the expenditure and impoverishes them. Wealth differences thus tend to be leveled down to a subsistence level.

The Indian receives low wages from a national agricultural system which, although being modernized, is the heir of the hacienda, and is based on low capital input, high labor input, and lack of mechanization. This agricultural system is Mestizo dominated and is admirably adjusted to the stabilities that are involved, since Indian wage work needs are short-term and Mestizo demands for Indian labor are temporary.

The Mestizos participate in the national money economy, function in an economically differentiated class society, and are highly mobile. They operate for profit, invest their surplus in capitalistic, wealth-producing ways, and adopt outward signs of status differential which are based on wealth. In the political realm, the Mestizo policy is dominated by the PRI, the national party which governs Mexico.

The Mestizos tend to be what an American would call authoritarian; the Indians are for most purposes and in most contexts highly democratic. The Indian subordinates his own desires and profits to those of the community; for the Mestizo every office is regarded as a profit-making opportunity for personal exploitation. Each segment considers the other to be alien and rejects participation in the activities of the other. Moreover, each benefits emotionally from the perception of the differences. A Mestizo is decent, clean, civilized, and Christian, according to a Mestizo, while the Indians are dirty, drunken, brutal, ignorant savage pagans. To the Indian, however, the Mestizo is dictatorial, exploits others, is arbitrary and selfish, while he sees himself as morally responsible, hard-working, and civic-minded. Notwithstanding these ethnocentric attitudes, each is largely ignorant of the nature and workings of the other segment.

In addition to the many basic differences, membership in each segment is publicly proclaimed by highly visible markers. For example, Indians speak an Indian language and dress in clothing distinctive of their village. Mestizos speak (and may read) only Spanish, and dress in ordinary western tailored clothing.

It is not unknown for individuals to migrate from one social segment to another, either for short periods of time or permanently. There has been a steady leakage of Indians (the subordinate segment) away from Indian life. It is in part these people who are swelling the ranks of the urban working class. In order to effect this migration not only must behavior change but the markers must change as well. Some Indians migrate to the Mestizo world to work or to learn something of the Mestizo culture. Some migrate permanently. Mestizos also migrate to the Indian culture when they become impoverished (although such cases are rare).

Interface Institutions

Despite the mobility between the segments, the system remains stably differentiated. This is due not only to the desire on both sides for a cultural status quo but to the conservative role behavior of the brokers who conduct the interaction between the two segments.

There are two types of brokers serving the interface institutions. One type resides in the Mestizo-dominated towns. The Indians either come to them for services (such as governmental officials in the *cabecera* or county seat) or they travel at infrequent intervals to the Indian communities. In the latter category may be included government inspectors and traveling merchants. These brokers can be very significant in the lives of Indians, but, typically, their role and the Indian response to it are highy impersonal.

Much more interesting is the second type of broker: those who are resident in the Indian town. This includes the *cacique* (political boss), the town secretary, on occasion some merchants, and the grammar school teachers. These are the individuals who are face to face with both Indians and Mestizos on a continual and continuing basis, who face or produce the most pressure for acculturation, and who often attempt to manipulate the economy and polity for their own benefit, something which the outside brokers do not, and can not, do.

Brokers can be recruited from either segment. In most cases, however, they come from the Mestizo segment or are Indians who at some point in their lives attempted to migrate to the Mestizo segment.

Eric Wolf has pointed out that the broker must operate competently with both segments; to be successful, he must satisfy to some degree the members of his own segment and the significant members of the other segment. In order to do this, he must know a considerable amount about the demand schedules of both segments.

The teacher is an excellent example of this. He is an employee of a large, urban-centered bureaucracy with a distinctive style of life, a representative of Mestizo culture to himself, to other Mestizos, and to the Indians, and he has to somehow get along with the Indian population whose co-operation is necessary if his career is to advance.

Ever since the era of Porfirio Diaz (1876–1910), the national education bureaucracy (among others) has been strongly oriented toward progress, which generally has meant "opening" the Indian community and integrating the individual Indian into the national state. To this end, it has tried to teach the Indians the Spanish language, Mexican history, geography, and culture, modern farming methods, and crafts, and has promoted their conversion into Mexican nationals.

It is immediately apparent, of course, that the goals of the national political elite are directly opposed to the goals of the local populace, or at least a powerful portion of it, among both

Indians and Mestizos. It is not surprising, then, to find that the
teachers are caught on the horns of a dilemma and that getting
off gracefully is not easily accomplished.

In the typical Indian society, the period from the beginning
of latency to the beginning of puberty is the time in which the
child learns from his parents the skills required of competent
adults in his community. Learning is gradual and occurs by the
slow increase of task responsibilities given to the child. The
process is an informal one and adjusted to the individual child's
speed of learning. At the same time, in the typical Indian view,
this is the period in which the most play and socially useless
behavior are permissible in the life cycle. The contradiction with
the school program becomes evident. Learning, attention span, and
increased responsibility are imposed by the demands of a bureaucratic schedule and a crowded school and are not adjusted to
the individual child's needs. As the formal school becomes more
and more demanding, the child is also subject to heavier work
demands from the home, for he is becoming an economic asset.
Children respond first to the demands of the agricultural cycle
and family, and, secondly, if at all, to the demands of the school
year. This combination does not promote parental pressure to
keep the children in school nor does it lead them to take the
school seriously. School attendance is thus a source of constant
conflict between the teacher and the community.

The information that is presented in school, while highly
relevant from the point of view of the nation and the national
culture, are supremely irrelevant when they are not boring to the
Indian. Arithmetic, Spanish grammar, Aztec myths and dances,
the meaning of national holidays, and all the other bits of information which every civilized Mexican knows have no place in
Indian culture, which has its own items of received knowledge
regarding history, religion, technology, etc.

Because of the justifiable lack of interest of the pupils, the
teachers typically regard the Indians as stupid and incapable of
learning not only the national culture but anything. Many are
very open about communicating this information to the Indians,
both pupils and parents. Slighting (even if unconscious) remarks
about the lack of civilization and intelligence of the Indians, of
their dirty habits, their self-imposed poverty, their outrageous
language, all combine to both openly and more subtly com-

municate the basic attitude of the teacher to the Indians: rejection.

In many ways the teachers are often worse in these attitudes than many other brokers. Many teachers in these rural Indian towns are either newcomers to the Mestizo lower-middle class or upwardly mobile Indians whose objective in becoming teachers is to raise themselves in ethnic terms. Both typically are unsure of their own ethnic or class identities. Thus they have more of a stake than anyone else in preserving the distance, and the difference, between the Indian and the Mestizo. The danger of slipping (back) into the cultural state of the Indian is personally threatening; they are the most vigorous in rejecting it. (The upper-class urban Mexican tends, on the contrary, to idealize the Indian as a Rousseauian primitive.)

Under the circumstances, the teachers are most closely allied with the local conservative Mestizos whose culture they consciously adopt as their own. If they were to be successful in carrying out the demands (realistically put as suggestions) of the national bureaucracy concerning acculturating the Indians, they would be violating the demands of the local Mestizos and their own outlook. In this conflict between an urban, progressive education bureaucracy and the local, conservative populace, it is the demands of the village that are met first.

Schooling, which is supposed to be presenting the Indian children with information which will help them to become Mexicans and integrate their communities into the nation and the national culture, does not succeed. Not only is the information irrelevant to the life of the Indian but the teacher, often the first systematic contact a youngster has with Mestizo culture, actively rejects and despises him. In addition, because of his own personal identity struggles, the teacher is not psychologically prepared to accept Indians. The system has the further covert function of teaching most Indian children, very early in the game, that there is nothing to be gained from identifying with and trying to join the Mestizo world, for in that world the Indian is despised, rejected, and kept at the bottom of the heap. Given all the above reasons, the teacher rarely serves as a significant source of identity formation for the children. On the contrary, his behavior creates social distance. He serves the needs of the Mestizo world. His presence in the community pacifies members of the national segment who think that the Indian should be civilized, or at least offered the benefits of civilization. He is also extremely useful to the local society (whether Indian or Mestizo) since a minimum knowledge of Spanish acquired in school allows some Indians to become hired laborers in the Mestizo market or to act as interpreters for the monolinguals in the community.

The role is useful to the teacher himself, as well. If he has little ambition, then he has a fairly comfortable formal position which clearly marks him as an important local figure. If he has ambition, however, the teacher post is a popular job in which to learn the skills to eventually become a political boss, or *cacique*. The *cacique,* like the teacher, must live and work with both cultures if he is to prosper. He has to have an intimate knowledge of the opposite segment which the teacher role allows him to acquire. Thus an ambitious young man of obscure background can learn both about national bureaucracies and the local Indian culture by temporarily becoming a schoolteacher. The apprenticeship is usually quite long, taking upward of ten to fifteen years, but is a stepping stone to a political role. The dynamic is to be found in the career of the teacher, and not in the careers of the pupils, which is where attention is usually focused.

Education which is supposed to be fomenting significant culture change is in fact organized (consciously or unconsciously) to accomplish the exact opposite. Thus Indian children "prefer" to remain Indians and later contacts in life reinforce their preference. The school as an interface institution, and the teacher as its broker, are successful in preserving social and cultural distance.

American Inner-City Schools as Interface Institutions

A comparison of American inner-city school systems and the Mexican system turns up some interesting similarities. The American public school system is a bureaucracy largely staffed by middle-class personnel and is designed to provide the children of the nation with a large range of skills which are useful to them in an industrial society. These skills, which are largely but not entirely picked up in school, include the three R's and certain bodies of myth and knowledge. But in addition to these that are widely recognized, other skills are learned in school. These include the ability to be bored without rebellion (pacific boredom), to perform adequately an intellectual task in which there is no great interest, and to divide the working part of the day into relatively small and inflexible periods of time to meet the demands of externally imposed timetables. In concrete, the modern school teaches what Mannheim called self-rationalization. It is immediately obvious that these skills are required of all those who would perform satisfactorily in the bureaucratic and the automated and skilled labor activities which make up the major employment environment of an industrial society. The public schools, then, are at least consistent with the demands that the system makes as it envelops adults.

In the schools, the children are exposed to (and expected to learn) the technical skills, the psychological skills, and the information about society as a whole which are part and parcel of successful adult life in the United States.

The public schools have also been given another job: to prepare the immigrants to this country for life as Americans. According to the melting-pot theory, it is in the schools that children of foreigners learn to be Americans, through exposure to the American adult models who staff the schools, through American peers, and through the information which is transmitted in the schools in books and lectures. Here is an institution conceived and staffed by middle-class Americans, which has been given the job of converting the young into viable members of our industrial society. For the middle-class youngsters, the school is an extension of the home and the later job and is largely consistent with them. For the cultural immigrant (foreign or rural), at least some of them, it represents an effective route for cultural migration. It is in the latter case where our schools are interface institutions.

Recently, attention has been focused on the inability of the inner-city school to effectively cope with its pupils. Like the Mexican school, it maintains social distance rather than reduces it. The problem which this poses for the society as a whole is enormous and very serious, and it appears to be organized as a vicious circle. There is a large-scale alienation in the inner city from industrial middle-class society. In part, it comes about due to low prestige and low-paid and intermittent employment. This, partly, is a result of lack of education and understanding of the urban mode of life. Family structure, in turn, is fragmented and depressed by the employment situation which discourages

educational effort. It has often been said that education is the
solution to these problems, for with better education comes better
jobs, with stronger family structure and better housing following.
(The above is of course highly simplified. We give it as an
example of the way that people tend to talk and think about
these problems today, not for its objective truth value concerning
the organization of American society.) The inner-city schools
should play a crucial role for the population they serve and
bear very importantly upon our most serious, and potentially
most explosive, social problems. But overwhelming evidence points
out that these schools are not achieving their social goals.

We can then ask two questions: why are the inner-city schools
not doing their job, and what can be done to help them? We
have no obvious solutions. What we propose to do is to organize
some of our knowledge about what is happening in terms of
the theory of interface institutions. This analysis should be read
as an addition to the voluminous literature on the solutions to
these problems, not as a replacement of it. Institutions are complex and must be approached from many points of view.

There has been considerable general discussion of the differences
between the culture of the inner-city residents and middle-class
America. Differences in values, motivations, behavior patterns,
and expectations have all been claimed. There has been lamen-
tably little solid empirical work on these cultural differences. It
appears that what we have is a case of structural ignorance, just
as in the Mexican example. The superordinate segment of the
culture remains largely ignorant of the other segment, and what
it perceives (or projects) it despises. The two populations therefore remain opaque to, and reject, each other. Our statements
about the cultural differences of the two segments in what follows
is therefore general and tentative.

The Northern inner-city child shares with his Indian counterpart a language which is significantly different from that of the
dominant segment. Although in the Mexican situation the Indian
speech is a distinct language, the Negro inner-city child is told
that he speaks a corrupt and deficient version of English. There
is mounting evidence that the inability to perform middle-class
tasks, such as abstraction in canonical English, does not reflect
an impoverished mind but merely the inability to perform in
what is almost certainly a foreign language. The culture of the

subordinate segment is rich and sophisticated, and not merely an "impoverished" version of the dominant one.

It has been said that the inner-city pupil does not perform well in school in part because the home environment does not support the school objectives. The Mexican Indian knows that he can use the school to move into the Mestizo world if he desires. The change of markers is sufficient, since racially the populations are indistinguishable. The Negro child is confronted with the fact that learning the markers of the superordinate segment is not sufficient for mobility, since the major marker, skin color, cannot be changed. If the Indian learns the proper skills, he can be integrated into the Mestizo world. For the Negro, this is much more problematic. It is not surprising therefore to find that the Negro home does not support the objectives of the middle-class public school. It could hardly be expected to support an experience which is painful and, sorrowfully, irrelevant to adult Negro life. The same sense of alienation from the school situation and the curriculum that exists between the Indian and Mestizo also exists between the recent Negro migrant from rural areas and the middle-class white urbanite.

One can question the genuineness of the local superordinate segment's desire to integrate Negroes into the middle-class culture even though the national policies may point (at least in the North) in that direction. But as the relative and absolute number of Negro migrants to the middle class increases, the attractiveness of the move will increase as well, for both segments.

Finally, we can suggest that the role of teacher in the Mexican Indian town and in the American inner-city school is very similar. That is, an understanding of the functions of the school in the inner city cannot be gained without understanding the nature of the confrontation of members of two different social segments, middle-class teachers (usually white) and lower-class pupils (frequently not white). It is important of course to understand the culture that the child brings to the school, but an understanding of the school cannot be had without an understanding of the kinds of communications that take place between teacher and pupil, as representatives of two different cultural segments, both in school and out. In this case, the segmentary opposition is even more definite than that between Mestizo and Indian in Mexico. Our schools are staffed by middle-class personnel. They have been through college, which proves that they can meet the demands of the middle-class bureaucratized world. If only recently arrived in the middle class, they tend to hold rather rigidly to the values and behavior patterns of the middle class. Like the teacher in Mexico, if there is some danger of the teacher being identified with his pupils (especially if the teacher is a Negro himself), he will reject the pupils and what they stand for to the degree that he has recently migrated from their culture. The teachers who were raised in a middle-class environment feel justified in making middle-class demands of the pupils. These who were not are forced to do so to avoid threats to their own change of identity. These demands include a taboo on physical aggression, giving overt signs of paying attention and respect, and meeting middle-class standards of language, cleanliness, and obedience.

We have then a school which is definitely middle class in subject matter, in expectations, and in staff. But not in pupils. And our teachers, as well as their Mexican counterparts, are trapped in a net of cultural oppositions where the wrong choice is personally threatening.

One possible solution to the problem involves primarily some changes in the school structure itself, which offers an intervention point relatively little intermeshed with much more intractable problems such as the job market, housing, and family structure.

We would like to propose making teachers sensitive to the consequences of their own behavior and attitudes. They should be made aware of the importance of their feelings toward their own culture and that of their pupils, and the distance between them.

Second, the teachers should acquire information about the culture of their pupils. They should become aware of their own resistances, so that they can exercise conscious restraint. Programs to this effect can be incorporated either during training or later. The sensitivity training techniques for adult re-education being developed by those associated with the National Training Laboratory seem admirably suited to accomplishing these two tasks.

Once an ethnographic knowledge of their own and their pupils' culture is attained, it should become possible for the teachers to become a source of positive rather than negative identity for the students. When this sort of communication is established, it should be possible to start the learning process that will make the inner-city child an eager pupil. (We are assuming that most members of this social system want to become members of the dominant segment and will do so if given half a chance. Some will not want to do so, but that is another matter entirely.)

The solution then is, in part, to present the pupils with tasks which will be both *interesting* to them and *effective* in changing them, and to present them in a communication network which involves positive human models. It has been argued that the usual curriculum in schools is not attractive to the average inner-city pupil. We suggest that children are willing to learn many disagreeable tasks when their adult models are positive affective figures, and perhaps herein lies an exit from the ghetto's vicious circle.

BIBLIOGRAPHY

Aberle, D. F.
1951 *The Psychosocial Analysis of a Hopi Life-history*. (Comparative Psychology Monographs 21), Berkeley, University of California.
Adair, J. and E. Z. Vogt
1949 "Navaho and Zuni veterans: a study of contrasting modes of culture change," *American Anthropologist* 51:547–61.
Alldridge, T. J.
1901 *The Sherbo and its Hinterland*. London.
Alldridge, T. J.
1910 *A Transformed Colony*. London.
Allport, G. W.
1951 "The personality trait," in M. H. Marx (editor), *Psychological Theory: Contemporary Readings*, New York, Macmillan: 503–7.
Ammar, H.
1954 *Growing Up in an Egyptian Village*. London, Routledge and Kegan Paul.
Asch, S. E.
1952 *Social Psychology*. New York, Prentice-Hall.
Ausubel, D. P.
1961 *Maori Youth*. Wellington. Price, Milburn (published New York, Holt, Rinehart & Winston, 1965).
Barnes, C. A.
1952 "A statistical study of the Freudian theory of levels of psychosexual development," *Genetic Psychological Monographs* 45:105–74.
Barnes, J. A.
1947 "The collection of genealogies," *Rhodes-Livingston Journal* 5:48–56.
Bartlett, F. C.
1923 *Psychology and Primitive Culture*. Cambridge, Cambridge University Press.
Bartlett, F. C.
1932 *Remembering*. Cambridge, Cambridge University Press.
Bartlett, F. C.
1939 *The Study of Society*. London, Trench, Trubner.

Bateson, G. and M. Mead
  1942 *Balinese Character: a Photographic Analysis.* New York, New York Academy of Sciences.
Benedict, R.
  1934 *Patterns of Culture.* Boston, Houghton Mifflin.
Benedict, R.
  1938 "Continuities and discontinuities in cultural conditioning," *Psychiatry* 1:161–67.
Benedict, R.
  1946a *The Chrysanthemum and the Sword.* Boston, Houghton Mifflin.
Benedict, R.
  1946b "The study of cultural patterns in European nations," *Transactions, New York Academy of Sciences* 8:274–79.
Blacking, J.
  1964 *Black Background: the Childhood of a South African Girl.* New York, Abelard-Schuman.
Blum, G. S.
  1949 "A study of the psychoanalytic theory of psychosexual development," *Genetic Psychoanalytic Monographs* 39:3–99.
Blum, G. S.
  1953 *Psychoanalytic Theory of Personality.* New York, McGraw-Hill.
Bohannan, L.
  1952 "A genealogical charter," *Africa* 22:301–15.
Brameld, T.
  1959 *The Remaking of a Culture: Life and Education in Puerto Rico.* New York, Harper.
Brandt, R. B.
  1954 *Hopi Ethics: a Theoretical Analysis.* Chicago, University of Chicago Press.
Bruner, E. M.
  1956a "Cultural transmission and cultural change," *Southwestern Journal of Anthropology* 12:191–99.
Bruner, E. M.
  1956b "Primary group experience and the process of acculturation," *American Anthropologist* 58:605–23.
Busia, K. A.
  1950 *Report on a Social Survey of Sekondi-Takoradi.* London, Crown Agents.
Carney, R. J. and W. Ferguson
  1965 *A Selected and Annotated Bibliography on the Sociology of Eskimo Education.* Edmonton, University of Alberta Press.
Chiang, Y.
  1952 *A Chinese Childhood.* New York, John Day.
Child, I. L.
  1954 "Socialization," in G. Lindzey (editor), *Handbook of Social Psychology,* Cambridge, Addison-Wesley.

Childs, G. M.
1949 *Umbundu Kinship and Character.* London, Oxford University Press.
Cohen, Y. A.
1964 *The Transition from Childhood to Adolescence.* Chicago, Aldine.
Davis, A.
1949 *Social Class Influences on Learning.* Cambridge, Harvard University Press.
Davis, K.
1949 *Human Society.* New York, Macmillan.
DeLaguna, F.
1965 "Childhood among the Yakutat Tlingit," in M. E. Spiro (editor), *Context and Meaning in Cultural Anthropology,* New York, Harper.
Dennis, W.
1940 *The Hopi Child.* New York, Wiley.
Dennis, W.
1941 "The socialization of the Hopi child," in L. Spier, A. I. Hallowell, S. S. Newman (editors), *Language, Culture, and Personality,* Menasha, Sapir Memorial Publication Fund: 259–71.
DeRidder, J. C.
1961 *The Personality of the Urban African in South Africa.* New York, Humanities Press.
Devereux, G.
1949 "Magic substances and narcotics of the Mohave Indians," *British Journal of Medical Psychology* 22:115.
Dewey, J.
1961 *Democracy and Education.* New York, Macmillan.
Dore, R. P.
1965 *Education in Tokugawa Japan.* Berkeley, University of California Press.
Dozier, E. P.
1954 *The Hopi-Tewa of Arizona.* University of California Publications in American Archaeology and Ethnology No. 44, Berkeley, University of California Press.
Dozier, E. P.
1955 "Forced and permissive acculturation," *American Anthropologist* 56:973–1002.
Driberg, J. H.
1932 *At Home with the Savage.* London, Routledge and Kegan Paul.
DuBois, C.
1941 "Attitudes toward food and hunger in Alor," in L. Spier, A. I. Hallowell, S. S. Newman (editors), *Language, Culture, and Personality,* Menasha, Sapir Memorial Publication Fund: 272–81.
DuBois, C.
1944 *The People of Alor.* Minneapolis, University of Minnesota Press.
DuBois, C.
1955 "Some notions on learning intercultural understanding," in G.

Spindler (editor), *Education and Anthropology*, Stanford, Stanford University Press: 89–126.

Dundas, C.
1924 *Kilimanjaro and its People*. London.

Durkheim, E.
1897 *Le Suicide*. Paris.

Durkheim, E.
1915 *The Elementary Forms of the Religious Life*. London, Macmillan.

Durkheim, E.
1925 *L'Education morale*. Paris, Alcan.

Durkheim, E.
1933 *The Division of Labor in Society*. Glencoe, Free Press.

Durkheim, E. and M. Mauss
1902–3 "De quelques formes primitives de classification," *L'Année Sociologique* 7:1–72.

Earle, E. and E. A. Kennard
1938 *Hopi Kachinas*. New York, Augustin.

Earle, M. J.
1958 *Rakau Children: from Six to Thirteen Years*. Wellington, Victoria University College.

Eggan, D.
1948 "The general problem of Hopi adjustment," in C. Kluckhohn and H. A. Murray (editors), *Personality in Nature, Society, and Culture*, New York, Knopf: 220–35.

Eggan, D.
1955 "The personal use of myth in dreams," *Journal of American Folklore* 68:445–53.

Eggan, D.
1956 "Instruction and affect in Hopi cultural continuity," *Southwestern Journal of Anthropology* 12 (4):347–70.

Eggan, F.
1950 *Social Organization of the Western Pueblos*. Chicago, University of Chicago Press.

Eisenstadt, S. N.
1956 *From Generation to Generation*. Glencoe, Free Press.

Erikson, E. H.
1943 *Observations on the Yurok: Childhood and World Image*. University of California Publications in American Archaeology and Ethnology 35, No. 10.

Erikson, E. H.
1948 "Childhod and tradition in two American Indian tribes," in C. Kluckhohn and H. A. Murray (editors), *Personality in Nature, Society, and Culture*, New York, Knopf: 176–203.

Evans-Pritchard, E. E.
1934 "Levy-Bruhl's theory of primitive mentality," *Bulletin of the Faculty of Arts, University of Cairo* 2:1–36.

Evans-Pritchard, E. E.
1937 *Witchcraft, Oracles, and Magic among the Azande.* Oxford, Clarendon Press.
Evans-Pritchard, E. E.
1940a *The Nuer.* Oxford, Clarendon Press.
Evans-Pritchard, E. E.
1940b "The Nuer of the Southern Sudan," in M. Fortes and E. E. Evans-Pritchard, *African Political Systems,* London, Oxford University Press.
Evans-Pritchard, E. E.
1948 *The Divine Kingship of the Shilluk of the Nilotic Sudan.* Cambridge, Cambridge University Press.
Fei, H. T.
1939 *Peasant Life in China.* London, Routledge and Kegan Paul.
Fenichel, O.
1945 *The Psychoanalytic Theory of Neurosis.* New York, Norton.
Firth, R.
1936 *We, the Tikopia.* London, Allen and Unwin.
Firth, R.
1956 "Function," in W. L. Thomas (editor), *Current Anthropology,* Chicago, University of Chicago Press: 237–58.
Fleming, C. M.
1948 *Adolescence.* London, Routledge and Kegan Paul.
Fortes, M.
1936a "Ritual festivals and social cohesion in the hinterland of the Gold Coast," *American Anthropologist* 38 (4).
Fortes, M.
1936b "Kinship, incest and exogamy in the Northern Territories of the Gold Coast," in J. D. Buxton (editor), *Custom Is King,* London, Hutchinson.
Fortes, M.
1938 *Social and Psychological Aspects of Education in Taleland.* Supplement to *Africa* 11 (4).
Fortes, M.
1944 "Descent in the social structure of the Tallensi," *Africa* 14:362–85.
Fortes, M.
1945 *The Dynamics of Clanship among the Tallensi.* London, Oxford University Press.
Fortes, M.
1949 *The Web of Kinship among the Tallensi.* London, Oxford University Press.
Fortes, M.
1951 "Parenthood in primitive society," *Man* 51:65.
Fortes, M. and S. L. Fortes
1936 "Food in the domestic economy of the Tallensi," *Africa* 9:237–76.
Foster, P.
1966 *Education and Social Change in Ghana.* Chicago, Chicago University Press.

Freud, S.
1950 *Totem and Taboo*. London, Routledge and Kegan Paul.
Fromm, E.
1948 *Man for Himself*. London, Routledge and Kegan Paul.
Gay, J.
1967 *The New Mathematics and an Old Culture: a Study of Learning among the Kpelle of Liberia*. New York, Holt, Rinehart & Winston.
Geertz, H.
1961 *The Javanese Family: a Study of Kinship and Socialization*. New York, Free Press.
Gillin, J.
1951 *The Culture of Security in San Carlos*. New Orleans: Middle American Research Institute Publication 15.
Gluckman, M.
1949–50 "Social beliefs and individual thinking in primitive society," *Memoirs and Proceedings of the Manchester Literary and Philosophical Society* 91:73–98.
Gluckman, M.
1952 *Rituals of Rebellion in South-east Africa*. Manchester, Manchester University Press.
Gluckman, M. (editor)
1962 *The Ritual of Social Relations*. Manchester, Manchester University Press.
Gold Coast Government
1942 *Report of the Education Committee*. Accra, Government Printer.
1947 *Ten Year Plan of Development and Welfare*. Accra, Government Printer.
1951 *Accelerated Development Plan for Education*. Accra, Government Printer.
1954 *Progress in Education in the Gold Coast*. Accra, Government Printer.
Goldfrank, E.
1945 "Socialization, personality, and the structure of Pueblo society," *American Anthropologist* 47:516–539.
Goldman, F.
1948–50 "Breast feeding and character formation," *Journal of Personality* 17:83–103; 19:189–96.
Goldman-Eisler, F.
1951 "The problem of orality and its origin in early childhood," *Journal of Mental Science* 97:765–82.
Gorer, G.
1938 *Himalayan Village*. London, Michael Joseph.
Gorer, G.
1948 *The American People*. New York, Norton.
Gorer, G.
1950 *The Concept of National Character*. Harmondsworth, Penguin Books.

Gorer, G. and J. Rickman
1949 *The People of Great Russia.* London, Cresset Press.
Granqvist, H.
1947 *Birth and Childhood among the Arabs.* Helsinki, Soderstrom.
Granqvist, H.
1950 *Child Problems among the Arabs.* Helsinki, Soderstrom.
Griaule, M.
1952 "Etendue de l'instruction traditionnelle au Soudan," *Zaire* 6:563–68.
Gruber, F.
1961 *Anthropology and Education.* Philadelphia, University of Pennsylvania Press.
Guthrie, G. M.
1961 *The Filipino Child and Philippine Society.* Manila.
Guthrie, G. M. and P. J. Jacobs
1966 *Child Rearing and Personality Development in the Philippines.* University Park, Pennsylvania State University Press.
Gutmann, B.
1926 *Das Recht der Dschagga.* München, Beck.
Gutmann, B.
1932–35 *Die Stammeslehren der Dschagga.* München, Beck.
Hailey, Lord
1957 *An African Survey* (Revised edition). London, Oxford University Press.
Hallowell, A. I.
1953 "Culture, personality, and society," in A. L. Kroeber (editor), *Anthropology Today.* Chicago, University of Chicago Press: 597–620.
Hallowell, A. I.
1955 *Culture and Experience.* Philadelphia, University of Pennsylvania Press.
Haring, D. G.
1956 *Personal Character and Cultural Milieu* (3rd edition). Syracuse, Syracuse University Press.
Haury, E. W.
1950 *The Stratigraphy and Archeology of Fontana Cave, Arizona.* Tucson, University of Arizona Press.
Havinghurst, R. J.
1957 "Education among American Indians: individual and cultural aspects," *Annals of the American Academy of Political and Social Science* 311:105–15.
Havinghurst, R. J. and B. L. Newgarten
1955 *American Indian and White Children.* Chicago, University of Chicago Press.
Heinicke, C. and B. Whiting
1953 *Bibliographies on Personality and Social Development of the Child.* New York, Social Science Research Council.

Helser, A. D.
1934 *Education of Primitive People.* New York, Columbia University Press.
Henry, J.
1955 "Culture, education, and communications theory," in G. Spindler (editor), *Education and Anthropology,* Stanford, Stanford University Press: 188–215.
Henry, J.
1960 "A cross-cultural outline of education," *Current Anthropology* 1 (4):267–305.
Henry, J.
1961 "More on cross-cultural education," *Current Anthropology* 2 (3): 255–64.
Herskovits, M. J.
1938 *Dahomey.* New York, Knopf.
Herskovits, M. J.
1941 *The Myth of the Negro Past.* New York, Harper.
Herskovits, M. J.
1943 "Education and cultural dynamics," *American Journal of Sociology* 48:737–49.
Herskovits, M. J.
1950 *Man and His Works.* New York, Knopf.
Hilger, I.
1957 *Araucanian Child Life and its Cultural Background.* Washington, Smithsonian Miscellaneous Collections, 133.
Hilger, I.
1960 *Field Guide to the Ethnological Study of Child Life.* New Haven, Human Relations Area Files.
Hoernlé, A. W.
1931 "An outline of the native conception of education in Africa," *Africa* 4:145–63.
Hogbin, H. I.
1931 "Education at Ontong-Java," *American Anthropologist* 33:601–14.
Hogbin, H. I.
1935–36 "Adoption in Wogeo," *Journal of the Polynesian Society* 44; 45.
Hogbin, H. I.
1938 "Tillage and collection," *Oceania* 9:128–51.
Hogbin, H. I.
1940 "The father chooses his heir," *Oceania* 11:1–39.
Hogbin, H. I.
1943 "A New Guinea Infancy," *Oceania* 13:285–309.
Hogbin, H. I.
1944a "Trading voyages in northern New Guinea," *Oceania* 15.
Hogbin, H. I.
1944b "Marriage in Wogeo," *Oceania* 15.
Hogbin, H. I.
1946 "A New Guinea infancy: from weaning till the eighth year in Wogeo," *Oceania* 16:275–96.

Honigmann, J. J.
1954 *Culture and Personality*. New York, Harper.
Hough, W.
1915 *The Hopi Indians*. Cedar Rapids, Torch Press.
Hsu, F. L. K.
1952 "Anthropology or psychiatry: a definition of objectives and their implications," *Southwestern Journal of Anthropology* 8:227–50.
Hsu, F. L. K. (editor)
1961 *Psychological Anthropology*. Homewood, Dorsey.
Hunt, R. (editor)
1967 *Personalities and Cultures*. New York, Natural History Press.
Hunt, R. and E. Hunt
1967 "Education as an interface institution in rural Mexico and the American inner city," *Midway* 8 (2):99–109.
Inkeles, A. and D. J. Levinson
1954 "National character: the study of model personality and sociocultural systems," in G. Lindzey (editor), *Handbook of Social Psychology*, Cambridge, Addison-Wesley, II:977–1021.
Isaacs, S.
1930 *Intellectual growth of young children*. London, Routledge and Kegan Paul.
Isaacs, S.
1933 *Social development of young children*. London, Routledge and Kegan Paul.
Joseph, A., R. Spicer, and J. Chesky
1949 *The Desert People*. Chicago, University of Chicago Press.
Kapadia, K. M.
1957 *Marriage and Family in India*. New York, Oxford University Press.
Kaplan, B. (editor)
1961 *Studying Personality Cross Culturally*. Evanston, Row, Peterson.
Kardiner, A.
1939 *The Individual and His Society*. New York, Columbia University Press.
Kardiner, A.
1940 *The Psychological Frontiers of Society*. New York, Columbia University Press.
Kaye, B.
1962 *Bringing Up Children in Ghana*. London, Allen and Unwin.
Keesing, F. M.
1953 *Culture Change*. Stanford, Stanford University Press.
Keur, J. Y. and D. L. Keur
1961 *Windward Children: a Study in Human Ecology of the Three Dutch Windward Islands in the Caribbean*. New York, Humanities Press.
Kidd, D.
1906 *Savage Childhood: a Study of Kafir Children*. London, Black.

King, A. R.
1967 *The School at Mopass: a Problem of Identity.* New York, Holt, Rinehart & Winston.
Kluckhohn, C.
1948 "Some aspects of Navaho infancy and early childhood," in D. G. Haring (editor), *Personal Character and Cultural Milieu,* Syracuse, Syracuse University Press: 472–85.
Kluckhohn, C.
1951 "Values and value-orientations in the theory of action," in T. Parsons and E. A. Shils, *Toward a General Theory of Action,* Cambridge, Harvard University Press: 388–433.
Kluckhohn, C.
1954 "Culture and behavior," in G. Lindzey (editor), *Handbook of Social Psychology,* Cambridge, Addison-Wesley, II:921–76.
Kluckhohn, C. and F. R. Kluckhohn
1947 "American culture: generalized orientations and class patterns," in *Conflicts of Power in Modern Culture.*
Kluckhohn, C. and H. A. Murray (editors)
1949 *Personality in Nature, Society, and Culture.* New York, Knopf.
Knapen, M-T.
1962 *L'Enfant Mukongo.* Louvain, Publications Universitaires.
Koffka, K.
1928 *The Growth of the Mind.* London, Kegan Paul, Trench, Trubner.
Krige, E. J.
1937 "Individual development," in I. Schapera (editor), *The Bantu-speaking Tribes of South Africa,* London, Routledge and Kegan Paul: 95–118.
La Barre, W.
1945 "Some observations on character structure in the Orient (the Japanese)," *Psychiatry* 8:319–42.
La Barre, W.
1946 "Some observations on character structure in the Orient (the Chinese)," *Psychiatry* 9:375–95.
Landy, D.
1959 *Tropical Childhood: Cultural Transmission and Learning in a Rural Puerto Rican Village.* Chapel Hill, University of North Carolina Press.
Lantis, M.
1960 *Eskimo Childhood and Interpersonal Relationships.* Seattle, University of Washington Press.
Leighton, D. and C. Kluckhohn
1947 *Children of the People.* Cambridge, Harvard University Press.
Levine, D. L.
1965 *Wax and Gold: Tradition and Innovation in Ethiopian Culture.* Chicago, University of Chicago Press.
LeVine, R. A. and B. LeVine
1966 *Nyansongo: a Gusii Community in Kenya.* New York, Wiley.

Levi-Strauss, C.
1962 *La Pensée Sauvage*. Paris, Plon.
Levy, M. J.
1952 *The Structure of Society*. Princeton, Princeton University Press.
Linton, R.
1947 *Cultural Background of Personality*. London, Kegan Paul, Trench, Trubner.
Little, K. L.
1951 *The Mende of Sierra Leone*. London, Routledge and Kegan Paul.
Mair, L. P.
1943 *An African People in the Twentieth Century*. London, Routledge and Kegan Paul.
Malinowski, B.
1922 *Argonauts of the Western Pacific*. London, Routledge and Kegan Paul.
Malinowski, B.
1925 "Magic, science and religion," in J. Needham (editor), *Science, Religion and Reality*. New York.
Malinowski, B.
1926 *Myth in Primitive Psychology*. New York, Norton.
Malinowski, B.
1936 "Native education and culture contact," *International Review of Missions* 25:480–517.
Malinowski, B.
1945 *The Dynamics of Culture Change*. New Haven, Yale University Press.
Margai, M. A. S.
1948 "Welfare work in a secret society," *African Affairs*.
McGlashan, N.
1964 "Indigenous Kikuyu education," *African Affairs* 63:47–57.
Mead, M.
1928 *Coming of Age in Samoa*. New York, Morrow.
Mead, M.
1930 *Growing up in New Guinea*. New York, Morrow.
Mead, M.
1931 "The primitive child," in *A Handbook of Child Psychology*, Worcester, Clark University Press: 669–87.
Mead, M.
1935 *Sex and Temperament in Three Primitive Societies*. New York, Morrow.
Mead, M.
1940 "Social change and cultural surrogates," *Journal of Educational Sociology* 14:92–109.
Mead, M.
1942 "Educational effects of social environment as disclosed by studies of primitive societies," in E. W. Burgess, W. L. Warner, F. Alexander, M. Mead (editors), *Symposium on Environment and Education*, Chicago, University of Chicago Press: 48–61.

Mead, M.
1943 "Our education emphases in primitive perspective," *American Journal of Sociology* 48:633–39.
Mead, M.
1946 "Research on primitive children," in L. Carmichael (editor), *Manual of Child Psychology*, New York, Wiley: 667–706.
Mead, M.
1947 "The implications of culture change for personality development," *American Journal* of *Orthopsychiatry* 17:633–66.
Mead, M.
1948 "Social change and cultural surrogates," in C. Kluckhohn and H. A. Murray (editors), *Personality in Nature, Society, and Culture*, New York, Knopf: 511–22.
Mead, M.
1949 *Male and Female.* New York, Morrow.
Mead, M.
1953 "National character," in A. L. Kroeber (editor), *Anthropology Today*, Chicago, University of Chicago Press: 642–77.
Mead, M.
1956 *New Lives for Old.* New York, Morrow.
Mead, M.
1964 *Continuities in Cultural Evolution.* New Haven, Yale University Press.
Mead, M. and F. C. MacGregor
1951 *Growth and Culture: a Photographic Study of Balinese Childhood.* New York, Putnam's.
Mead, M. and M. Wolfenstein
1954 *Childhood in Contemporary Cultures.* Chicago, University of Chicago Press.
Mencher, J.
1963 "Growing up in South Malabar," *Human Organization* 22:54–65.
Merton, R. K.
1949 *Social Theory and Social Structure.* Glencoe, Free Press.
Miller, N. and J. Dollard
1941 *Social Learning and Imitation.* New Haven, Yale University Press.
Minturn, L. and J. T. Hitchcock
1966 *The Rajputs of Khalapur, India.* New York, Wiley.
Minturn, L. and W. W. Lambert
1964 *Mothers of Six Cultures: Antecedents of Child Rearing.* New York, Wiley.
Mumford, W. B.
1930 "Malangali school," *Africa* 3 (3):265–92.
Murphy, G.
1937 *Experimental Social Psychology.* New York, Harper.
Murphy, G.
1947 *Personality: a Biosocial Approach to Origins and Structure.* New York, Harper.

Musgrove, F.
1953 "Education and the culture concept," *Africa* 23 (2):110–26.
Nadel, S. F.
1942 *A Black Byzantium.* London, Oxford University Press.
Nadel, S. F.
1951 *The Foundations of Social Anthropology.* London, Cohen and West.
Narain, D.
1964 "Growing up in India," *Family Process* 3:127–54.
Nash, M.
1961 "Education in a new nation. The village school in Upper Burma," *International Journal of Comparative Sociology* 2 (2):135–43.
Neubauer, P. B.
1965 *Children in Collectives: Childrearing Aims and Practices in the Kibbutz.* Springfield, Thomas.
Nuffield Foundation
1952 *African Education.* London, Her Majesty's Stationery Office.
Oliver, R.
1952 *The Missionary Factor in East Africa.* London, Longmans.
Opler, M.
1941 *An Apache Life Way.* Chicago, University of Chicago Press.
Orlansky, H.
1949 "Infant care and personality," *Psychological Bulletin* 46:1–48.
Park, E. E.
1950 *Race and Culture.* Glencoe, Free Press.
Passin, H.
1956 *Society and Education in Japan.* New York, Columbia University Press.
Paulsen, F. R.
1961 "Cultural anthropology and education," *Journal of Educational Sociology* 34 (7):2–29.
Pettitt, G. A.
1946 *Primitive Education in North America.* (University of California Publications in American Archaeology and Ethnology 43), Berkeley, University of California Press.
Phillips, H.
1965 *Thai Peasant Personality. The Patterning of Interpersonal Behavior in the Village of Bang Chan.* Berkeley, University of California Press.
Piaget, J.
1959 *Language and Thought of the Child.* New York, Humanities Press.
Piers, G. and M. B. Singer
1953 *Shame and Guilt.* Springfield, Thomas.
Polgar, S.
1960 "Biculturation of Mesquakie teenage boys," *American Anthropologist* 62:217.
Rabin, A. I.
1965 *Growing up in the Kibbutz.* New York, Springer.

Rattray, R. S.
1932 "The education of girls," in *The Tribes of the Ashanti Hinterland,* Oxford, Clarendon Press.
Raum, O.
1938 "Some aspects of indigenous education among the Chaga," *Journal of the Royal Anthropological Institute* 68:209–21.
Raum, O.
1940 *Chaga Childhood.* London, Oxford University Press.
Raum, O.
1956 "The demand for and support of education in African tribal society," *Yearbook of Education 1956:* 533–44.
Raum, O.
1957 "An evaluation of indigenous education," in P. A. Duminy (editor), *Trends and Challenges in the Education of the South African Bantu,* Pretoria: 89–105.
Read, M.
1953 *Africans and their Schools.* London.
Read, M.
1955a *Education and Social Change in Tropical Areas.* London, Nelson.
Read, M.
1955b "Education in Africa: its pattern and role in social change," *Annals of the American Academy of Political and Social Science* 298:170–79.
Read, M.
1956 *The Ngoni of Nyasaland.* London, Oxford University Press.
Read, M.
1968 *Children of their Fathers: Growing Up among the Ngoni of Malawi.* New York, Holt, Rinehart & Winston (originally published London, 1960).
Redfield, R.
1934 *Chan Kom, a Maya Village.* Washington, Carnegie Institute.
Redfield, R.
1941 *The Folk Culture of Yucatan.* Chicago, University of Chicago Press.
Redfield, R.
1943 "Culture and education in the Midwestern Highlands of Guatemala," *American Journal of Sociology* 48:640–48.
Redfield, R.
1950 *A Village that Chose Progress: Chan Kom Revisited.* Chicago, University of Chicago Press.
Redfield, R.
1953 *The Primitive World and its Transformations.* Ithaca, Cornell University Press.
Redfield, R.
1955 *The Little Community.* Chicago, University of Chicago Press.
Reichel-Dolmatoff, G. and A. Reichel-Dolmatoff
1961 *The People of Aritama.* Chicago, University of Chicago Press.

Rees, A. D.
1950 *Life in a Welsh Countryside*. Cardiff, University of Wales Press.
Richards, A. 1.
1932 *Hunger and Work in a Savage Tribe*. London, Routledge and Kegan Paul.
Richards, A. I.
1956 *Chisungu*. London, Faber.
Richie, G. E.
1963 *The Making of a Maori*. Wellington, Reed.
Sapir, E.
1949 "The emergence of the concept of personality in a study of culture," in D. G. Mandelbaum (editor), *Selected Writings of Edward Sapir in Language, Culture, and Personality*, Berkeley, University of California Press: 590–97.
Sargent, S. S. and M. W. Smith (editors)
1949 *Culture and Personality*. New York, Viking Fund.
Searcy, A. M.
1965 *Contemporary and Traditional Prairie Potawatomi Child Life*. Lawrence, University of Kansas Press.
Sewell, W. H.
1952 "Infant training and the personality of the child," *American Journal of Sociology* 58:150–59.
Simmons, L. O.
1942 *Sun Chief: the Autobiography of a Hopi Indian*. New Haven, Yale University Press.
Singleton, J.
1967 *Nichu: a Japanese School*. New York, Holt, Rinehart & Winston.
Slotkin, J. S.
1951 *Personality Development*. New York, Harper.
Smith, E. W.
1934 "Indigenous education in Africa," in *Essays Presented to C. G. Seligman*, London, Routledge.
Smithson, C. L.
1959 *The Havasupai Woman*. Salt Lake City, University of Utah Papers in Anthropology 38.
Social Science Research Council
1954 "Acculturation: an exploratory formulation," *American Anthropologist* 56:973–1002.
Sorel, G.
1941 *Reflections on Violence*. New York, Collier.
Spearman, C. E.
1923 *The Nature of Intelligence*. London, Macmillan.
Spencer, P.
1965 "The gerontocratic society among the Samburu," ch. 11 of *The Samburu*, London, Routledge and Kegan Paul.
Spindler, G. D. (editor)
1955 *Education and Anthropology*. Stanford, Stanford University Press.

Spiro, M. E.
1955 "The acculturation of American ethnic groups," *American Anthropologist* 57:1240–52.
Spiro, M. E.
1958 *Children of the Kibbutz.* Cambridge, Harvard University Press.
Stephen, A. M.
1940 *Hopi Indians of Arizona.* Highland Park, Los Angeles, Southwest Museum.
Stevens, E. S.
1931 *Folk Tales of Irak.* Oxford, Clarendon Press.
Steward, J. H.
1931 "Notes on Hopi ceremonies in their initiatory form in 1927–1928," *American Anthropologist* 33:56–79.
Tait, D.
1961 *The Konkomba of Northern Ghana.* London, Oxford University Press.
Tannous, A.
1942 "Group behavior in the village community of Lebanon," *American Journal of Sociology* 48:221–39.
Thompson, L.
1945 "Logico-aesthetic integration in Hopi culture," *American Anthropologist* 47:540–53.
Thompson, L. and A. Joseph
1944 *The Hopi Way.* Chicago, University of Chicago Press.
Tinker, H.
1959 *The Union of Burma* (2nd edition). Oxford, Clarendon Press.
Titiev, M.
1942 "Notes on Hopi witchcraft," *Papers of the Michigan Academy of Science, Arts, and Letters.* 28:549–57.
Titiev, M.
1944 *Old Oraibi.* (Papers of the Peabody Museum of American Archaeology and Ethnology 22 (1)).
Turnbull, C. M.
1960 "The Elima: a premarital festival among the Bambuti Pygmies," *Zaire* 14 (2–3):175–92.
Underhill, R.
1939 *Social Organization of the Papago Indians.* New York, Columbia University Contributions to Anthropology 30.
Underhill, R.
1940 *The Papago Indians of Arizona and Their Relatives the Pima.* Lawrence, U. S. Office of Indian Affairs (Sherman Pamphlets 3).
Underhill, R.
1946 *Papago Indian Religion.* New York, Columbia University Press.
Underwood, F. W. and I. A. Honigmann
1947 "A comparison of socialization and personality in two simple societies," *American Anthropologist* 49:557–77.

Van Gennep, A.
1909 *Les Rites de Passage.* Paris, Nourry. Translated as *The Rites of Passage* by M. B. Vizedom and G. L. Caffee, London, Routledge and Kegan Paul, 1960.
Vanhove, J.
1953 *L'Oeuvre de l'Education au Congo Belge at au Ruanda-Urundi.* Brussels.
Vincent, M.
1954 *L'Enfant au Ruanda-Urundi.* Brussels, Institut Royal Colonial Belge.
Vogt, E. Z.
1951 *Navaho Veterans, a Study of Changing Values.* (Papers of the Peabody Museum of American Archaeology and Ethnology 41 (1)).
Watkins, M. H.
1943 "The West African 'Bush School,'" *American Journal of Sociology* 48:666–75.
Wax, M. L., R. Wax, and R. Dumont
1964 *Formal Education in an American Indian Community.* Supplement to *Social Problems* 11 (4).
Whiting, J. W. M.
1941 *Becoming a Kwoma.* New Haven, Yale University Press.
Whiting, J. W. M. and I. L. Child
1953 *Child Training and Personality.* New Haven, Yale University Press.
Whorf, B. L.
1941 "The relation of habitual thought and behavior to language," in L. Spier, A. I. Hallowell, S. S. Newman (editors), *Language, Culture, and Personality: Essays in Memory of Edward Sapir,* Menasha, Sapir Memorial Publication Fund: 75–93.
Williams, T. R.
1954 *Papago Adaptability as a Product of the Culture Contact and Change Situation.* (Master's thesis, University of Arizona.)
Williams, T. R.
1957 *Socialization in a Papago Indian Village.* (Doctoral thesis, Syracuse University), University Microfilm, Ann Arbor.
Williams, T. R.
1958 "The structure of the socialization process in Papago Indian society," *Social Forces* 36:251–56.
Williams, T. R.
1969 *Borneo Childhood: Enculturation in Dusun Society.* New York, Holt, Rinehart & Winston.
Wilson, G. and M.
1945 *The Analysis of Social Change.* Cambridge, Cambridge University Press.
Wilson, M.
1951 *Good Company.* London, Oxford University Press.
Wolcott, H. F.
1967 *A Kwakiutl Village and School.* New York, Holt, Rinehart & Winston.

Worsley, P.
1957 *The Trumpet Shall Sound*. London, McGibbon and Kee.
Yee, C.
1963 *A Chinese Childhood*. New York, Norton.

DATE DUE

GAYLORD   PRINTED IN U.S.A.